married TO THE SEA

Victorian Newspaper Art Gone Wrong

by
DREW

Ulysses Press

Published by:
ULYSSES PRESS
P.O. Box 3440
Berkeley, CA 94703
www.ulyssespress.com

ISBN: 978-1-56975-905-9
Library of Congress Control Number: 2010939866

Acquisitions Editor: Keith Riegert
Managing Editor: Claire Chun
Proofreader: Lauren Harrison
Production: Judith Metzener
Cover design: what!design @ whatweb.com
Cover photographs: mirror © shutterstock.com/thumb; leather
    © shutterstock.com/Phecsone; gold texture © shutterstock.com/
    mangiurea
Cover illustration: Drew

10 9 8 7 6 5 4 3 2 1

Printed in Canada by Transcontinental Printing

Distributed by Publishers Group West

To Natalie,
who helped create the concept of Married To The Sea,
and without whom none of this would have been possible.

Introduction

Dearest reader, thank you for purchasing this book. You are entering a world where the past collides with the present. A hand reaches through the fibers of time to put words into the mouths of long-dead actors, words such as "Nutty Bars" and "Whoomp, There It Is." It's my hand, and it's manly, but soft, because I use the computer a lot.

The consequence of the technology surrounding us in the year 2011 is that we use it for precisely nothing: breakfast statuses, lunch statuses, "I hate my job" statuses. The dishonor I commit by making our ancestors say "bantam-weight slapboxer" is the tiniest pebble of shame upon the Jupiter of Wasting All We've Been Given.

So, in closing, I'll leave you with this reminder: Those who forget history are something something (look up and fill this in later).

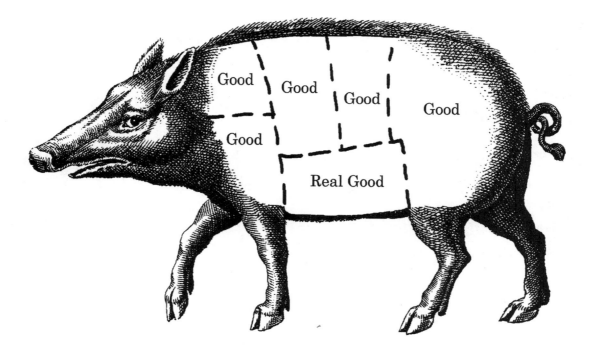

Tastes of the Portions of the Swine.

Good

Good

Good

Good

Good

Good

Real Good

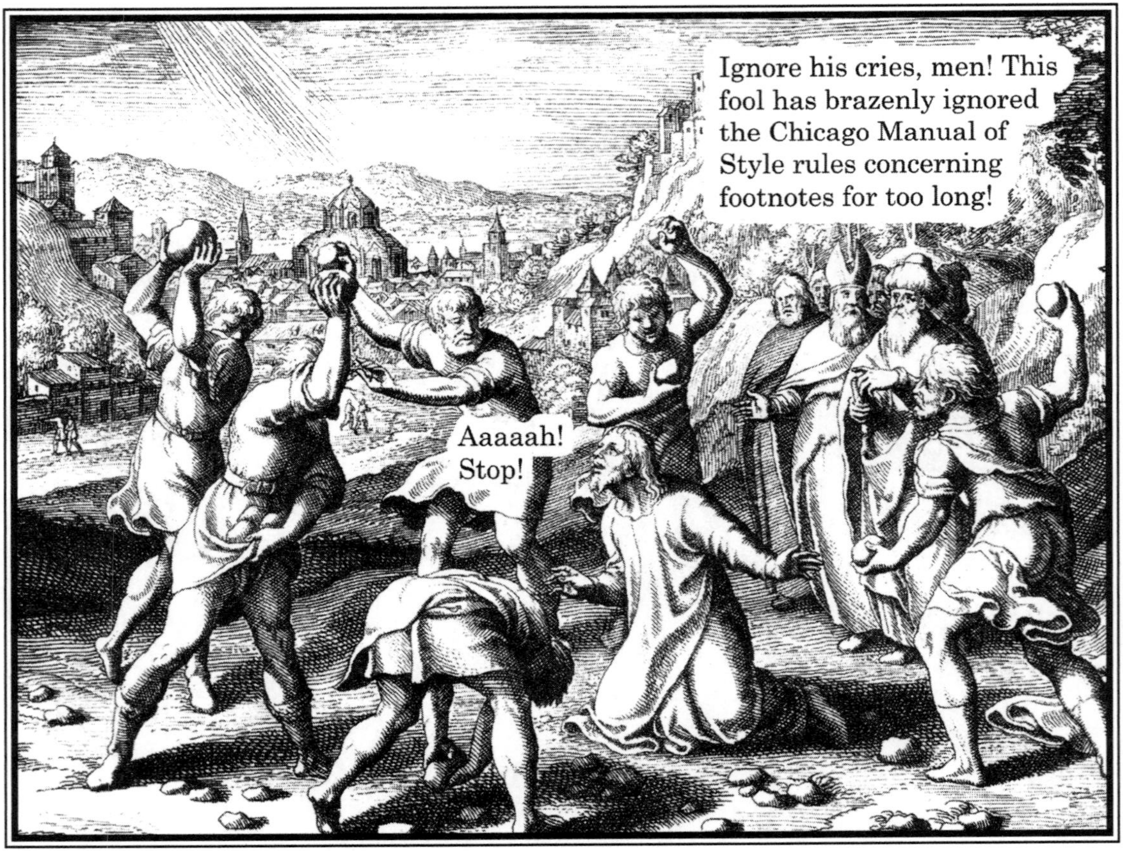
Ignore his cries, men! This fool has brazenly ignored the Chicago Manual of Style rules concerning footnotes for too long!
Aaaaah! Stop!

Heh heh. Dutch oven.

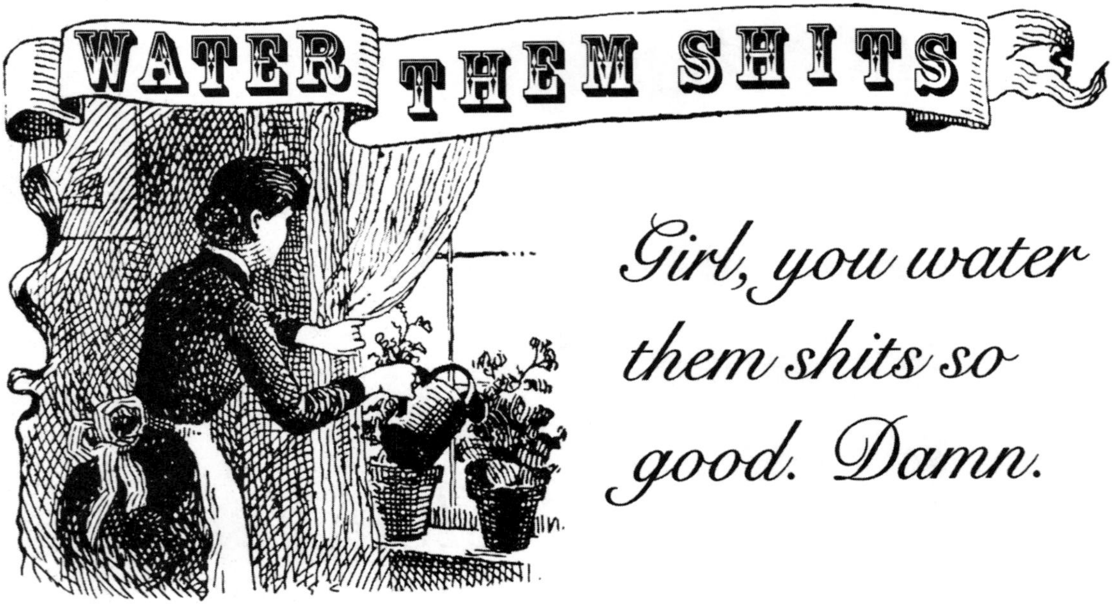
WATER THEM SHITS

Girl, you water them shits so good. Damn.

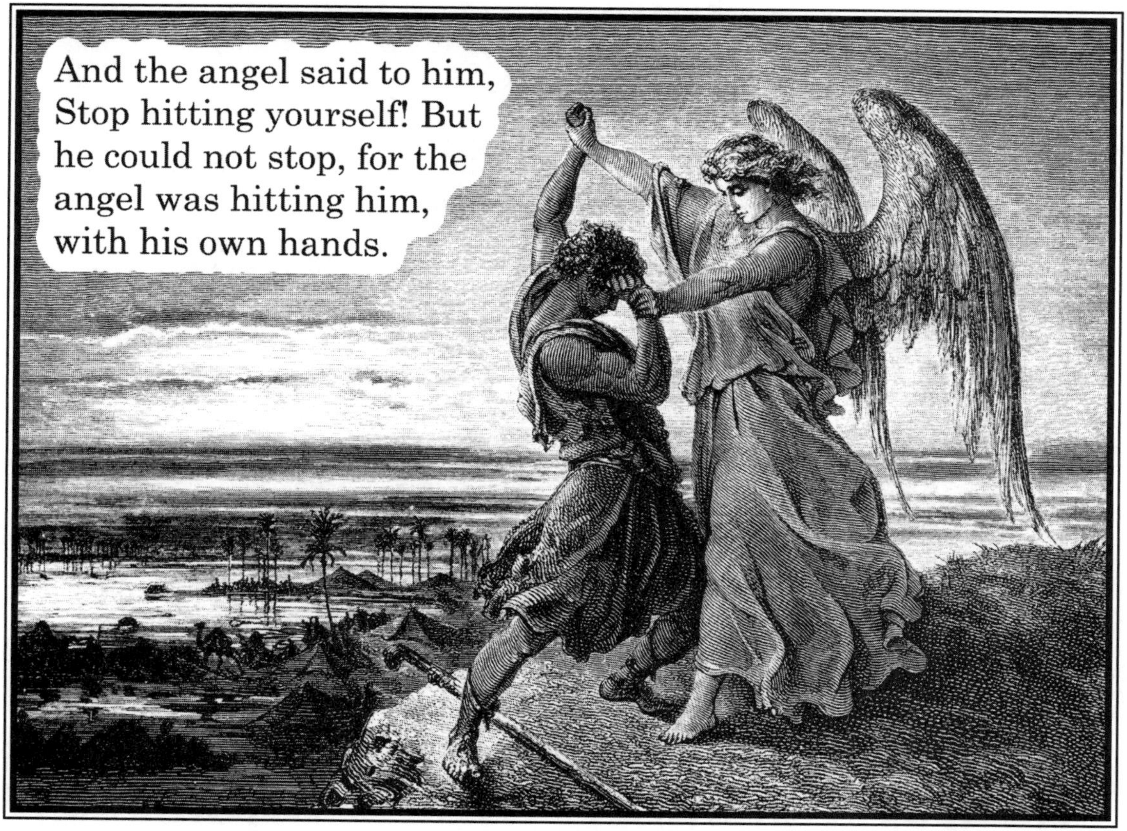
And the angel said to him, Stop hitting yourself! But he could not stop, for the angel was hitting him, with his own hands.

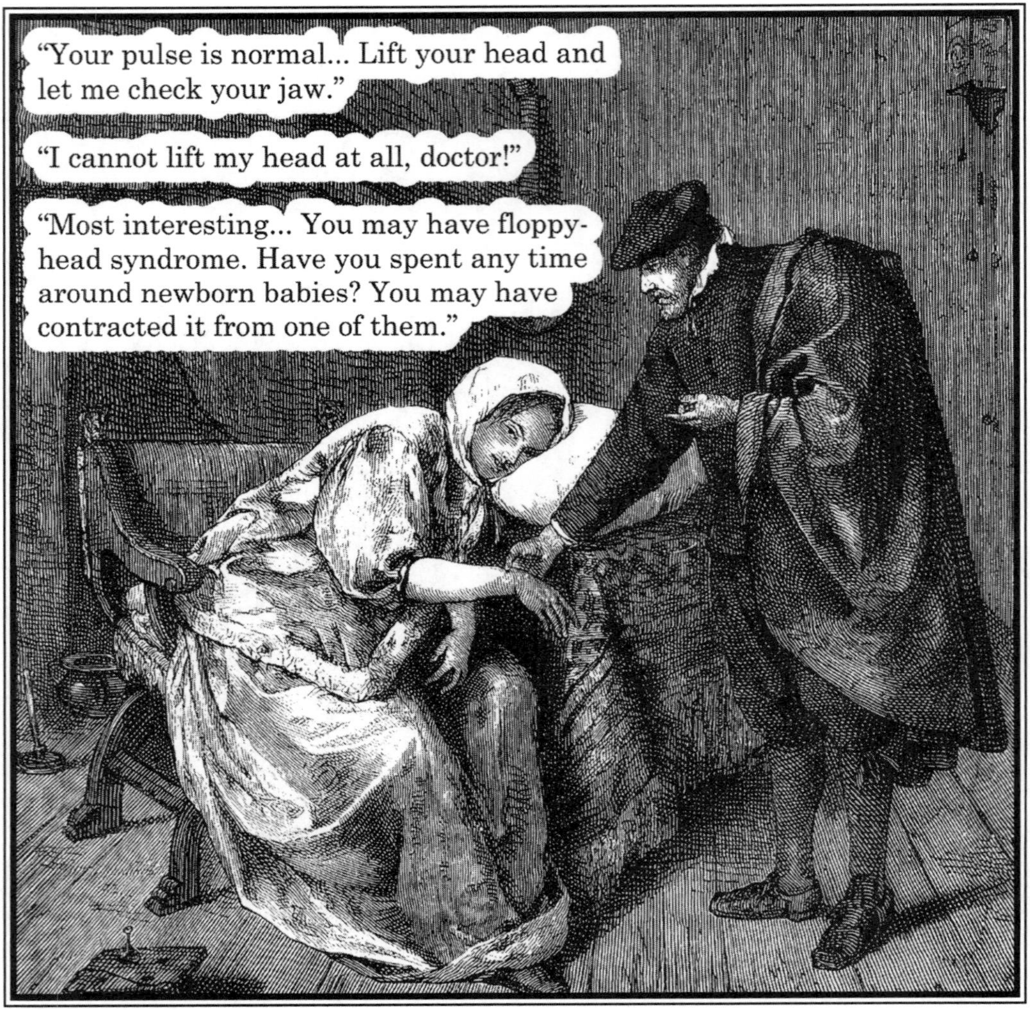
"Your pulse is normal... Lift your head and let me check your jaw."
"I cannot lift my head at all, doctor!"
"Most interesting... You may have floppy-head syndrome. Have you spent any time around newborn babies? You may have contracted it from one of them."

Champagne? Ugh... champagne has grapes in it too. I need some *soy wine*. I'm grapetose intolerant.

Your offer is generous, Craig... I'm just not sure I'm ready to
live in a cage in your living room, wear a dog collar, and
clean your house in exchange for room and board.
I'm sure you'll find someone... perhaps
you could start some sort of
listing service.

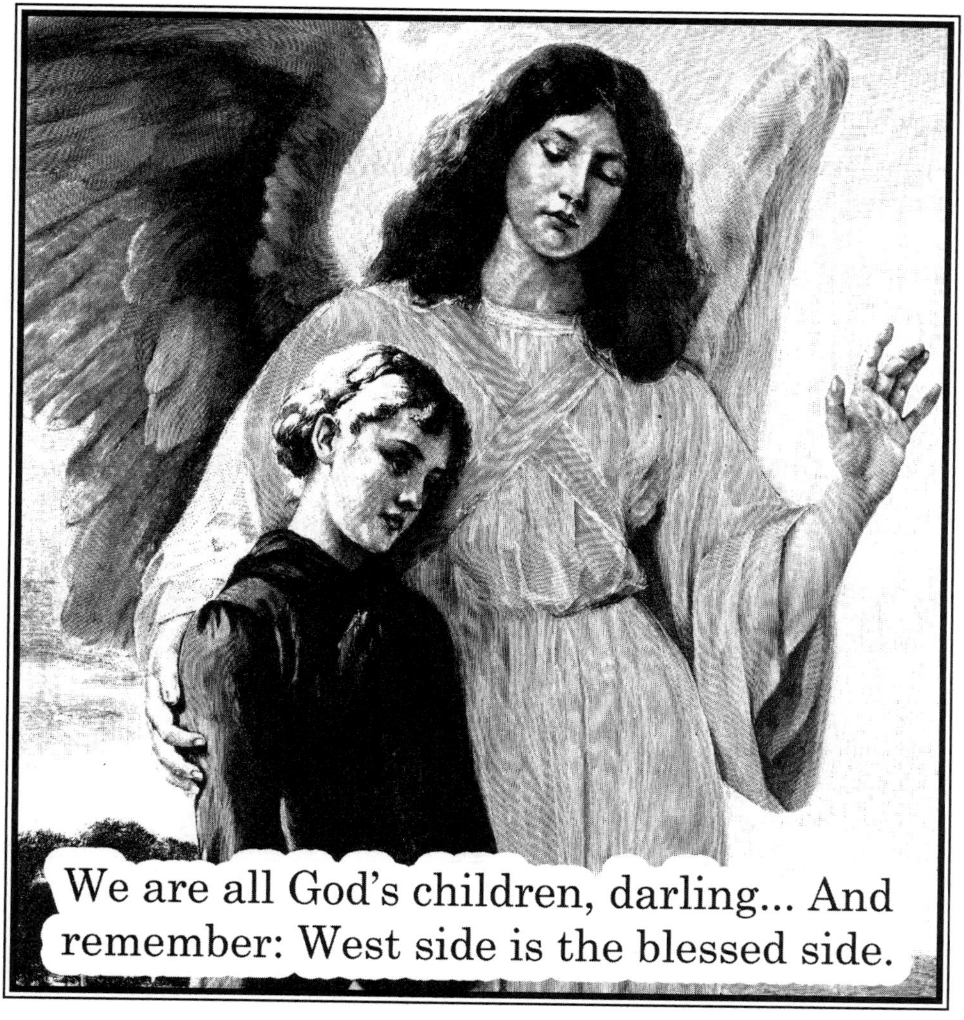
We are all God's children, darling... And remember: West side is the blessed side.

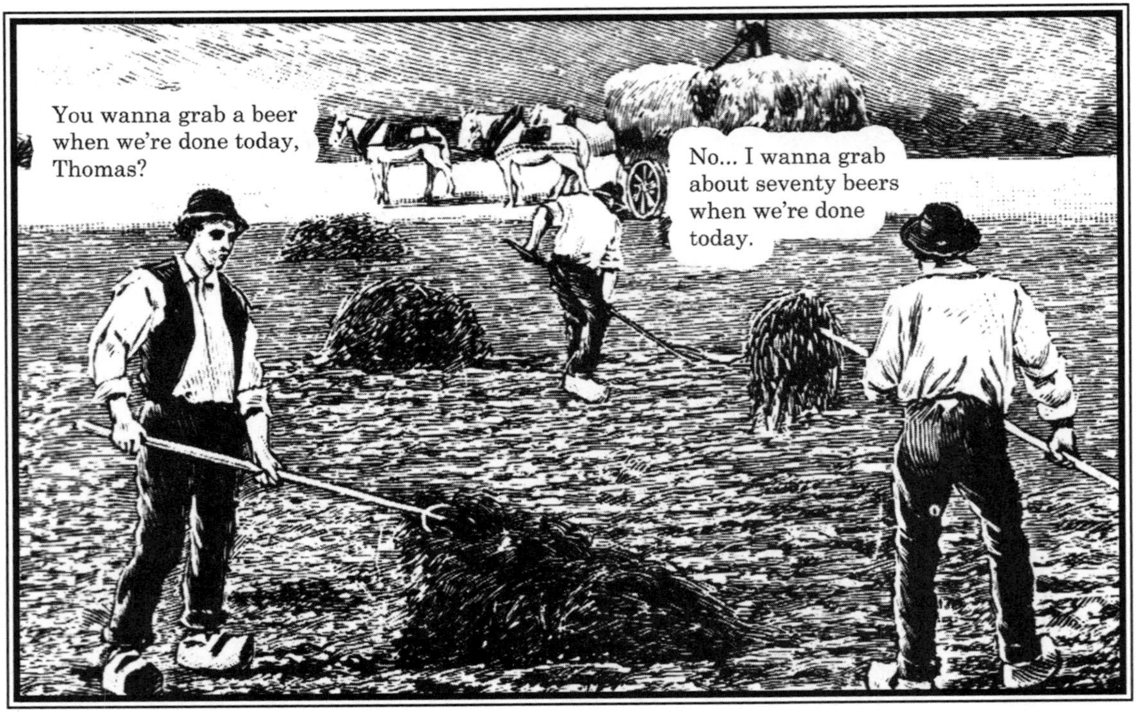
You wanna grab a beer when we're done today, Thomas?
No... I wanna grab about seventy beers when we're done today.

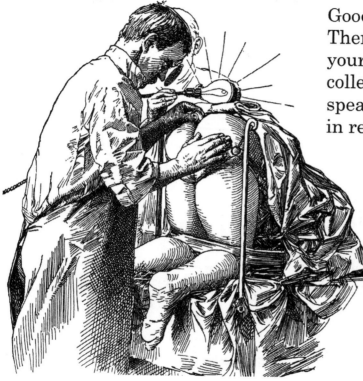

Good news, Mr. Atkinson!
There is nothing blocking
your colon at all... Your
colleague may have been
speaking idiomatically
in regards to the stick.

Please Read—
If you did not purchase plums
for the icebox, they are not
yours. This <u>means you</u>, William.
<u>Some of us</u> cannot eat poems
when we are hungry.

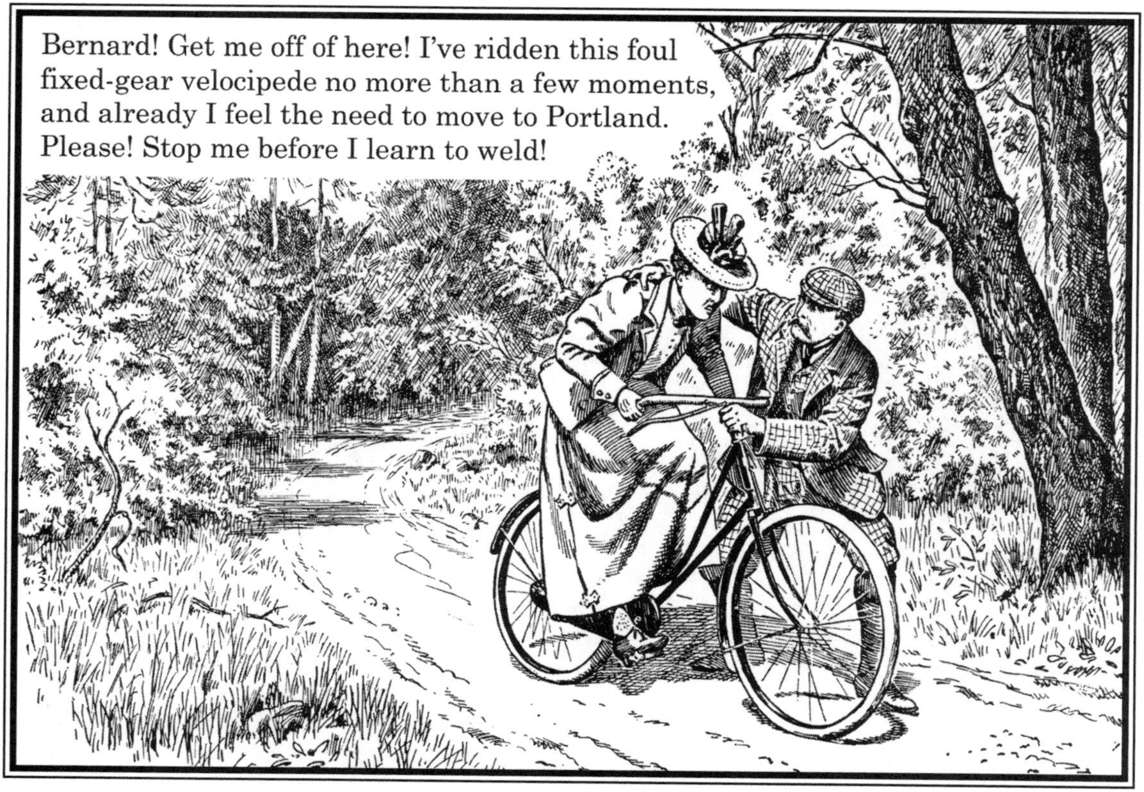
Bernard! Get me off of here! I've ridden this foul fixed-gear velocipede no more than a few moments, and already I feel the need to move to Portland. Please! Stop me before I learn to weld!

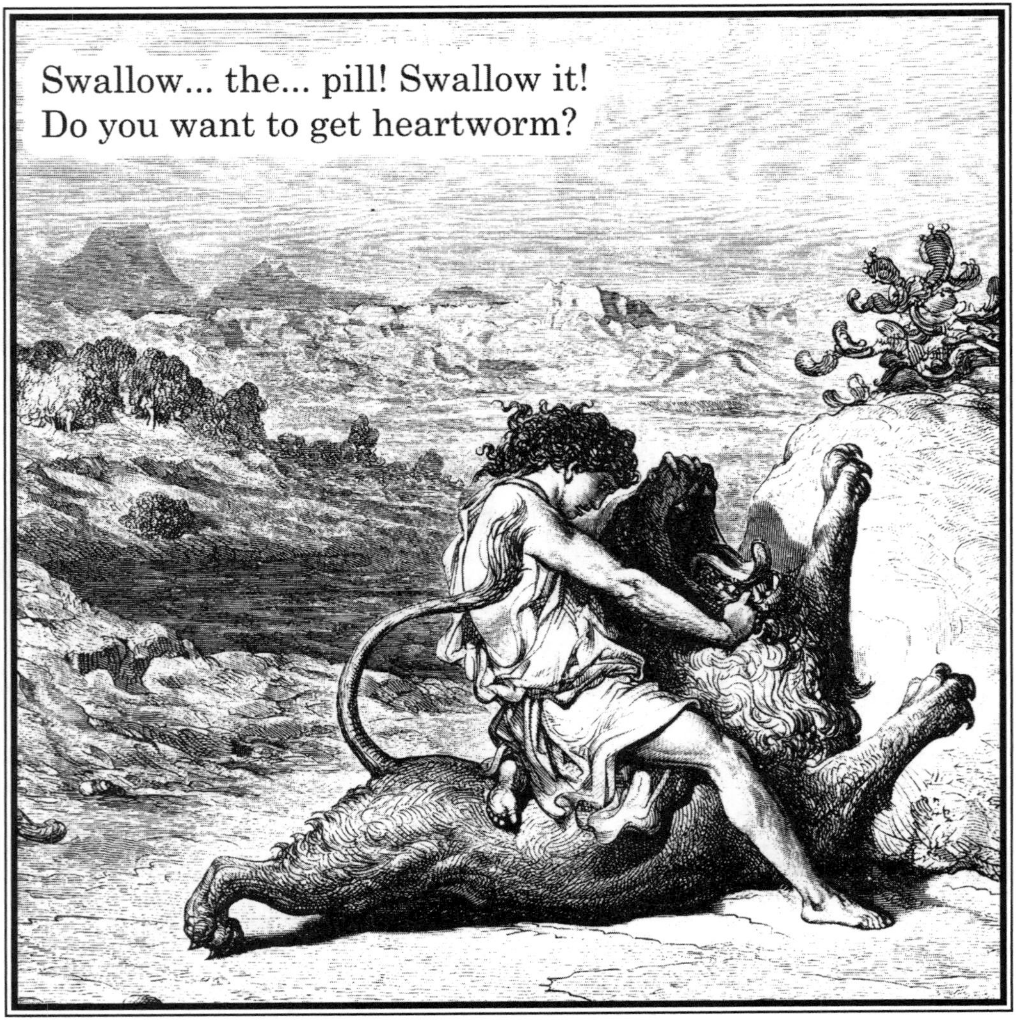
Swallow... the... pill! Swallow it!
Do you want to get heartworm?

Attention! Attention all townspeople! The King has declared that this village is now to be used for hipsters! If you are not a hipster, you will be subject to being scowled at... effective immediately!

Miss! Excuse me, miss... I simply can not let you pass without comment. Are you from that cult church in Texas? Because your sleeves are *mad puffy*. A man would marry his cousin for those sleeves, girl.

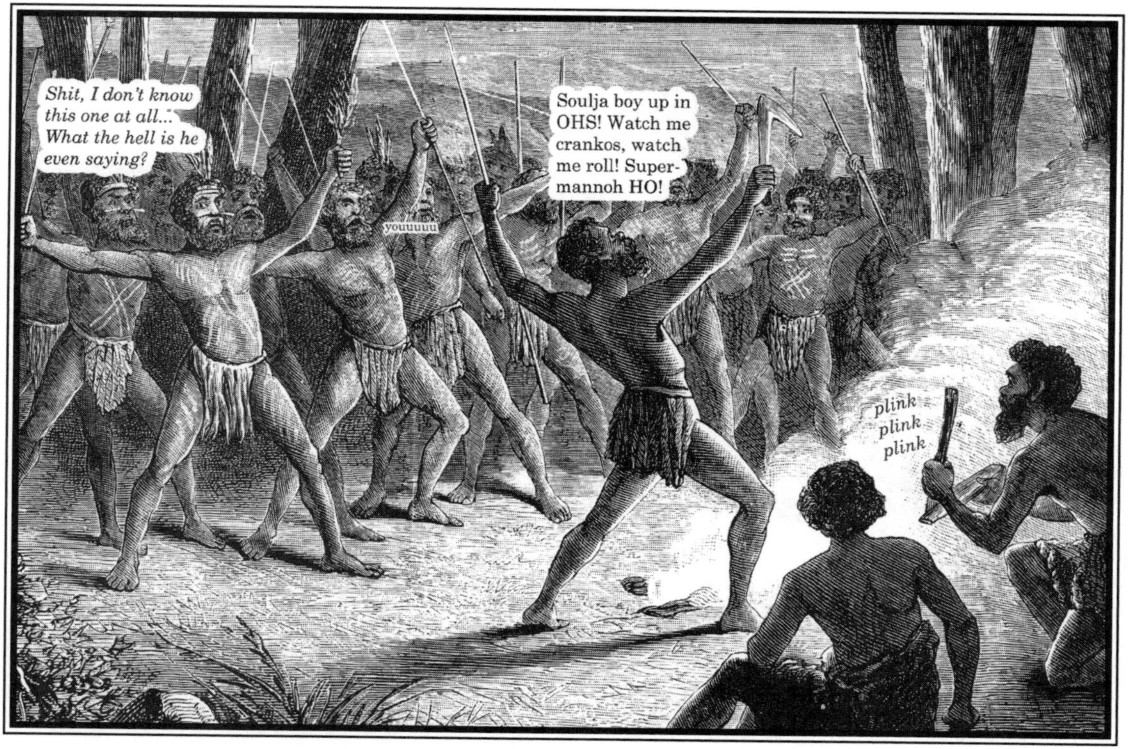
Shit, I don't know this one at all... What the hell is he even saying?
youuuuu
Soulja boy up in OHS! Watch me crankos, watch me roll! Super-mannoh HO!
plink plink plink

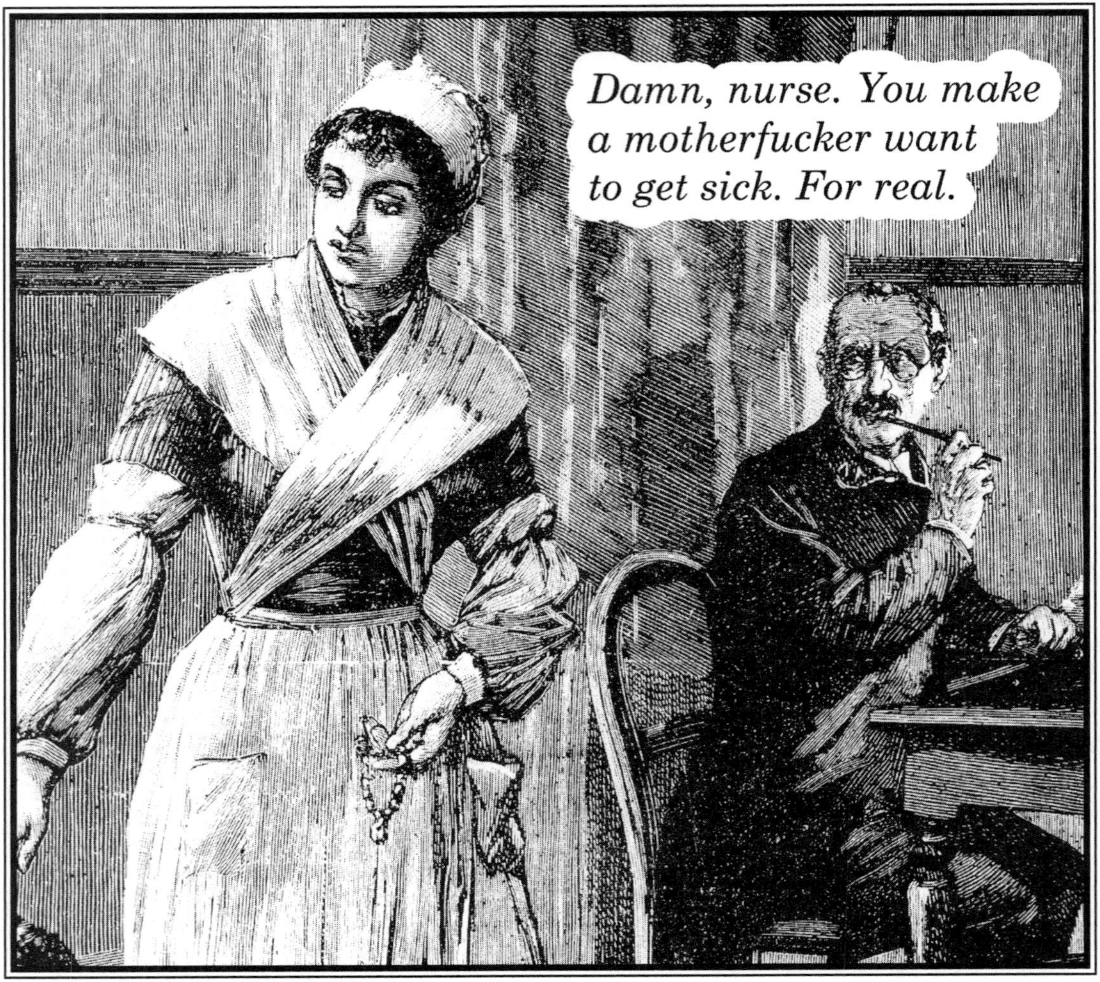
Damn, nurse. You make a motherfucker want to get sick. For real.

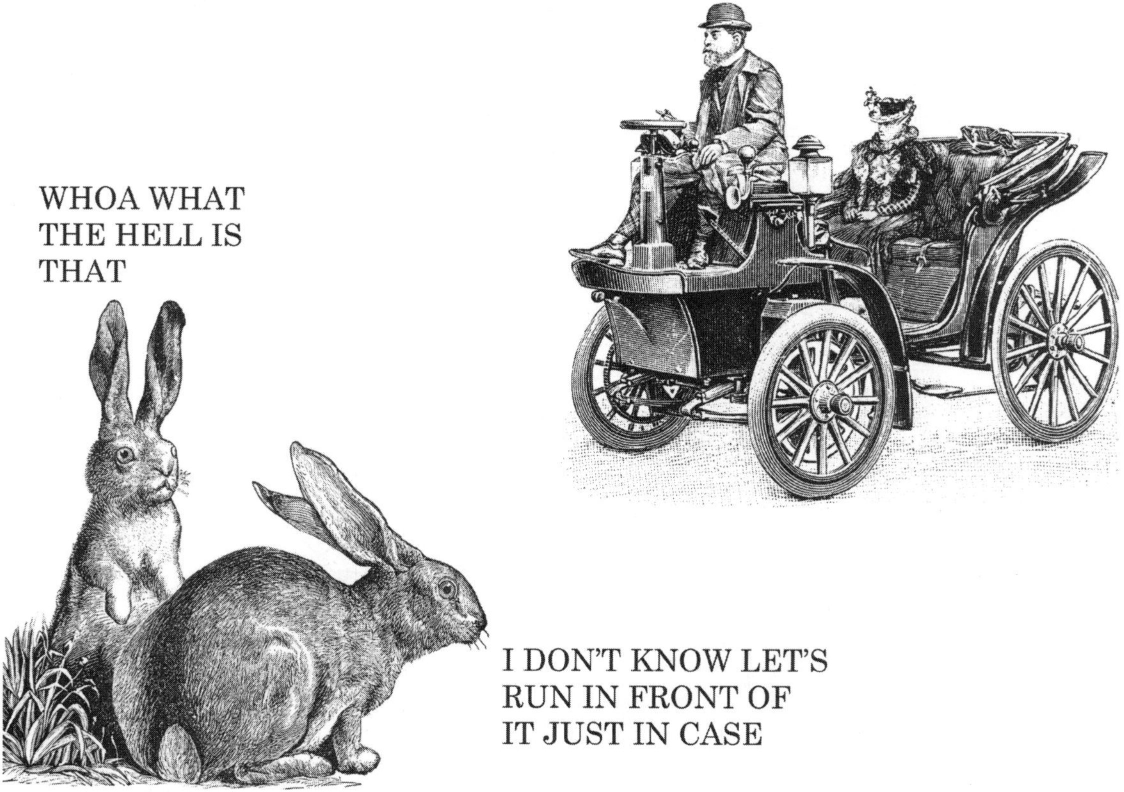
WHOA WHAT THE HELL IS THAT
I DON'T KNOW LET'S RUN IN FRONT OF IT JUST IN CASE

Hmm... What if I stomped on these a bunch and then let them rot in a barrel?

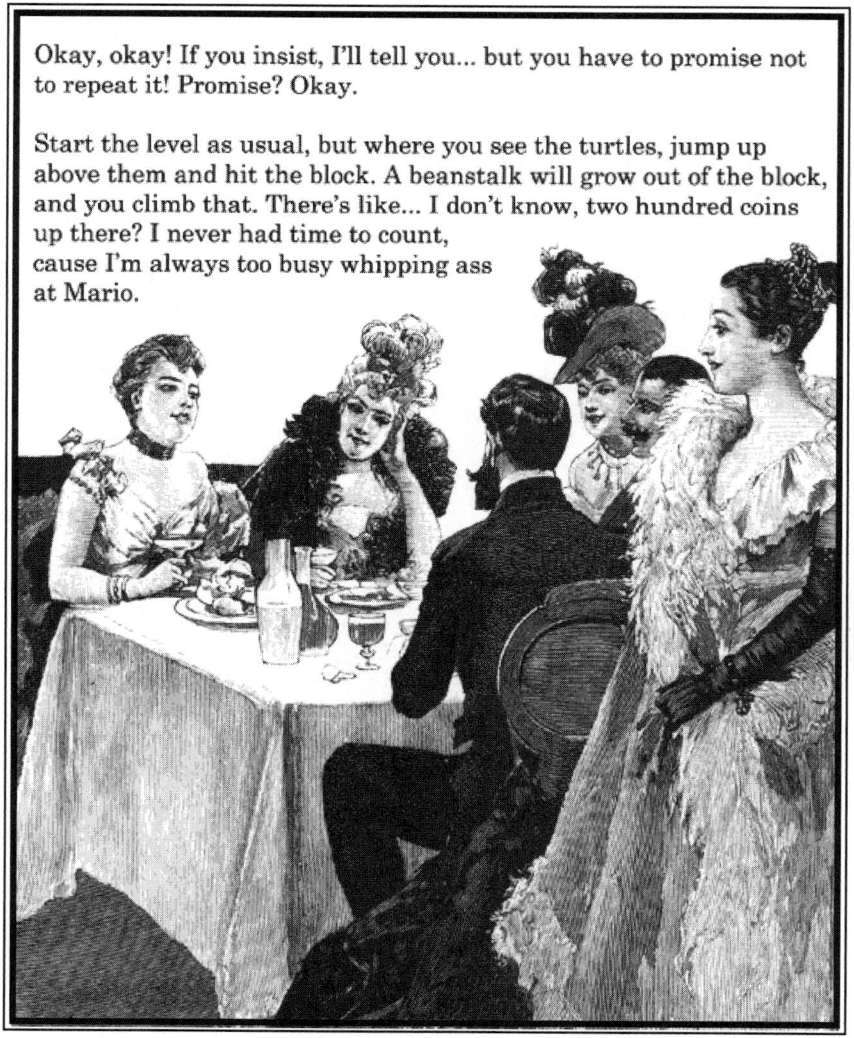
Okay, okay! If you insist, I'll tell you... but you have to promise not to repeat it! Promise? Okay.
Start the level as usual, but where you see the turtles, jump up above them and hit the block. A beanstalk will grow out of the block, and you climb that. There's like... I don't know, two hundred coins up there? I never had time to count, cause I'm always too busy whipping ass at Mario.

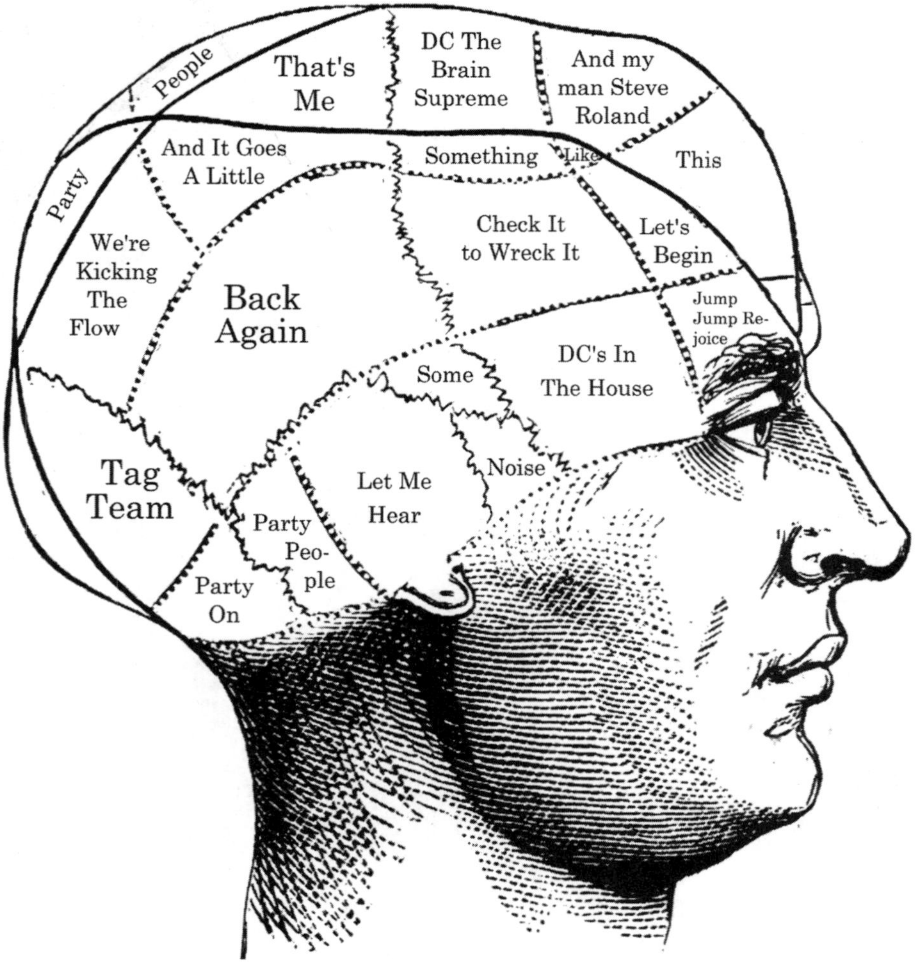
People
That's Me
DC The Brain Supreme
And my man Steve Roland
Party
And It Goes A Little
Something
Like
This
We're Kicking The Flow
Back Again
Check It to Wreck It
Let's Begin
Jump Jump Re-joice
Some
DC's In The House
Tag Team
Let Me Hear
Noise
Party People
Party On

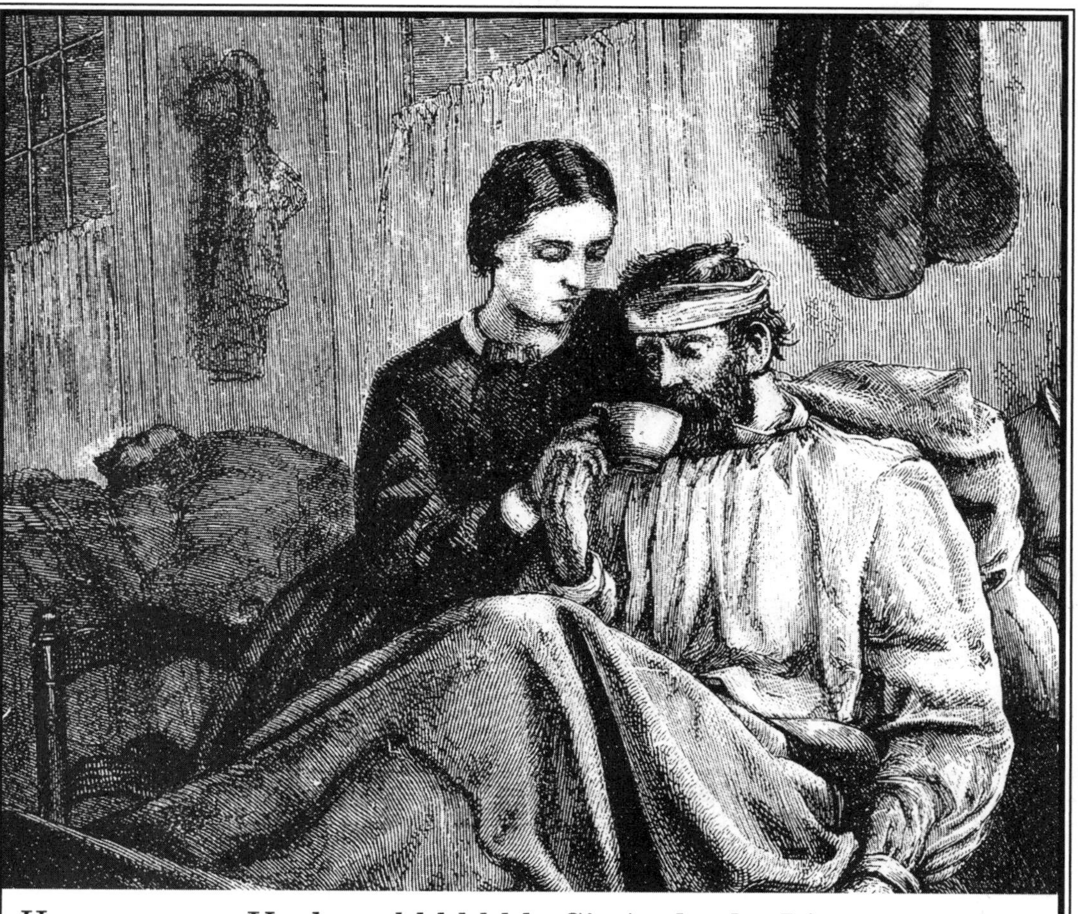

Here you are, Uncle... shhhhhhh. Sip it slowly. It's some purple drank. It taste good. Now lean... there you go. That's better.

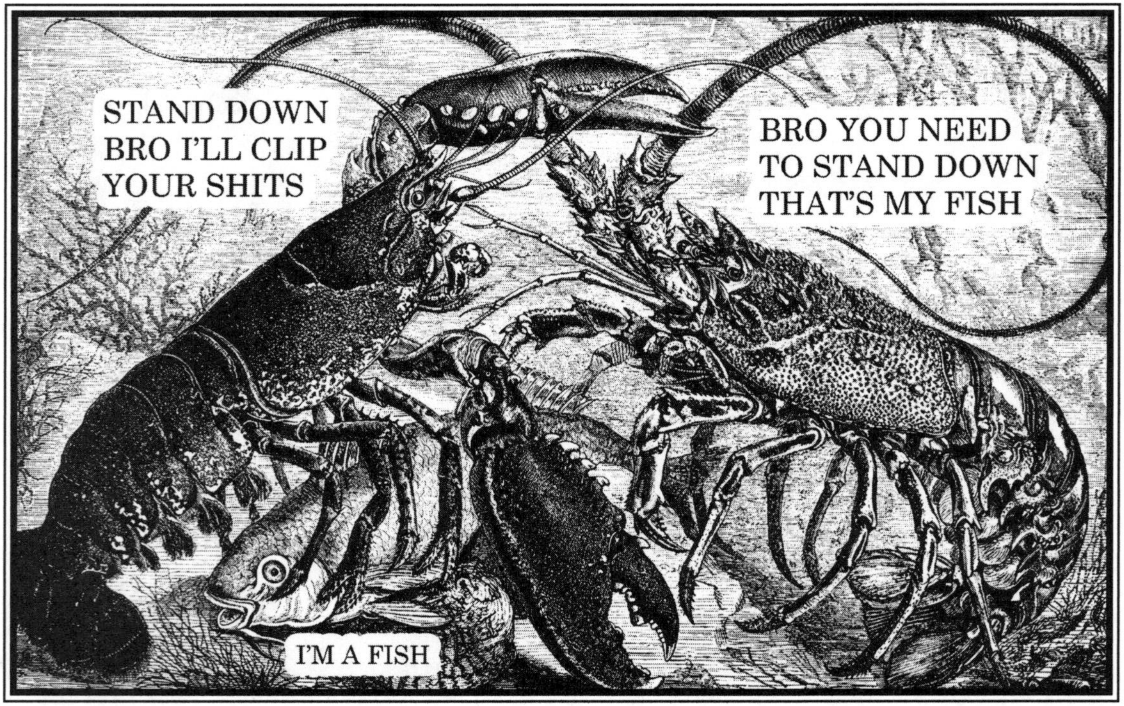
STAND DOWN BRO I'LL CLIP YOUR SHITS
BRO YOU NEED TO STAND DOWN THAT'S MY FISH
I'M A FISH

"It was nice to meet you. Here's my business card. Take care."

Guy who will stand behind
you at the post office and
whistle loudly

Telephone 5-2200

Ladies... Y'all interested in a man who can lead a horse to water *and* make him drink?

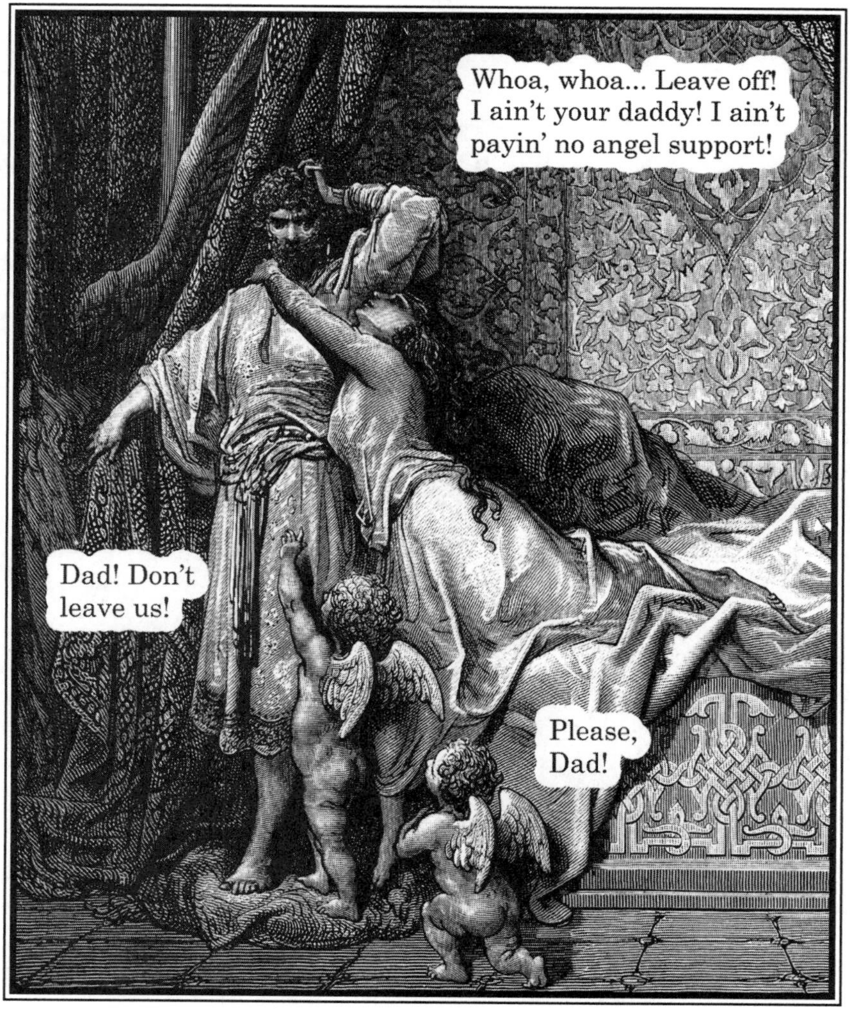
Whoa, whoa... Leave off! I ain't your daddy! I ain't payin' no angel support!
Dad! Don't leave us!
Please, Dad!

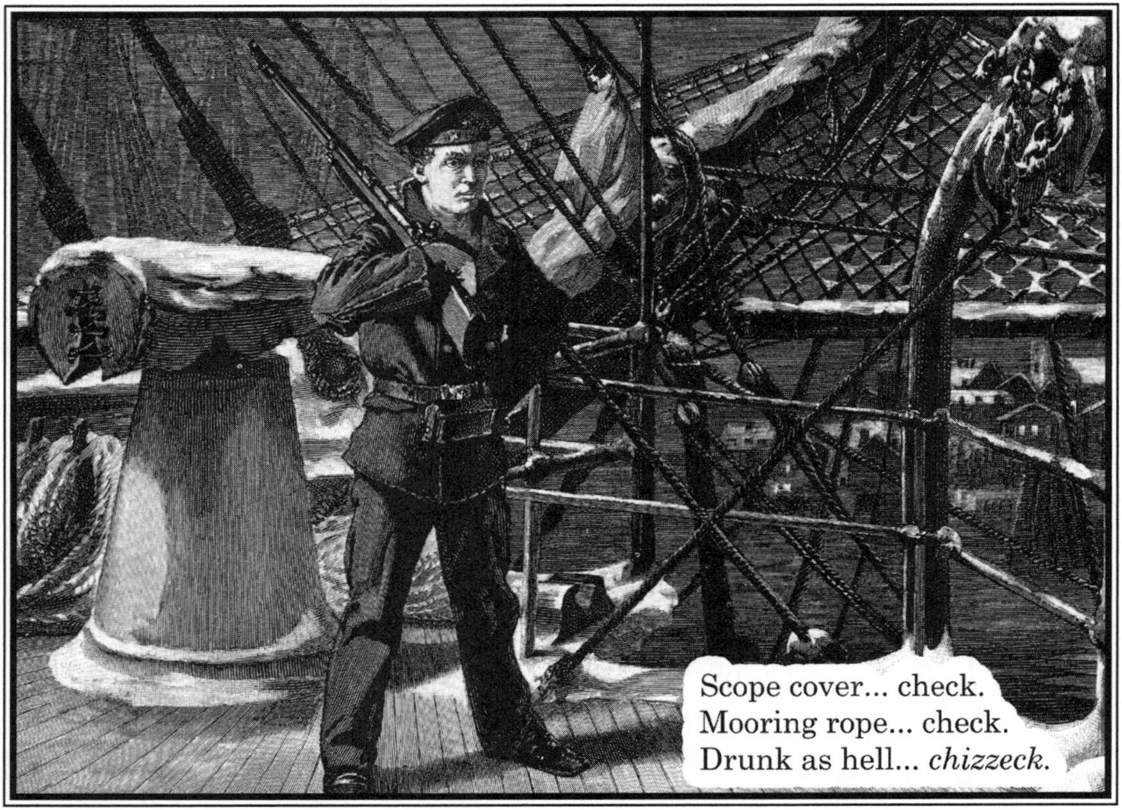
Scope cover... check.
Mooring rope... check.
Drunk as hell... *chizzeck*.

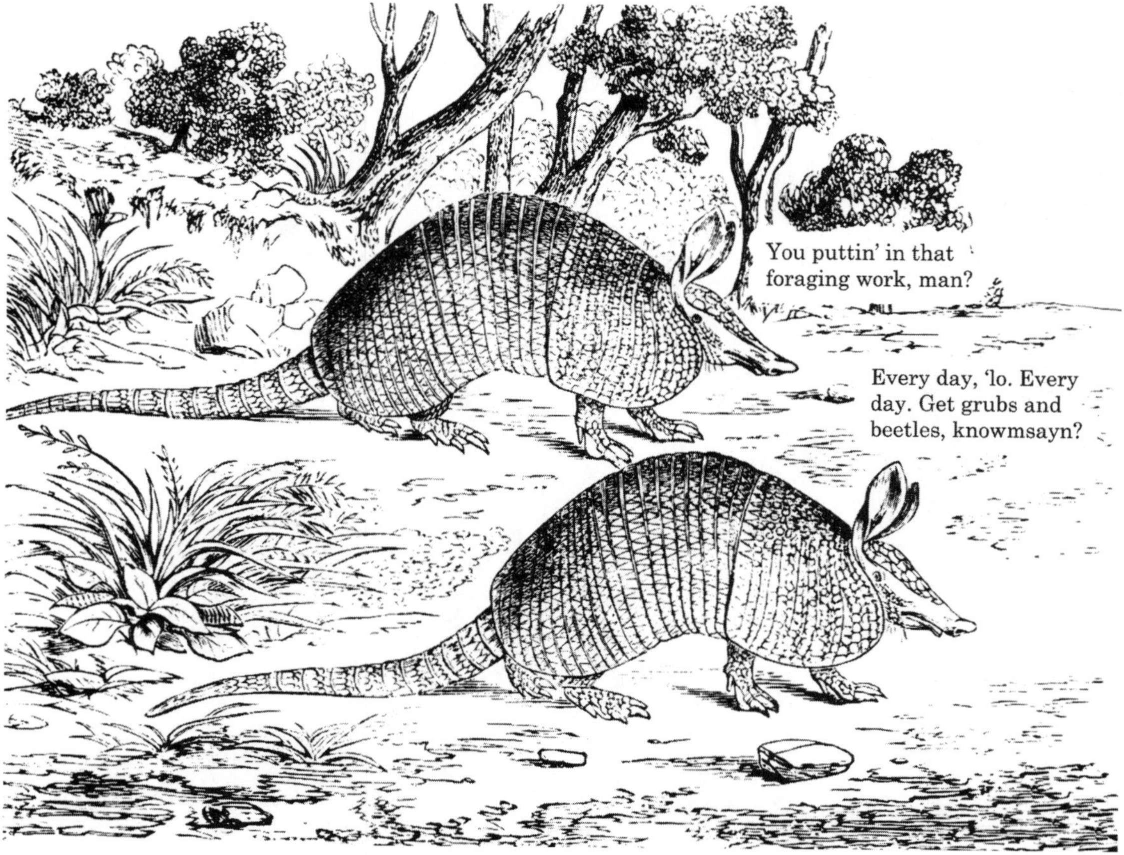
You puttin' in that foraging work, man?
Every day, 'lo. Every day. Get grubs and beetles, knowmsayn?

No... Mom! Listen! That's not mine. Come on, don't throw it out. It's not even my amphora. I'm holding onto it for someone.

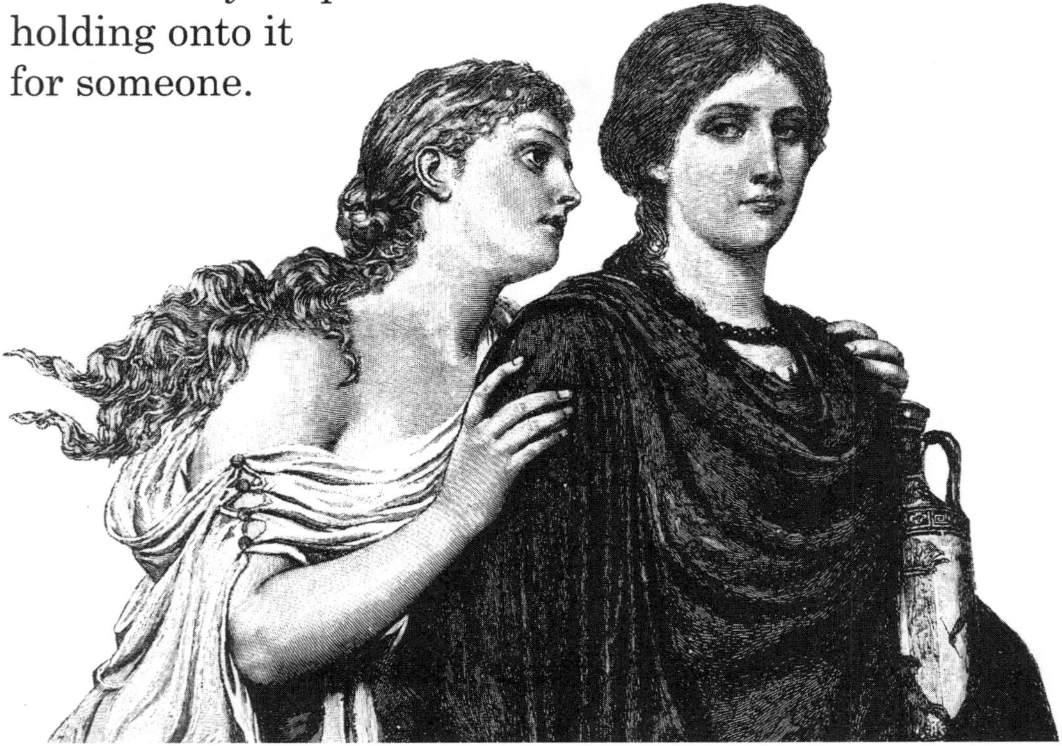

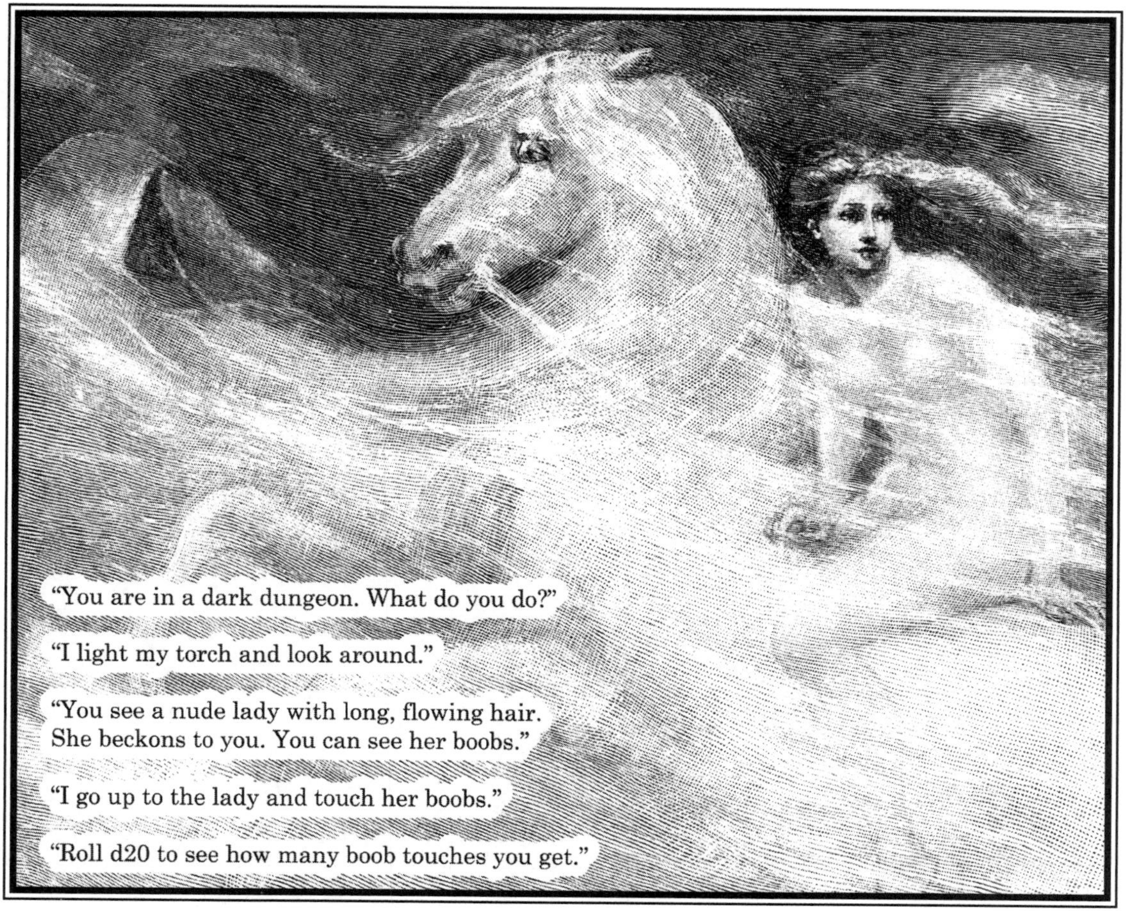
"You are in a dark dungeon. What do you do?"
"I light my torch and look around."
"You see a nude lady with long, flowing hair. She beckons to you. You can see her boobs."
"I go up to the lady and touch her boobs."
"Roll d20 to see how many boob touches you get."

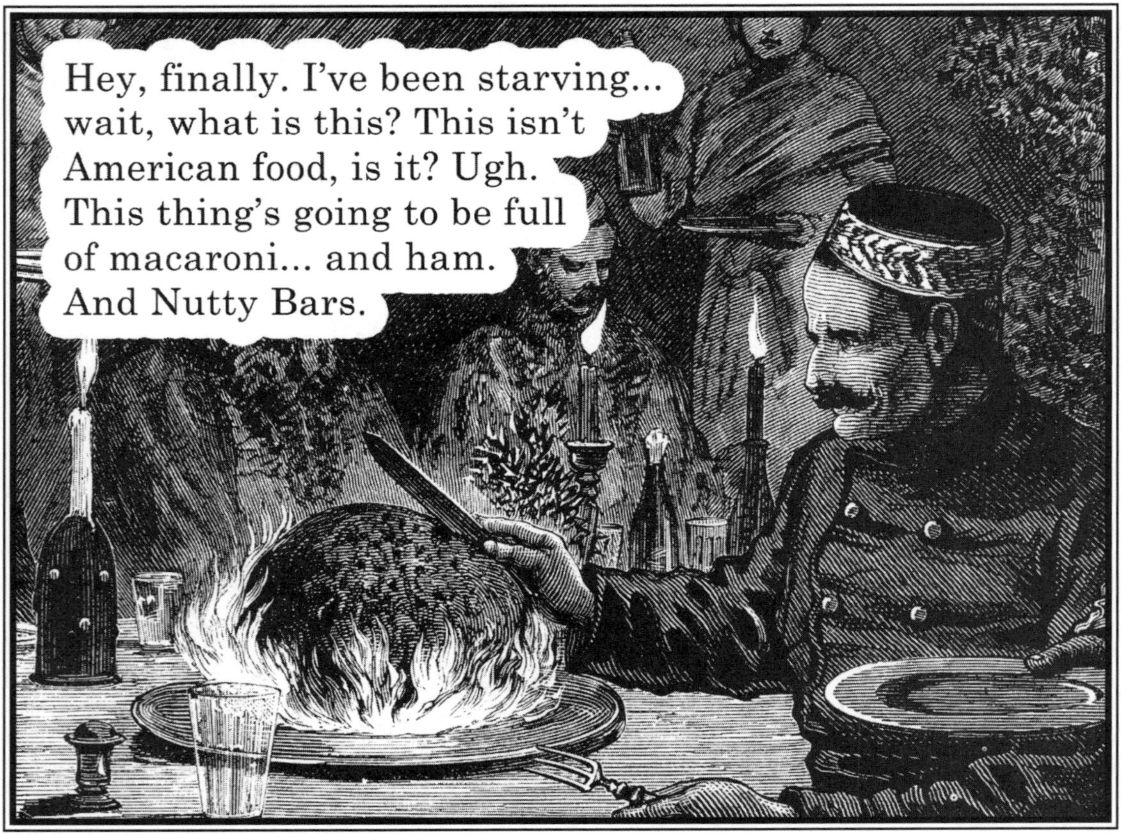
Hey, finally. I've been starving... wait, what is this? This isn't American food, is it? Ugh. This thing's going to be full of macaroni... and ham. And Nutty Bars.

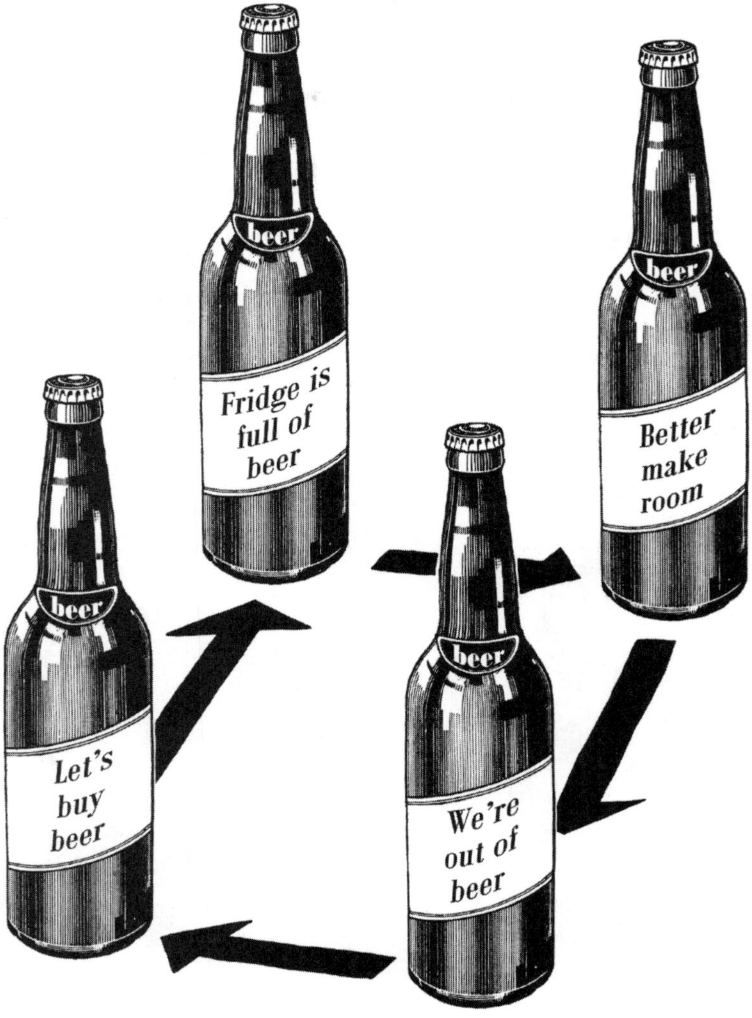
beer
Fridge is full of beer
beer
Better make room
beer
We're out of beer
beer
Let's buy beer

4 April. This Blog is going to have to go on hiatus for a while. The boss found out I have been using the town's only printing press to publish my writing. I hope he does not find any of the older entries.

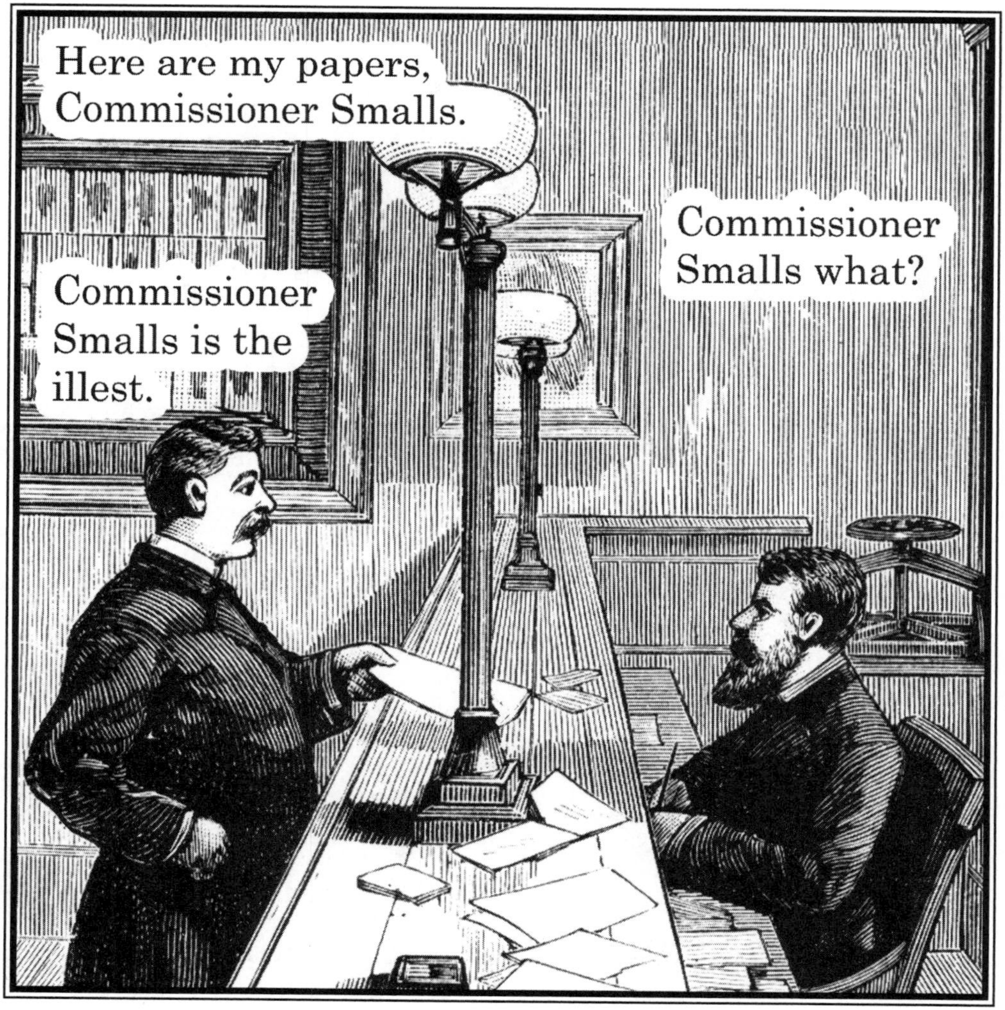
Here are my papers, Commissioner Smalls.
Commissioner Smalls what?
Commissioner Smalls is the illest.

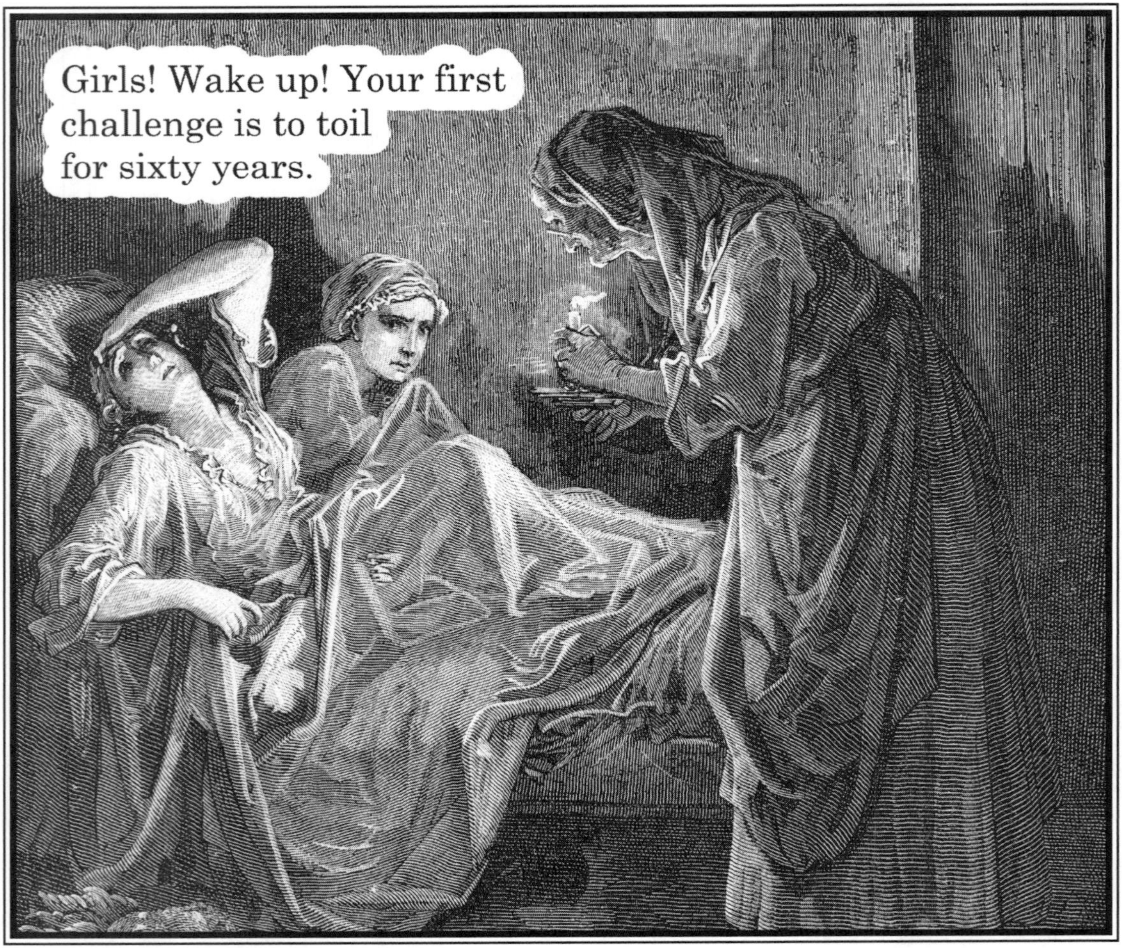
Girls! Wake up! Your first challenge is to toil for sixty years.

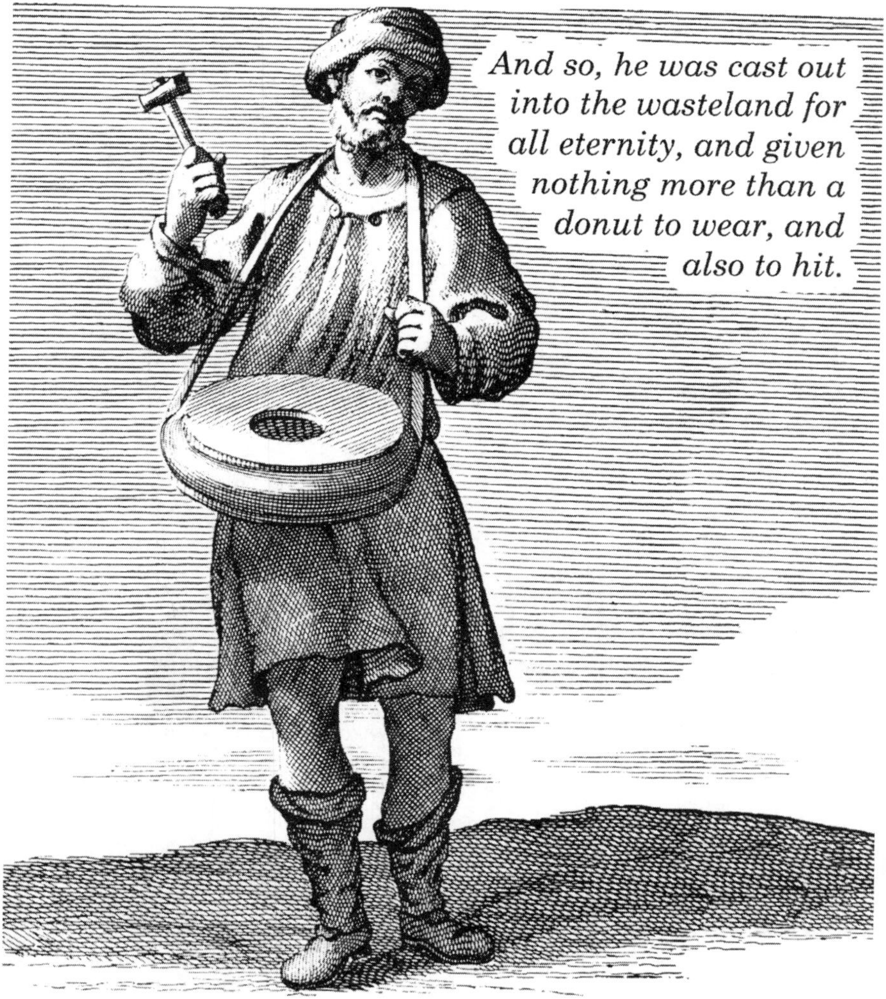
And so, he was cast out into the wasteland for all eternity, and given nothing more than a donut to wear, and also to hit.

To Whom It May Concern:
My pen is almost out of ink.

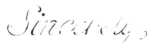

Sincerely,

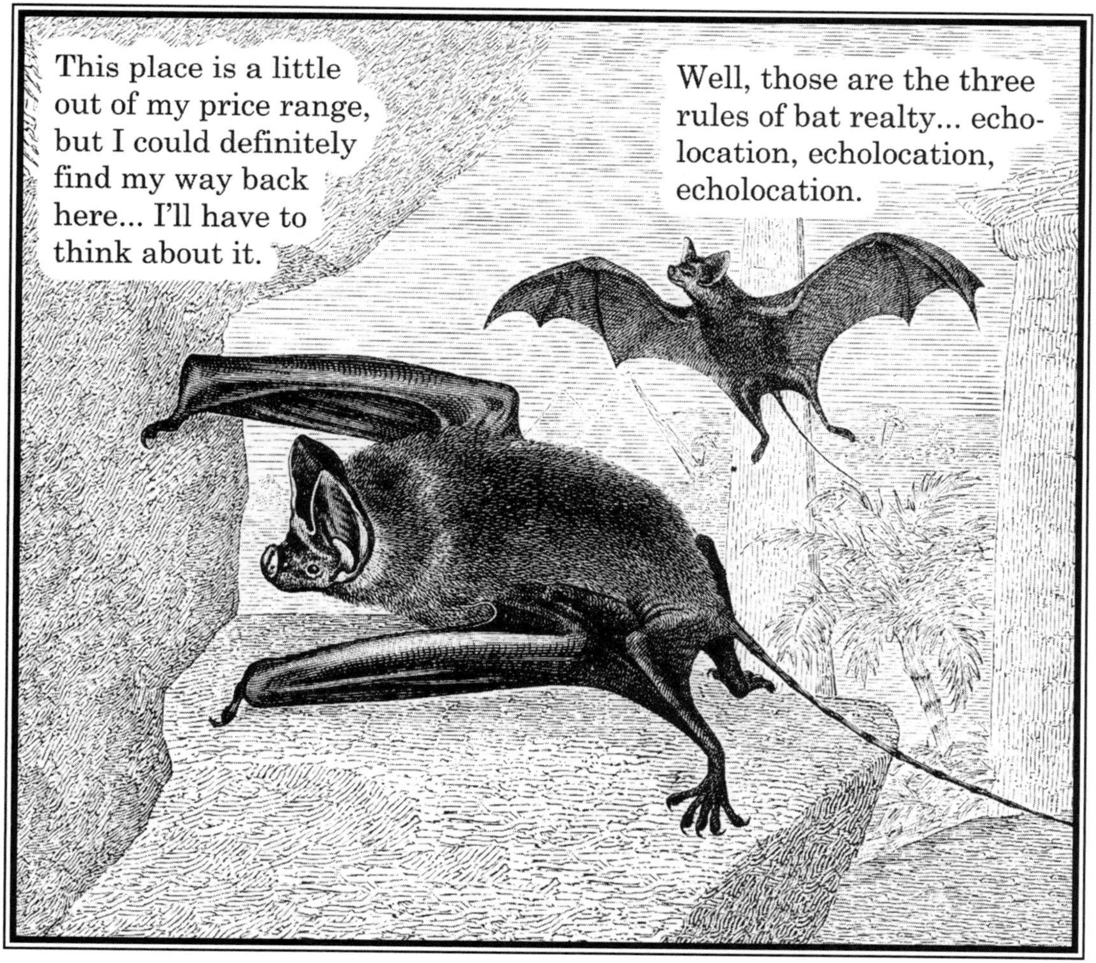
This place is a little out of my price range, but I could definitely find my way back here... I'll have to think about it.
Well, those are the three rules of bat realty... echo-location, echolocation, echolocation.

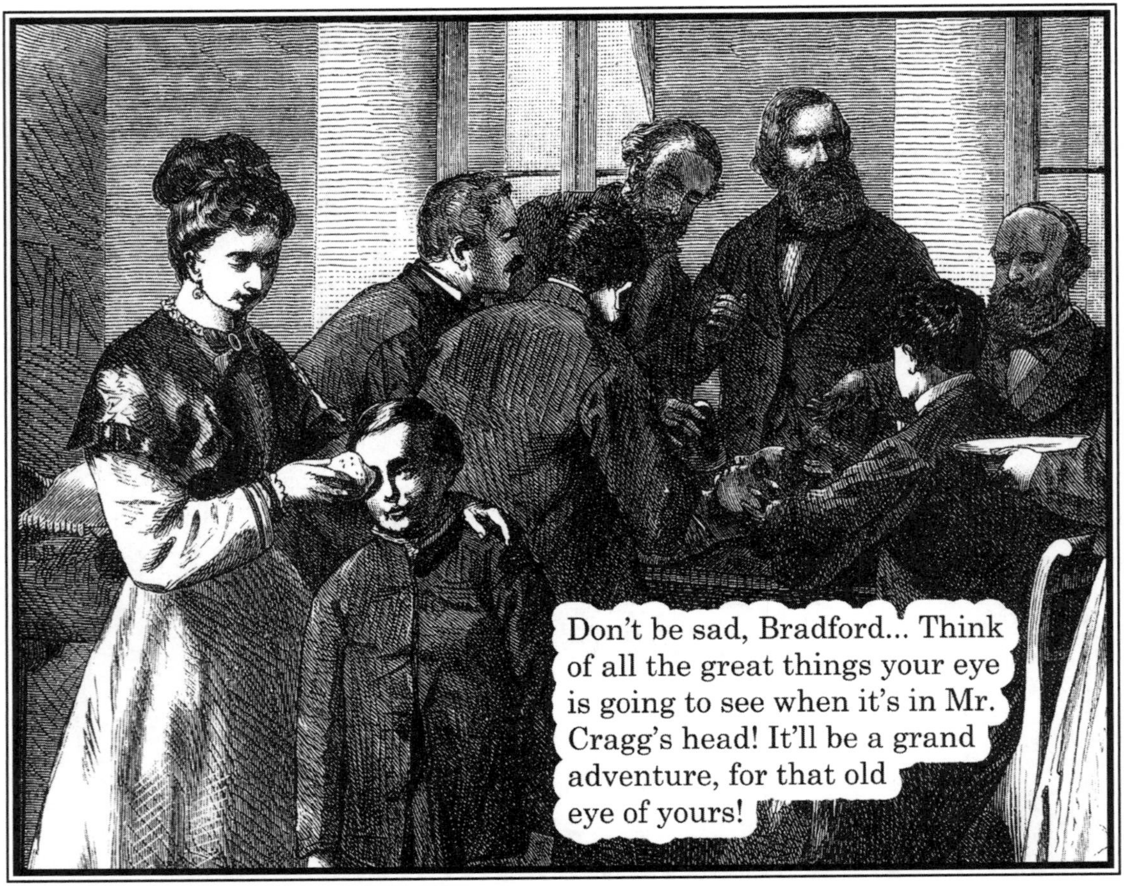
Don't be sad, Bradford... Think of all the great things your eye is going to see when it's in Mr. Cragg's head! It'll be a grand adventure, for that old eye of yours!

It's been over an hour! Have you told the cook that I've ordered pancakes?

Indeed I have, sir. He's almost done slaughtering them. Should be ready in a few minutes.

I will dress in the costume of a bear and dance seductively for you. Do you have a rough wooden pole upon which I may gyrate? And do you seek companionship from a bear-dressed man? Respond post-haste to me, and we shall convene.

AD #32

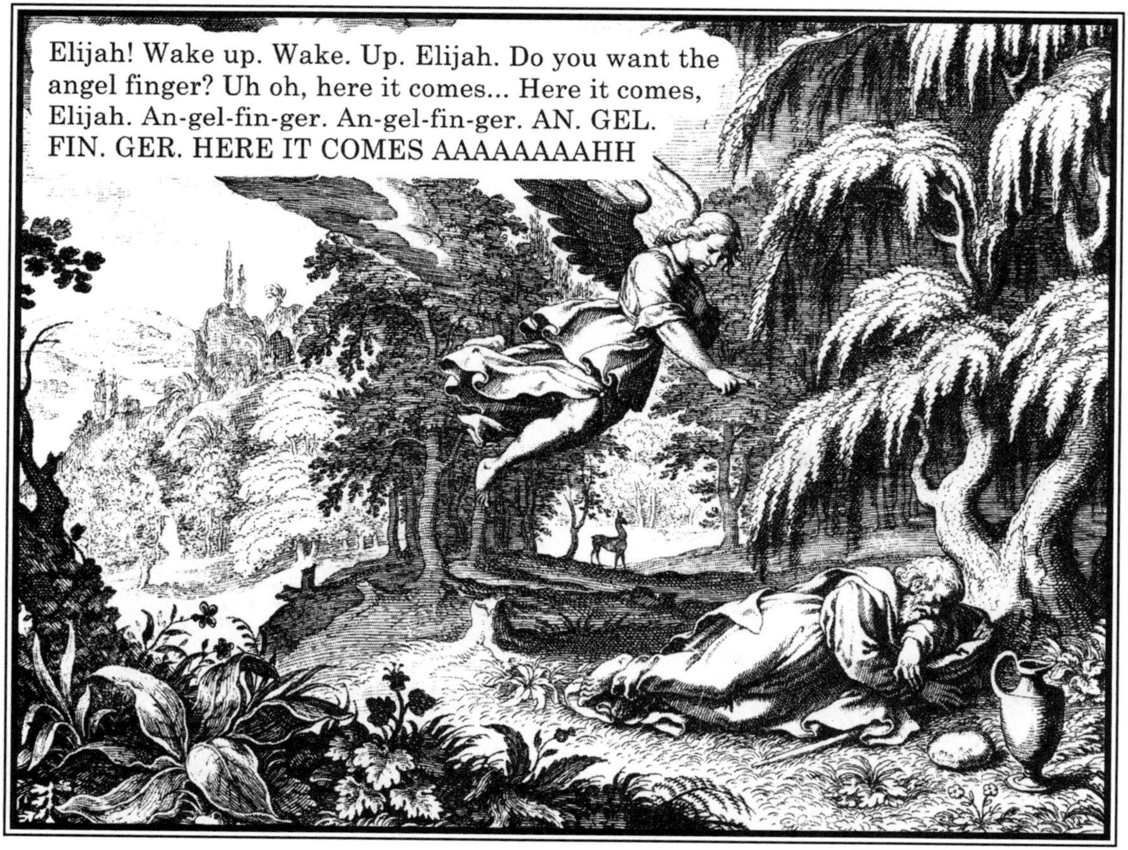
Elijah! Wake up. Wake. Up. Elijah. Do you want the angel finger? Uh oh, here it comes... Here it comes, Elijah. An-gel-fin-ger. An-gel-fin-ger. AN. GEL. FIN. GER. HERE IT COMES AAAAAAAAAHH

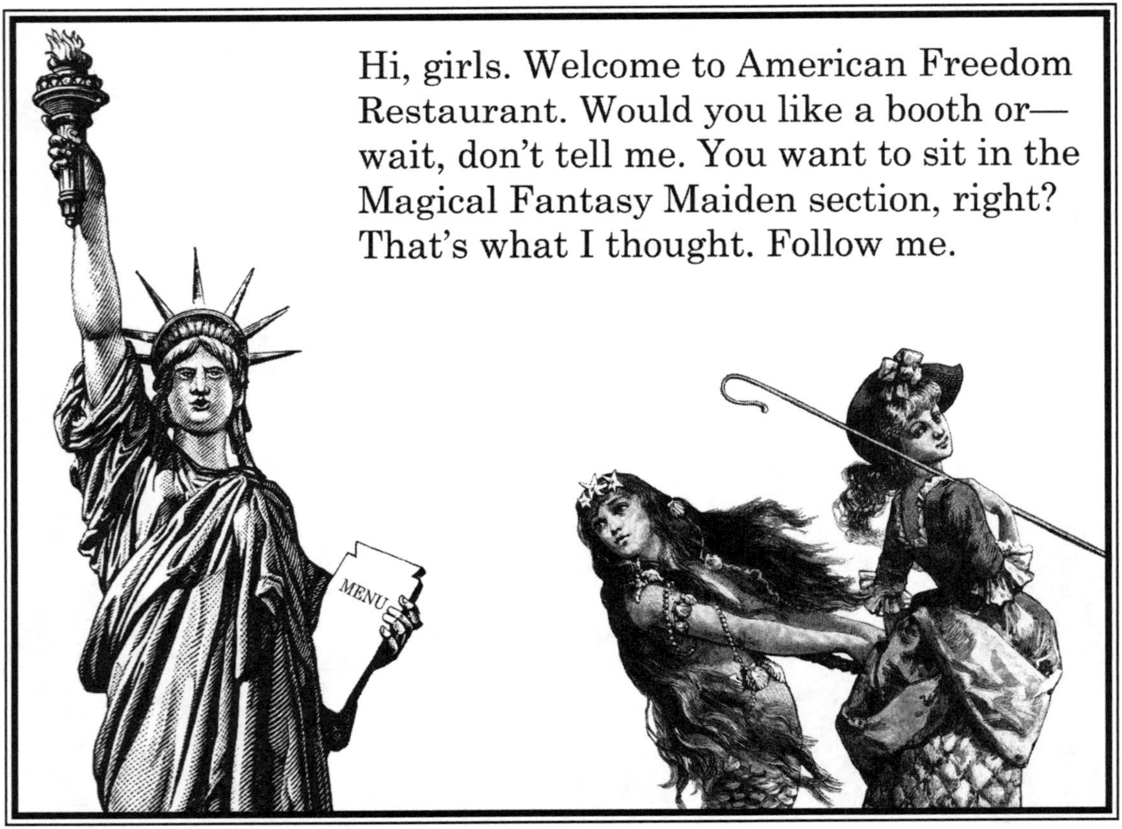
Hi, girls. Welcome to American Freedom Restaurant. Would you like a booth or—wait, don't tell me. You want to sit in the Magical Fantasy Maiden section, right? That's what I thought. Follow me.
MENU

Whoooops!

I accidentally made you in love with an insane person!

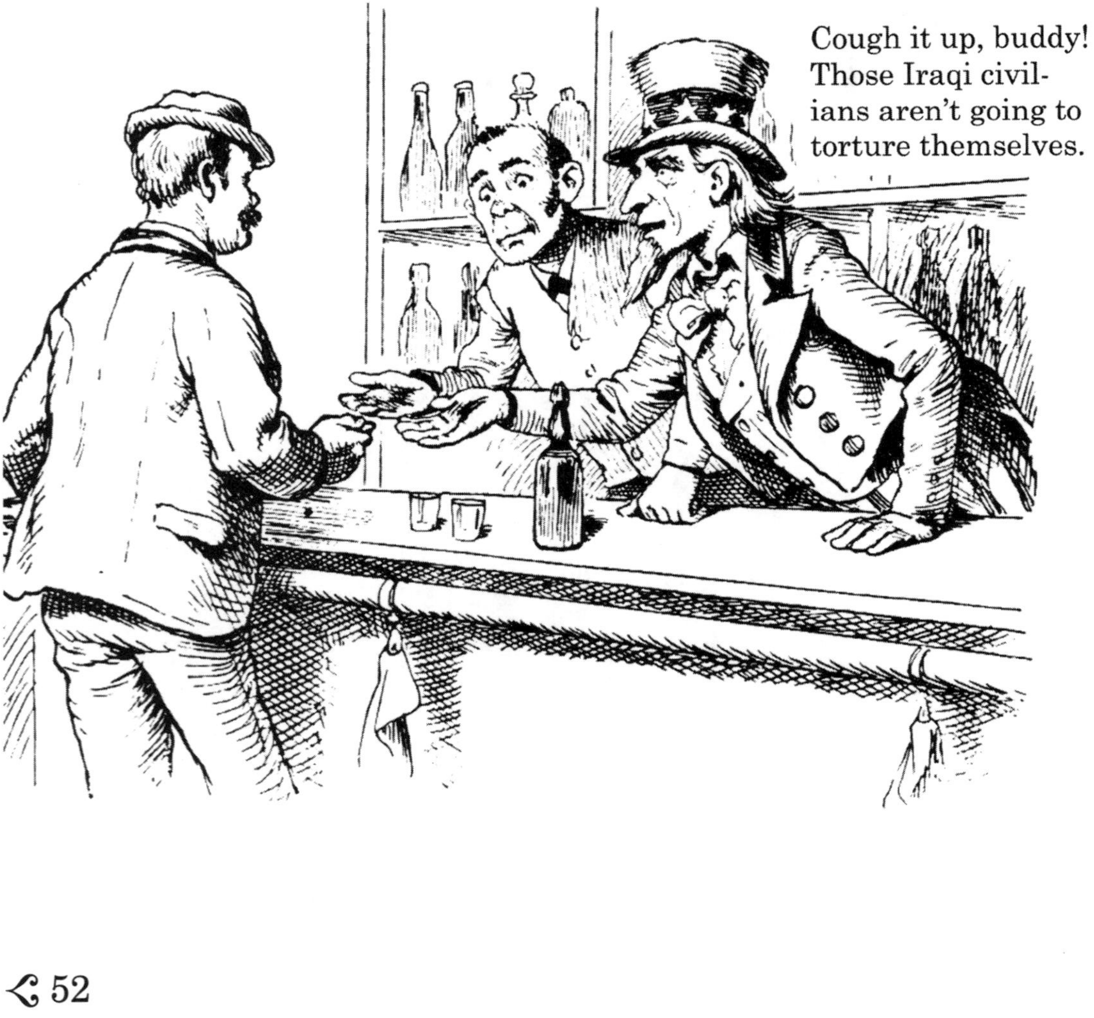
Cough it up, buddy! Those Iraqi civilians aren't going to torture themselves.

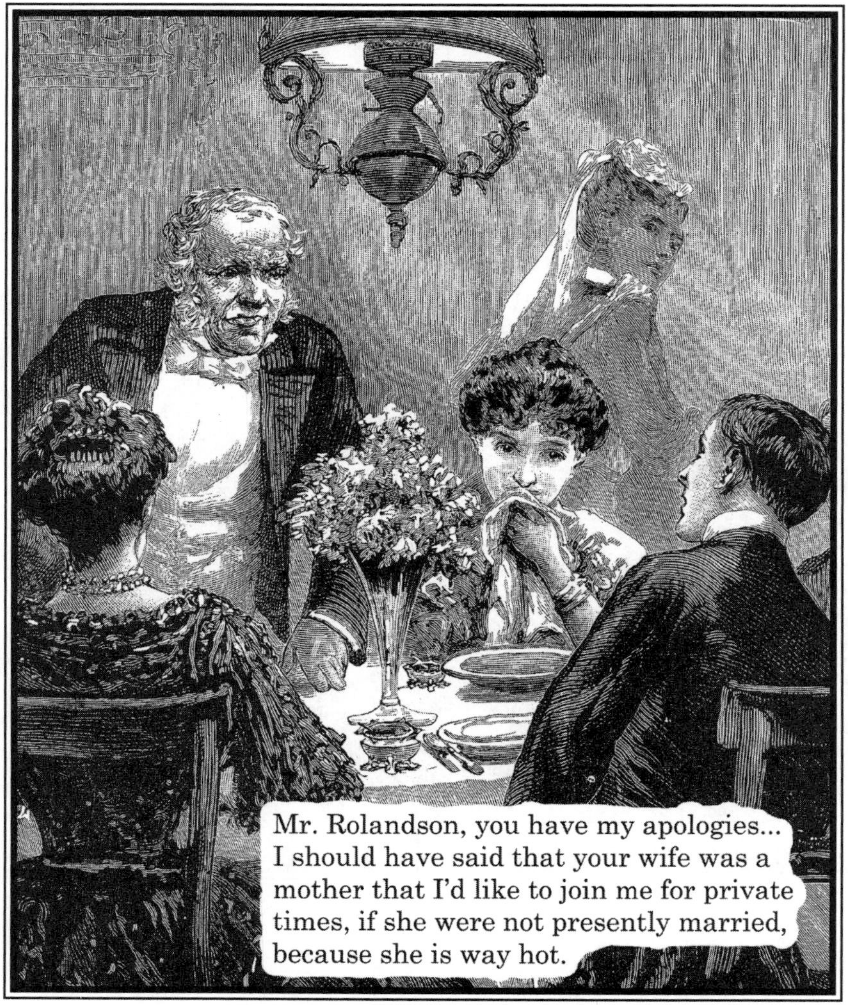
Mr. Rolandson, you have my apologies...
I should have said that your wife was a
mother that I'd like to join me for private
times, if she were not presently married,
because she is way hot.

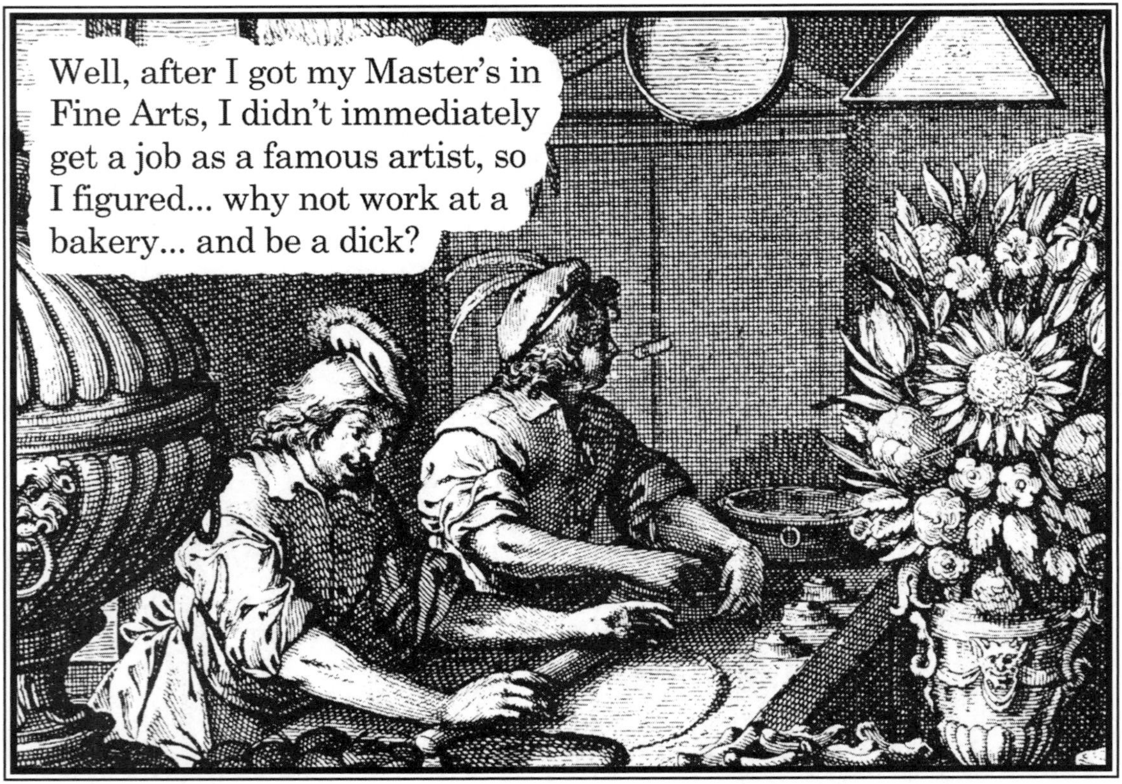
Well, after I got my Master's in Fine Arts, I didn't immediately get a job as a famous artist, so I figured... why not work at a bakery... and be a dick?

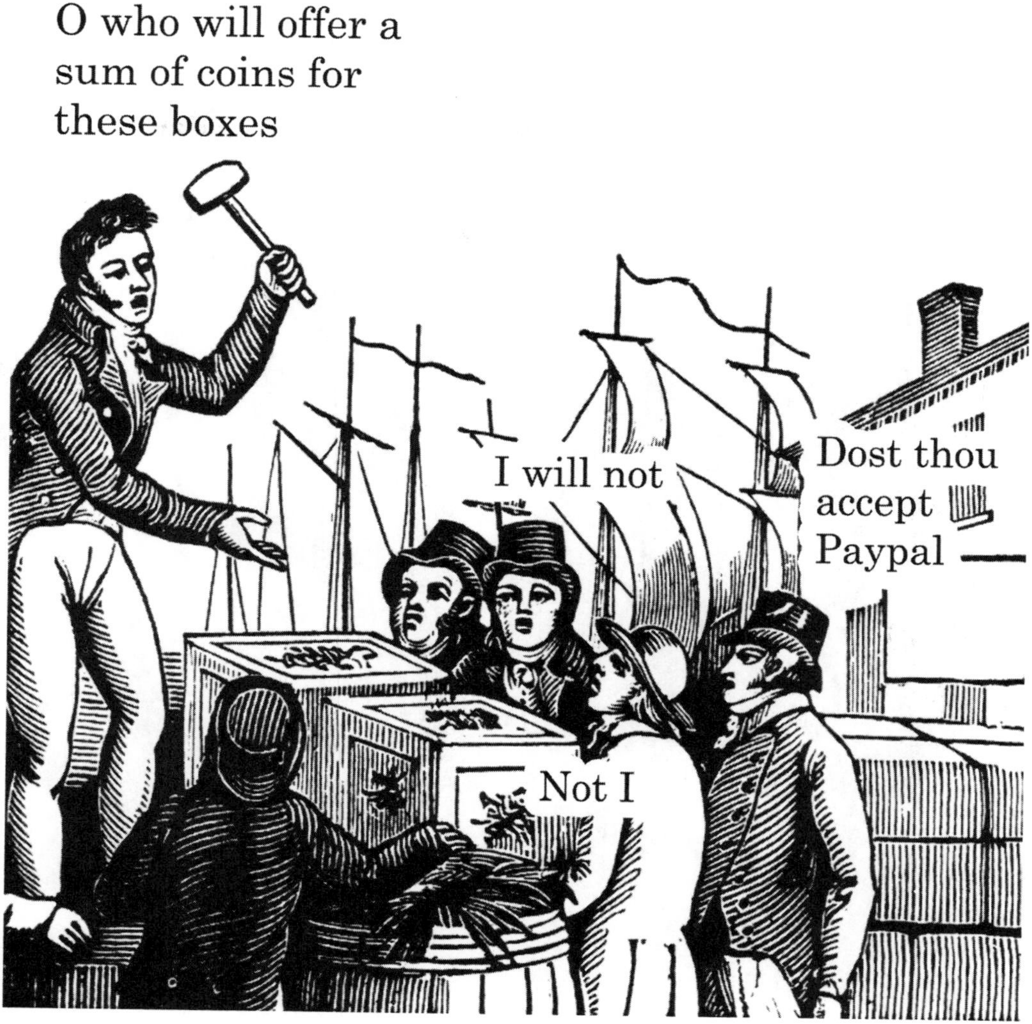
O who will offer a
sum of coins for
these boxes
I will not
Dost thou
accept
Paypal
Not I

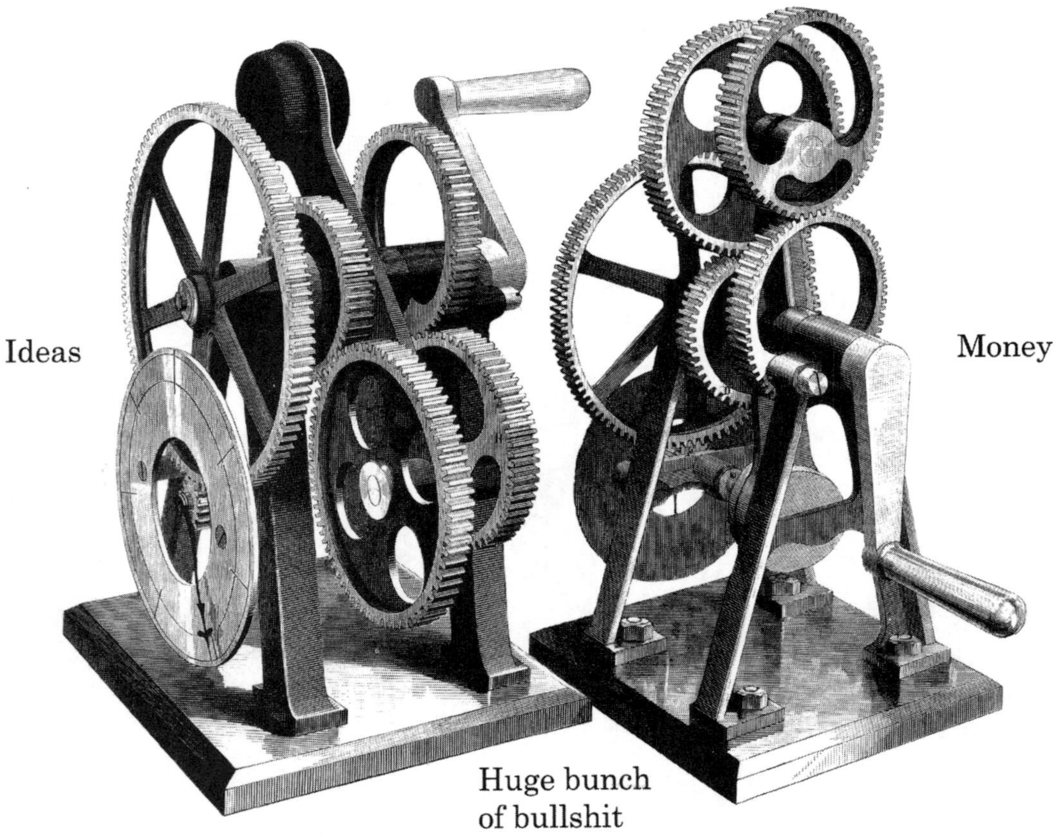
Ideas
Money
Huge bunch of bullshit

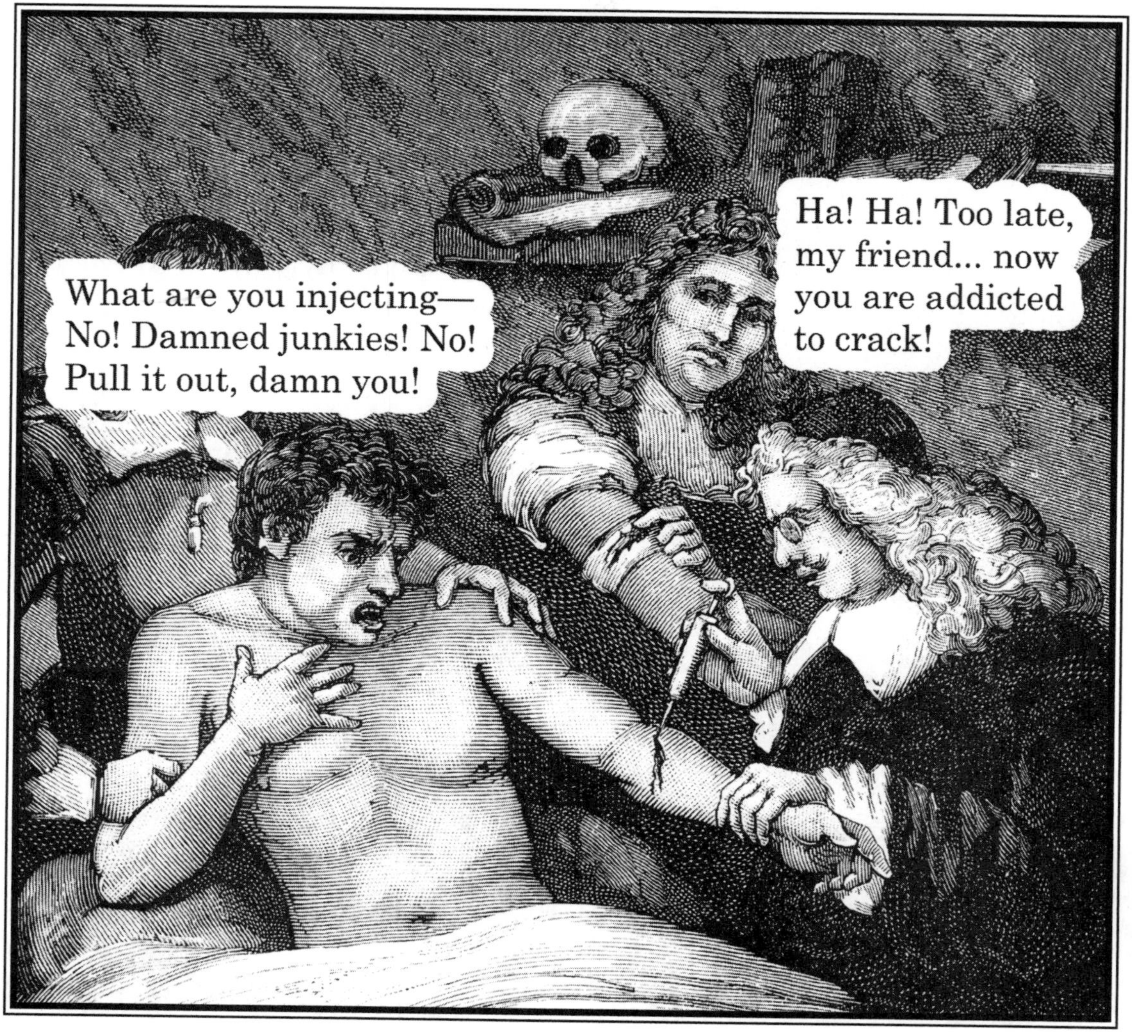
What are you injecting—
No! Damned junkies! No!
Pull it out, damn you!
Ha! Ha! Too late,
my friend... now
you are addicted
to crack!

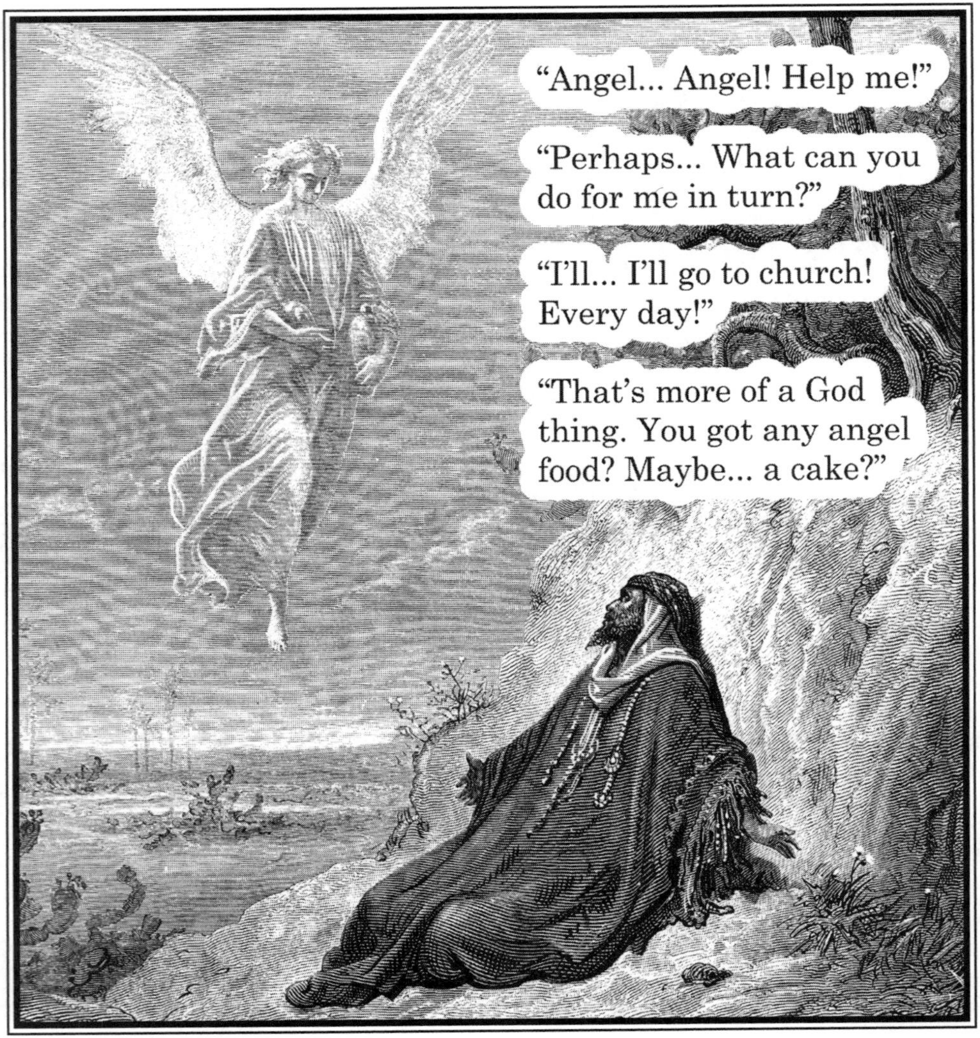
"Angel... Angel! Help me!"
"Perhaps... What can you do for me in turn?"
"I'll... I'll go to church! Every day!"
"That's more of a God thing. You got any angel food? Maybe... a cake?"

He ain't eatin' the bird, man...
he just testin' it to make sure
it a real one. Plenty of fake
birds in these parts.

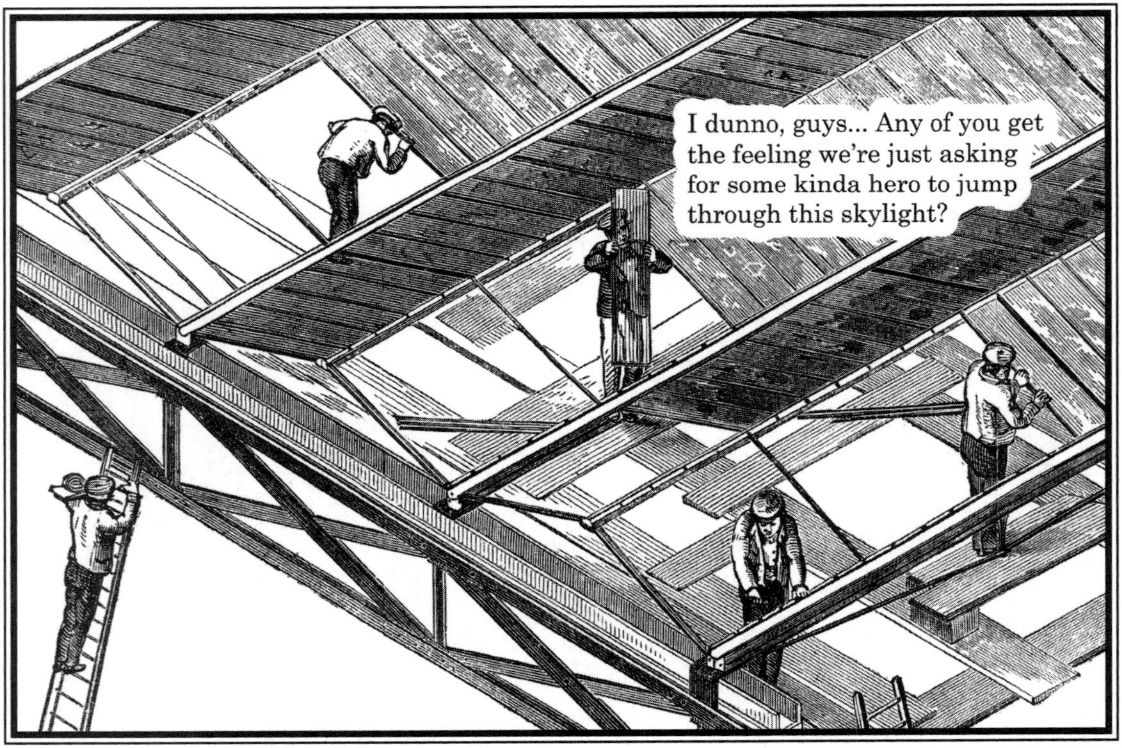
I dunno, guys... Any of you get the feeling we're just asking for some kinda hero to jump through this skylight?

Asparagus was miniaturized in 1889, which was a boon for asparagus farmers, but led directly to the bankruptcy of the Cincinnati Asparagus Lifts factory.

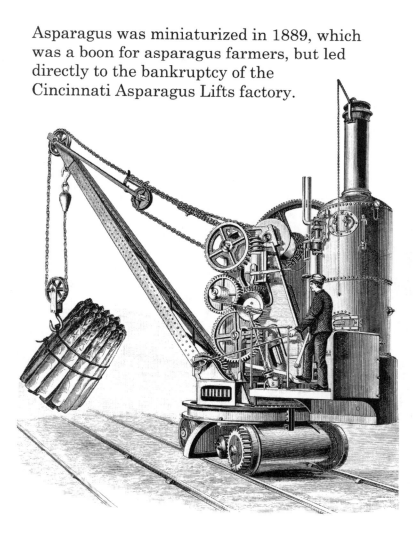

No, no, Conrad, you *do* want this medicine! It makes that... certain... part of the male anatomy bigger.

No, not your hand.
Another part.

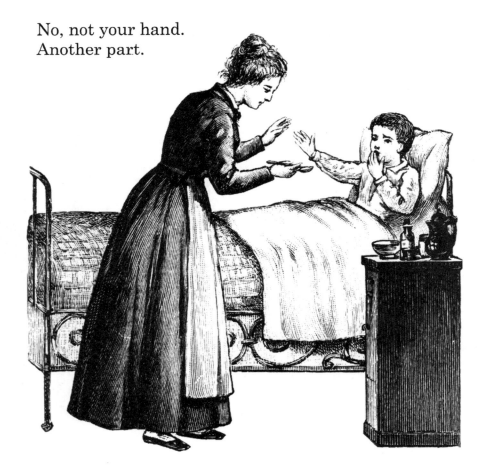

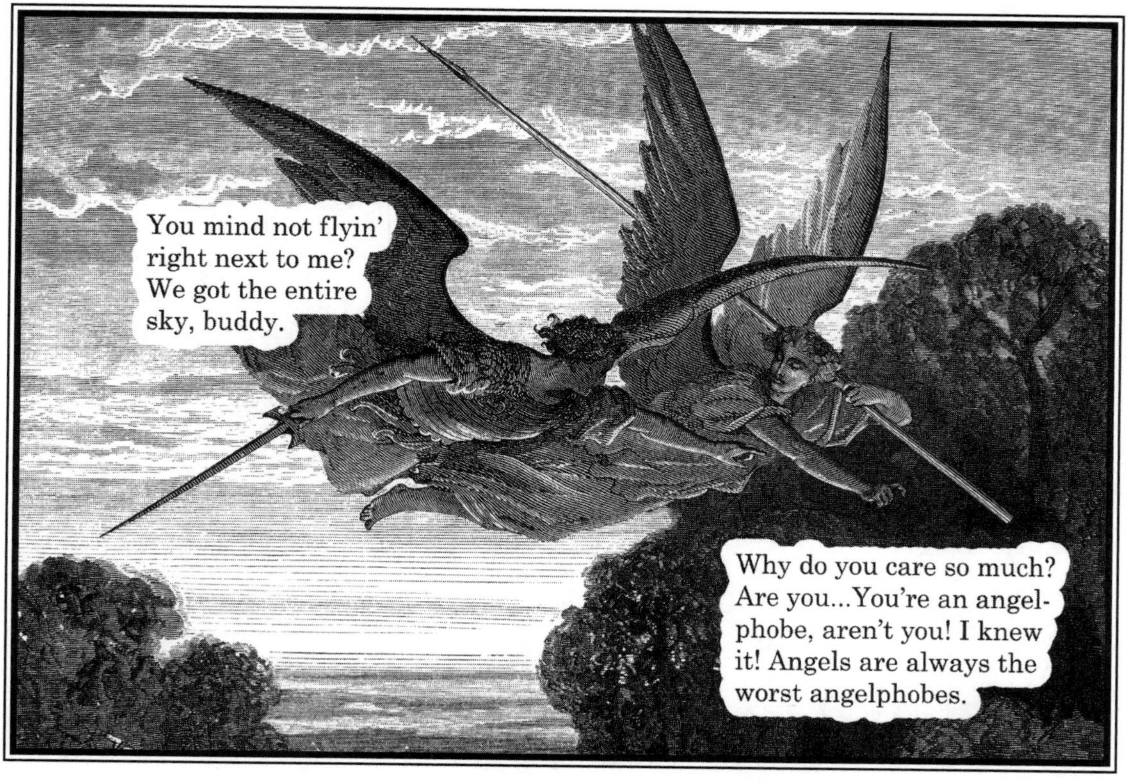
You mind not flyin' right next to me? We got the entire sky, buddy.
Why do you care so much? Are you...You're an angel-phobe, aren't you! I knew it! Angels are always the worst angelphobes.

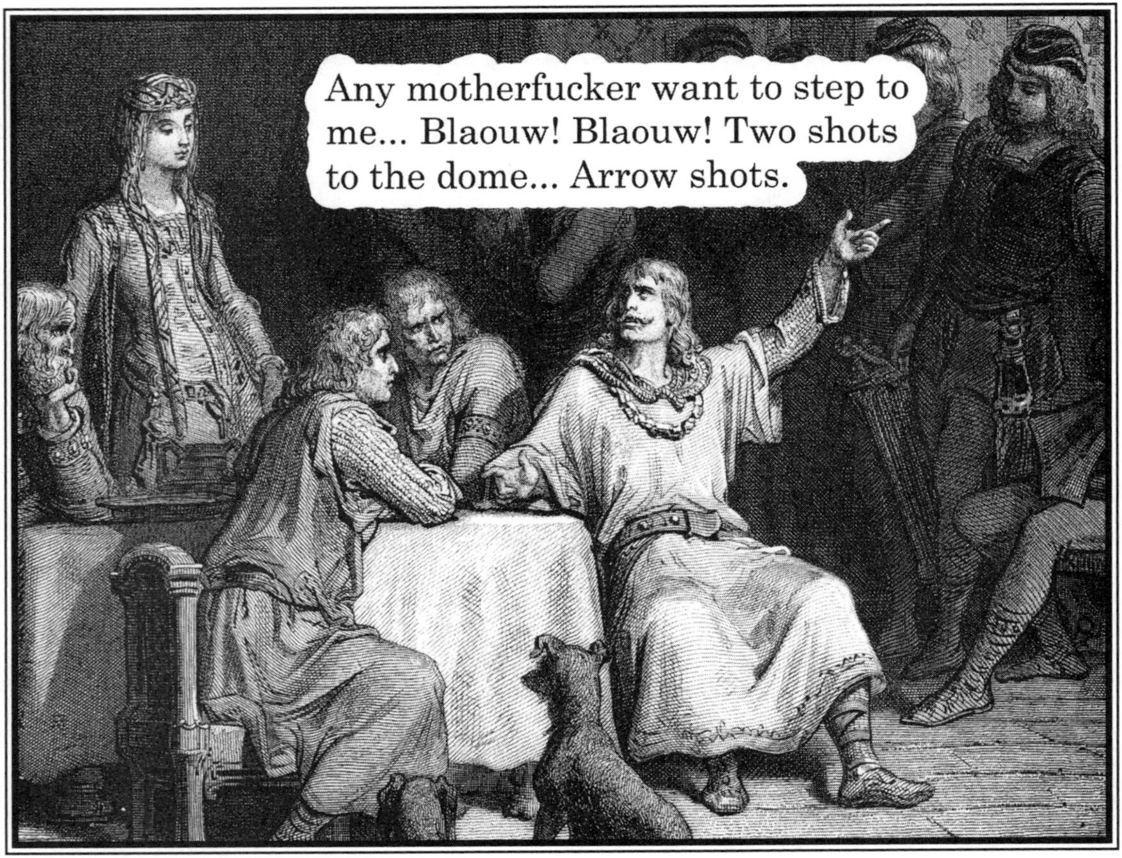
Any motherfucker want to step to me... Blaouw! Blaouw! Two shots to the dome... Arrow shots.

All right, dog, I've tallied today's sales...
We made just over nine thousand
dollars. You've done an excellent
job. We'd love to have you come
back and hold the sign
again tomorrow.

DOG PIPES
DOG TOBACCO
DOG ASHTRAYS
CRAZY DOGEYES

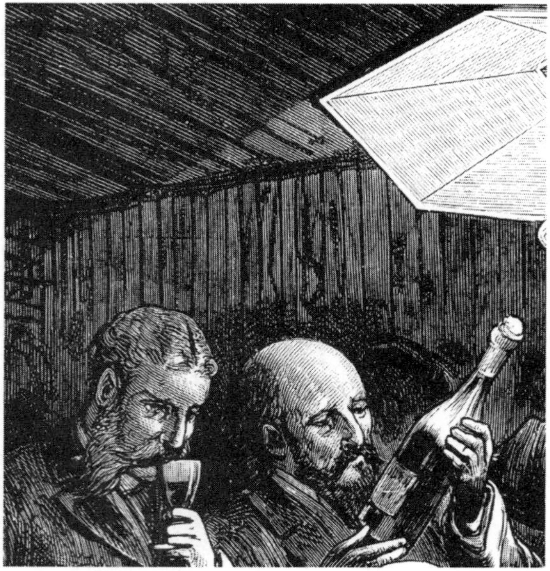

L'ESCAROLE POTARD

1898

Crab Wine

Drink somberly

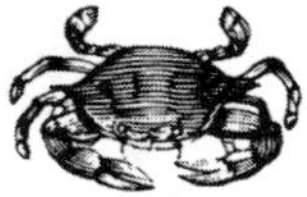

Potard & Sons, Montreal, PQ

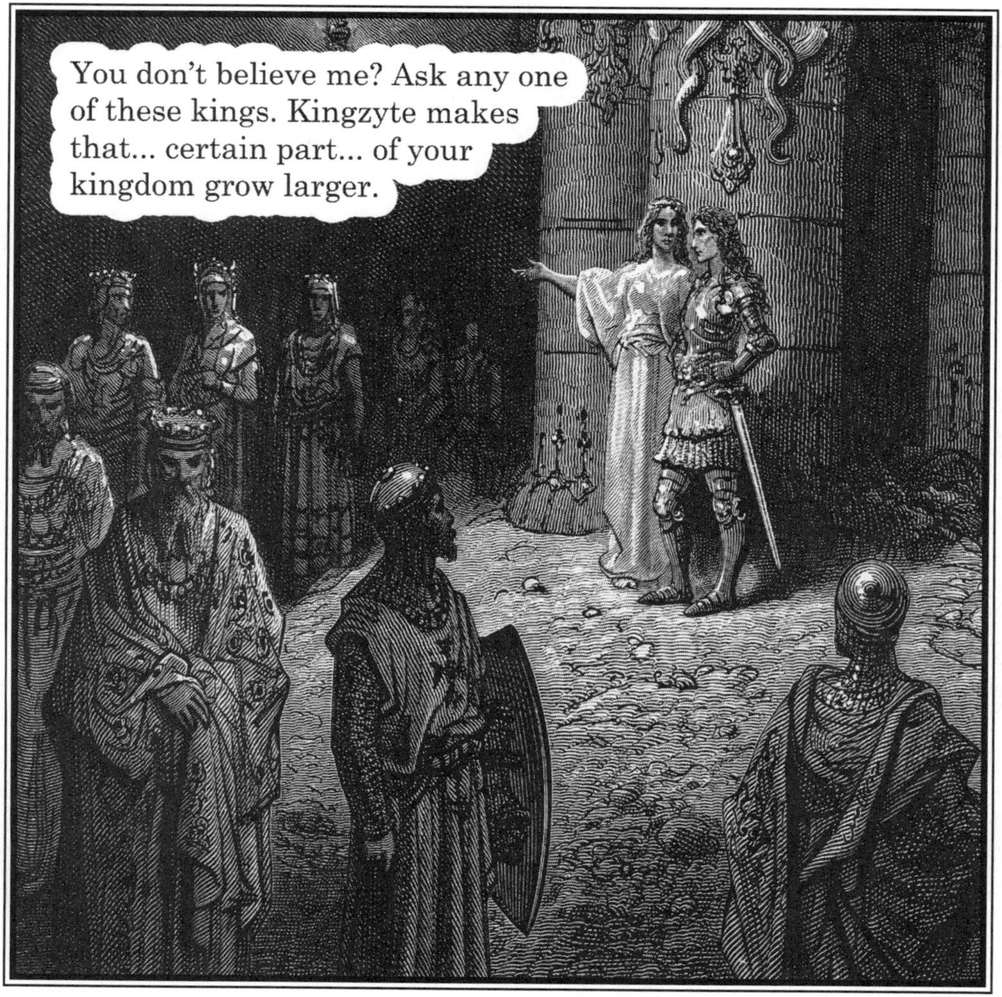
You don't believe me? Ask any one of these kings. Kingzyte makes that... certain part... of your kingdom grow larger.

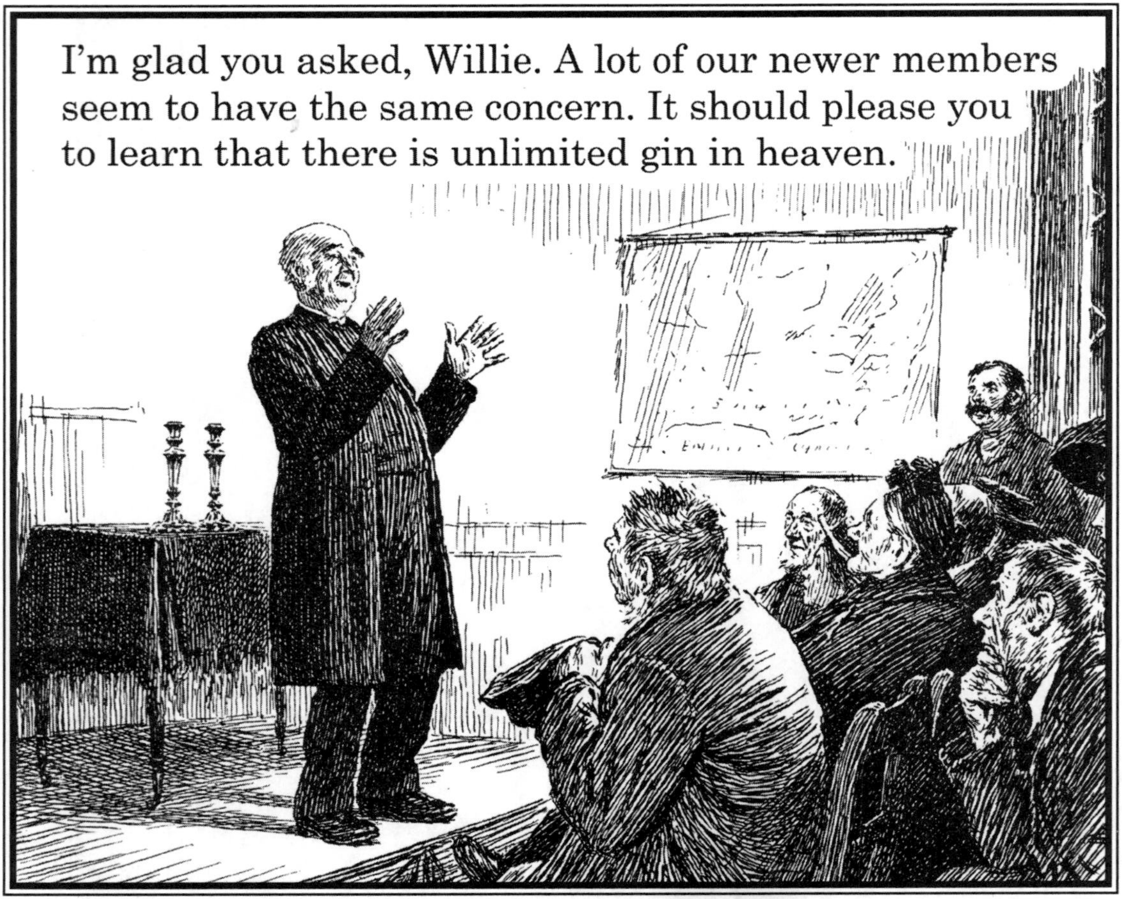
I'm glad you asked, Willie. A lot of our newer members seem to have the same concern. It should please you to learn that there is unlimited gin in heaven.

Thanks, man, but I can't hitch a ride. I appreciate the offer, but I'm *supposed* to ride a snail. My boss can hear me, so I'll leave it at that.

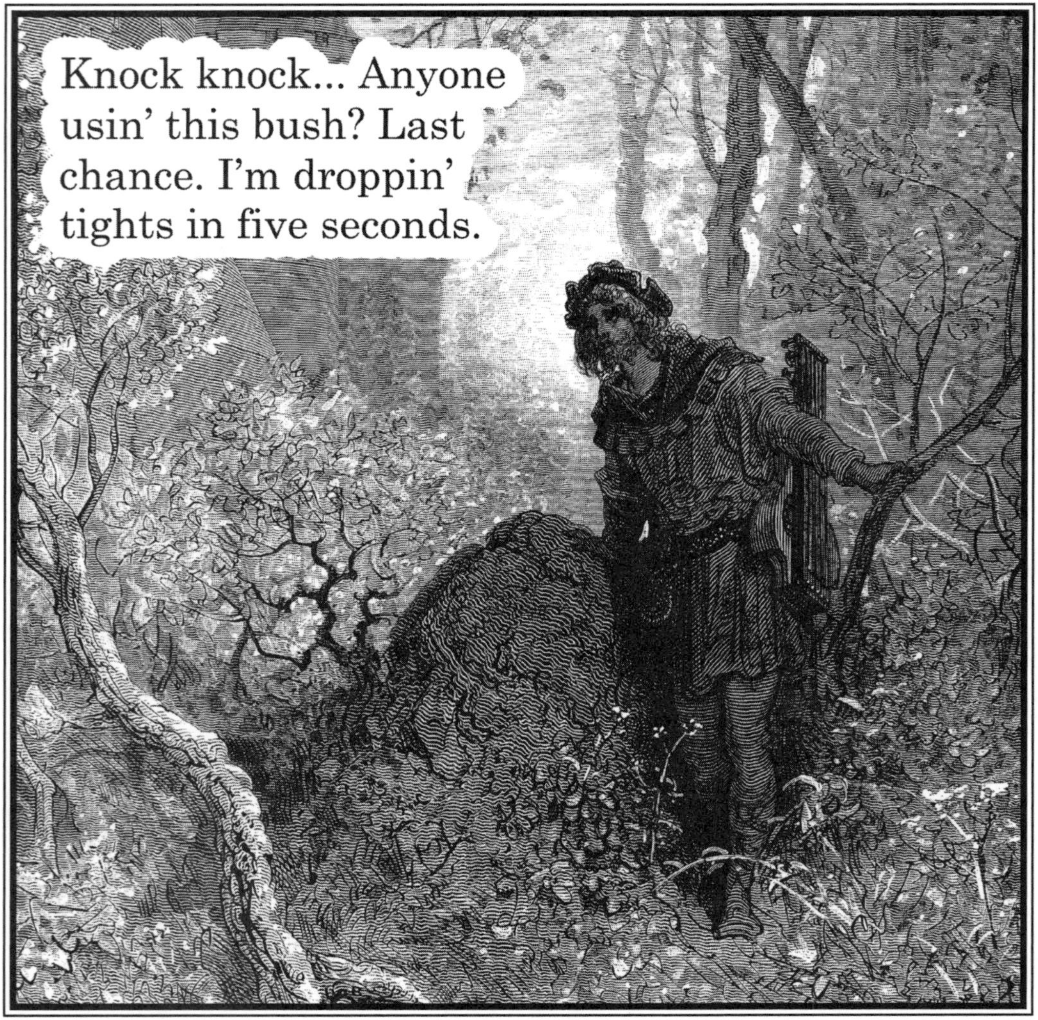
Knock knock... Anyone usin' this bush? Last chance. I'm droppin' tights in five seconds.

Oi, can I see that walkin' stick?
See with your spectacles, not with your handtacles, you cretin!

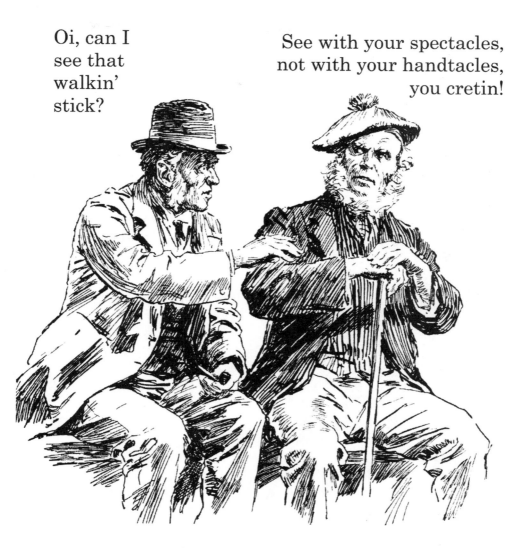

Ugh. It's already 6:30. Whoa, wait, it's six thirty at *night?* It's *dinner?* I... shit. I had it on the schedule, too. No drinking on October 22, because you gotta wake up on October 23rd, 4004 BC, and create the entire universe.

Okay... Let there be four Advil.

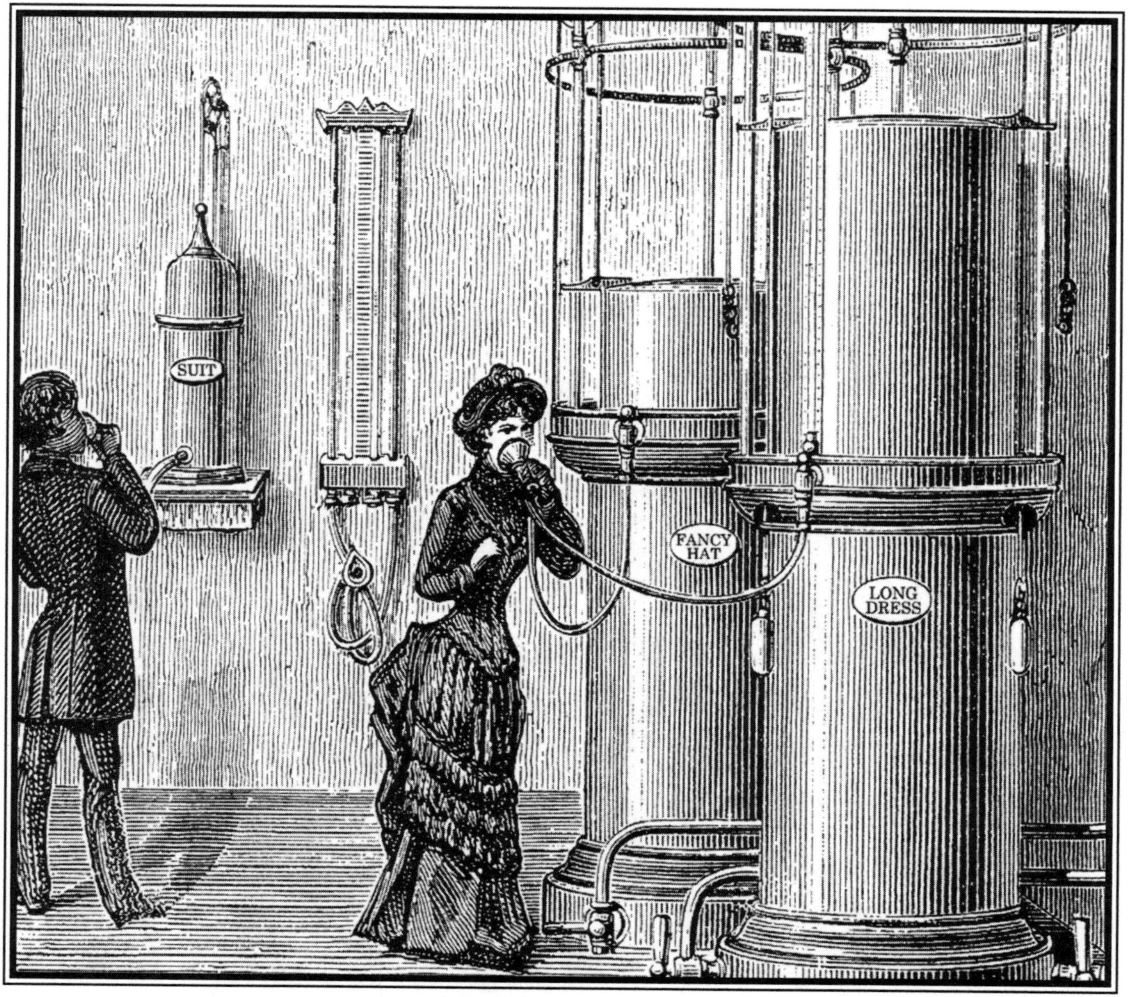
SUIT
FANCY HAT
LONG DRESS

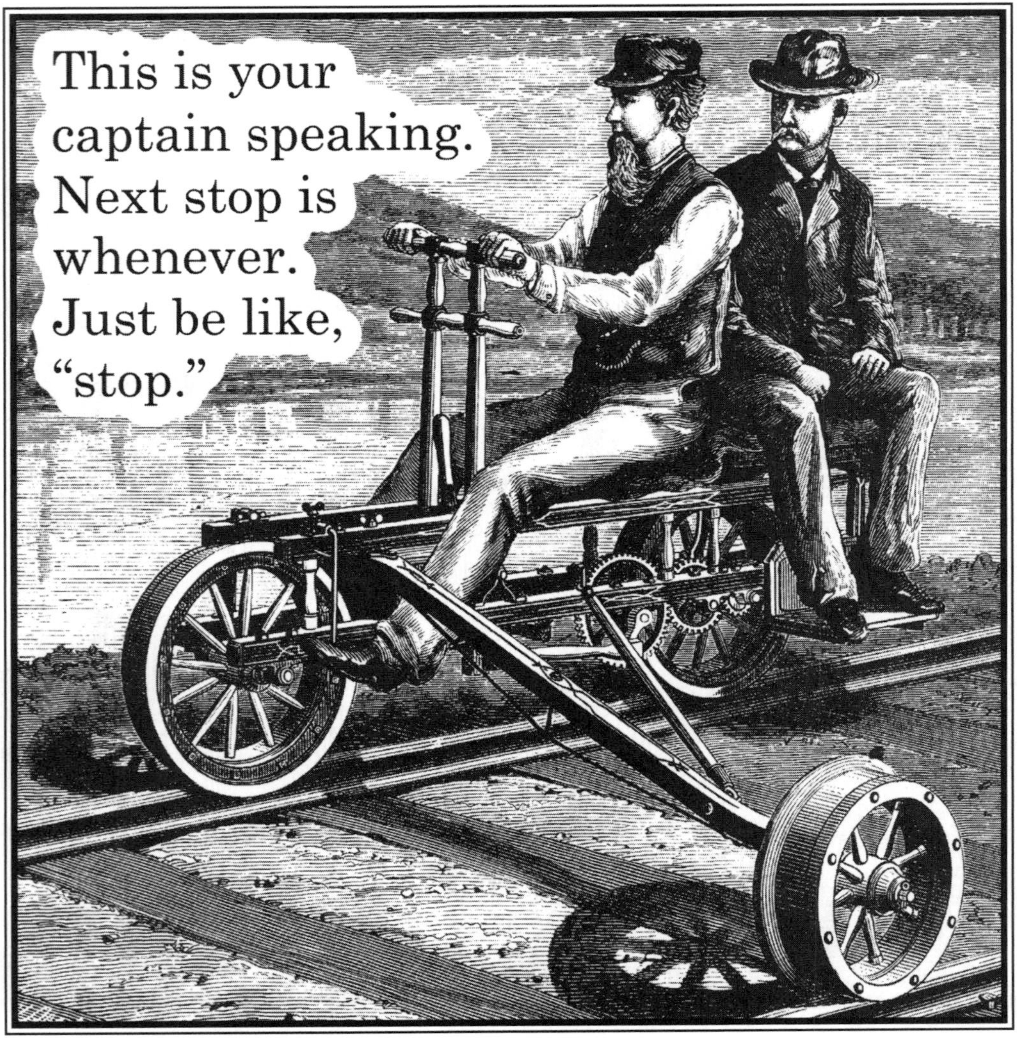
This is your captain speaking. Next stop is whenever. Just be like, "stop."

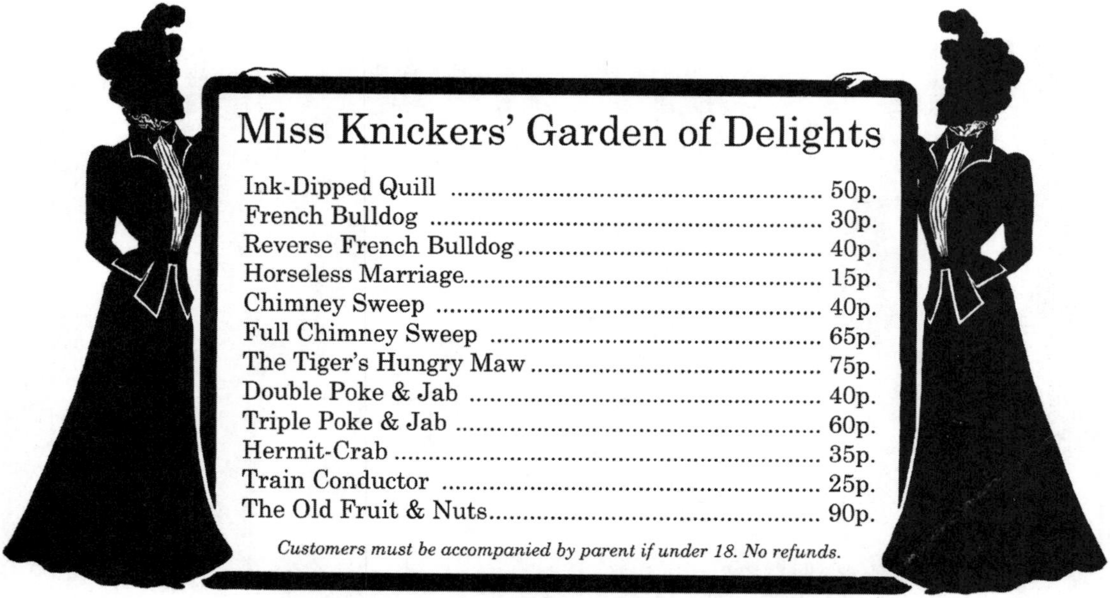
Miss Knickers' Garden of Delights
Ink-Dipped Quill .... 50p.
French Bulldog .... 30p.
Reverse French Bulldog .... 40p.
Horseless Marriage .... 15p.
Chimney Sweep .... 40p.
Full Chimney Sweep .... 65p.
The Tiger's Hungry Maw .... 75p.
Double Poke & Jab .... 40p.
Triple Poke & Jab .... 60p.
Hermit-Crab .... 35p.
Train Conductor .... 25p.
The Old Fruit & Nuts .... 90p.
Customers must be accompanied by parent if under 18. No refunds.

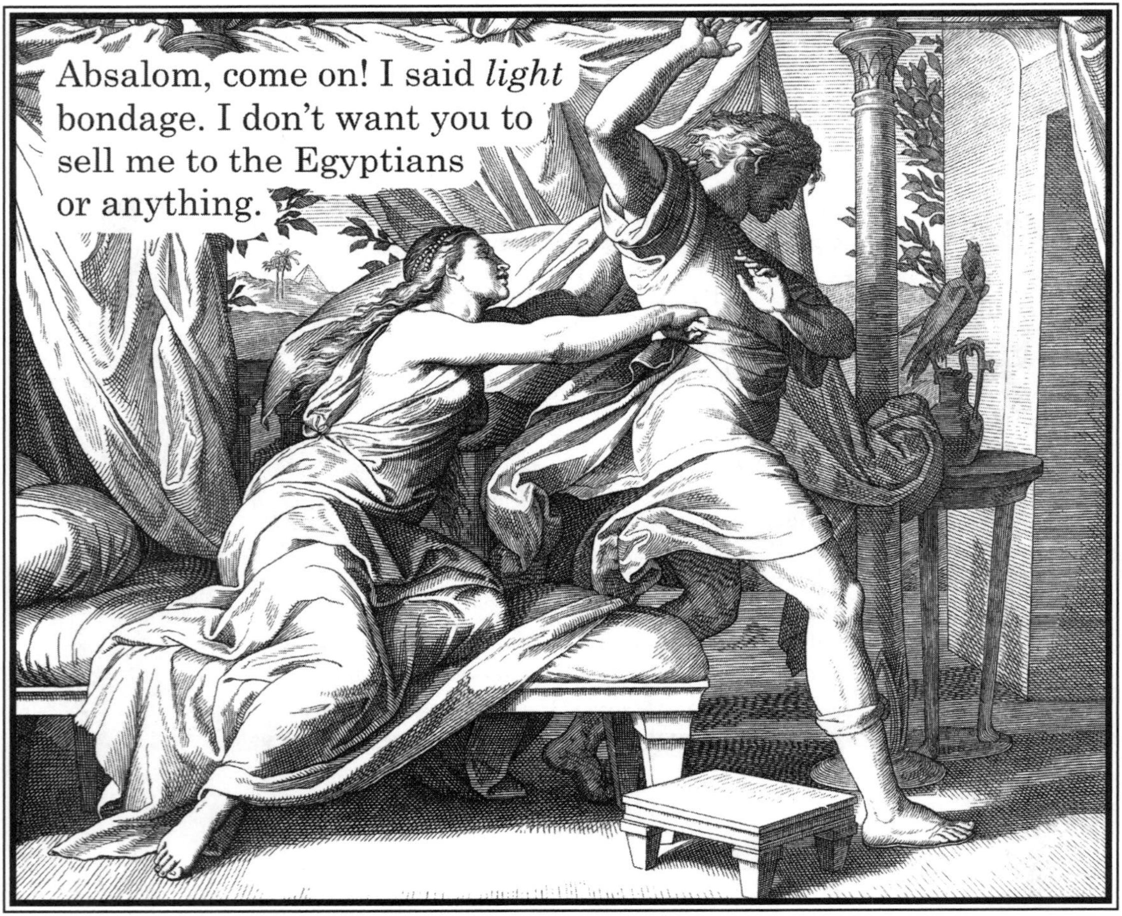
Absalom, come on! I said *light* bondage. I don't want you to sell me to the Egyptians or anything.

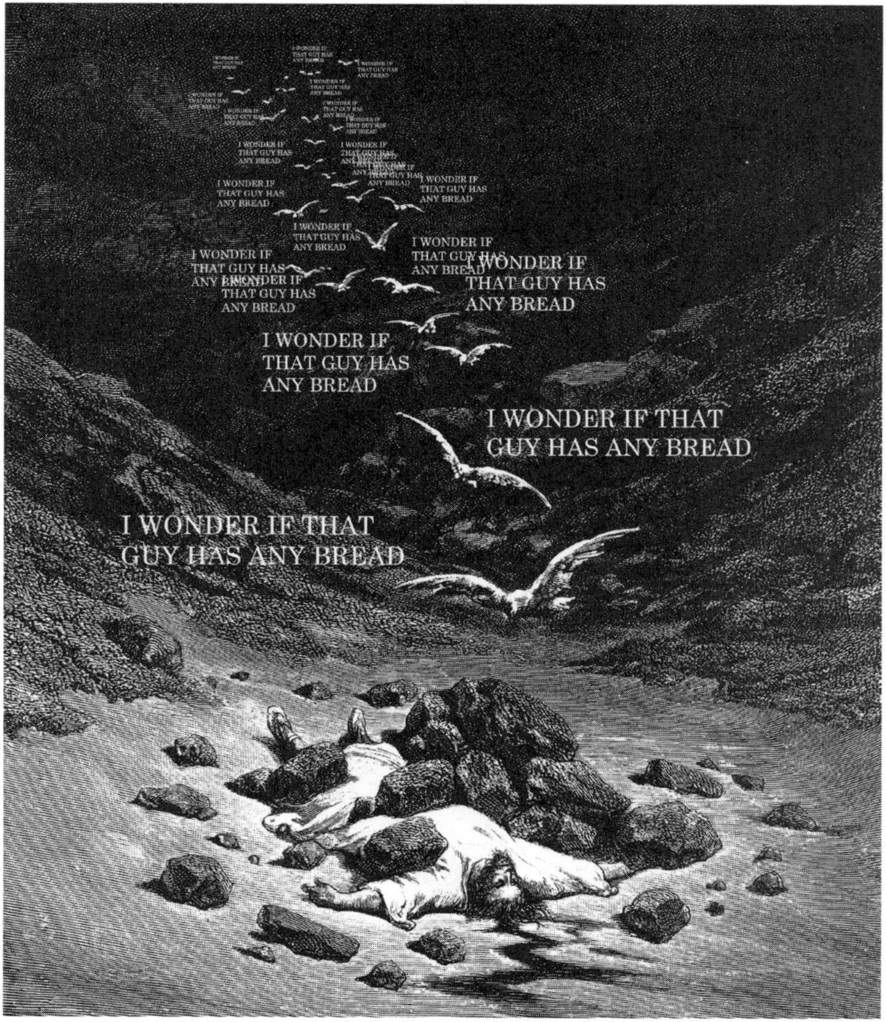
I WONDER IF
THAT GUY HAS
ANY BREAD
I WONDER IF
THAT GUY HAS
ANY BREAD
I WONDER IF
THAT GUY HAS
ANY BREAD
I WONDER IF
THAT GUY HAS
ANY BREAD
I WONDER IF
THAT GUY HAS
ANY BREAD
I WONDER IF
THAT GUY HAS
ANY BREAD
I WONDER IF THAT
GUY HAS ANY BREAD
I WONDER IF THAT
GUY HAS ANY BREAD

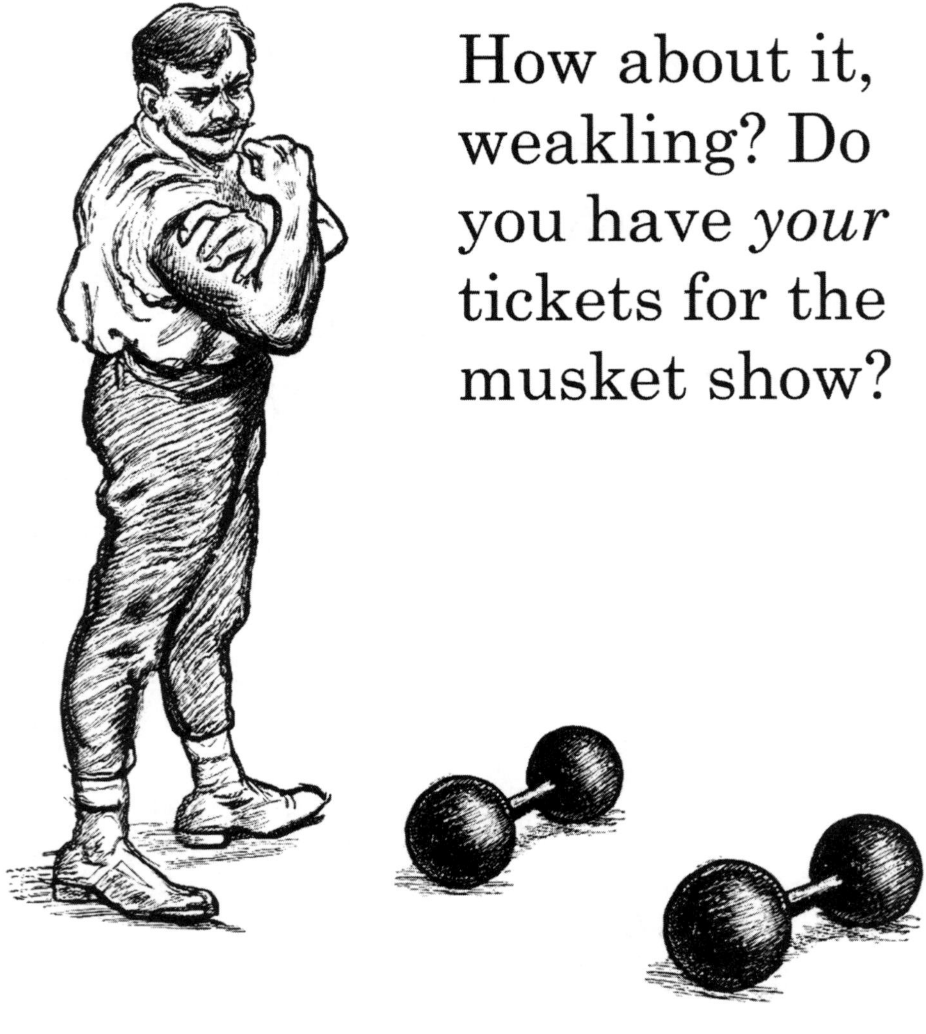

How about it, weakling? Do you have *your* tickets for the musket show?

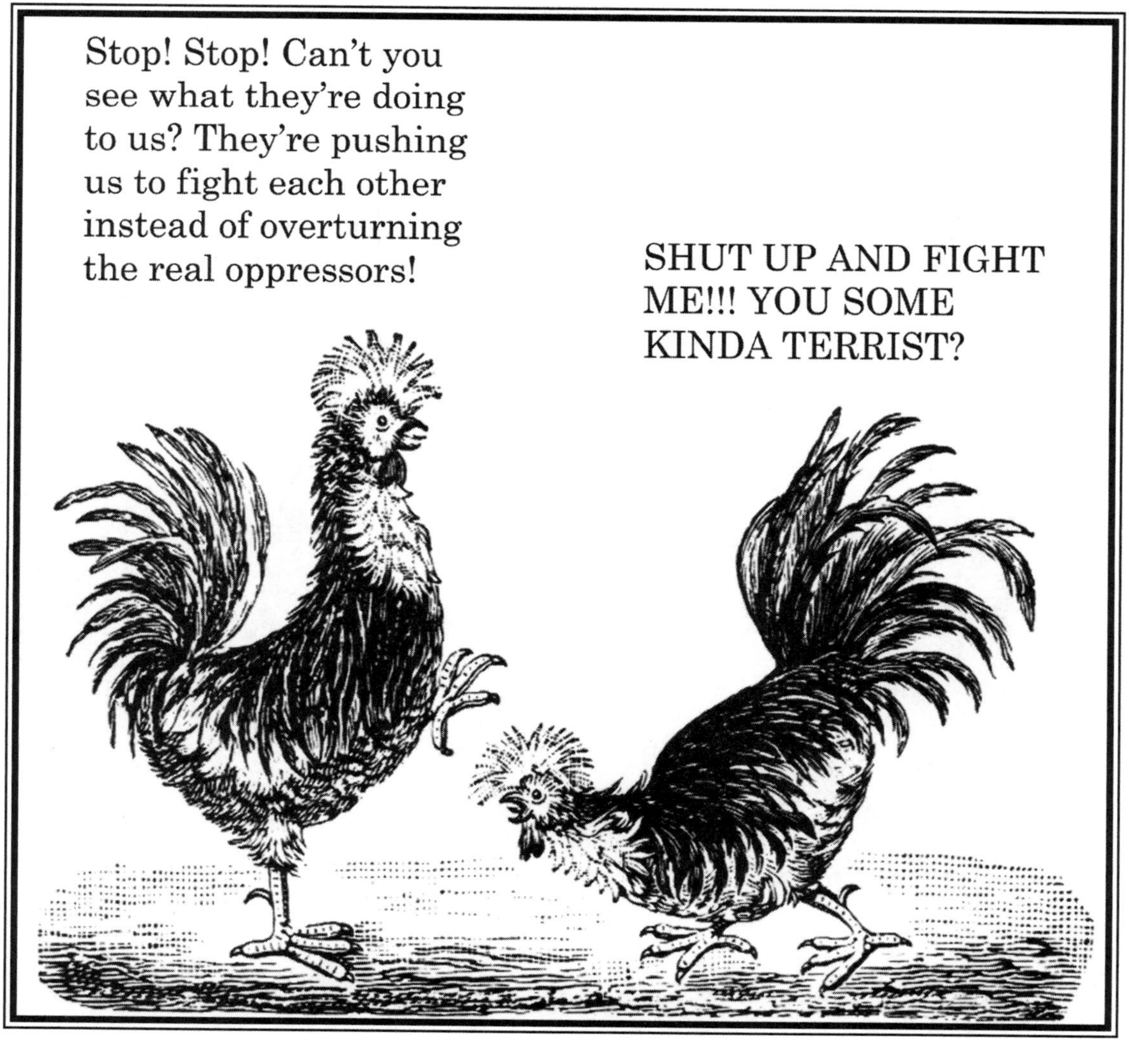
Stop! Stop! Can't you see what they're doing to us? They're pushing us to fight each other instead of overturning the real oppressors!
SHUT UP AND FIGHT ME!!! YOU SOME KINDA TERRIST?

Nooo... my hoes... My... my area codes...
Be still, Gaius Ludacris... You shall have all the women you desire once you come with me.

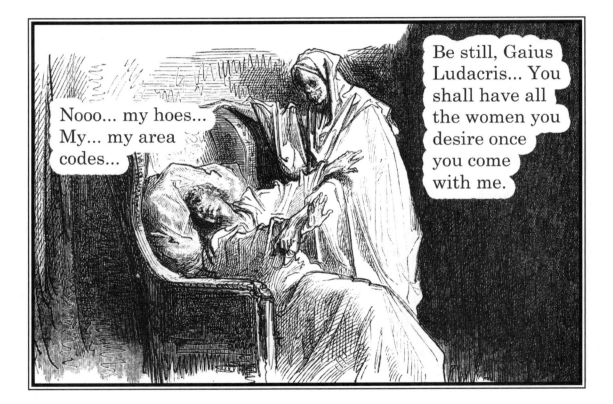

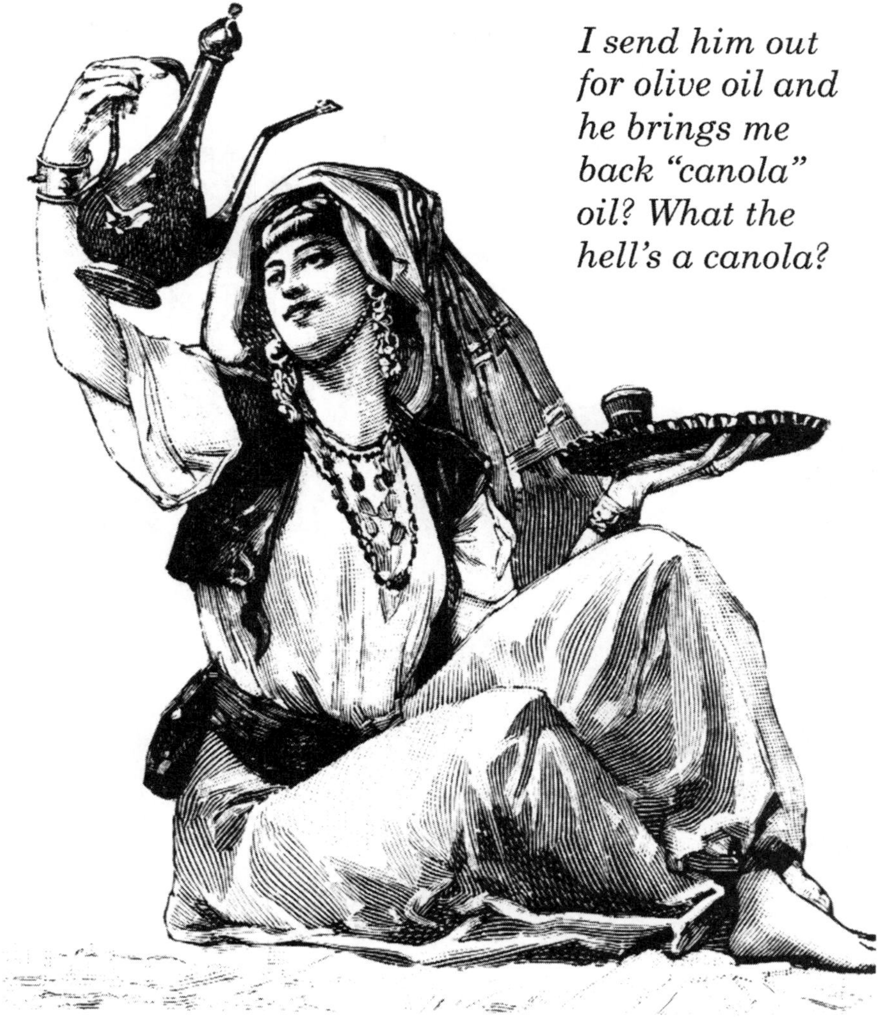

I send him out for olive oil and he brings me back "canola" oil? What the hell's a canola?

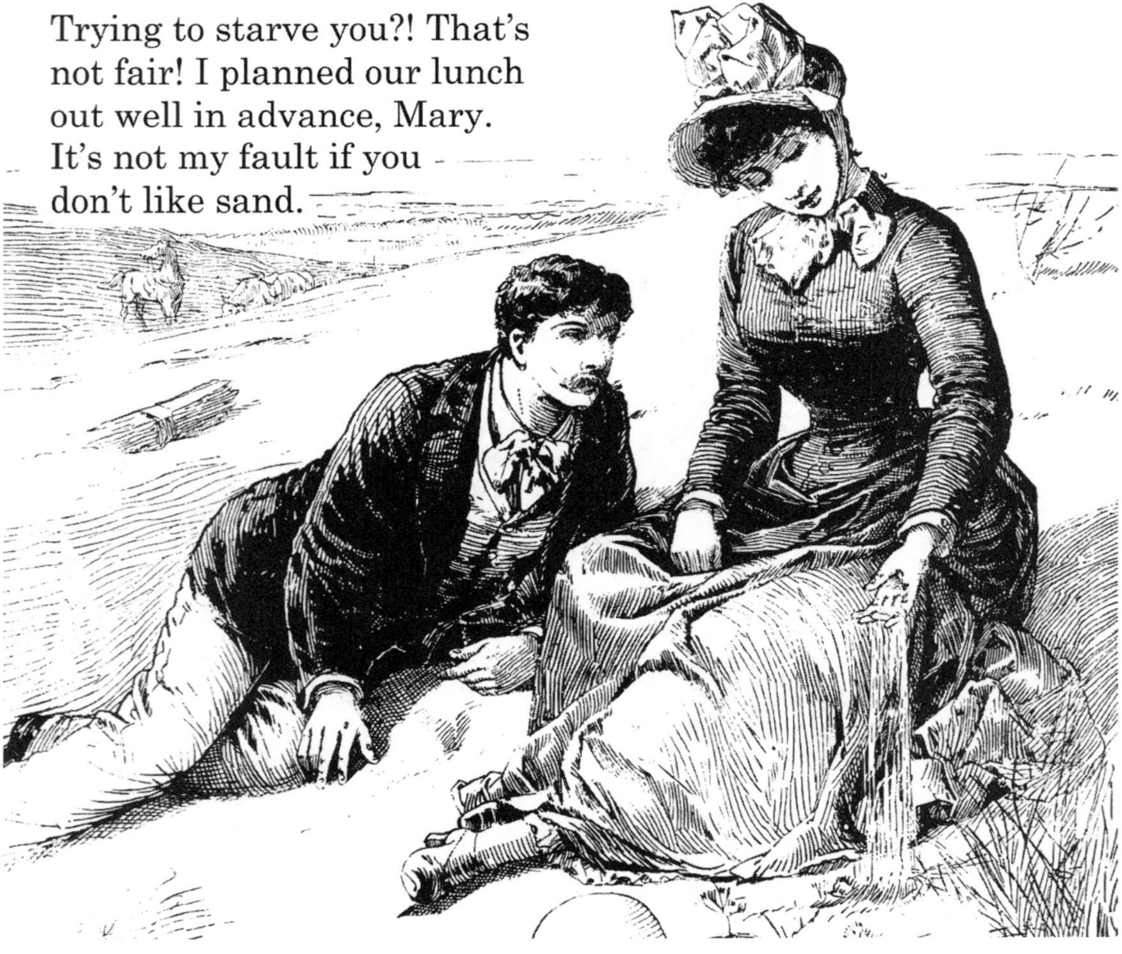
Trying to starve you?! That's not fair! I planned our lunch out well in advance, Mary. It's not my fault if you don't like sand.

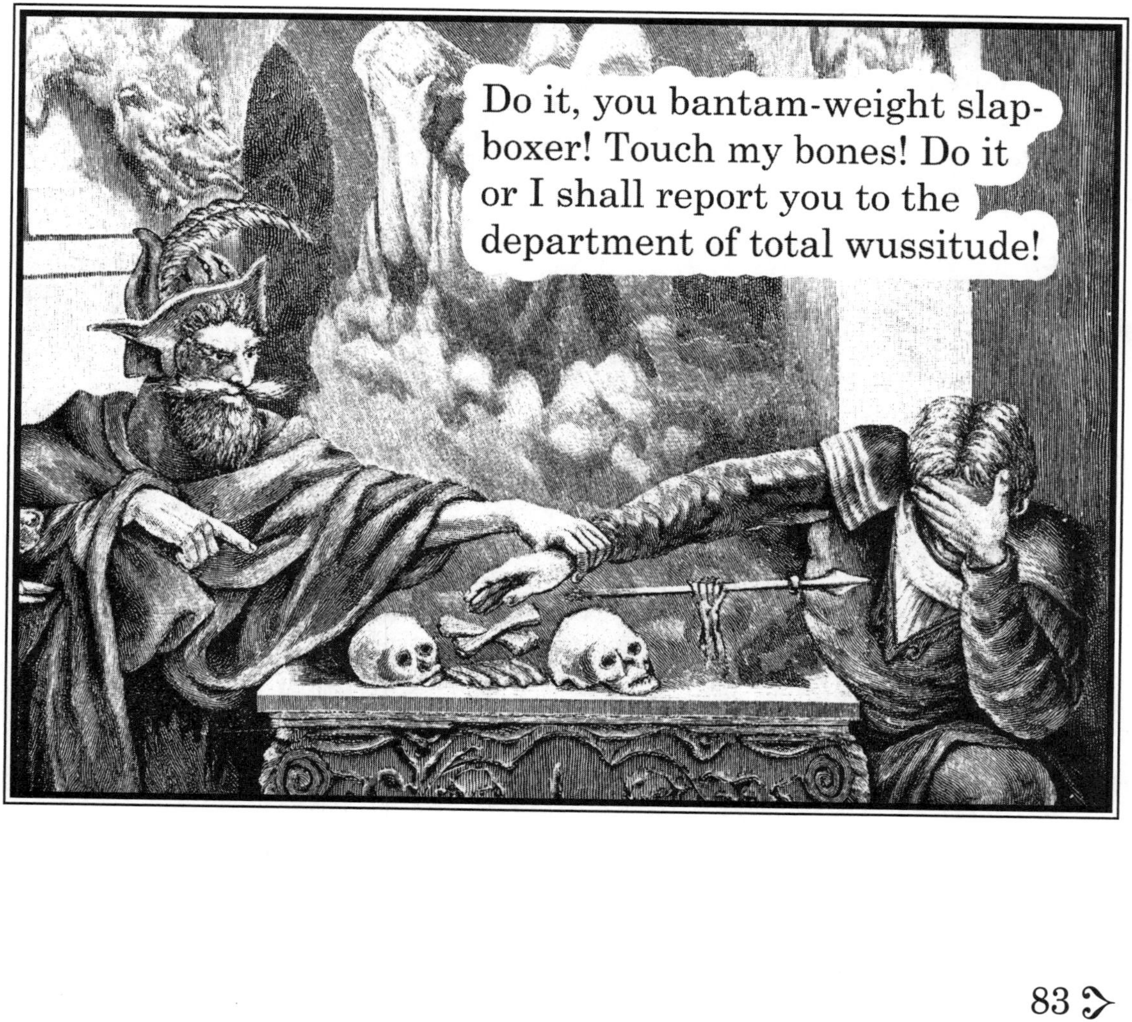
Do it, you bantam-weight slap-boxer! Touch my bones! Do it or I shall report you to the department of total wussitude!

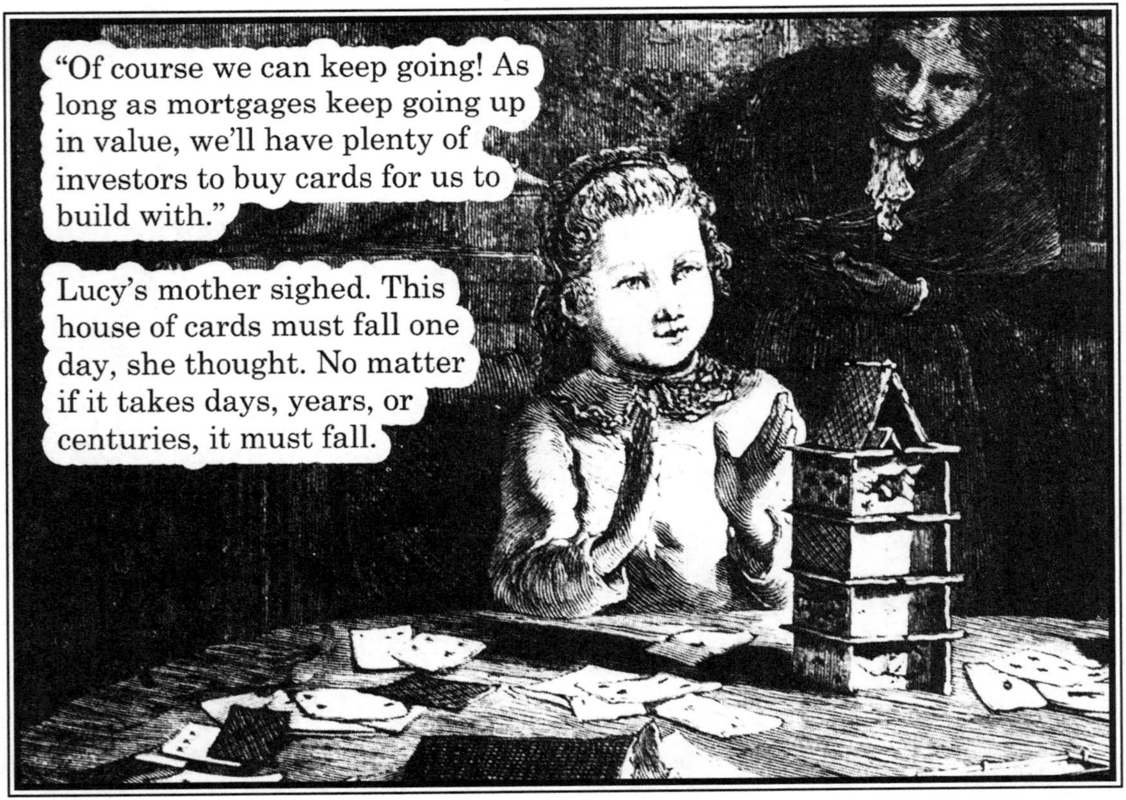
"Of course we can keep going! As long as mortgages keep going up in value, we'll have plenty of investors to buy cards for us to build with."
Lucy's mother sighed. This house of cards must fall one day, she thought. No matter if it takes days, years, or centuries, it must fall.

Voting day arrived, and the ballots were counted and the figures tallied and double-checked. By a thin margin, a wiremobile station was to be built, rather than an "air port." The wiremobile began running three years later, providing service across the Ohio River to northern Kentucky. Unfortunately, no other major cities constructed wiremobile stations, and in 1911, the Cincinnati Wiremobile Transit System ceased operations.

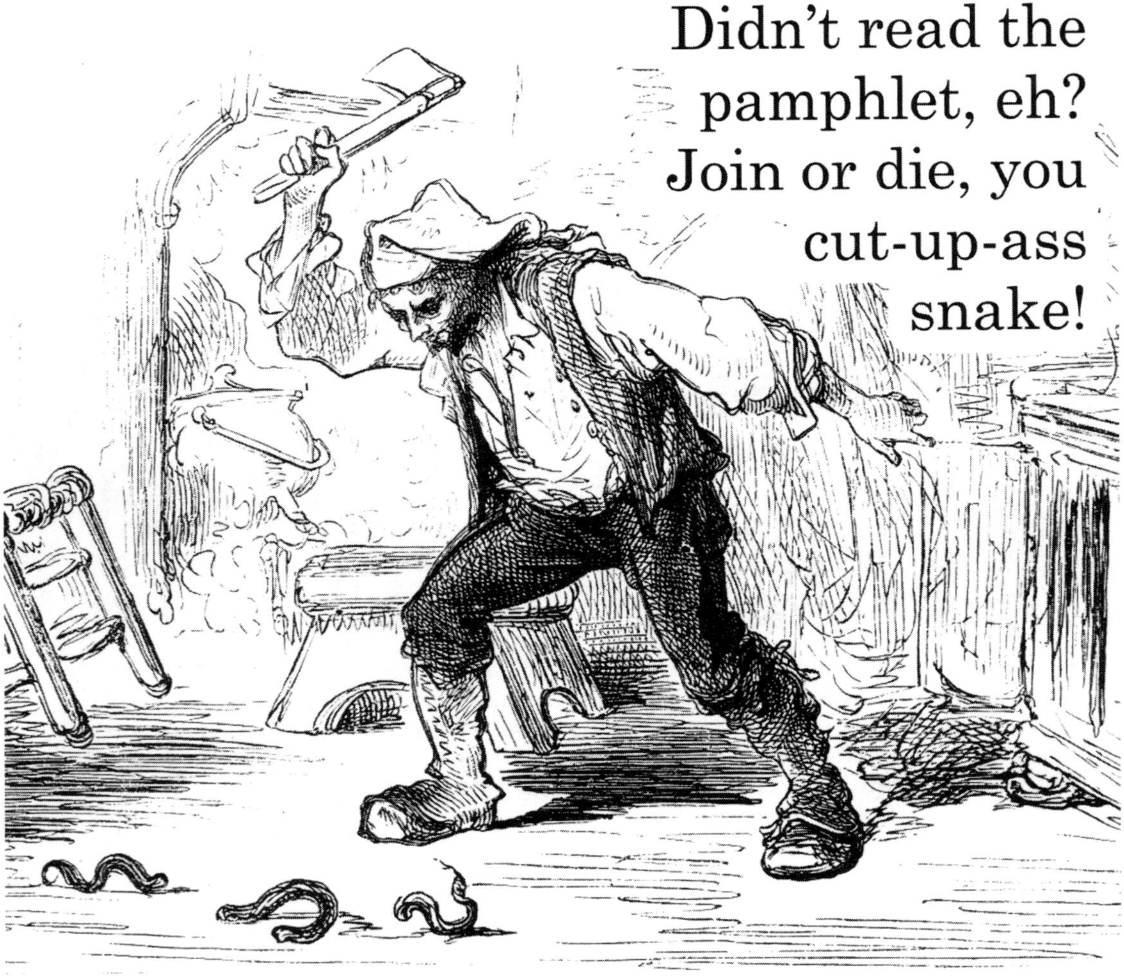
Didn't read the
pamphlet, eh?
Join or die, you
cut-up-ass
snake!

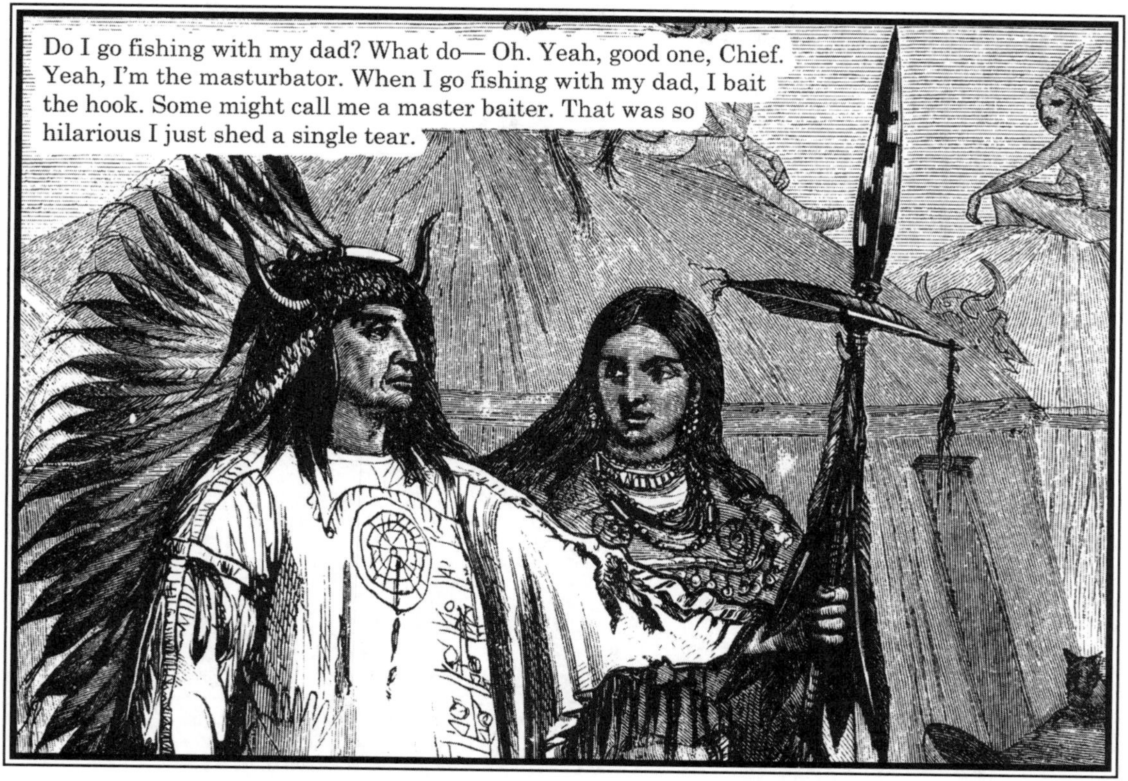
Do I go fishing with my dad? What do— Oh. Yeah, good one, Chief. Yeah, I'm the masturbator. When I go fishing with my dad, I bait the hook. Some might call me a master baiter. That was so hilarious I just shed a single tear.

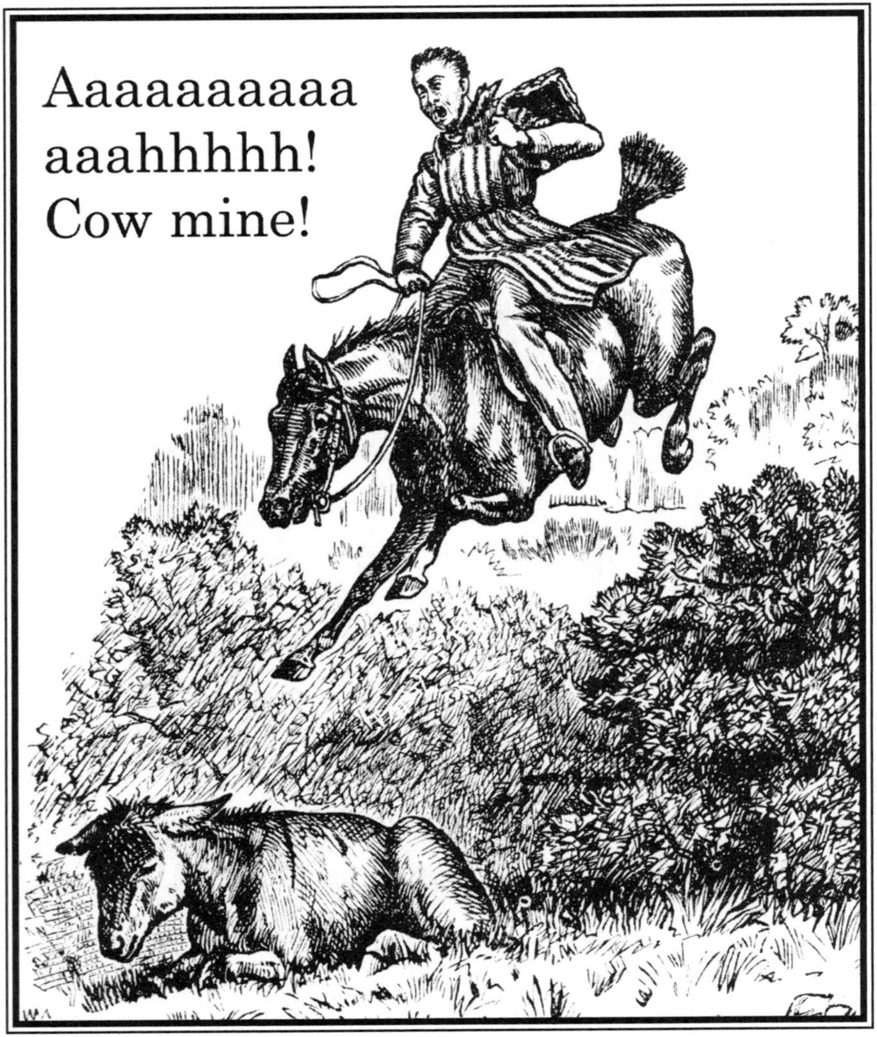
Aaaaaaaaaa
aaahhhhh!
Cow mine!

You want some cantaloupes?
Let me just special-order
them on my Blackberry. Tick-
a-tack-a-tack. There you go.
They'll be here in about
three hundred years.

Keep at it, chap!
These boots go
all the way up.

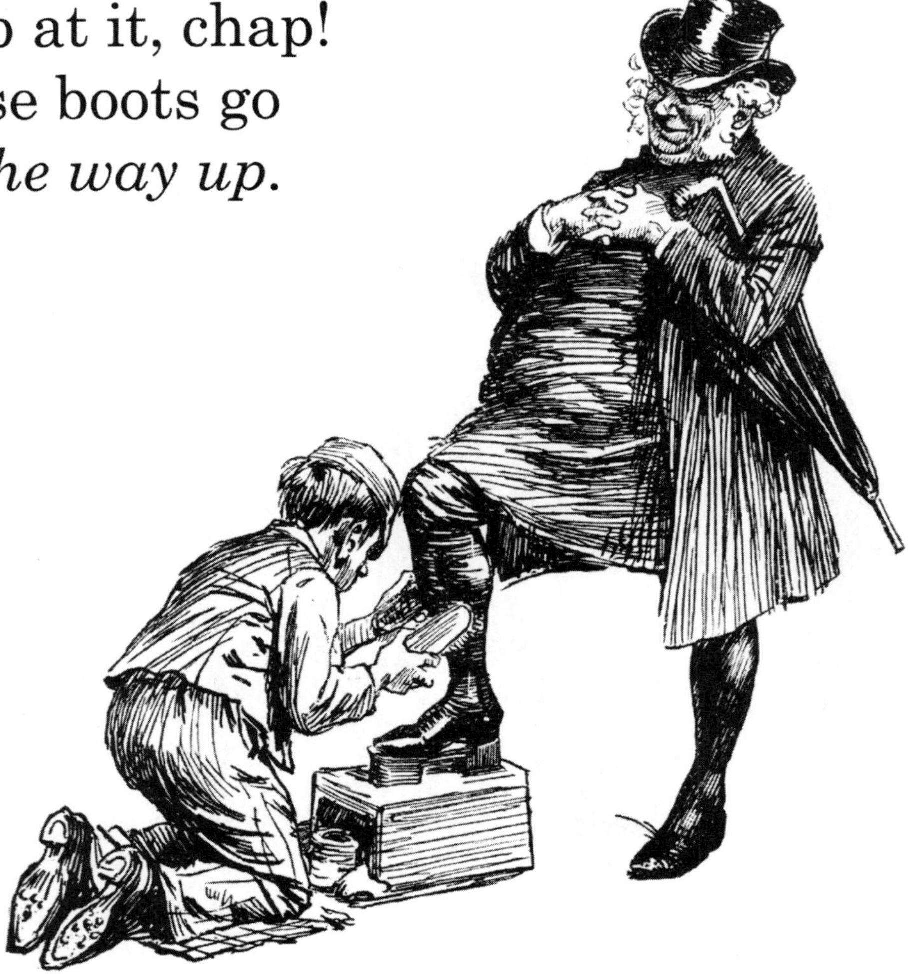

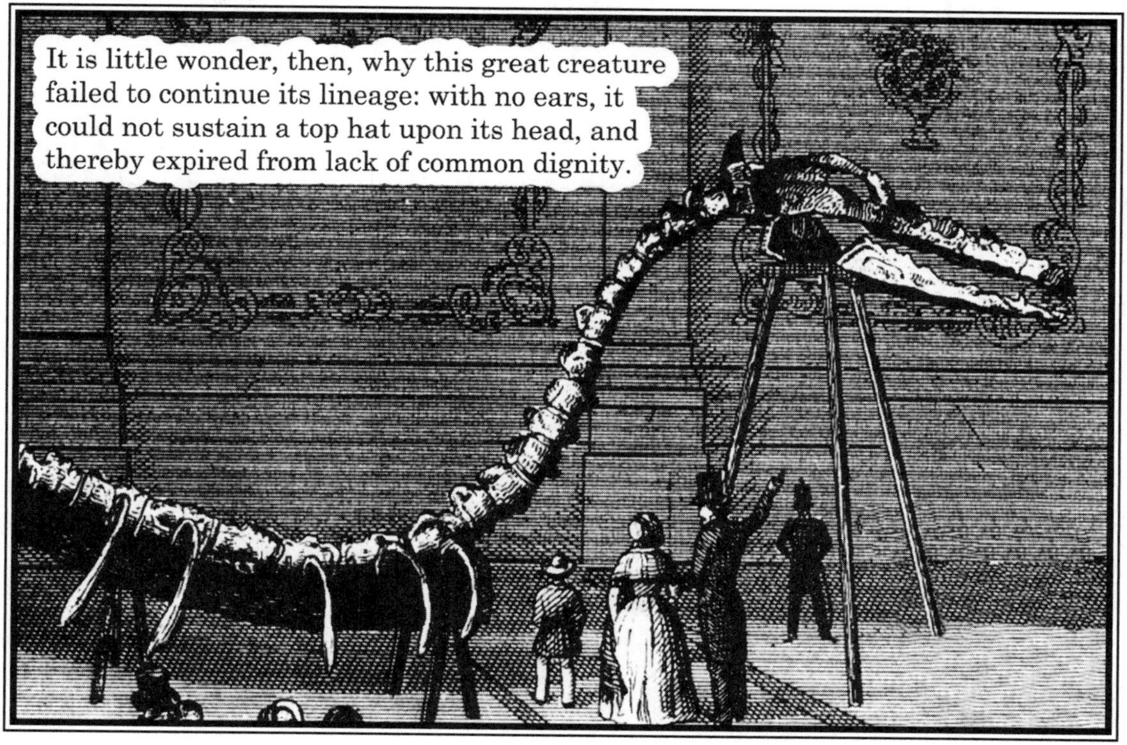
It is little wonder, then, why this great creature failed to continue its lineage: with no ears, it could not sustain a top hat upon its head, and thereby expired from lack of common dignity.

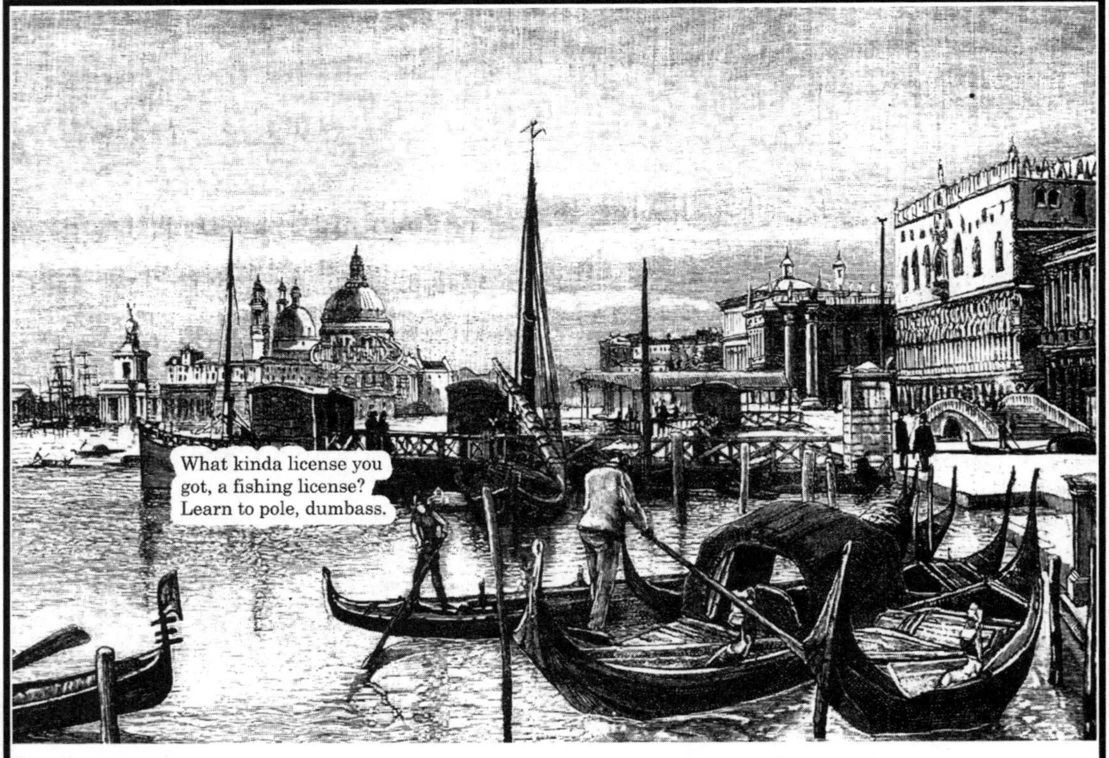
What kinda license you got, a fishing license? Learn to pole, dumbass.

As populations in the region increased, the reports of "boat rage" climbed exponentially.

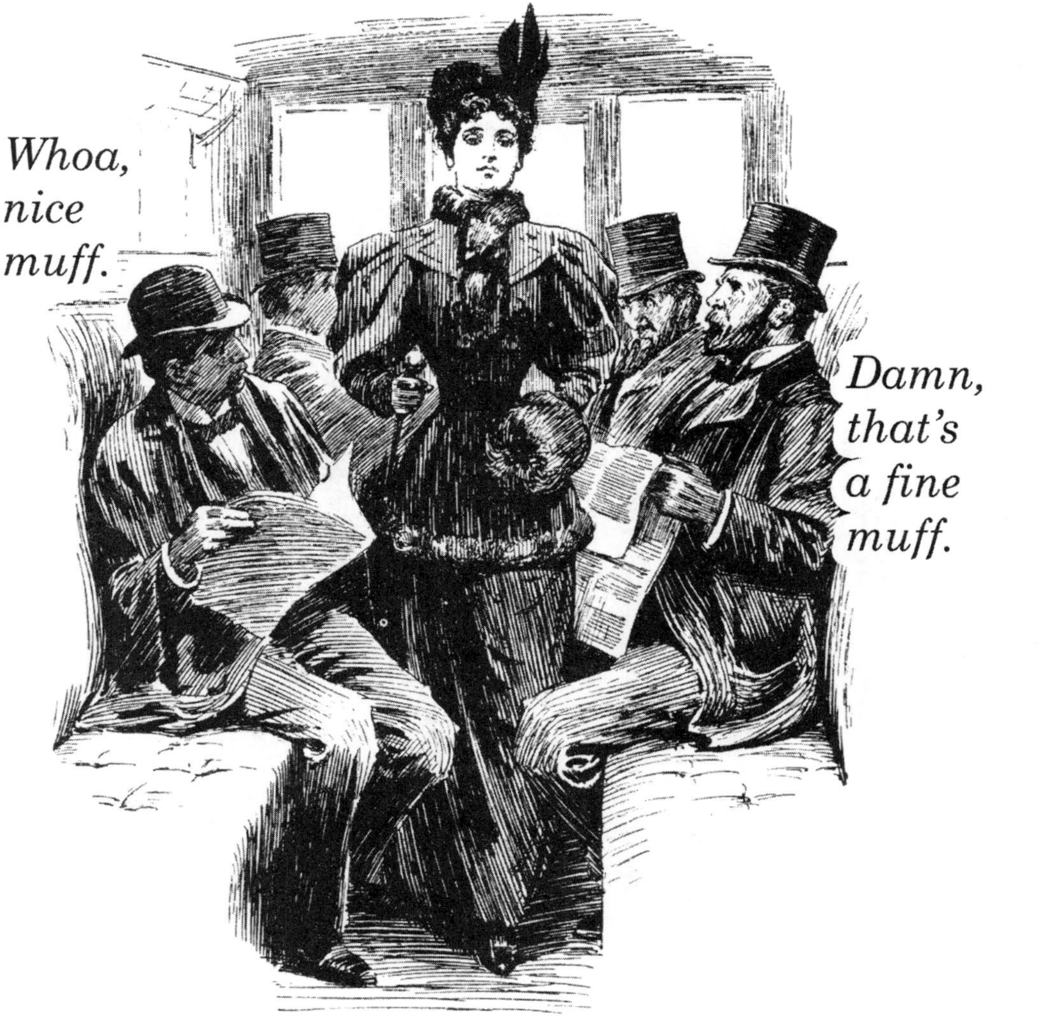
Whoa, nice muff.
Damn, that's a fine muff.

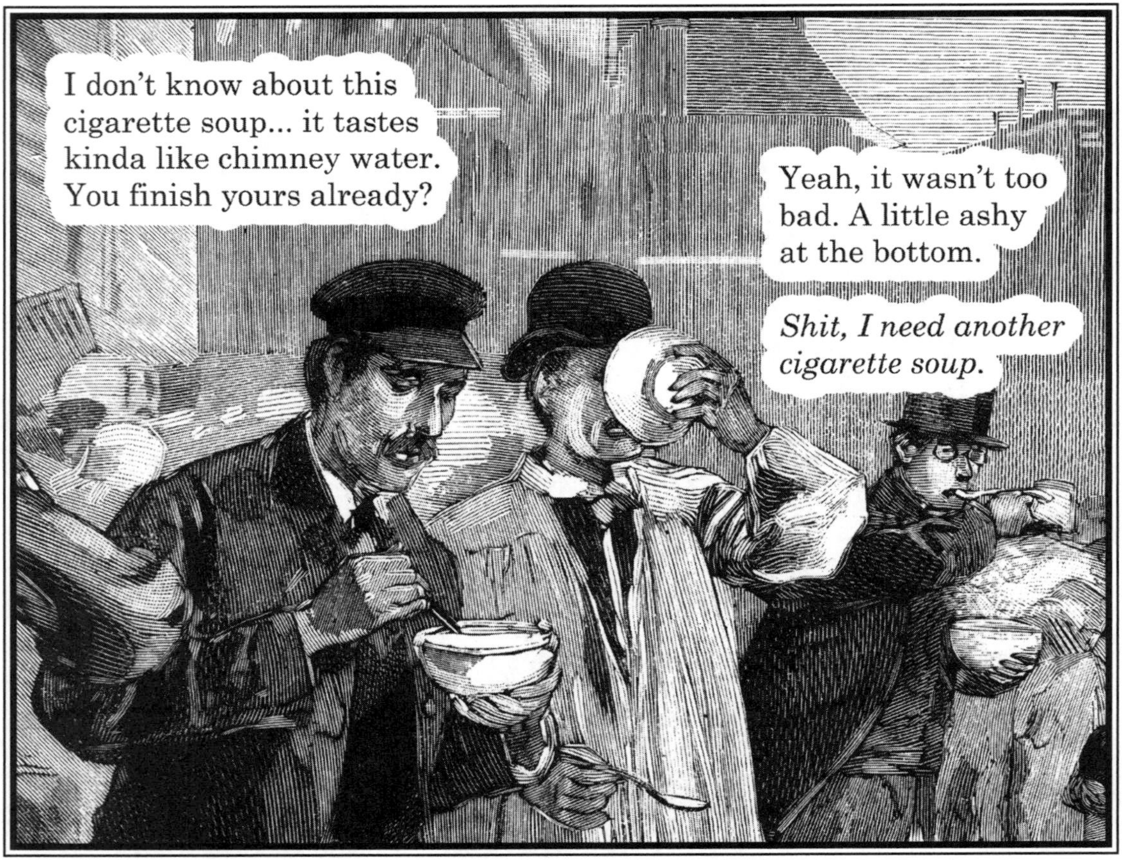
I don't know about this cigarette soup... it tastes kinda like chimney water. You finish yours already?
Yeah, it wasn't too bad. A little ashy at the bottom.
Shit, I need another cigarette soup.

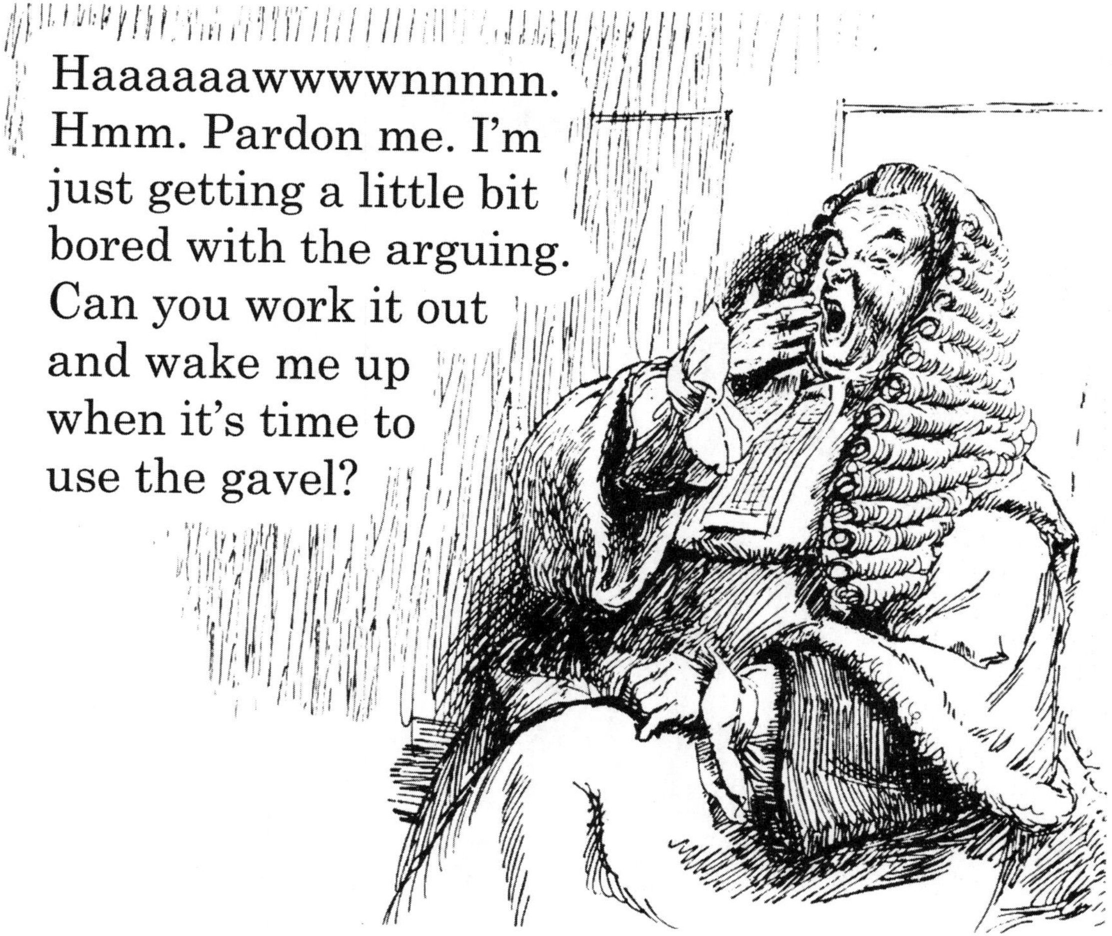
Haaaaaawwwwnnnnn. Hmm. Pardon me. I'm just getting a little bit bored with the arguing. Can you work it out and wake me up when it's time to use the gavel?

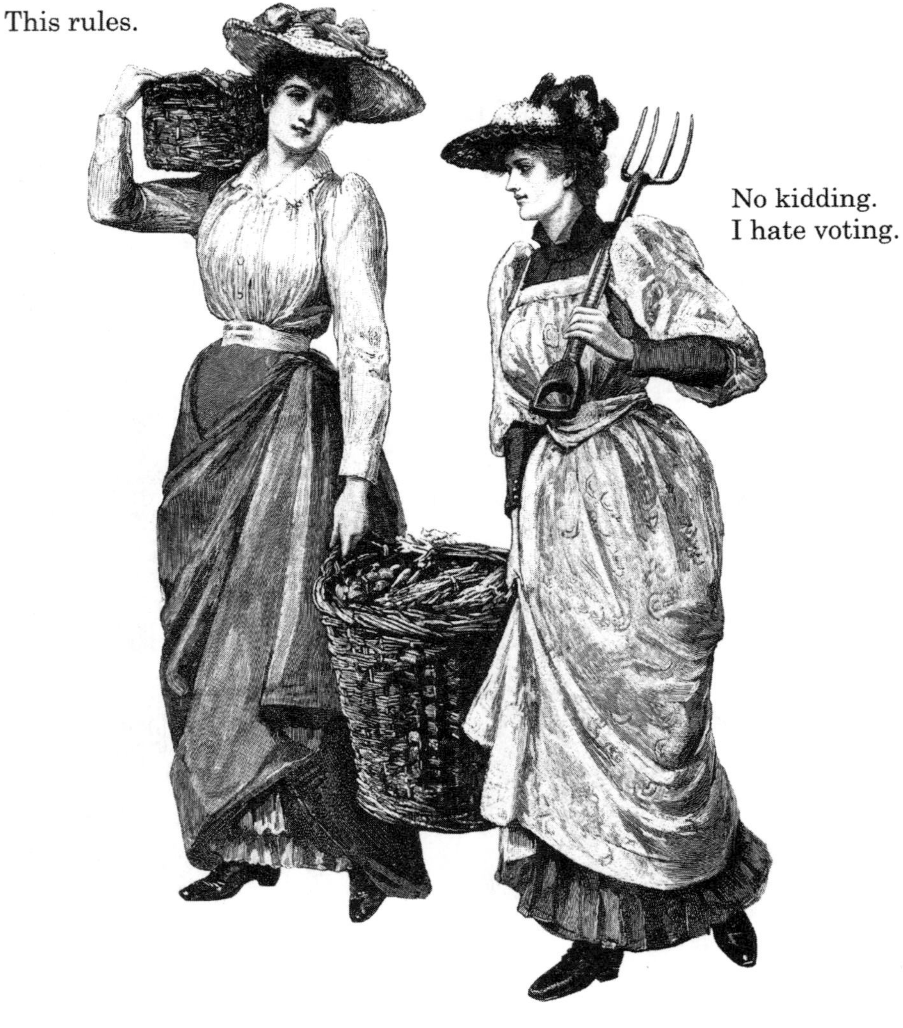
This rules.
No kidding.
I hate voting.

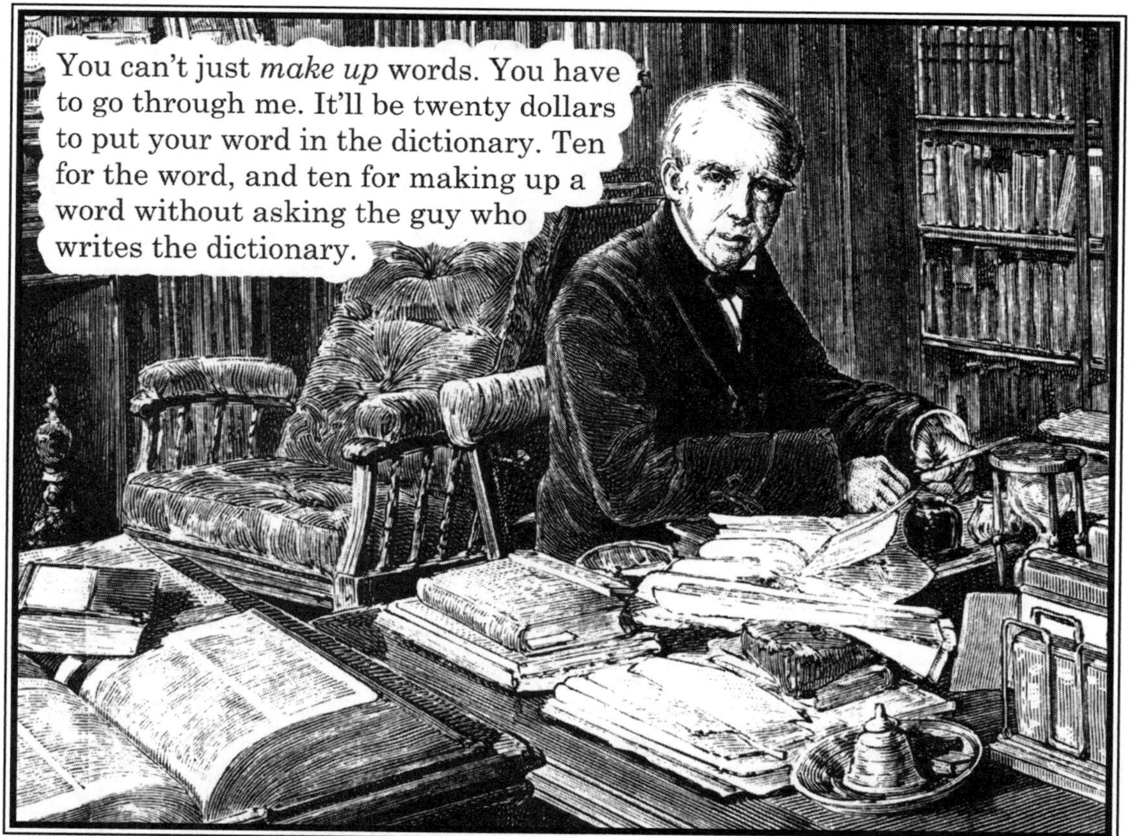
You can't just *make up* words. You have to go through me. It'll be twenty dollars to put your word in the dictionary. Ten for the word, and ten for making up a word without asking the guy who writes the dictionary.

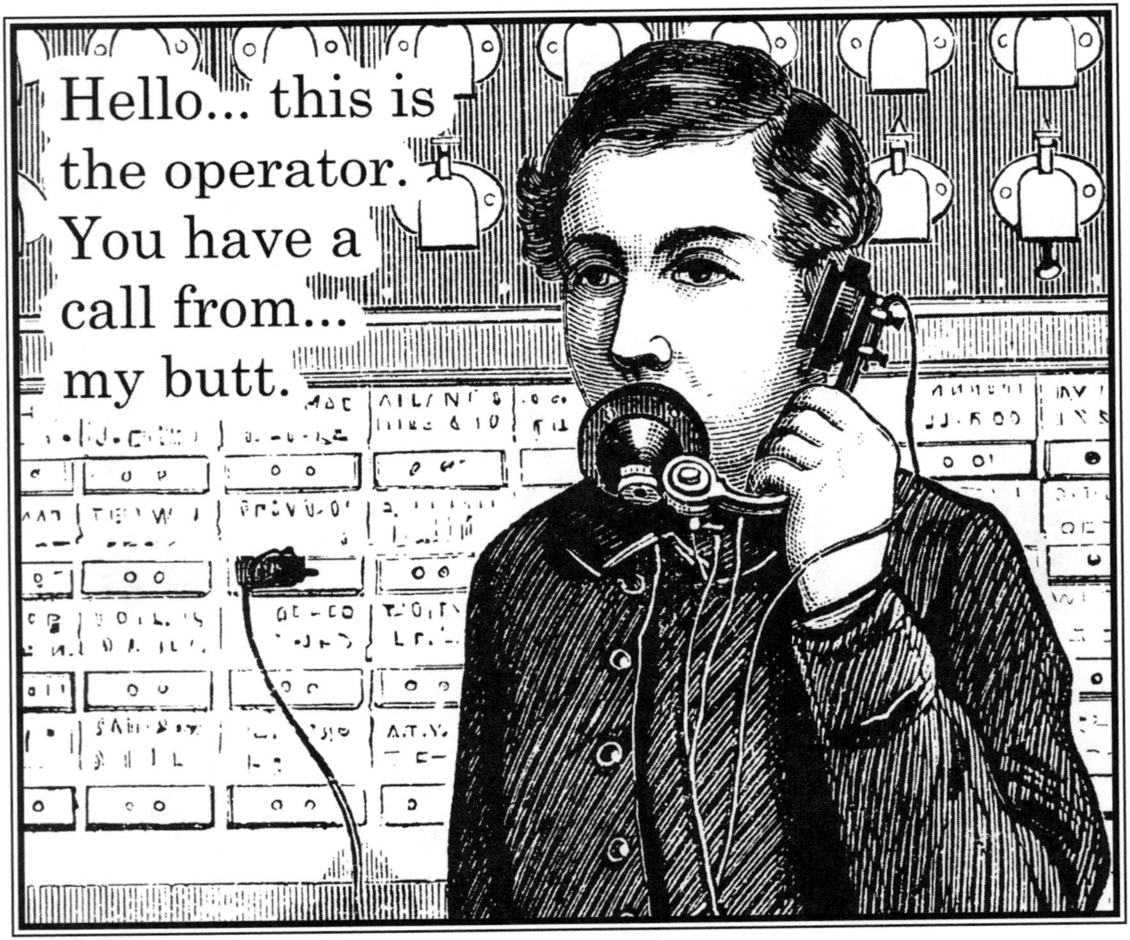
Hello... this is the operator. You have a call from... my butt.

Beat it, old man! This is my turf. I've been quackerying on this corner for years.

Shit! What is that thing?!
I'd better shoot blood out
of my eyes at it.

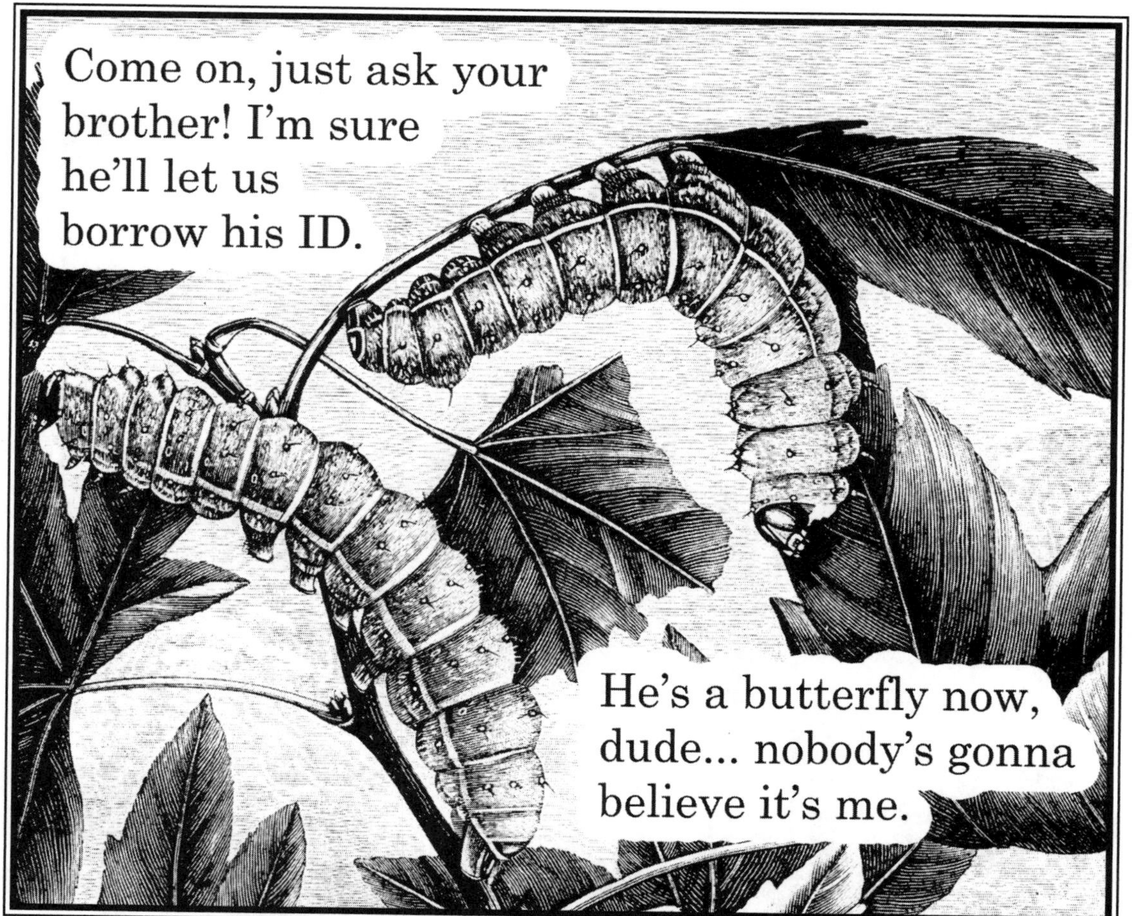
Come on, just ask your brother! I'm sure he'll let us borrow his ID.
He's a butterfly now, dude... nobody's gonna believe it's me.

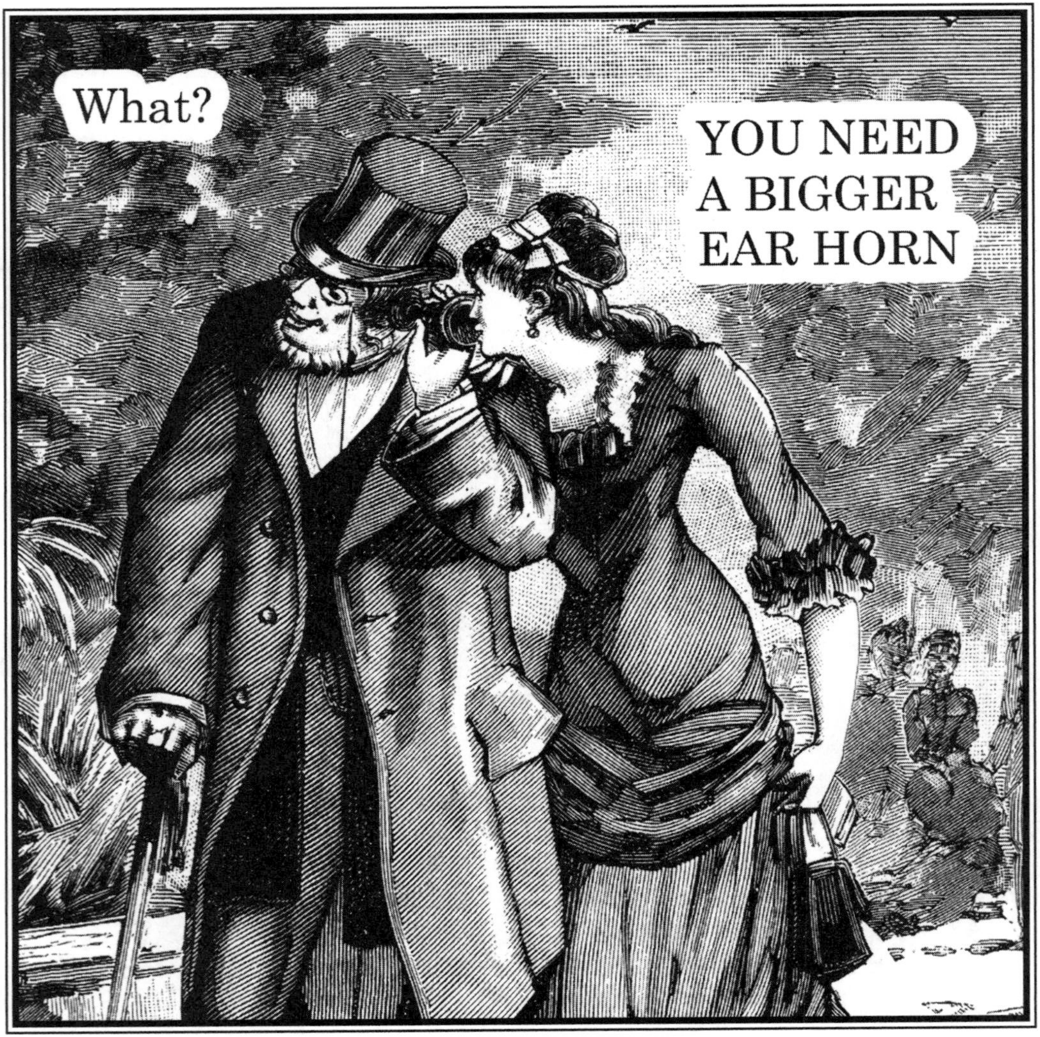
What?
YOU NEED A BIGGER EAR HORN

BITCH I
TOLD YOU

"Love Seat... in the case of one-year-old Padded Chair,
you are... *Not the father.*"

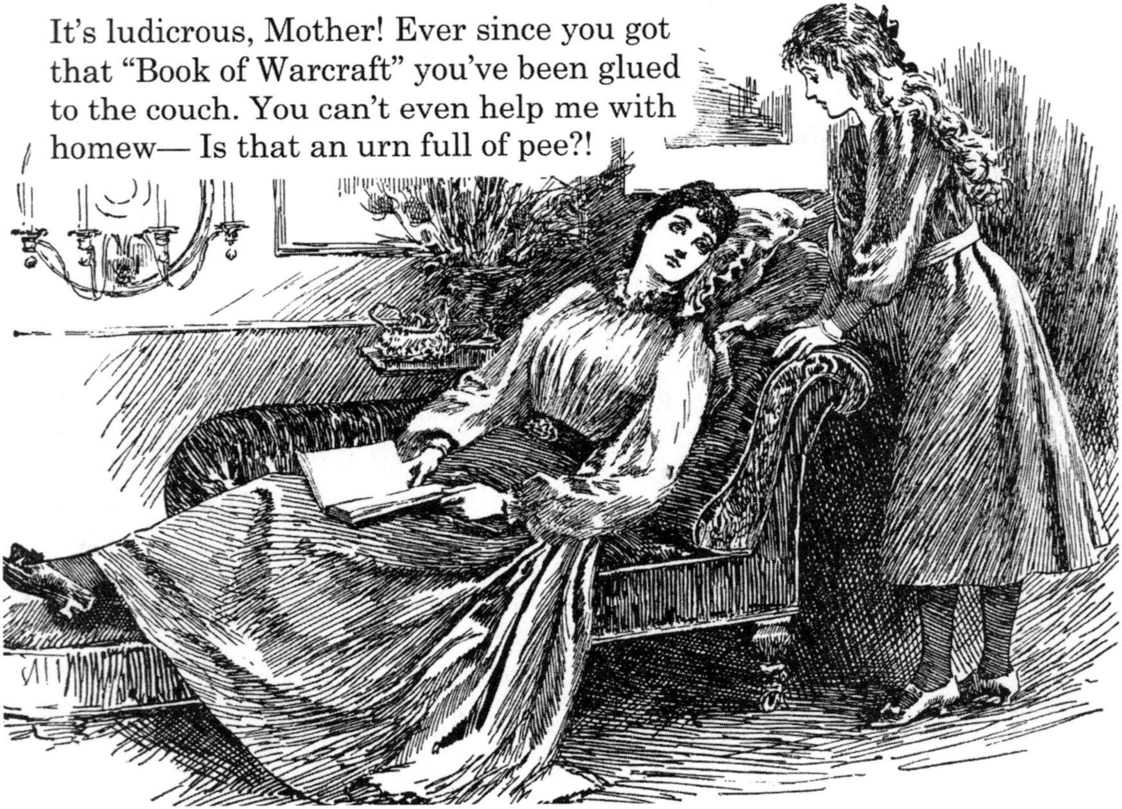
It's ludicrous, Mother! Ever since you got that "Book of Warcraft" you've been glued to the couch. You can't even help me with homew— Is that an urn full of pee?!

The world's first permanent photograph was produced in 1826 by Joseph Nicéphore Niépce, a French inventor. His early photographic experiments started in the late 18th century, but were hampered by his persistent failure to remember to remove the lens cap before exposing the plate.

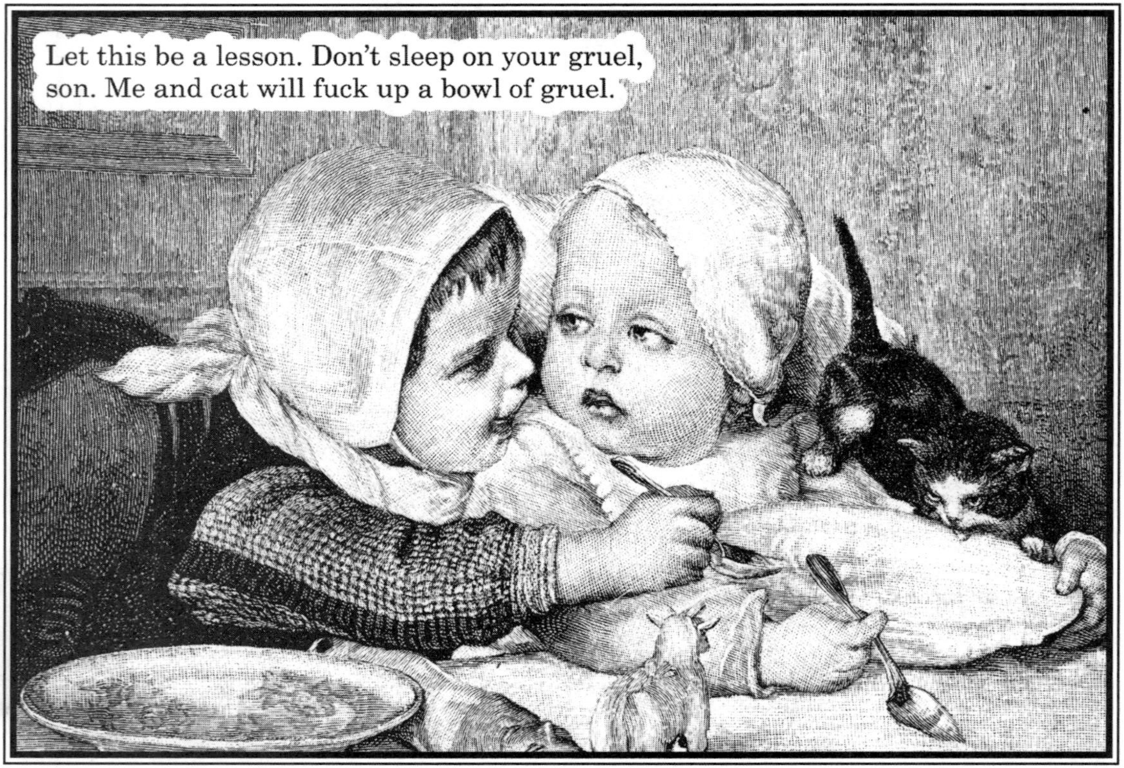
Let this be a lesson. Don't sleep on your gruel, son. Me and cat will fuck up a bowl of gruel.

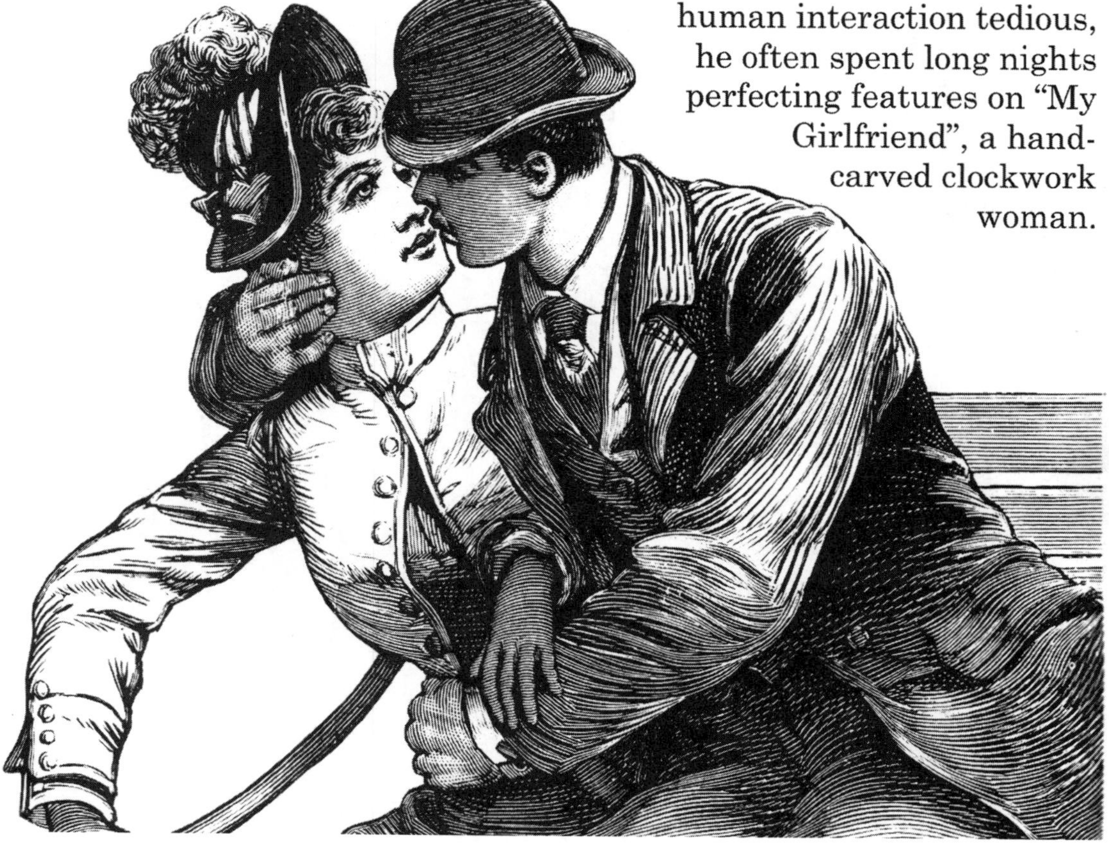

Although Randall found actual human interaction tedious, he often spent long nights perfecting features on "My Girlfriend", a hand-carved clockwork woman.

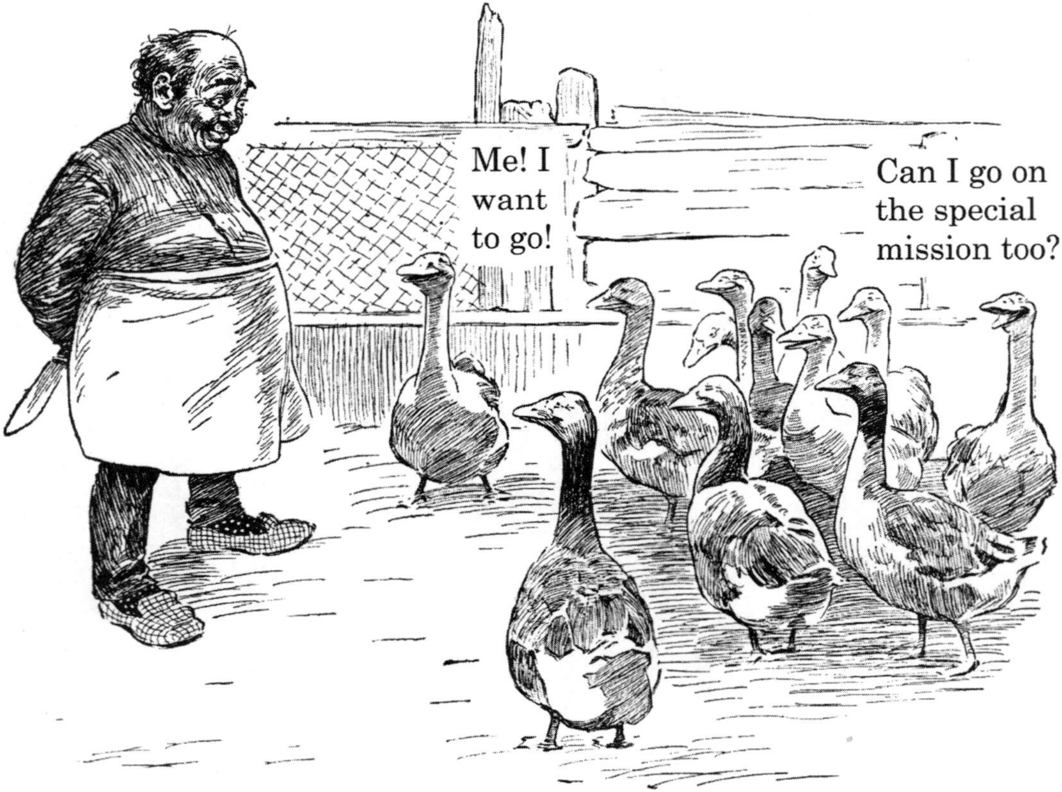
Me! I want to go!
Can I go on the special mission too?

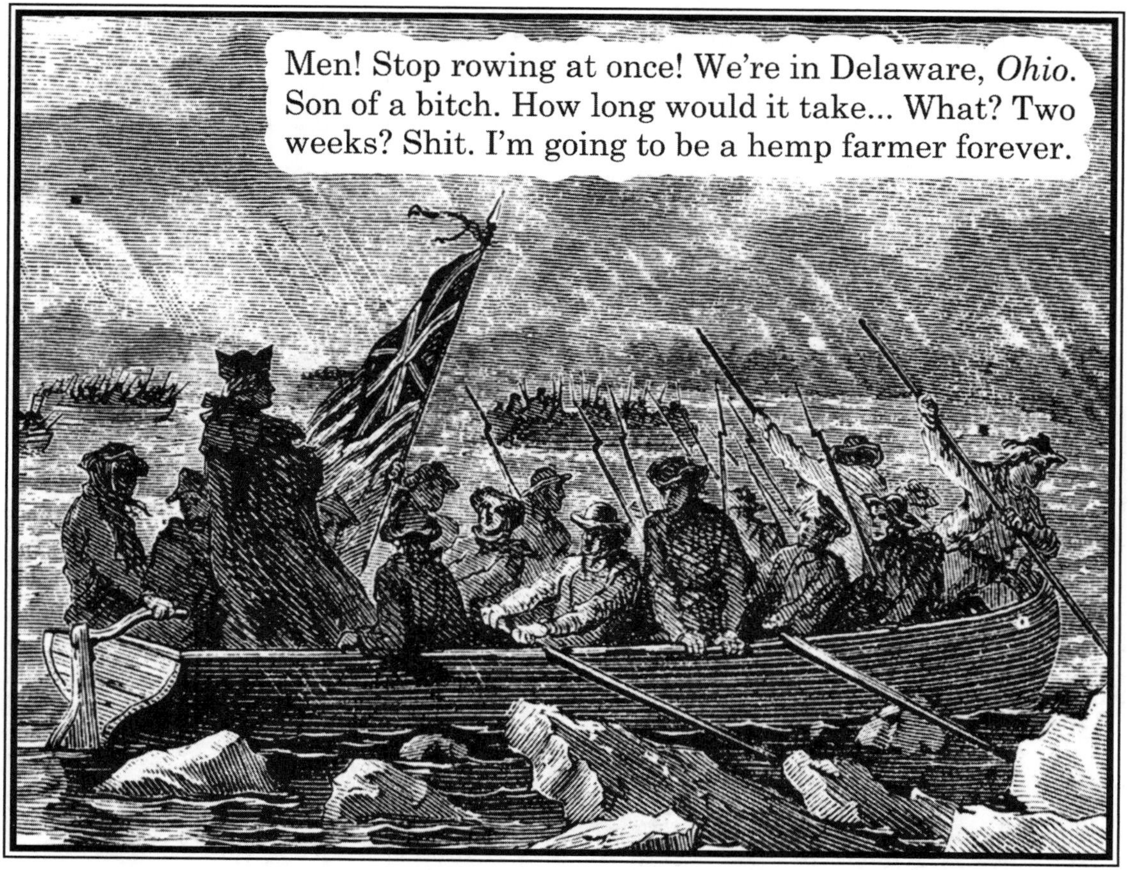
Men! Stop rowing at once! We're in Delaware, *Ohio*. Son of a bitch. How long would it take... What? Two weeks? Shit. I'm going to be a hemp farmer forever.

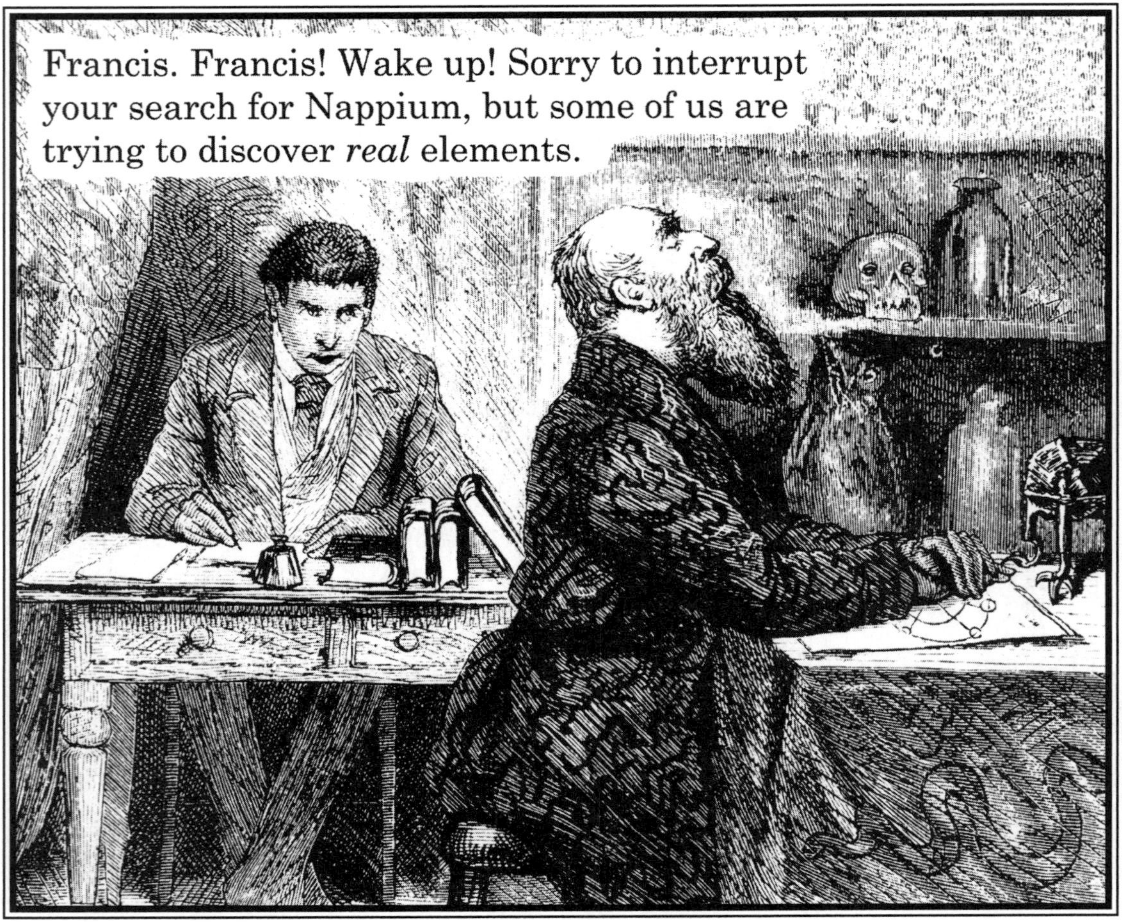
Francis. Francis! Wake up! Sorry to interrupt your search for Nappium, but some of us are trying to discover *real* elements.

Activist judges...
You'll pay for this!

HOOTING,
HOLLERING
LEGALIZED

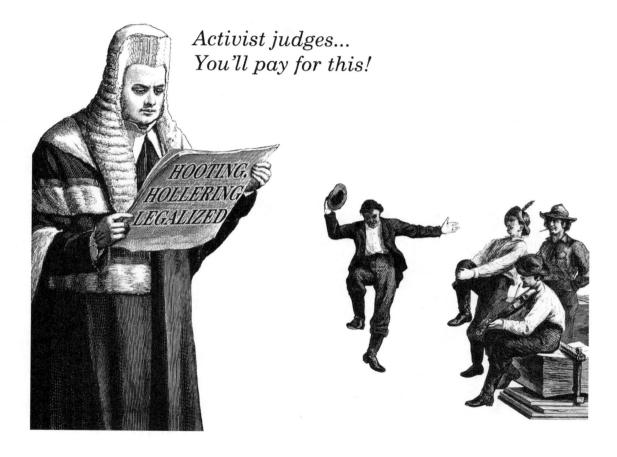

For the last time, Herbert! It's the help's job to close the gate. Do you truly wish to deprive them of the pleasure they get from their work?!

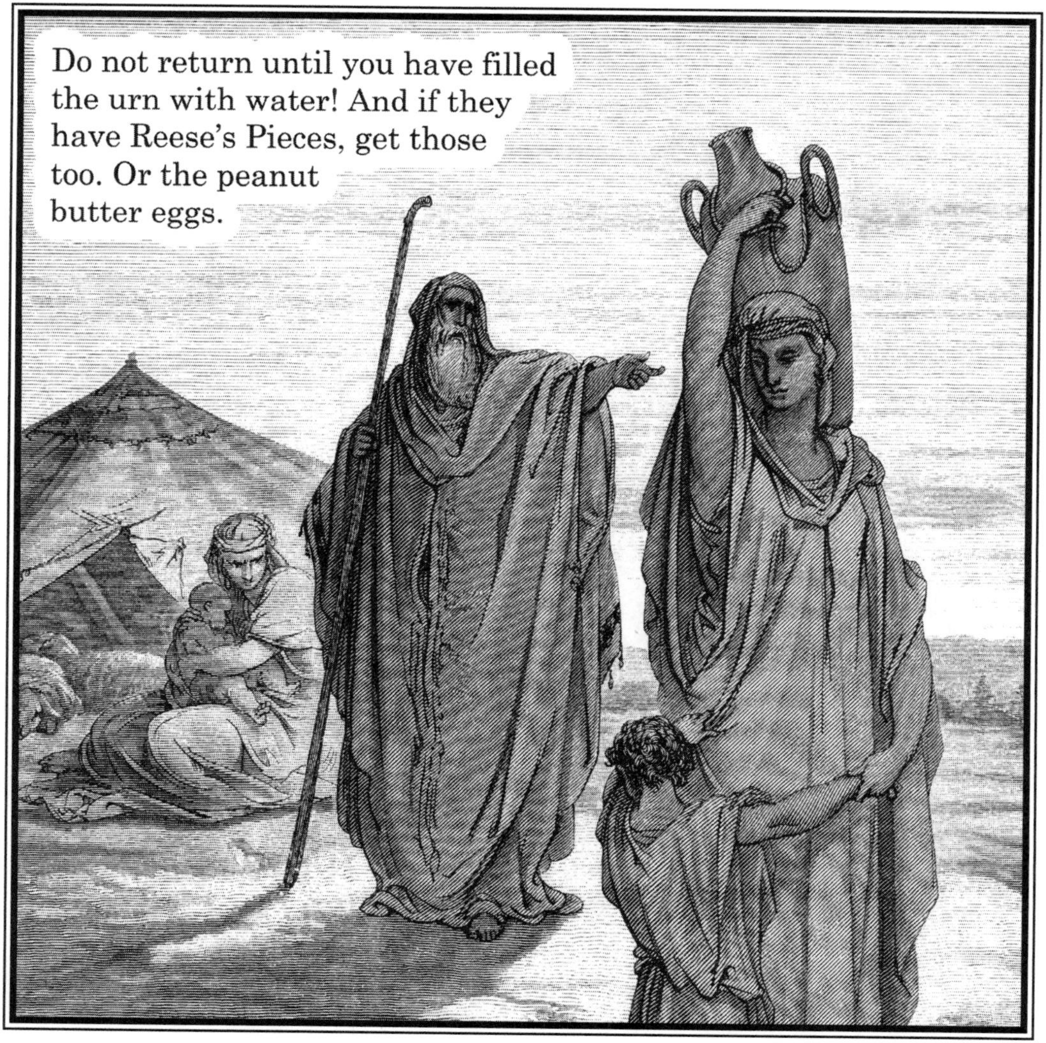
Do not return until you have filled the urn with water! And if they have Reese's Pieces, get those too. Or the peanut butter eggs.

Making flowers is such a pain...
I should figure out how to
grow these on plants.

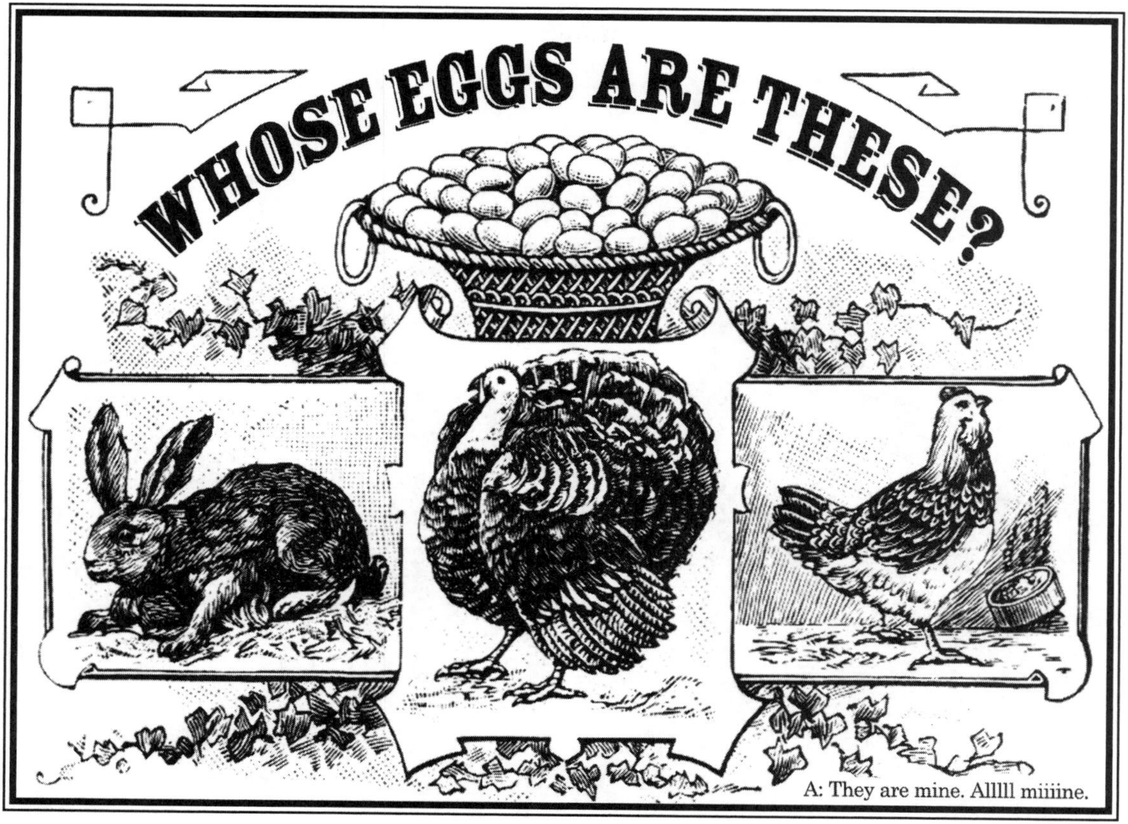
WHOSE EGGS ARE THESE?
A: They are mine. Alllll miiiine.

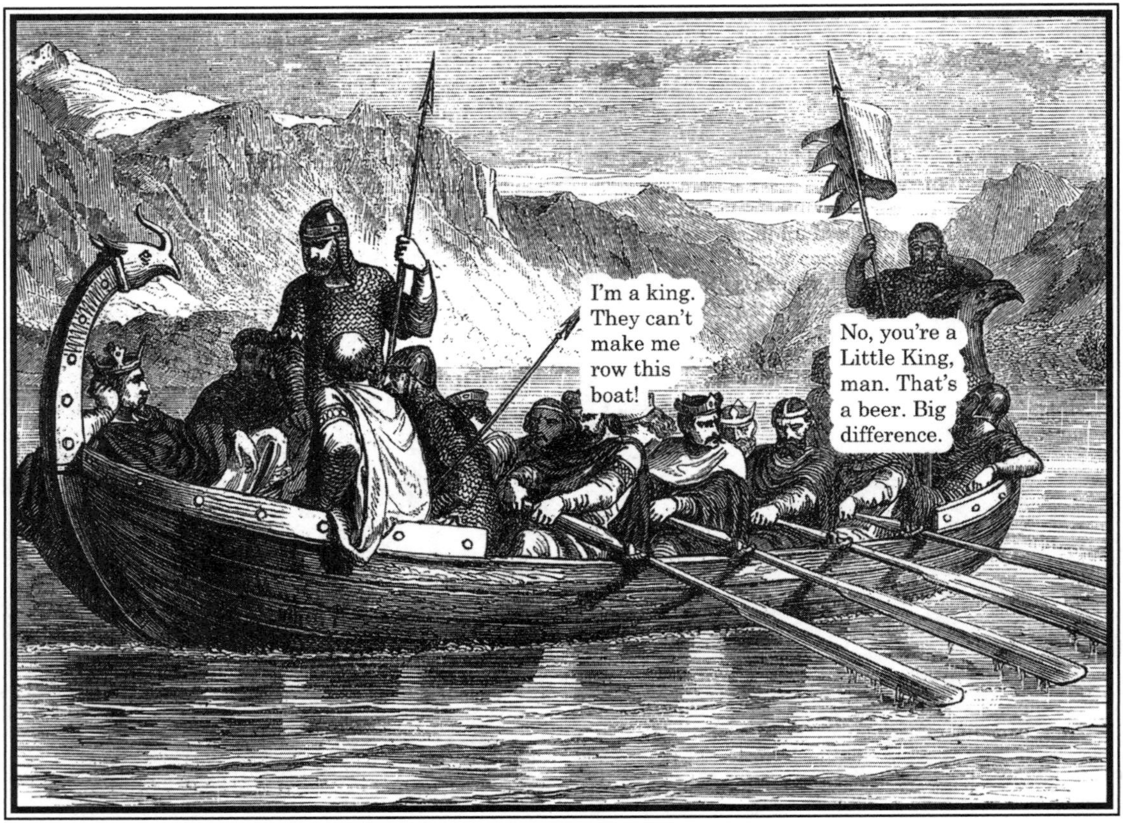
I'm a king. They can't make me row this boat!
No, you're a Little King, man. That's a beer. Big difference.

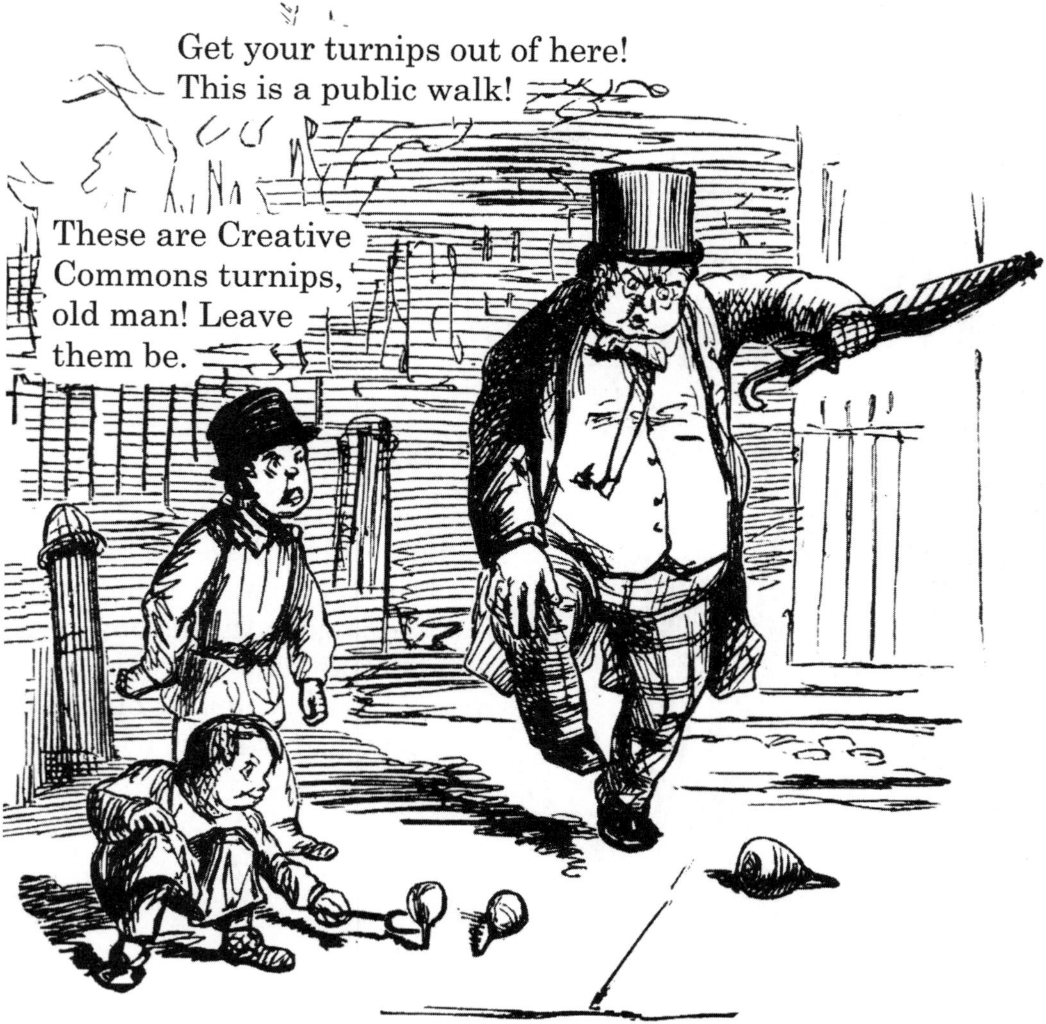
Get your turnips out of here! This is a public walk!
These are Creative Commons turnips, old man! Leave them be.

I should think there would be no argument, Maxwell! You'll have the plain one with the long dress, and I'll take the beauty in the hat. No use in courting outside your league, my socky friend.

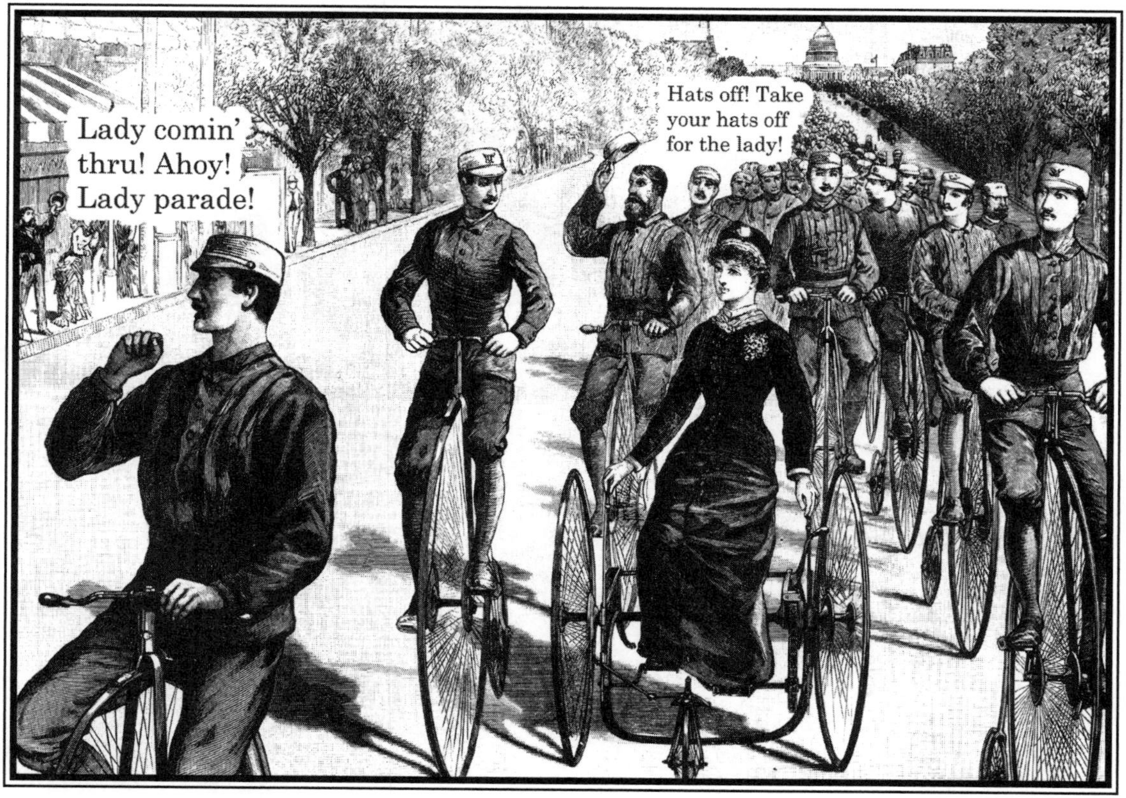
Lady comin' thru! Ahoy! Lady parade!
Hats off! Take your hats off for the lady!

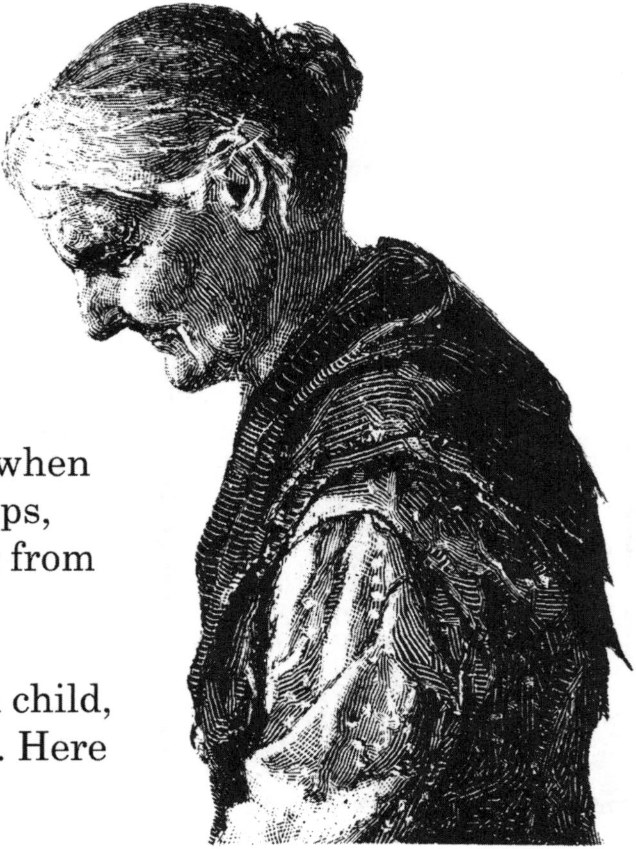

"Where were you, Lord, when I paid for two bags of chips, yet I pulled only one bag from the vending machine?"

"It was then, my beloved child, that I carried your chips. Here they are."

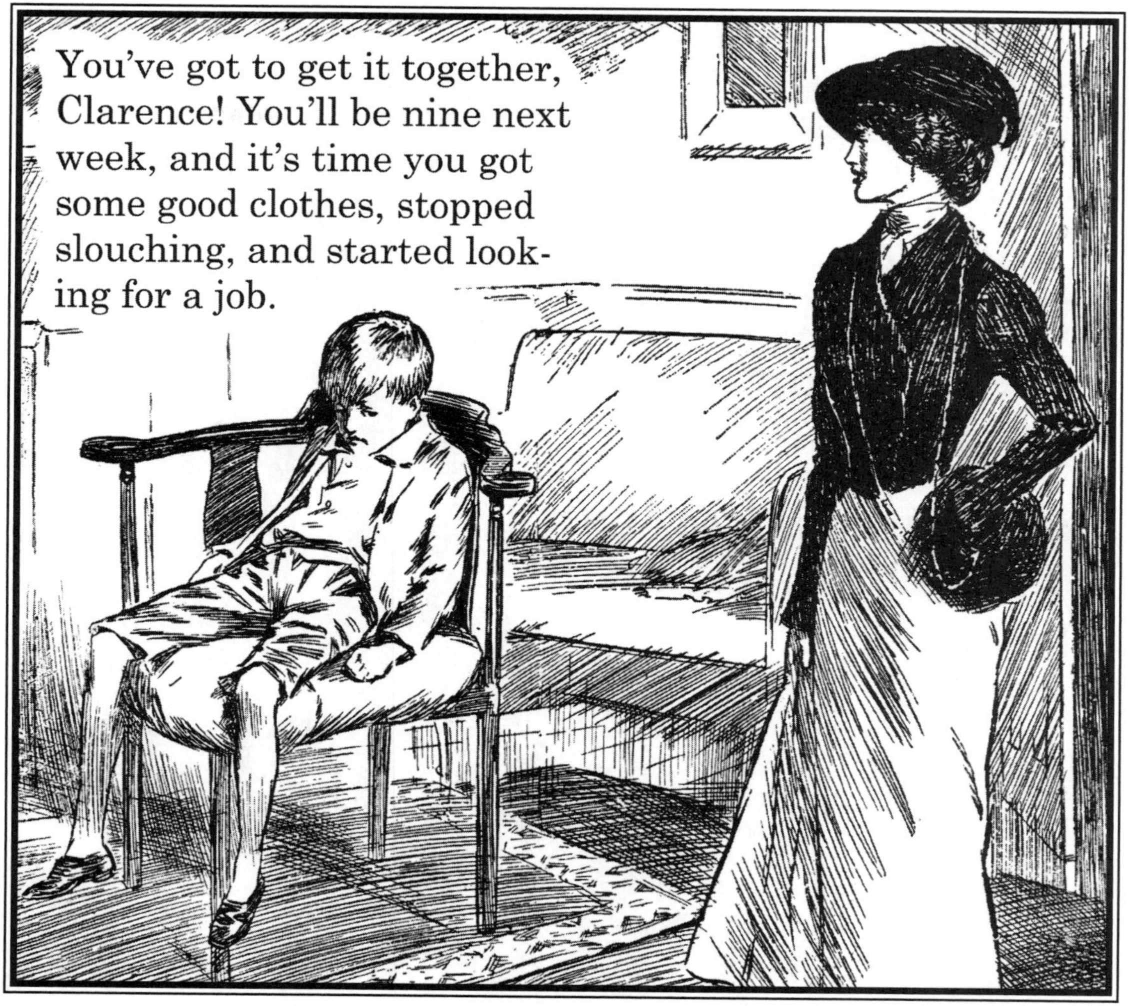
You've got to get it together, Clarence! You'll be nine next week, and it's time you got some good clothes, stopped slouching, and started looking for a job.

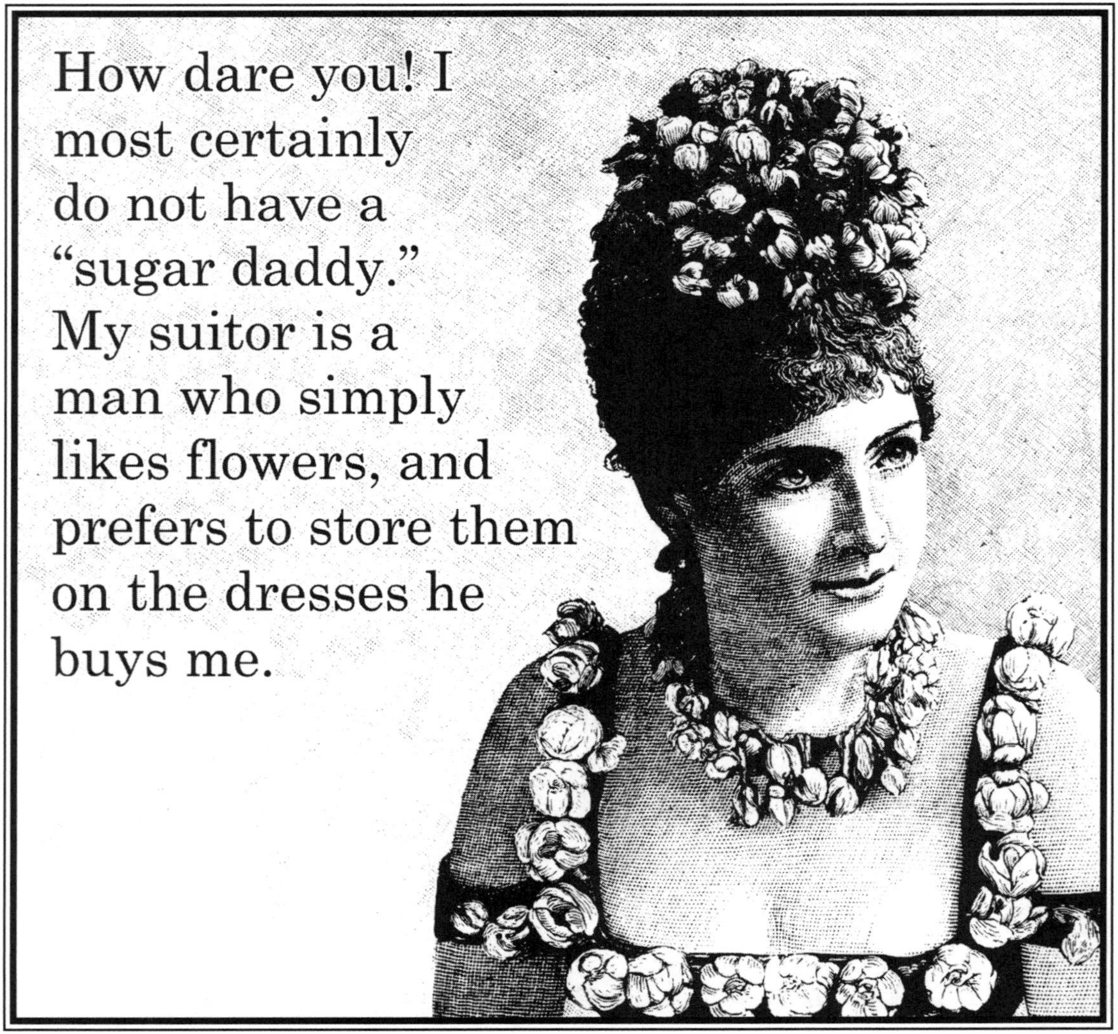
How dare you! I most certainly do not have a "sugar daddy." My suitor is a man who simply likes flowers, and prefers to store them on the dresses he buys me.

Well, it could be that when you die, your perception simply stops, and there is nothing. Or, you'll float through some clouds until you come to a podium, and if the angel at the podium lets you inside the cloud world, you'll learn that an invisible, omnipresent, omnipotent lord invented dinosaurs to test us. Either way.

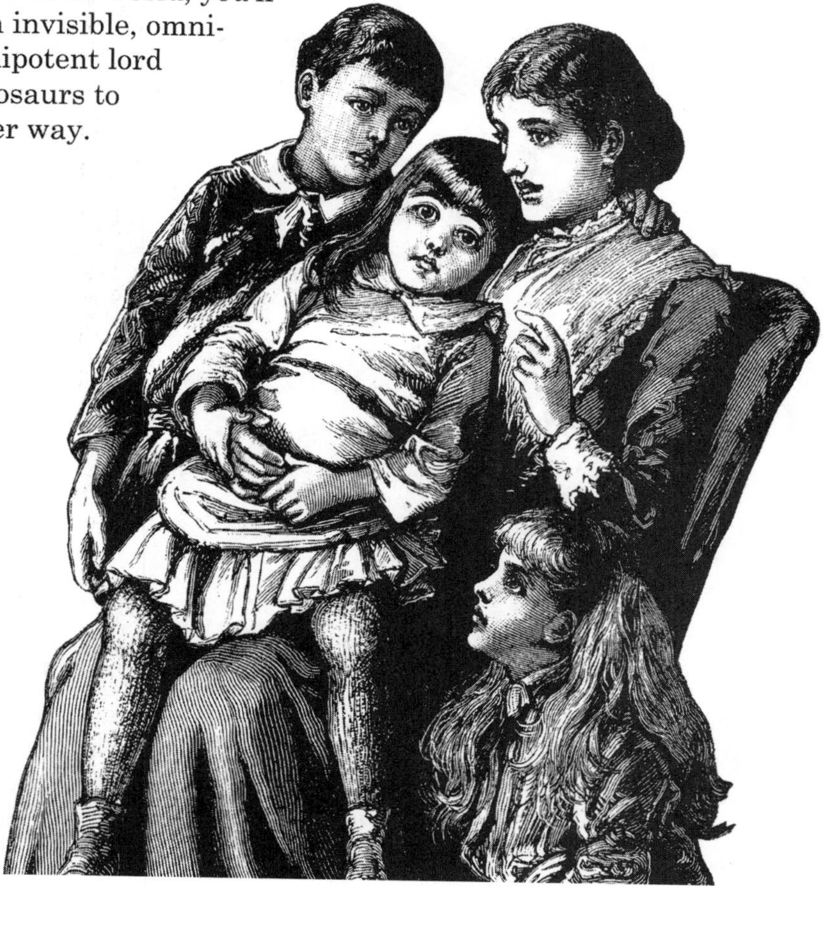

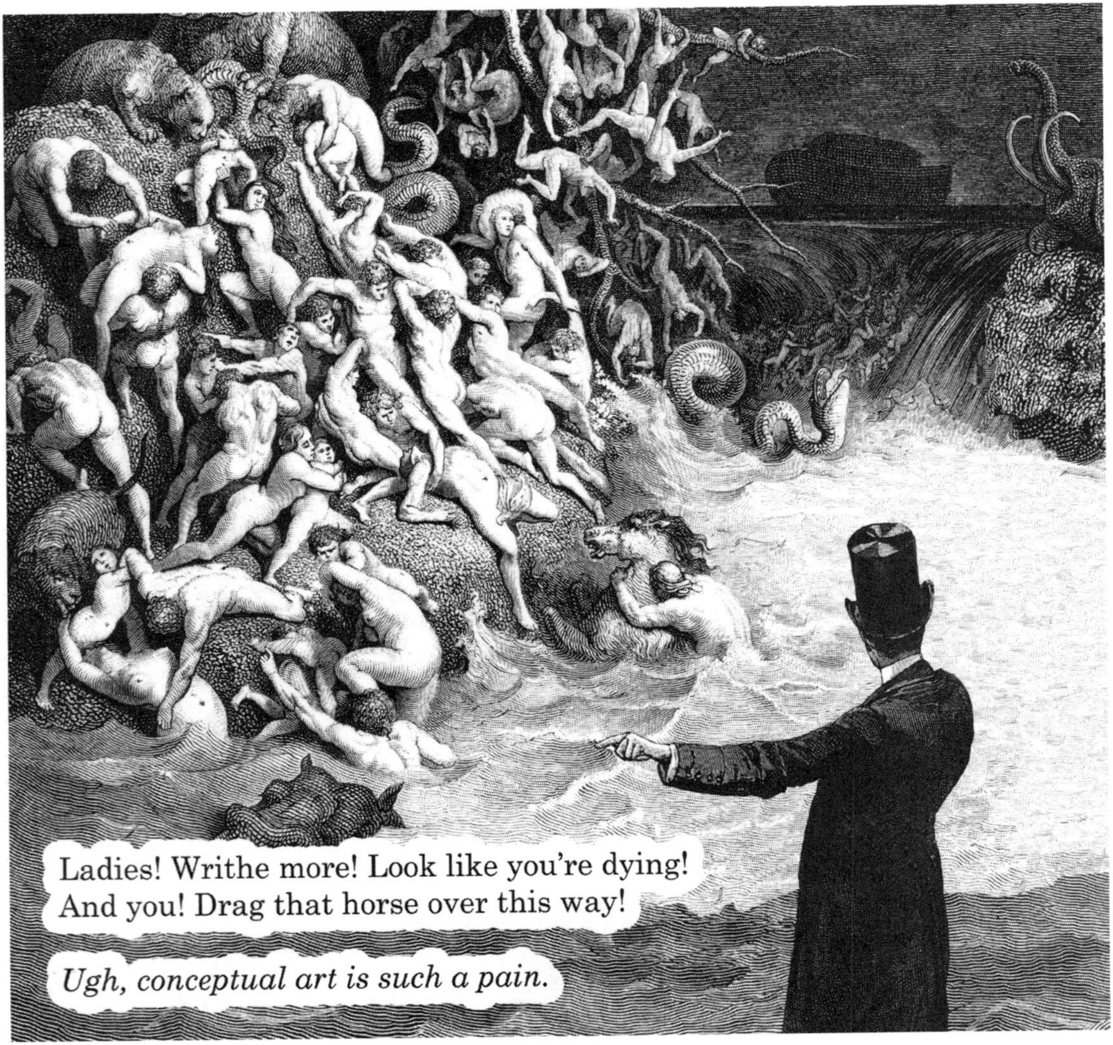
Ladies! Writhe more! Look like you're dying!
And you! Drag that horse over this way!
Ugh, conceptual art is such a pain.

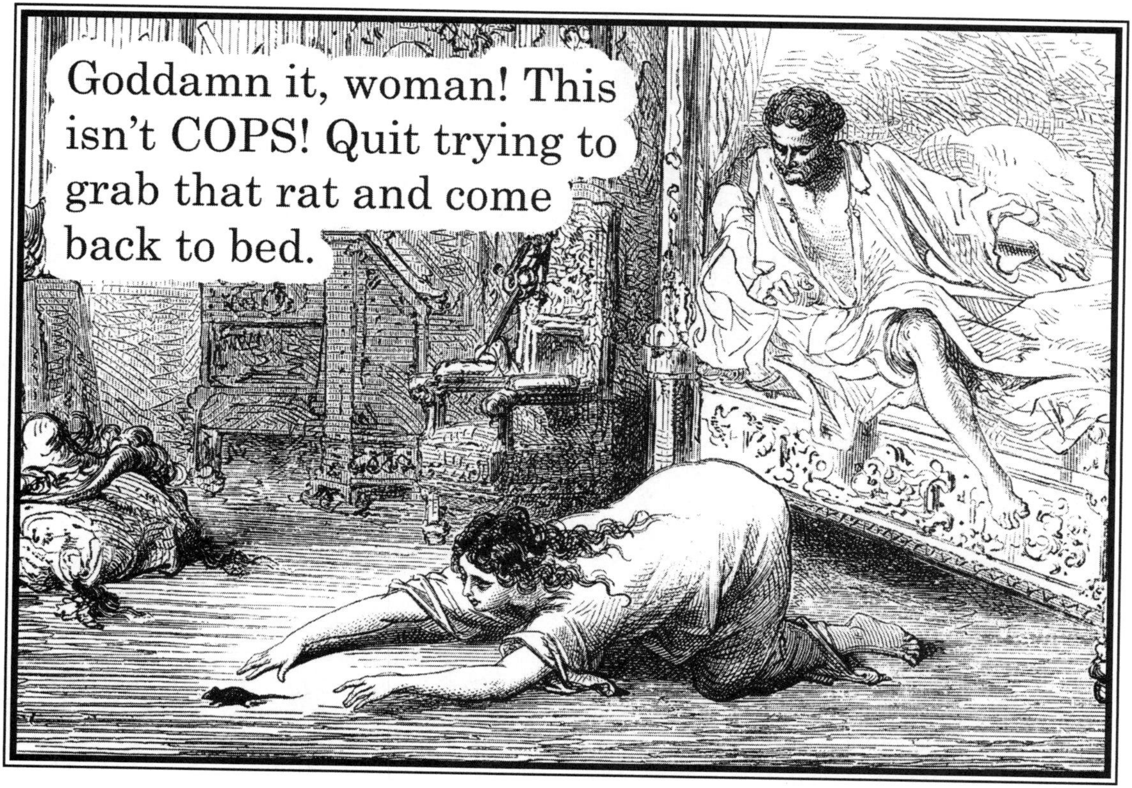
Goddamn it, woman! This isn't COPS! Quit trying to grab that rat and come back to bed.

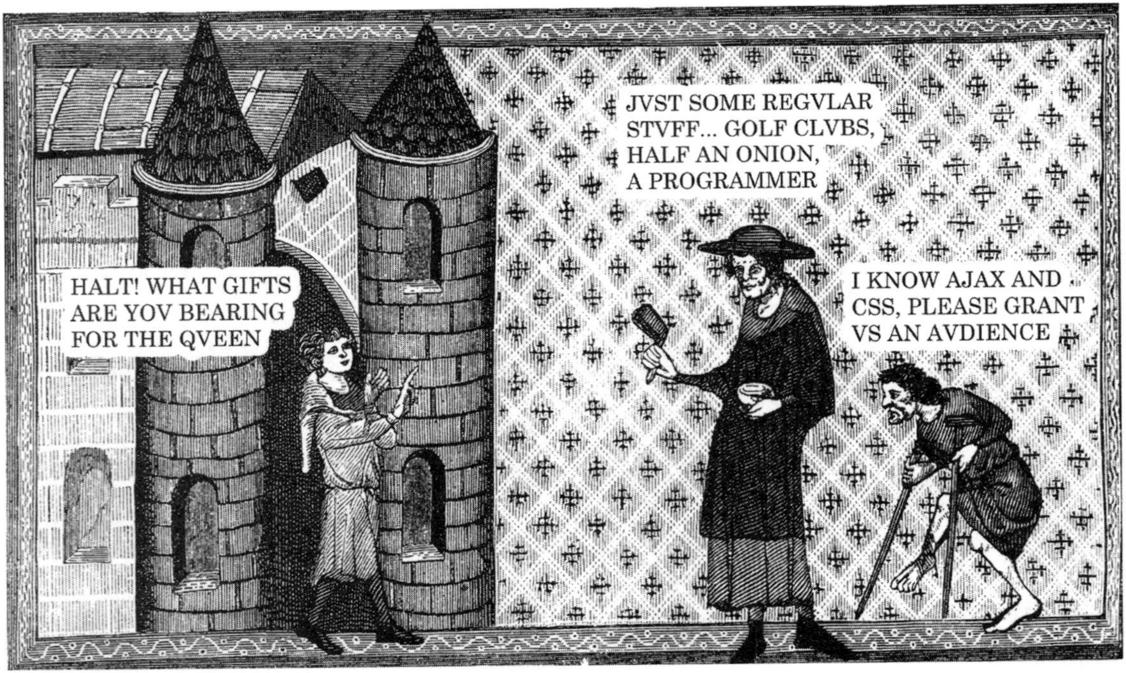
HALT! WHAT GIFTS ARE YOV BEARING FOR THE QVEEN
JVST SOME REGVLAR STVFF... GOLF CLVBS, HALF AN ONION, A PROGRAMMER
I KNOW AJAX AND CSS, PLEASE GRANT VS AN AVDIENCE

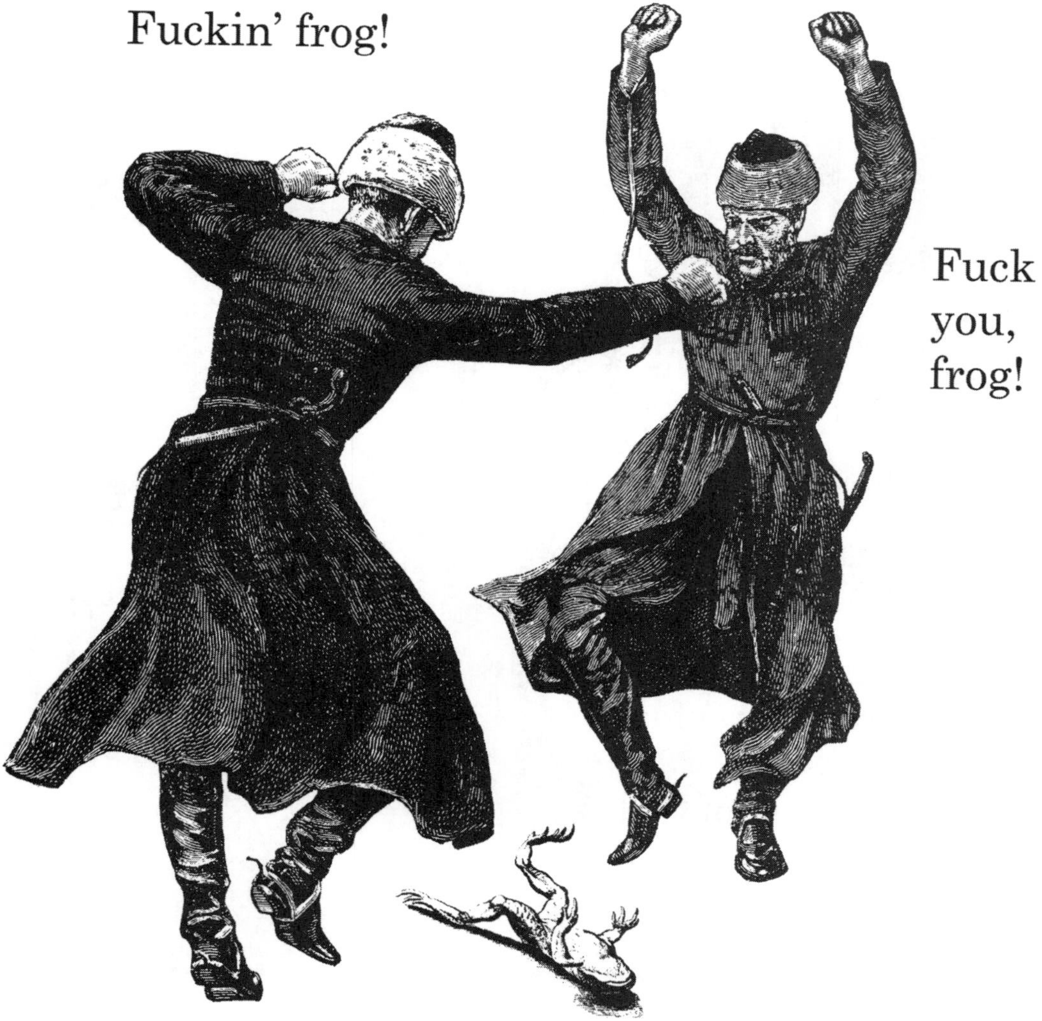
Fuckin' frog!
Fuck
you,
frog!

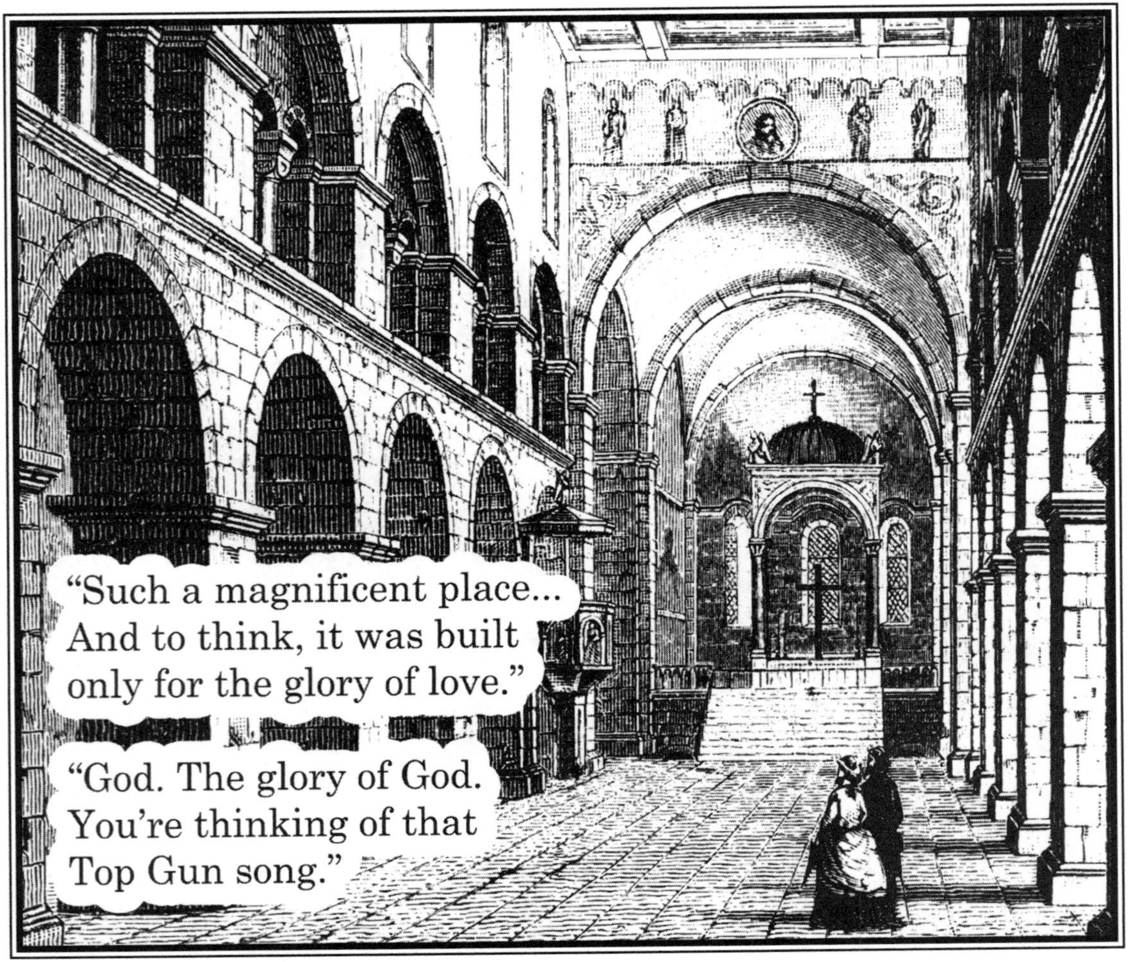
"Such a magnificent place... And to think, it was built only for the glory of love."
"God. The glory of God. You're thinking of that Top Gun song."

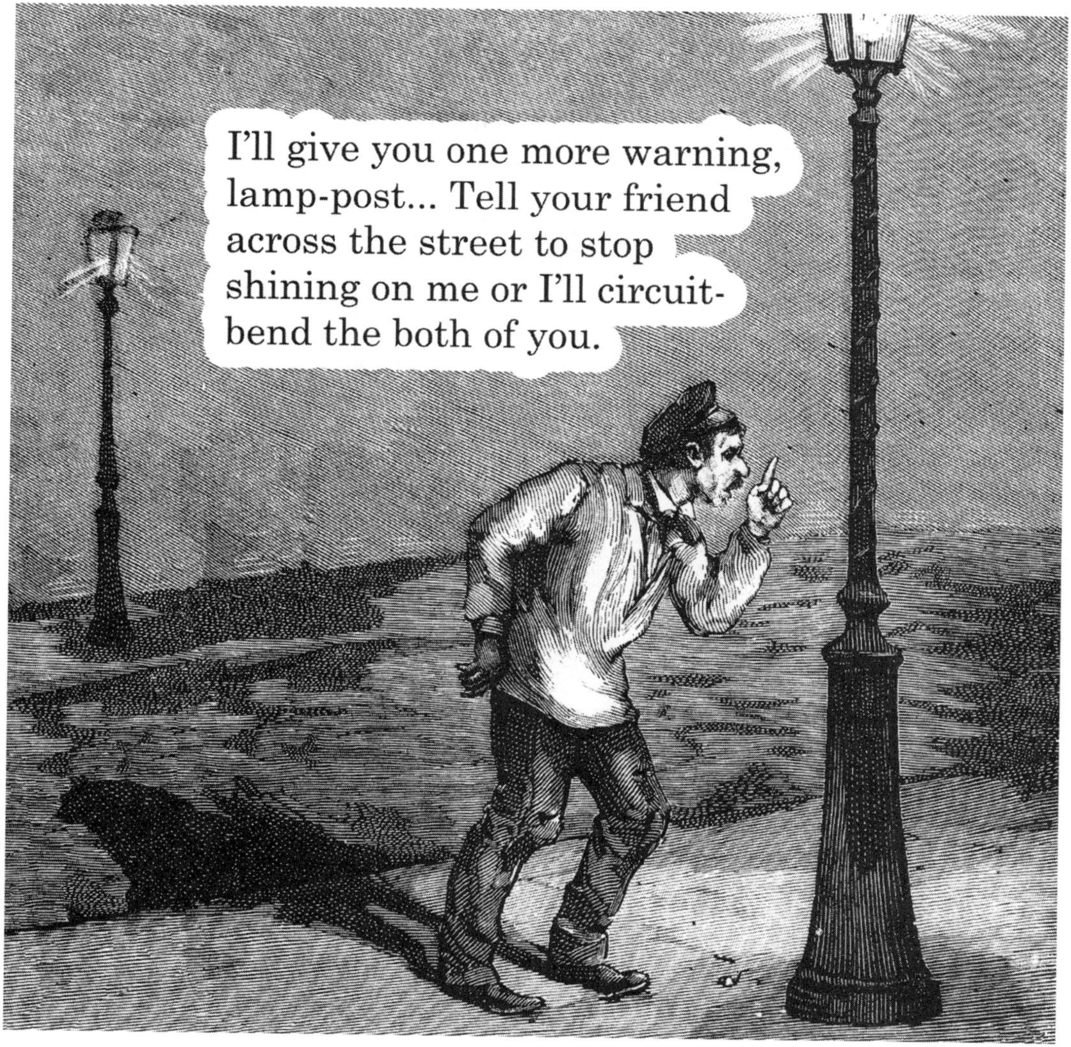
I'll give you one more warning, lamp-post... Tell your friend across the street to stop shining on me or I'll circuit-bend the both of you.

Wait. People are still reading Hamlet?! I wrote that in like one fortnight. I owed some people some money, you know? Shakespeare got to get paid, son.

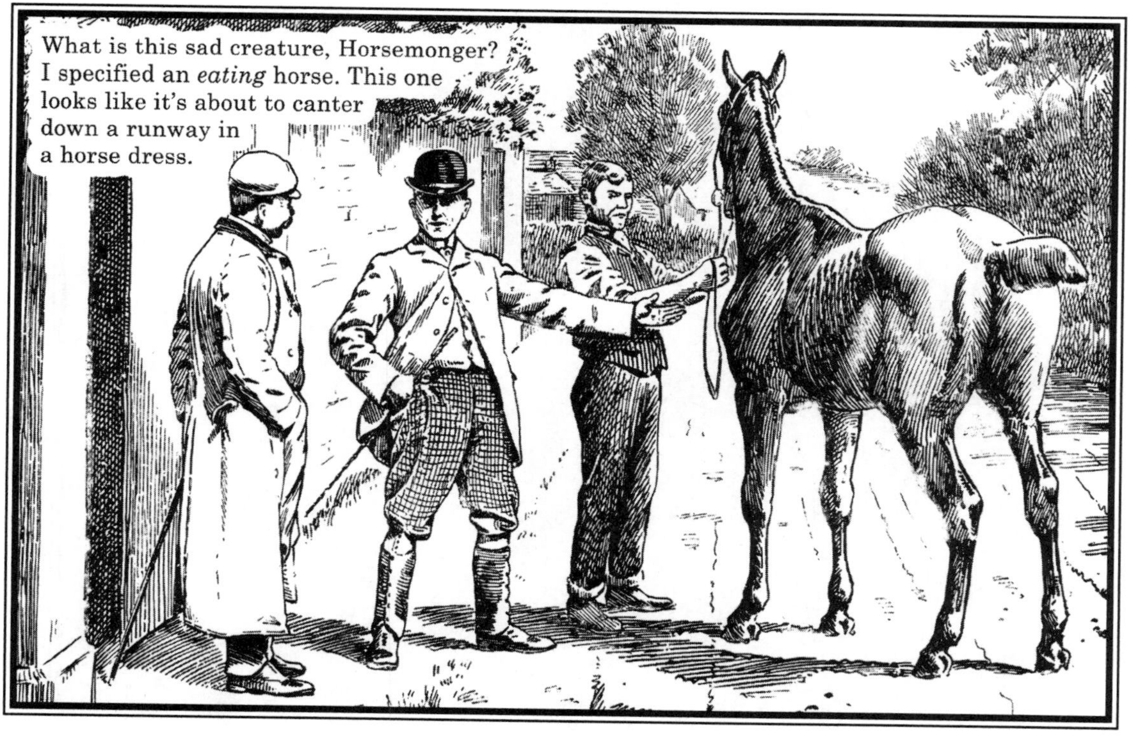
What is this sad creature, Horsemonger? I specified an *eating* horse. This one looks like it's about to canter down a runway in a horse dress.

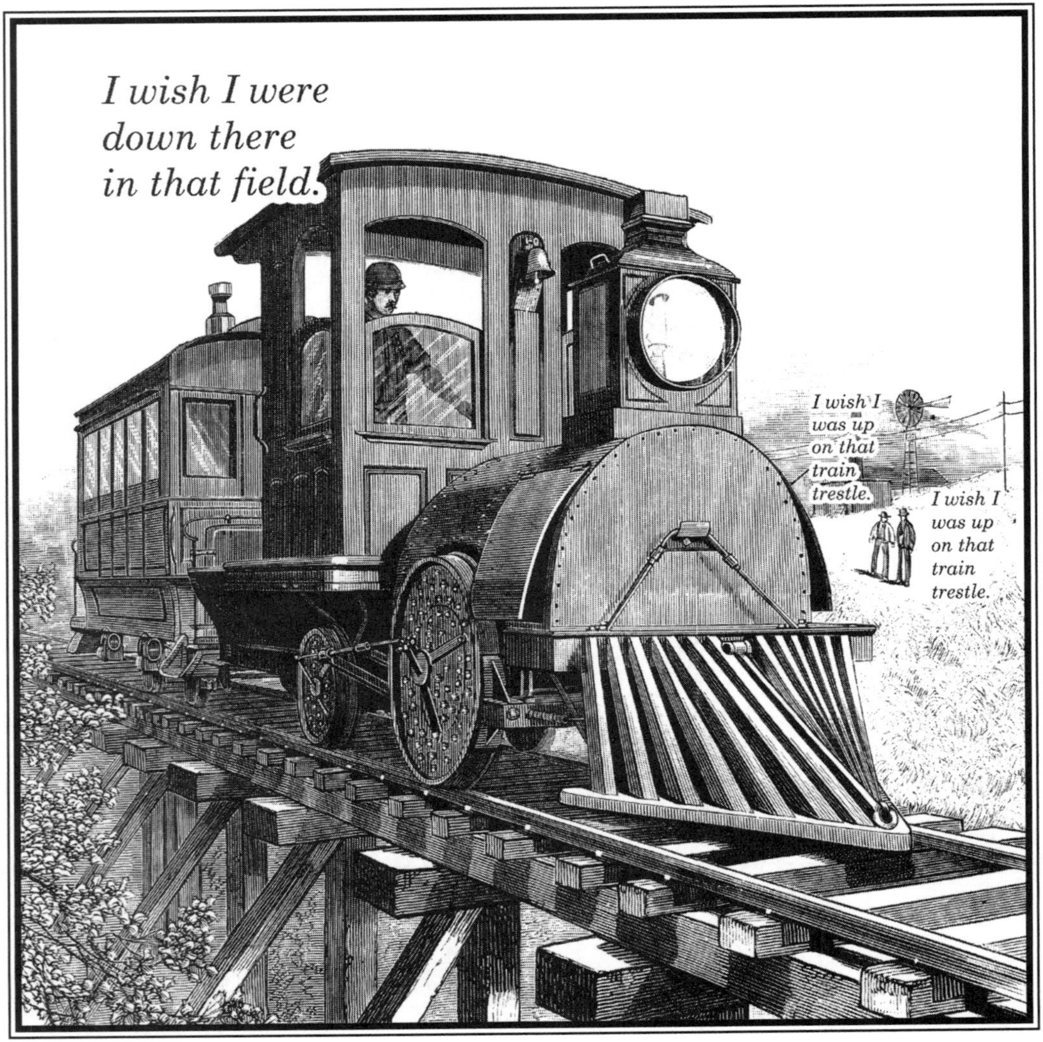
I wish I were
down there
in that field.
I wish I
was up
on that
train
trestle.
I wish I
was up
on that
train
trestle.

Is it okay to cuss on the green? Son, that's
why they invented golf. Nobody comes
out here 'cause they like
finding a tiny ball
over and over.

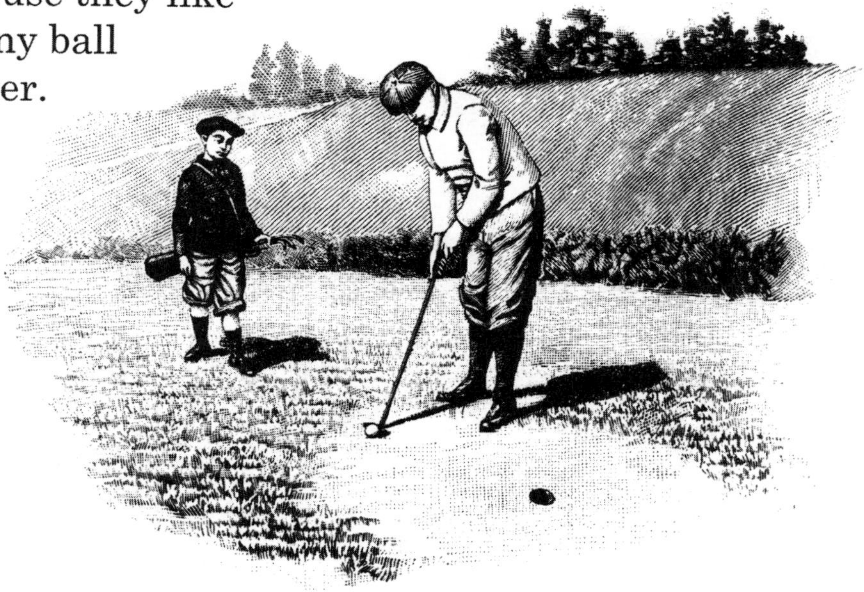

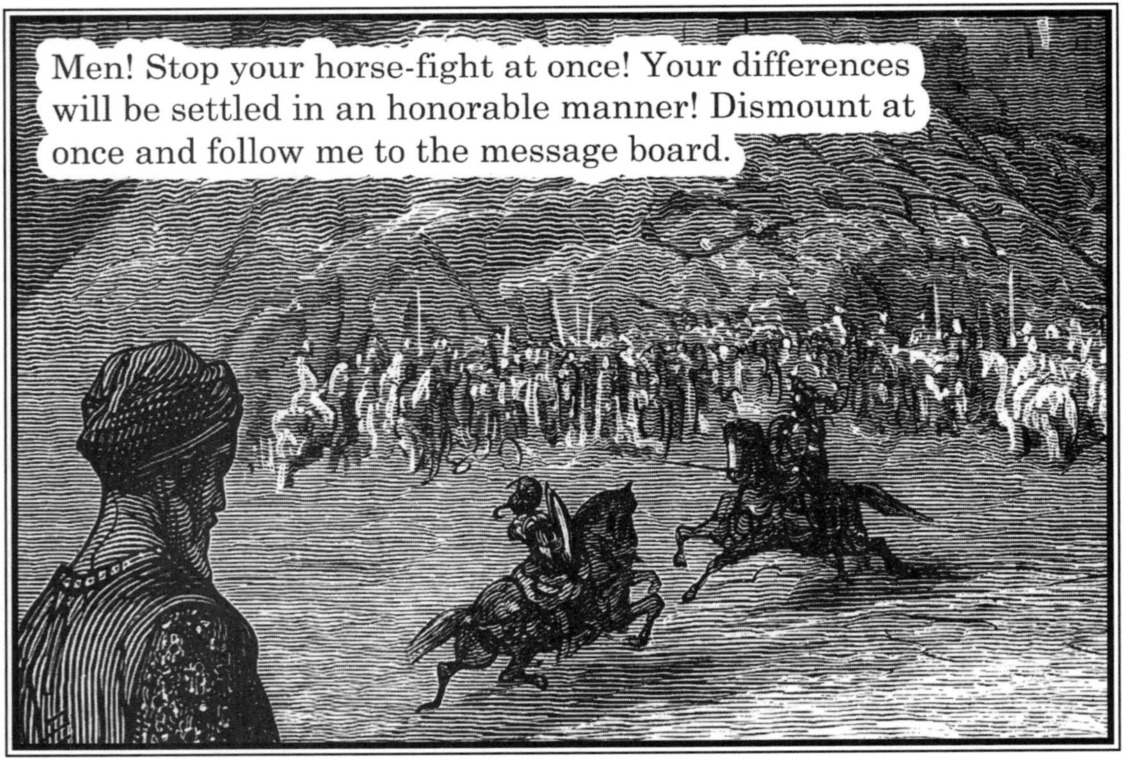
Men! Stop your horse-fight at once! Your differences will be settled in an honorable manner! Dismount at once and follow me to the message board.

Ladies! Ladies! Stop at once! Do you hear?
Stop! You are not to hit with fists. That is
not the fantasy. You are to *slap*. Open
hand slaps. I like the sound.

Hey! Breaking news! Reading the
newspaper gets you heckled!
Continue reading this story on
page you suck.

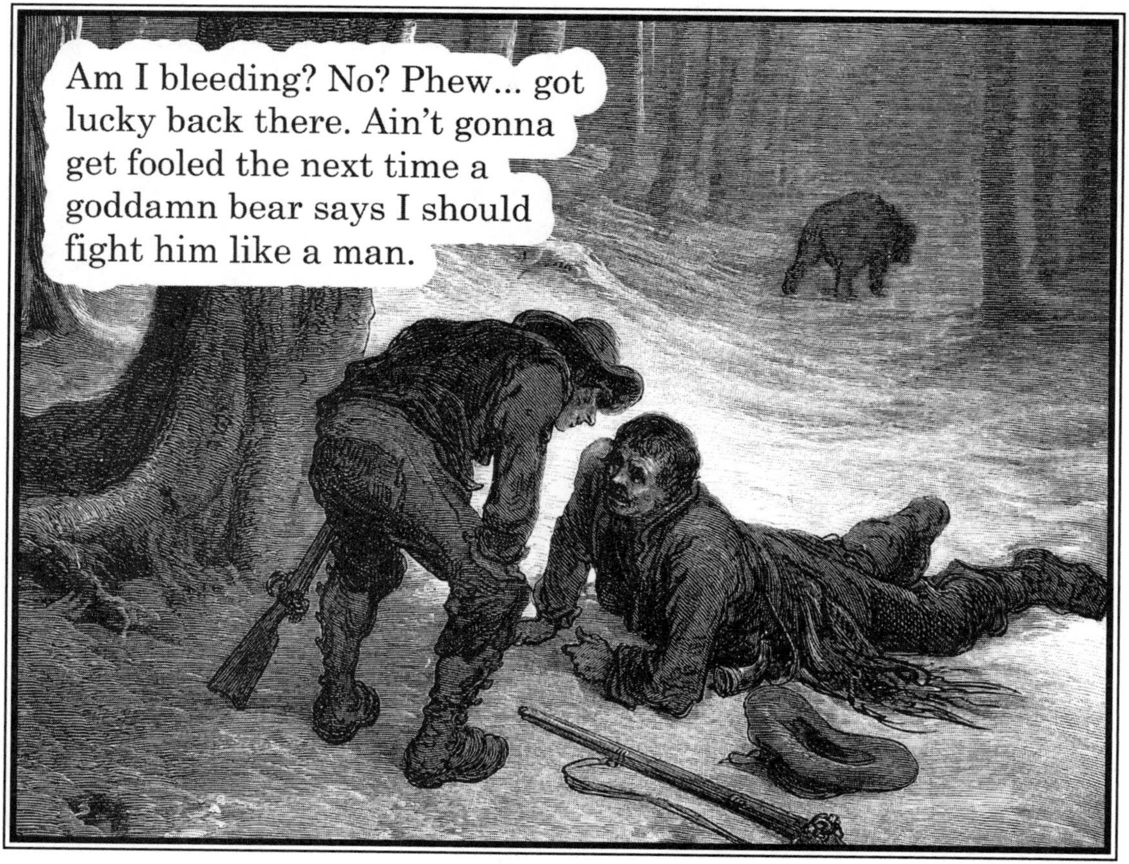
Am I bleeding? No? Phew... got lucky back there. Ain't gonna get fooled the next time a goddamn bear says I should fight him like a man.

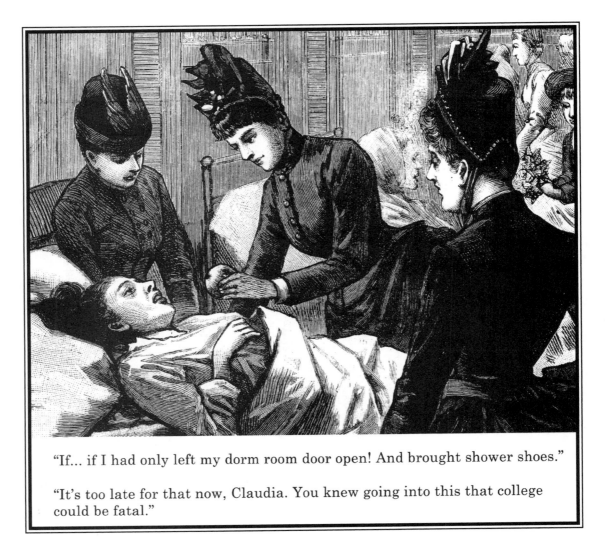

"If... if I had only left my dorm room door open! And brought shower shoes."

"It's too late for that now, Claudia. You knew going into this that college could be fatal."

I was fine with the hair soup, Helen. But this torn-up ass looking chicken leg... Where do you get this stuff? Do you own a bunch of stock in, like, Gross Animal Parts Limited?

Boy! I like your hoop... let me purchase it. I will give you five shillings.

No? Ten shillings, then. Ten! What say you!

Still no? How about a large package of mortgage-based securities?

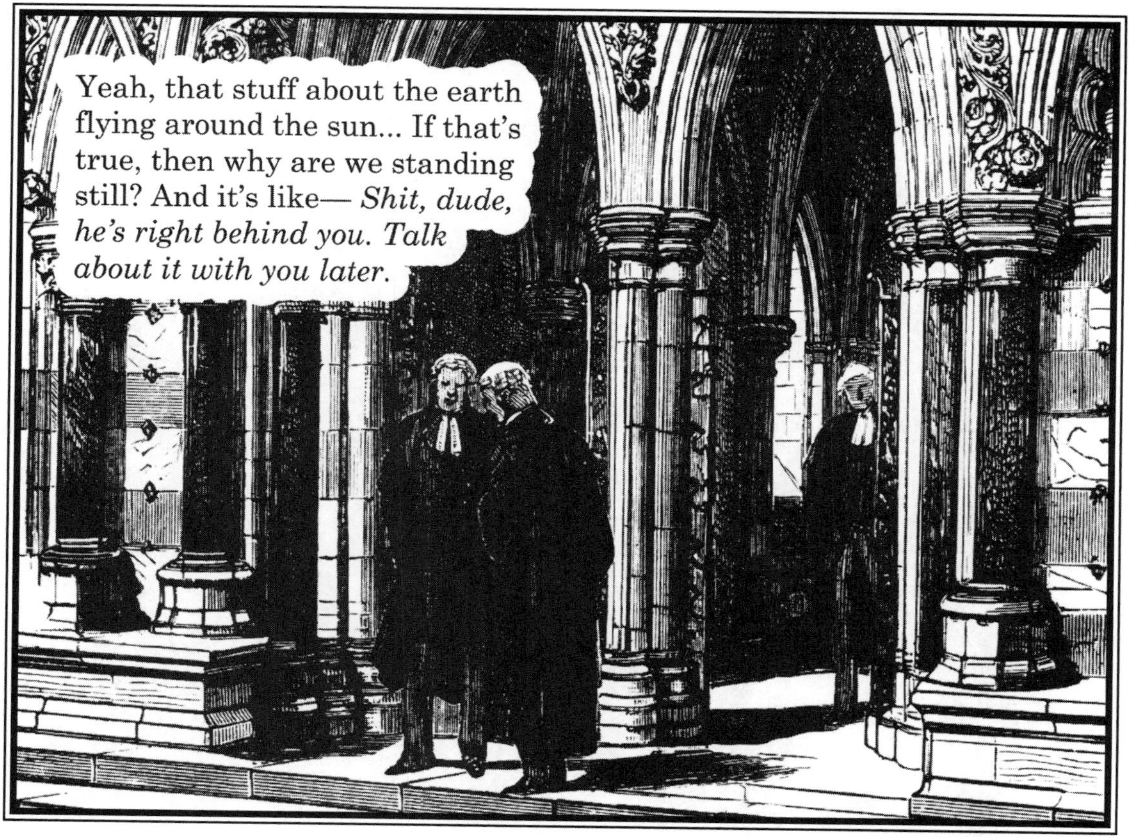
Yeah, that stuff about the earth flying around the sun... If that's true, then why are we standing still? And it's like— *Shit, dude, he's right behind you. Talk about it with you later.*

Oh!

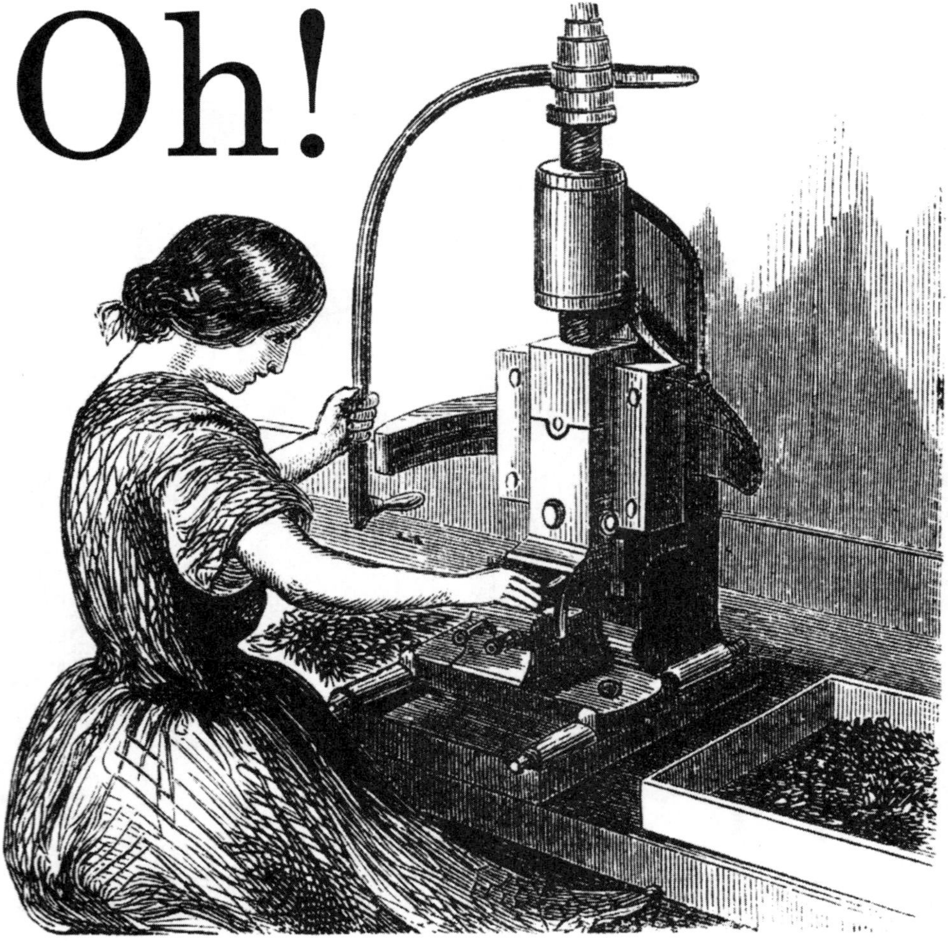

That's the third thumb this week.

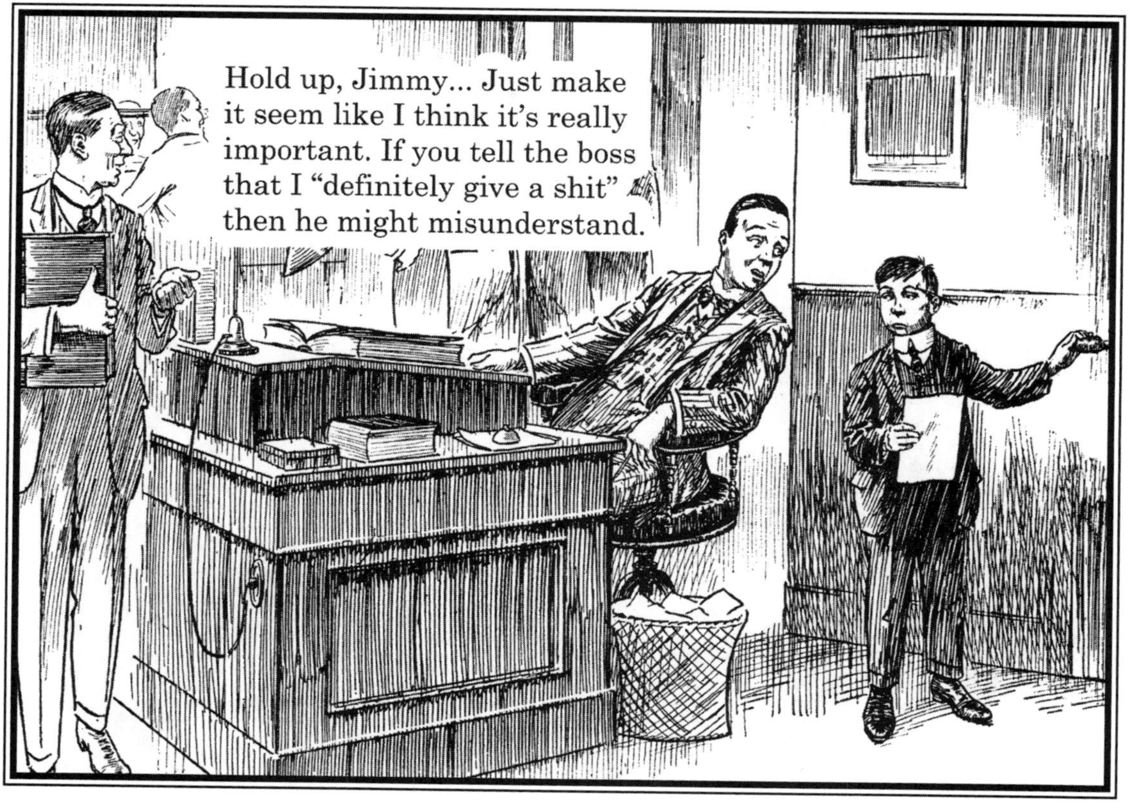
Hold up, Jimmy... Just make it seem like I think it's really important. If you tell the boss that I "definitely give a shit" then he might misunderstand.

New formulation!* 50% less dysentery!

"I preferred the old formulation."

Don't Fret!

Water Classic contains our originally-available amount of dysentery, and is available in drinking fountains across the country.

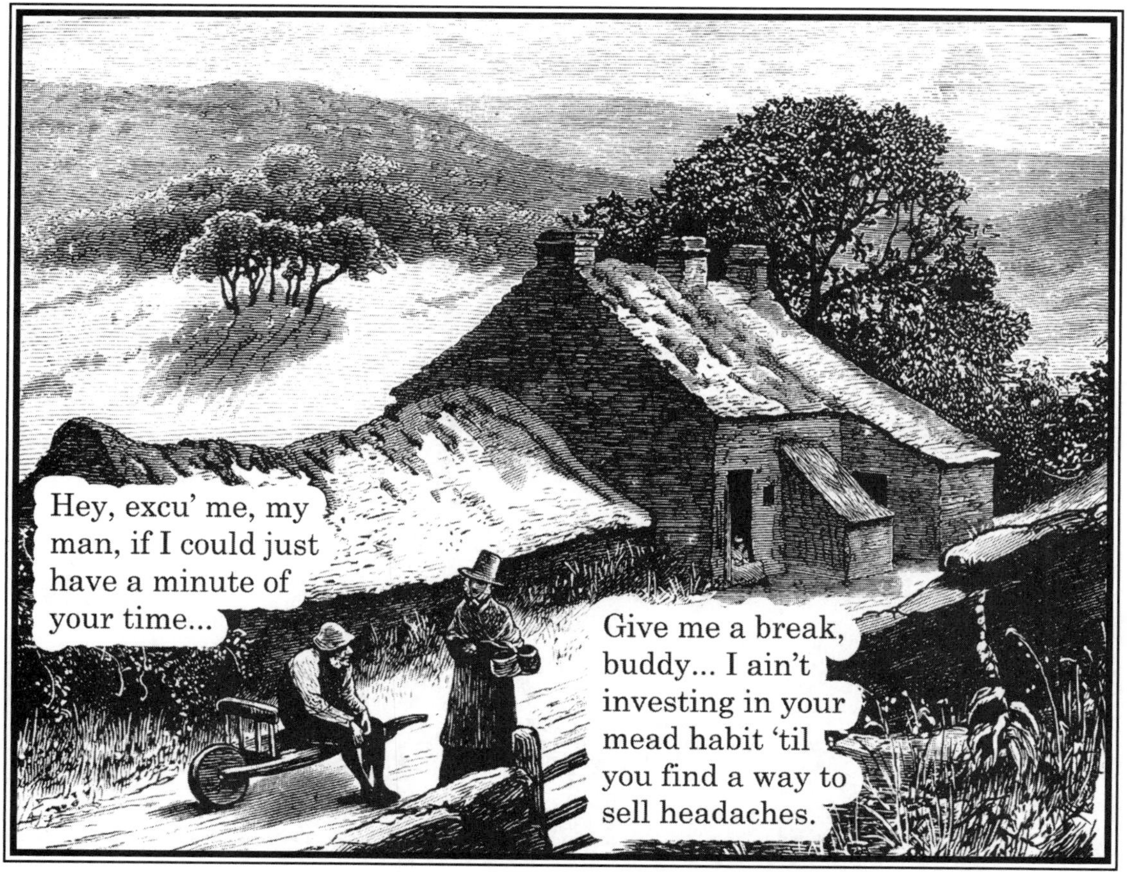
Hey, excu' me, my man, if I could just have a minute of your time...
Give me a break, buddy... I ain't investing in your mead habit 'til you find a way to sell headaches.

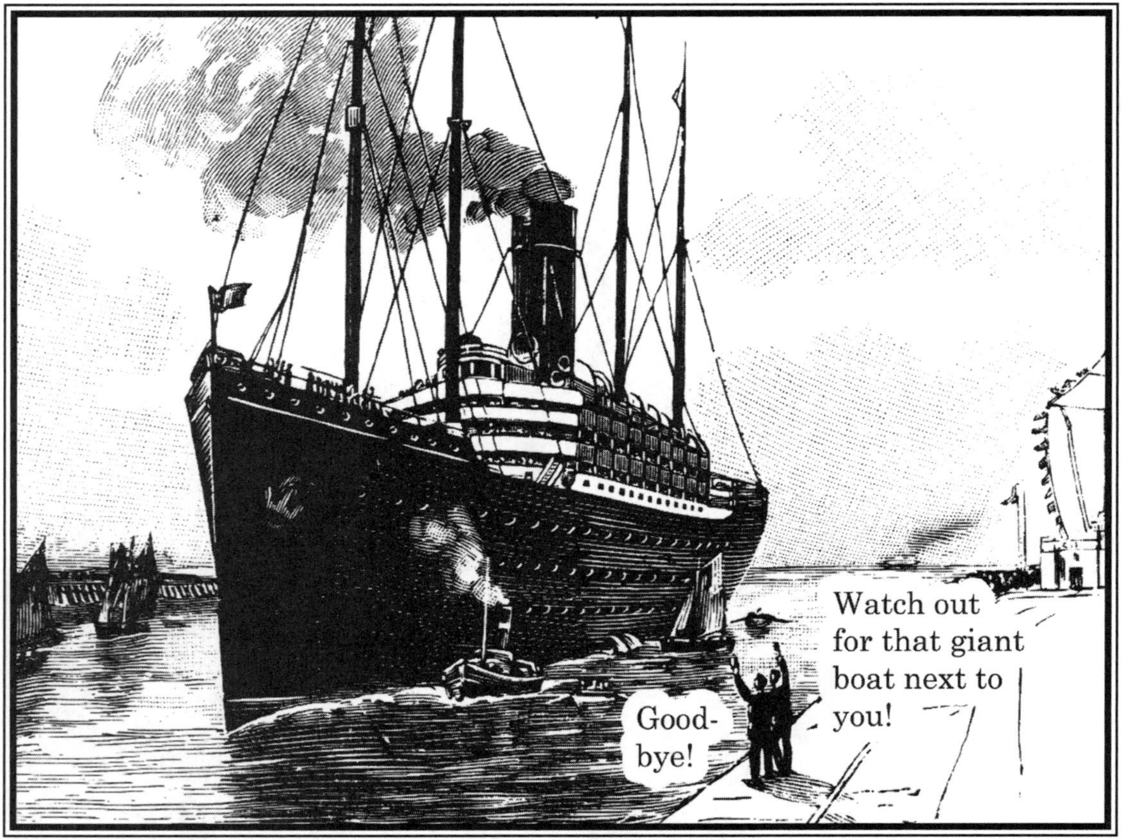
Good-
bye!
Watch out
for that giant
boat next to
you!

Bro, take it from me. If you want to pick up the saltiest ladies, you gotta learn the art of the pickup. You can't just say "nice frock," man. You gotta be like... Hey, nice frock, *tell your grandma to let you borrow her clothes more often.* Then slap the drink out of her hand and introduce yourself.

This... This is utterly fantastic! I'll be a million— no! I'll be a billionaire with this! I shall call my invention... "porno."

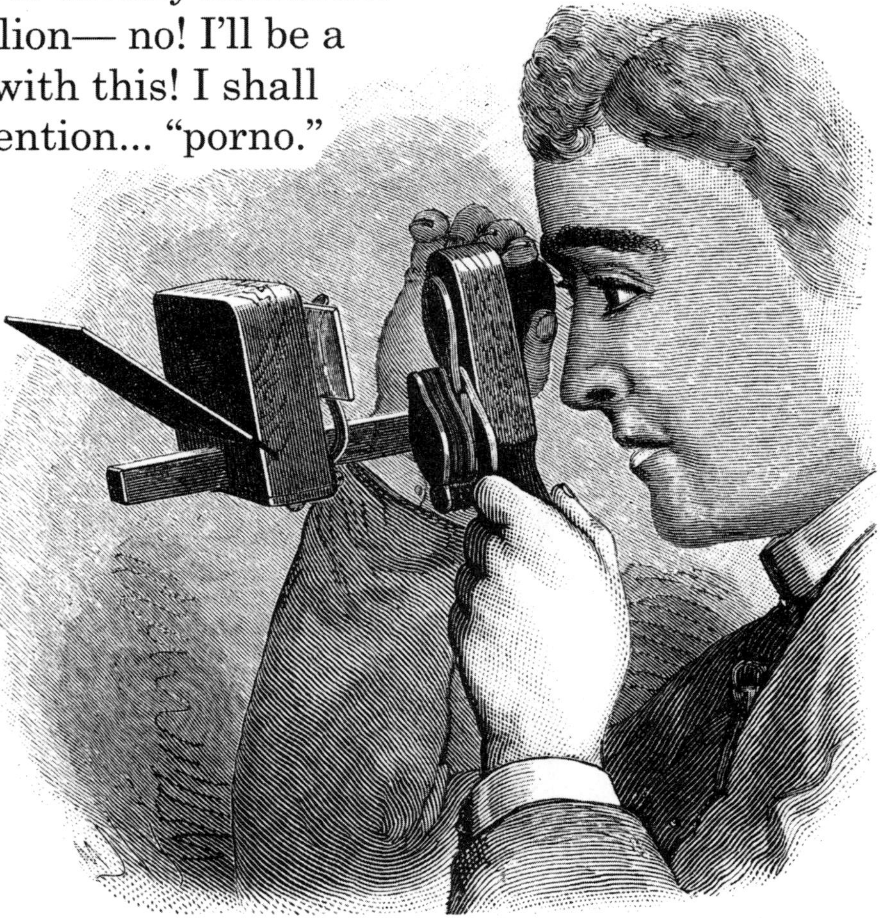

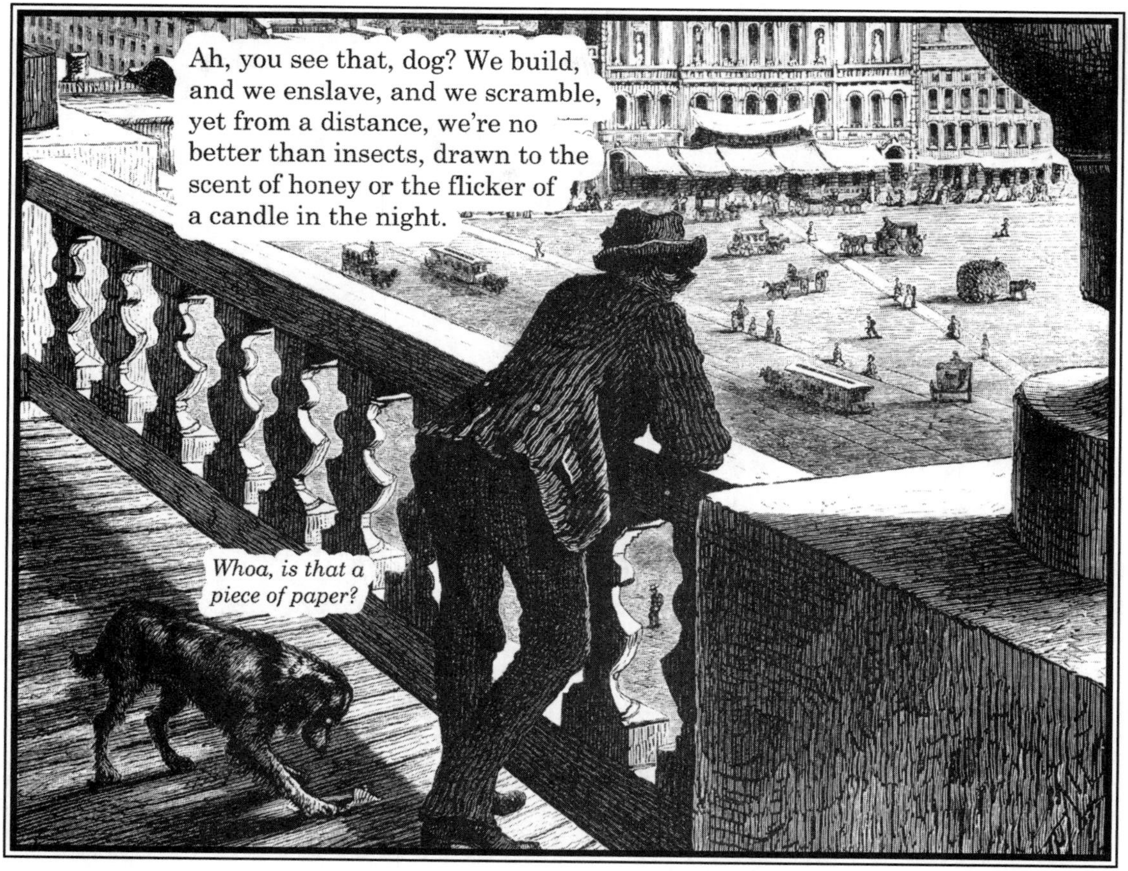
Ah, you see that, dog? We build, and we enslave, and we scramble, yet from a distance, we're no better than insects, drawn to the scent of honey or the flicker of a candle in the night.
Whoa, is that a piece of paper?

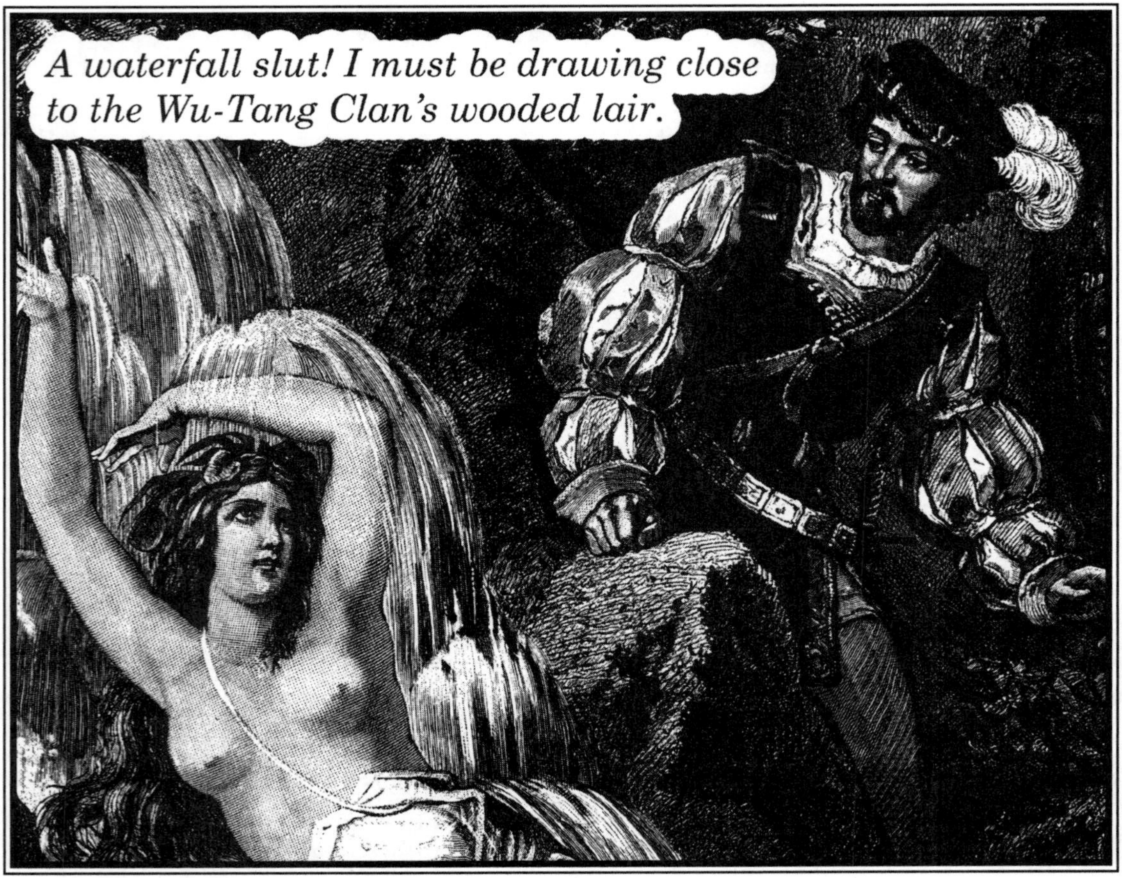
A waterfall slut! I must be drawing close to the Wu-Tang Clan's wooded lair.

"Little girl, you shan't be going from door to door! Some-one could grab you!"

"Oh, what you say could be true! I shall return to my home with my Thin Mints at once."

"No, darling, you shall return to your home with tuppence, and leave the Mints with me."

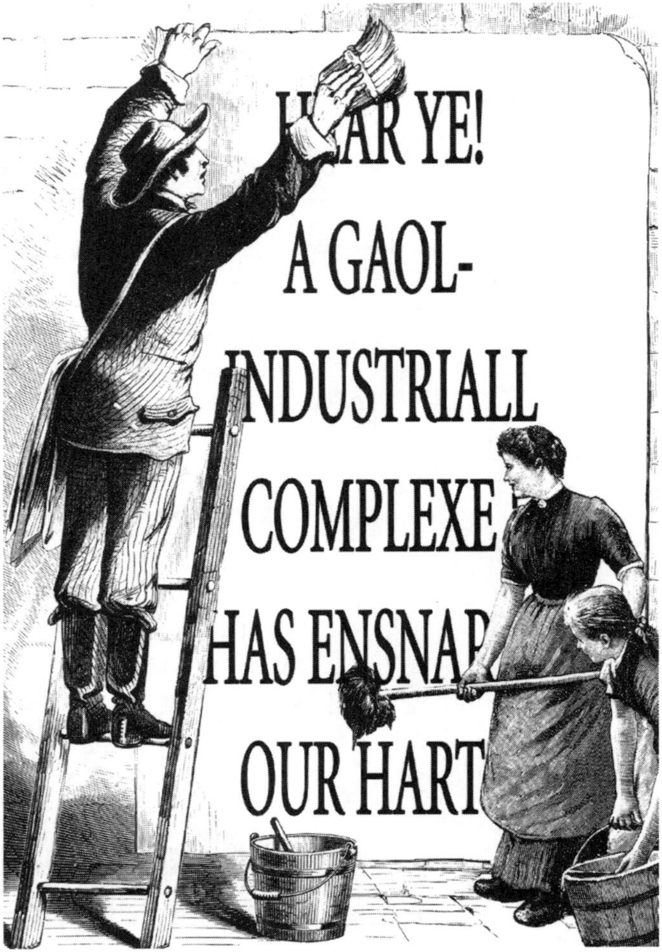
HEAR YE!
A GAOL-
INDUSTRIALL
COMPLEXE
HAS ENSNAR
OUR HART

Thanks for helping me paste up my poster, ladies...
my intellectual-graffiti poster, that is! Ha ha ha!

"Captain! Great news! There's an enormous waterspout ahead!"

"Great news?! We're likely doomed!"

"No! We'll be fine! Remember the rhyme? Tornado at night, sailor's delight."

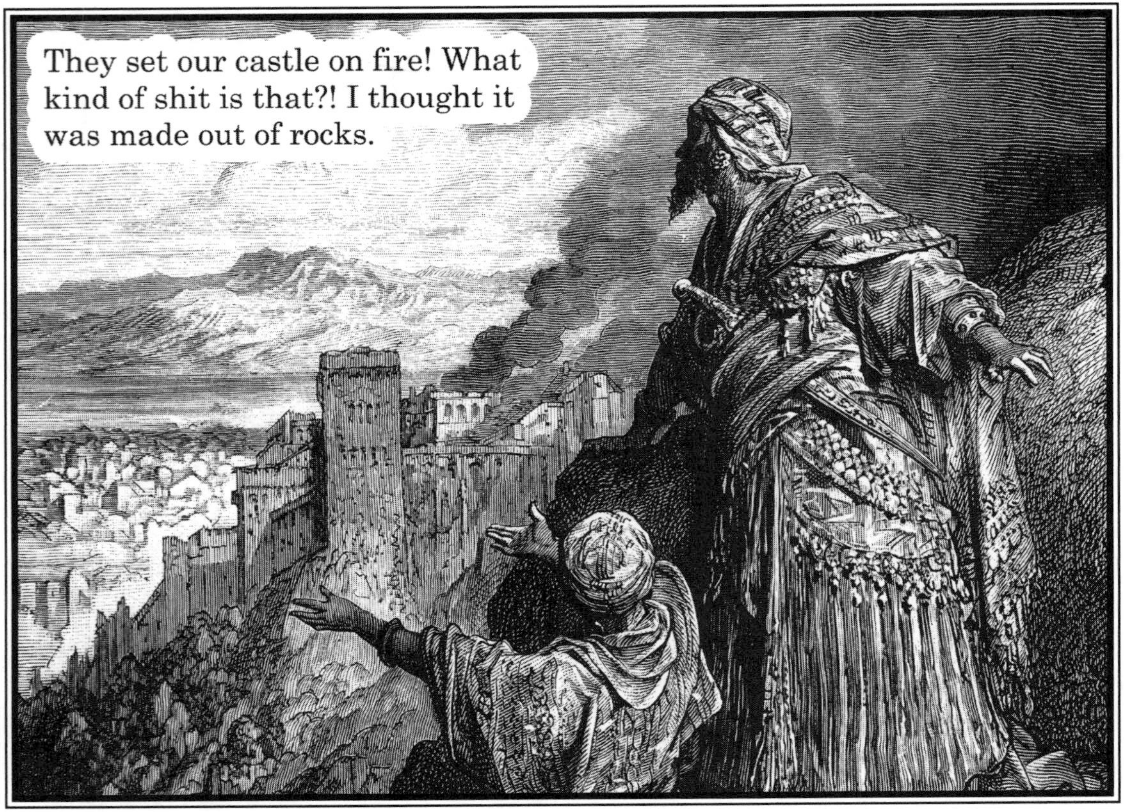
They set our castle on fire! What kind of shit is that?! I thought it was made out of rocks.

MAGIC FLAG

The more you wave it, the less you'll understand about civics! No electricity needed. Send 45¢ to "Flag", Box 12, Columbus, O.

Great job, dick. You fished me. What are you gonna do now? Put me in your truck and drive back home?

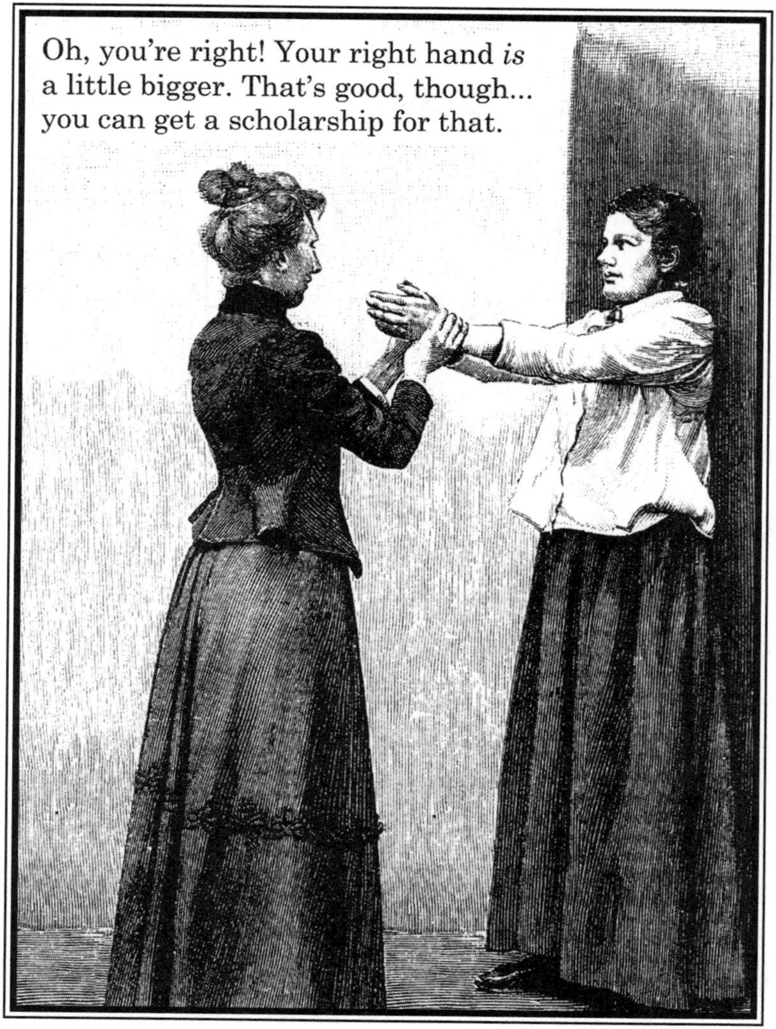
Oh, you're right! Your right hand *is* a little bigger. That's good, though... you can get a scholarship for that.

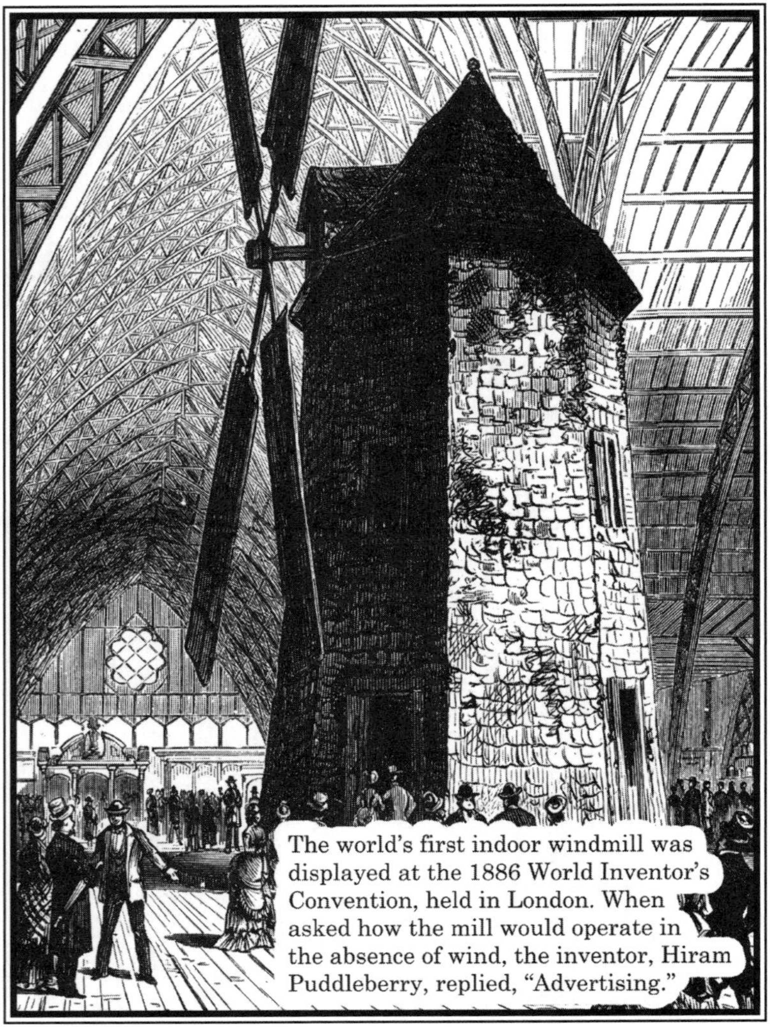
The world's first indoor windmill was displayed at the 1886 World Inventor's Convention, held in London. When asked how the mill would operate in the absence of wind, the inventor, Hiram Puddleberry, replied, "Advertising."

Okay... Looks-On-Red-River, Bison-Buffalo-Pants, I think it's time to switch to Plan B. We go undercover, blend in with the white man, invent Sam's Club, and exterminate them through obesity. You in?

Hey! I'm back from
the store. Help me
put the groceries
away.

Ooh! What kind of
cereal did you get?

What the fuck kind of
cereal do you think?

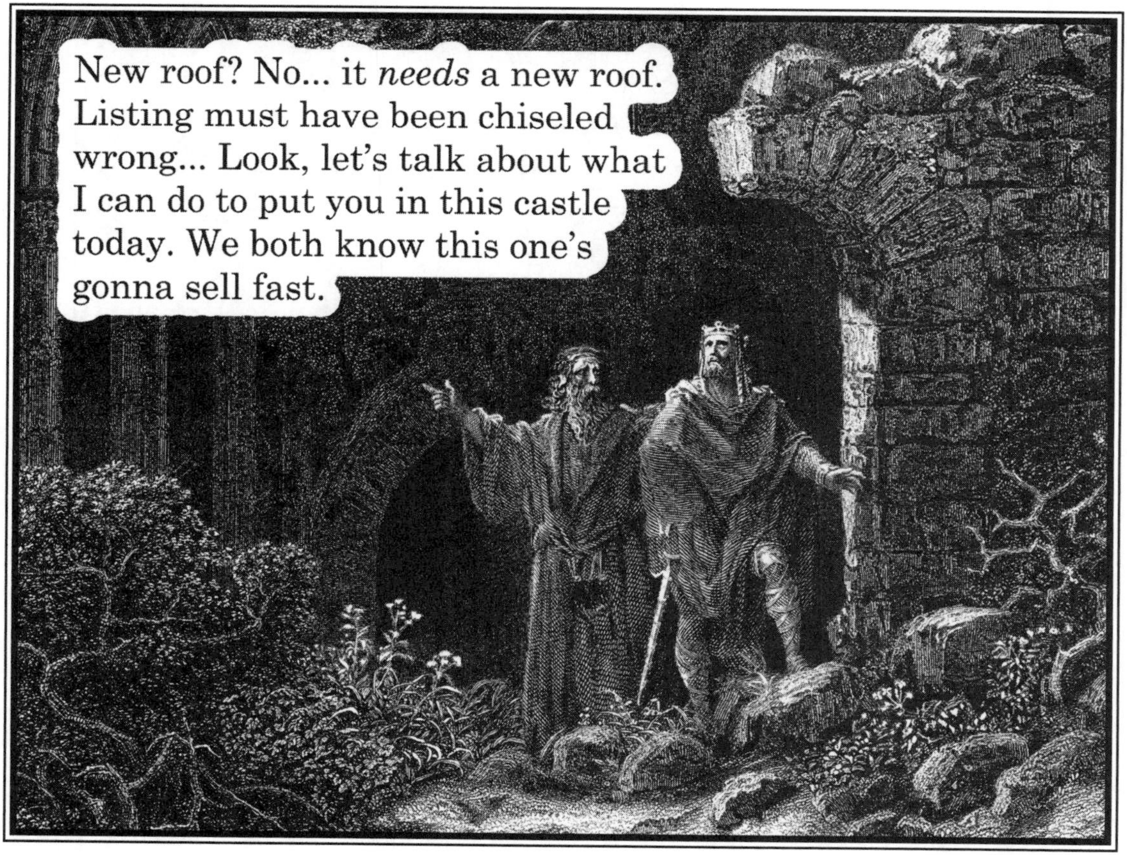
New roof? No... it *needs* a new roof. Listing must have been chiseled wrong... Look, let's talk about what I can do to put you in this castle today. We both know this one's gonna sell fast.

Dreams *can* come true!

Though nothing but a poor washerwoman, Charlotte dreamed that one day she would no longer have to do the laundry by hand. After fourteen years of hand-washing, her dream came true: She was now to use an automated washer!

Soon, she dreamed that one day, she would no longer have to use the laundry machine, and indeed, almost twenty years later, her dream came true! She no longer had to wash laundry at all, and instead, she toiled until death in the city factory, building laundry machines.

Honestly, Beatrix... You're either going to have to quit leaking this sick white stuff, or petition Congress to pass a healthcow bill. I can't afford to take you to the vet.

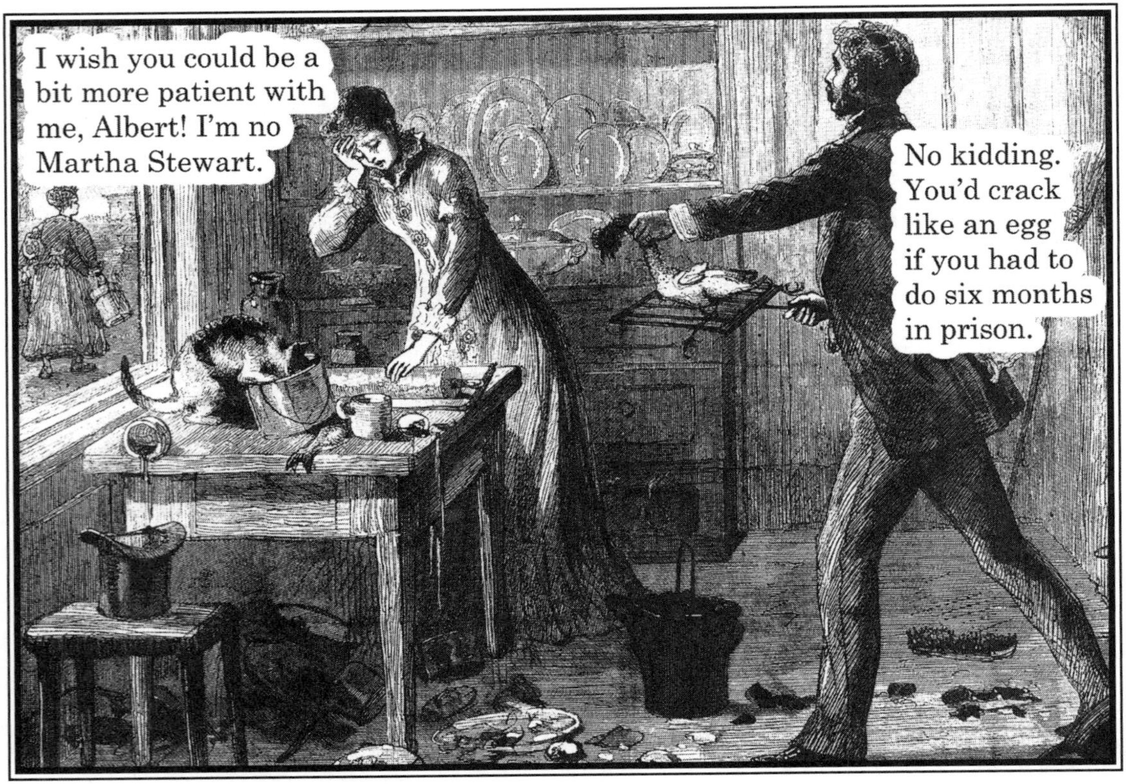
I wish you could be a bit more patient with me, Albert! I'm no Martha Stewart.
No kidding. You'd crack like an egg if you had to do six months in prison.

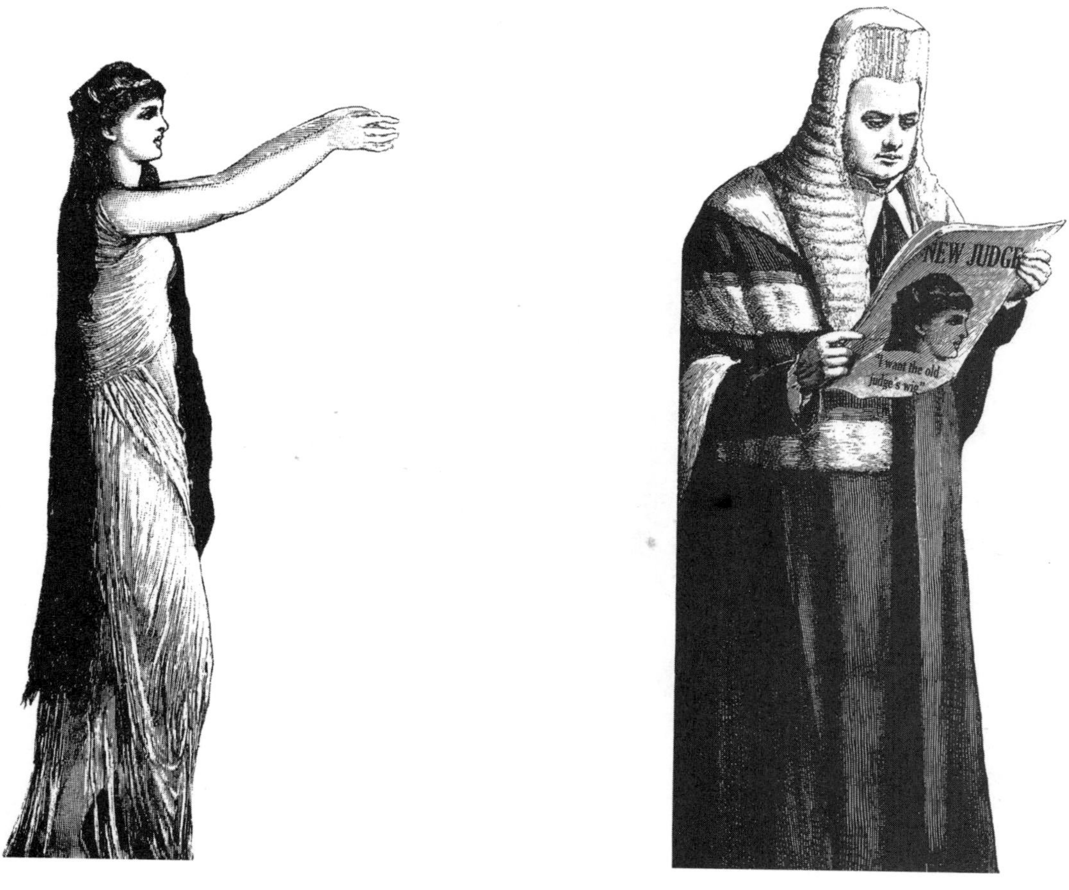
NEW JUDGE
"I want the old judge's wig"

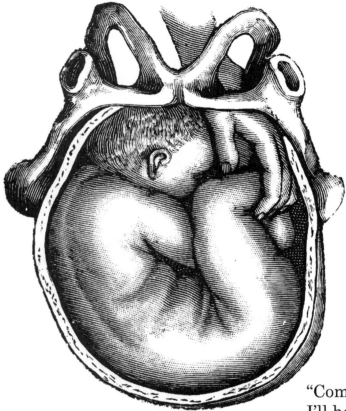

"Come on... it's time to go. I'll help you. Just slide on out. You can do it."

"No! I... I'm going to grad school! Leave me alone!"

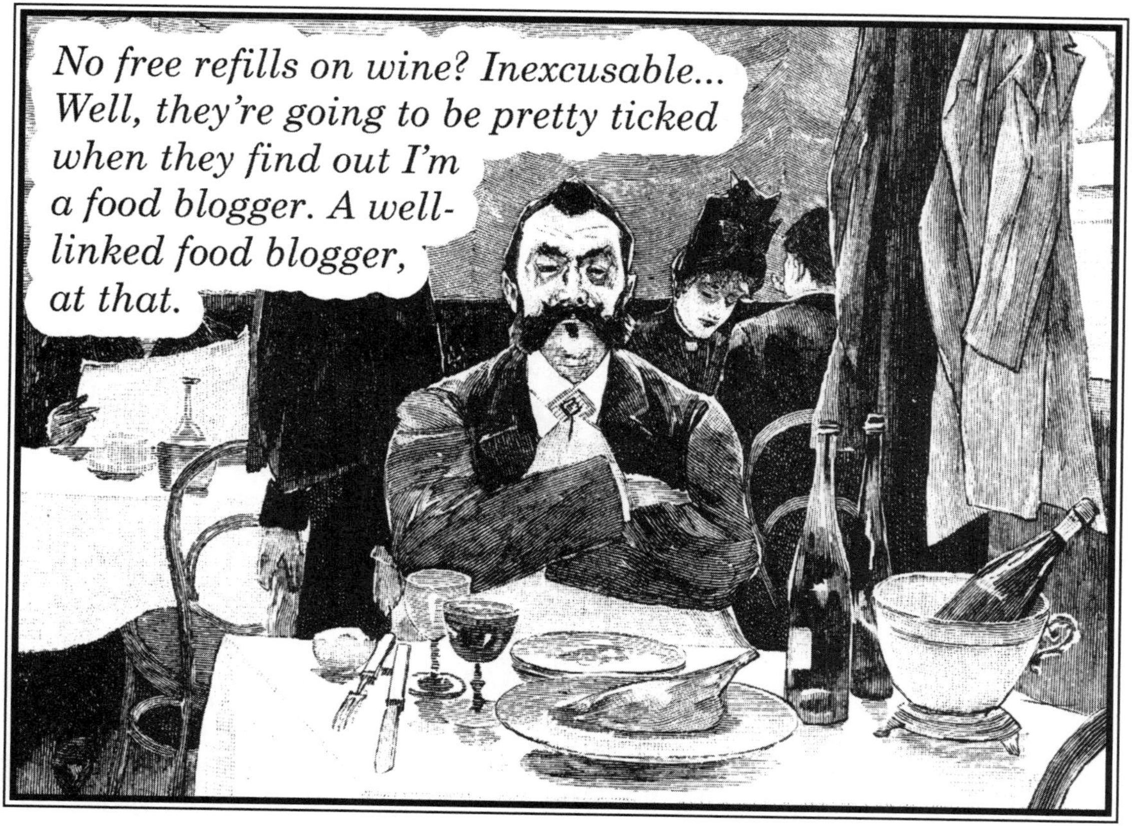
No free refills on wine? Inexcusable... Well, they're going to be pretty ticked when they find out I'm a food blogger. A well-linked food blogger, at that.

Whoa there, Lucy! You're supposed to sip it gently... you might wanna grab a bible and go on out to the latrine before it's too late. Last time I had a full cup of this stuff, I wasn't done shittin' till I was halfway through Revelations.

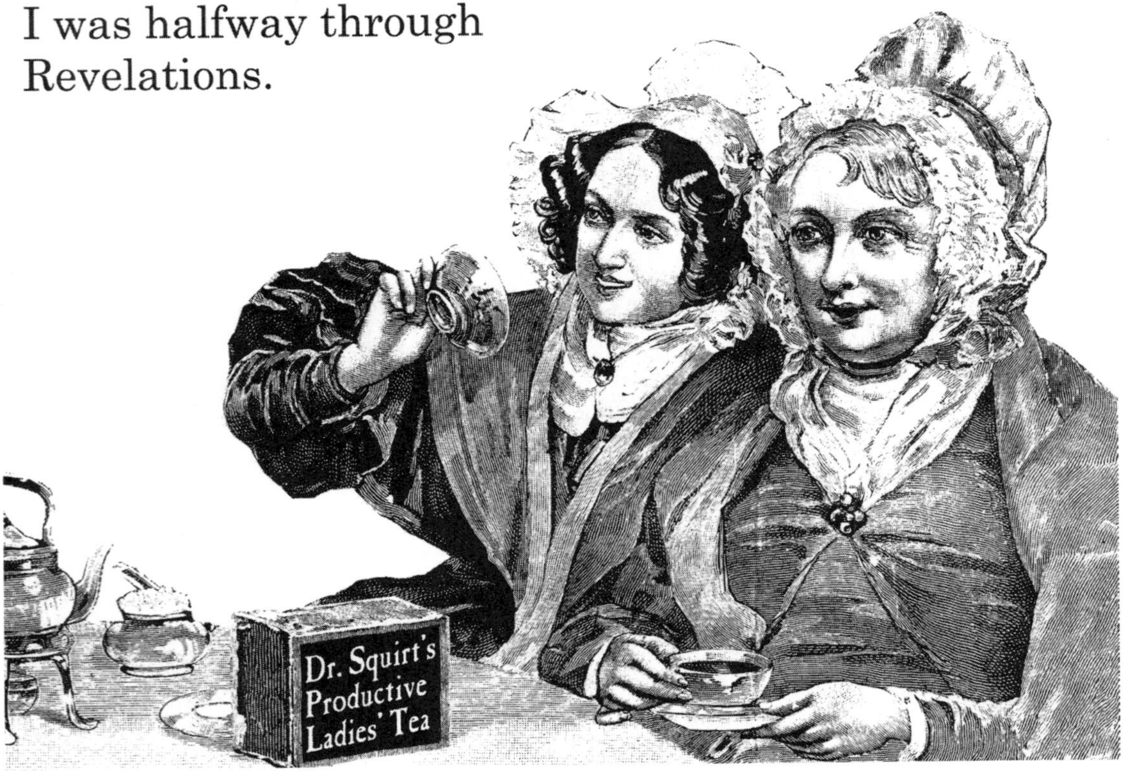
Dr. Squirt's
Productive
Ladies' Tea

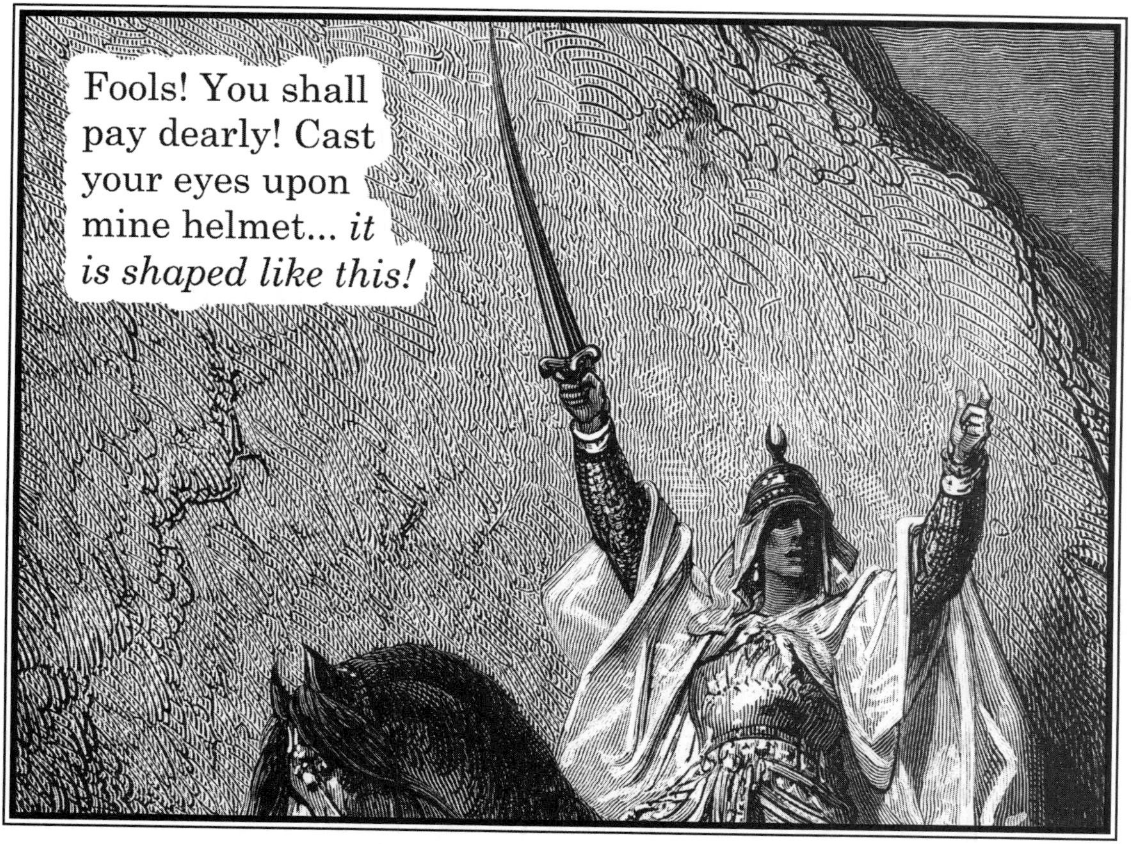
Fools! You shall pay dearly! Cast your eyes upon mine helmet... *it is shaped like this!*

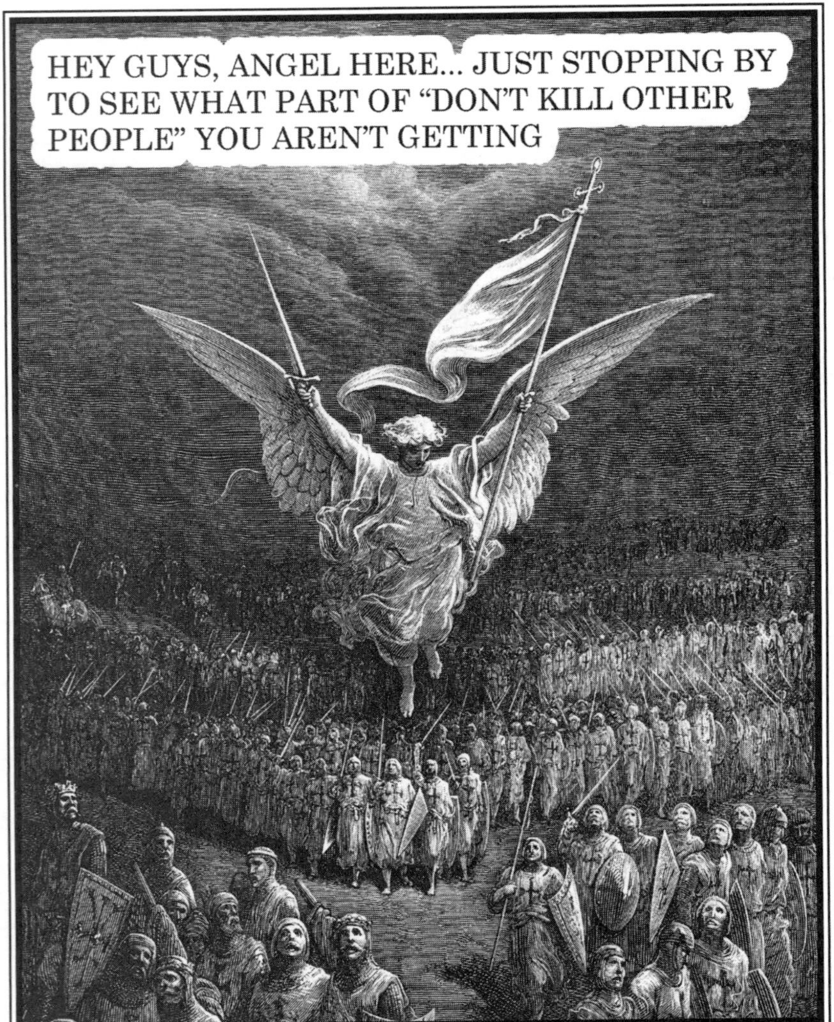
HEY GUYS, ANGEL HERE... JUST STOPPING BY TO SEE WHAT PART OF "DON'T KILL OTHER PEOPLE" YOU AREN'T GETTING

Mustrowski's Famous
Bed-Bender

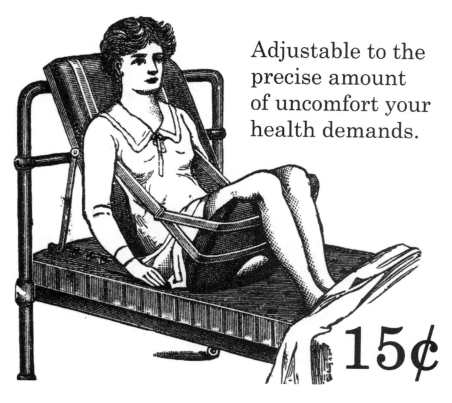

Adjustable to the
precise amount
of uncomfort your
health demands.

15¢

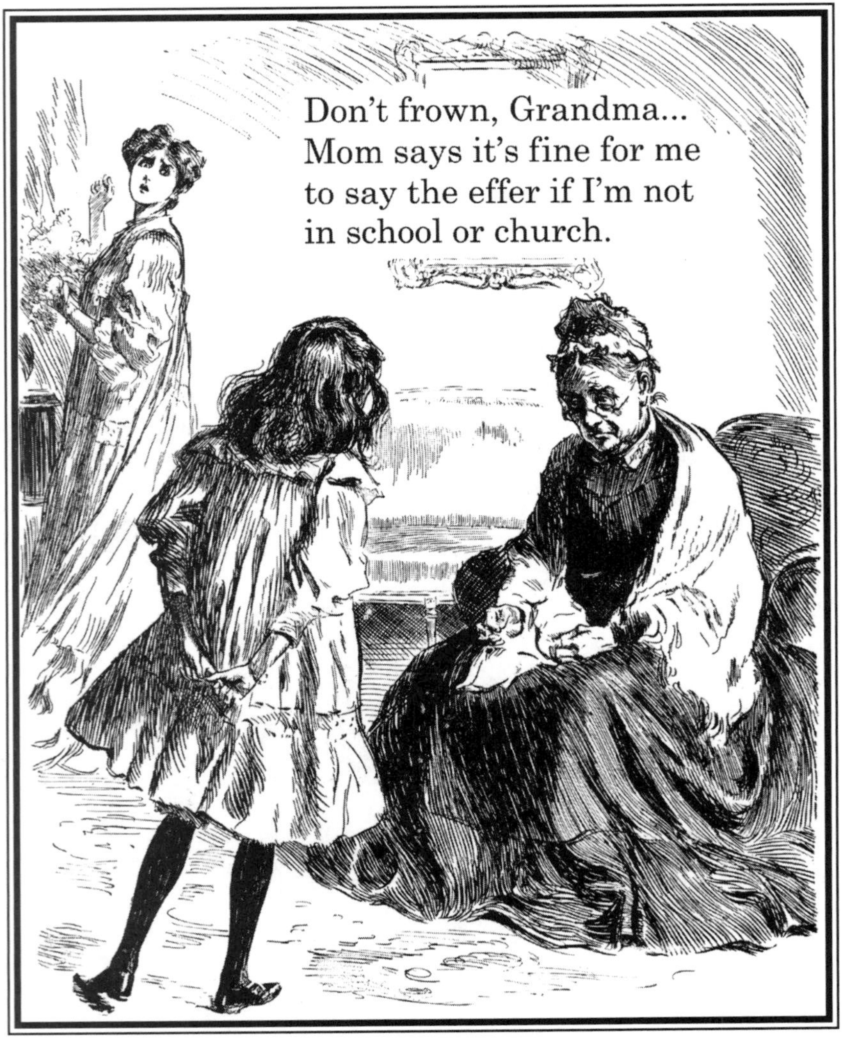
Don't frown, Grandma... Mom says it's fine for me to say the effer if I'm not in school or church.

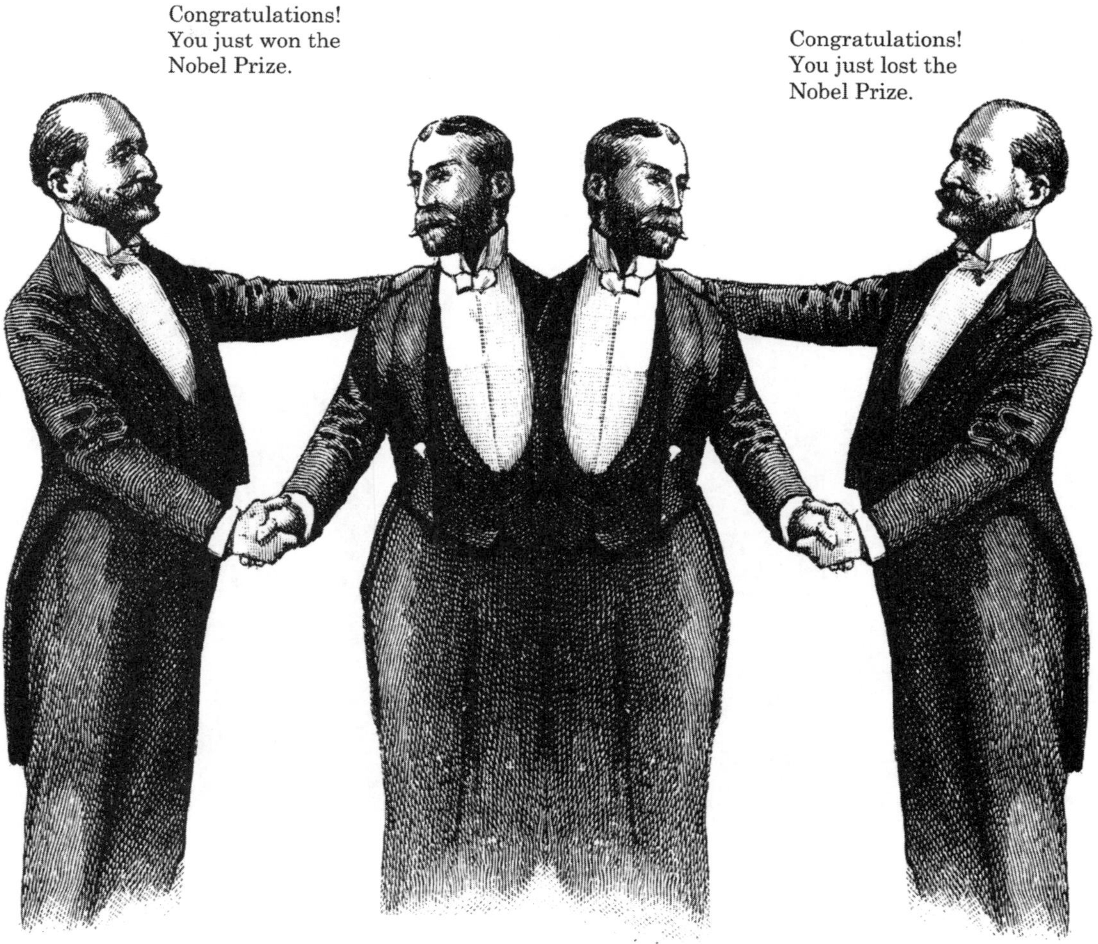
Congratulations!
You just won the
Nobel Prize.
Congratulations!
You just lost the
Nobel Prize.

You know anything *good?* I like pretty much everything... well, everything except country and ragtime.

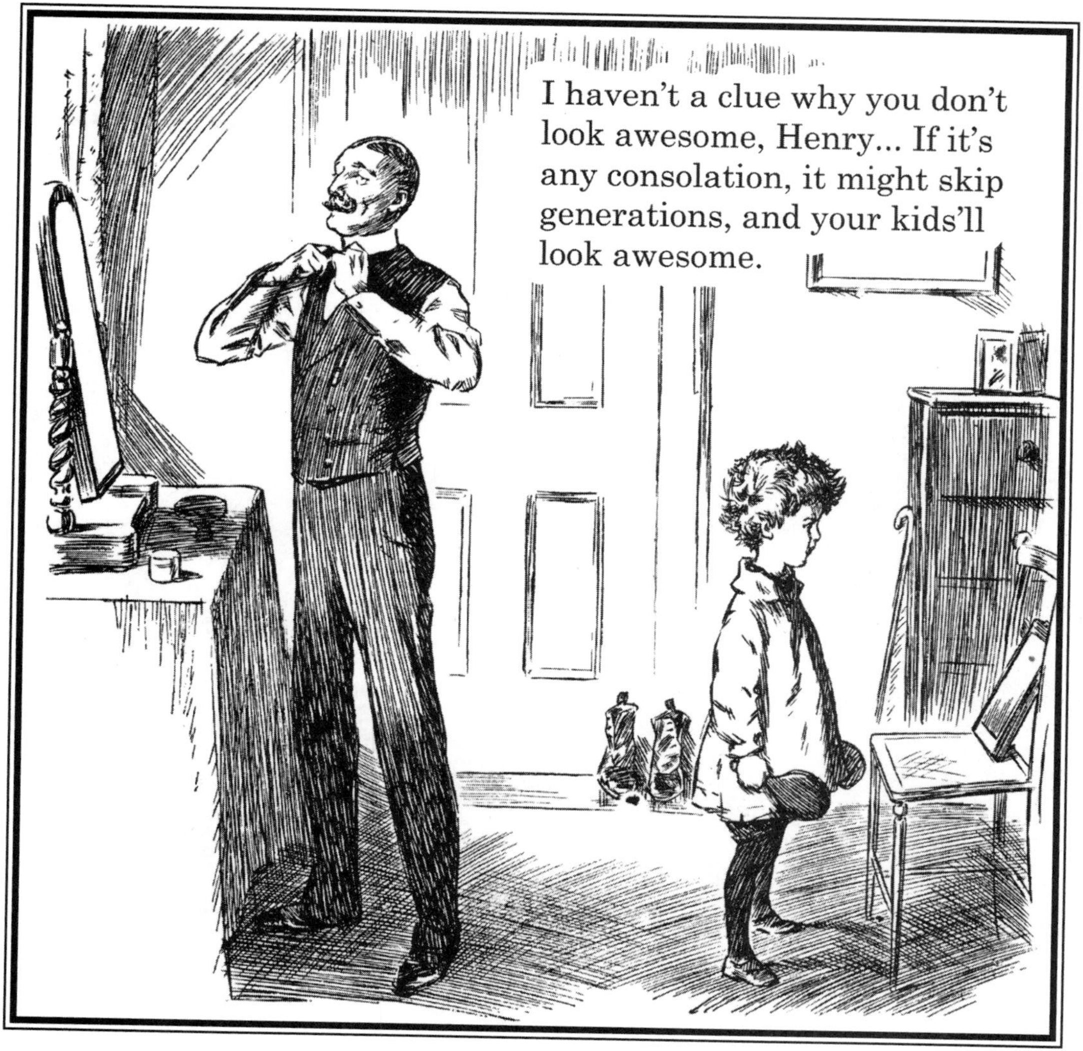
I haven't a clue why you don't look awesome, Henry... If it's any consolation, it might skip generations, and your kids'll look awesome.

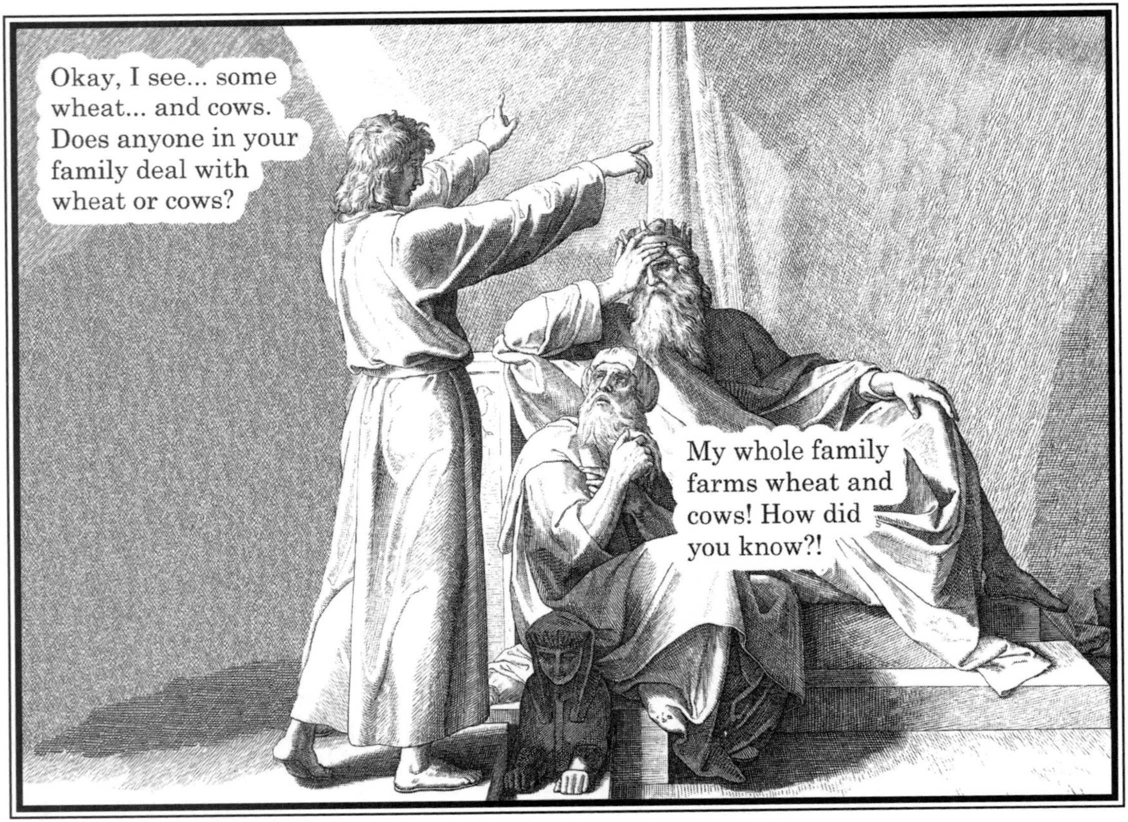
Okay, I see... some wheat... and cows. Does anyone in your family deal with wheat or cows?
My whole family farms wheat and cows! How did you know?!

"Okay... my castle shoots ether on your horse. Your horse died. Knock it over."

"Shit. Okay."

"I get an extra turn. This turn, my castle... shoots ether... on your other horse."

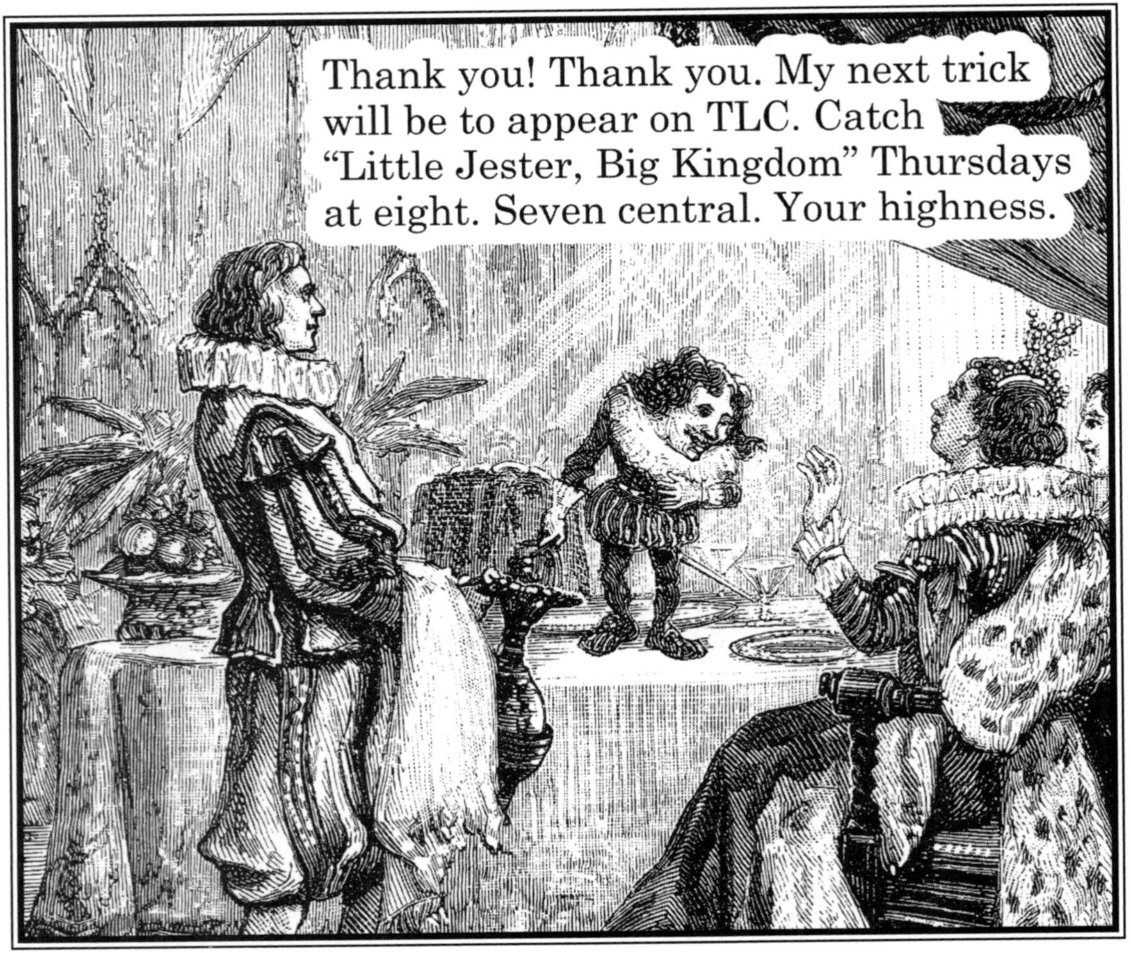
Thank you! Thank you. My next trick will be to appear on TLC. Catch "Little Jester, Big Kingdom" Thursdays at eight. Seven central. Your highness.

Your weiner-hat trick is fantastic! Tell me, between magicians, how you perform this illusion!

There's, uh... well... there's just a hole in the top. I stick my finger through, and—

Yes! Just like that! You must teach me how to create this Weiner-Hat. I beg of you!

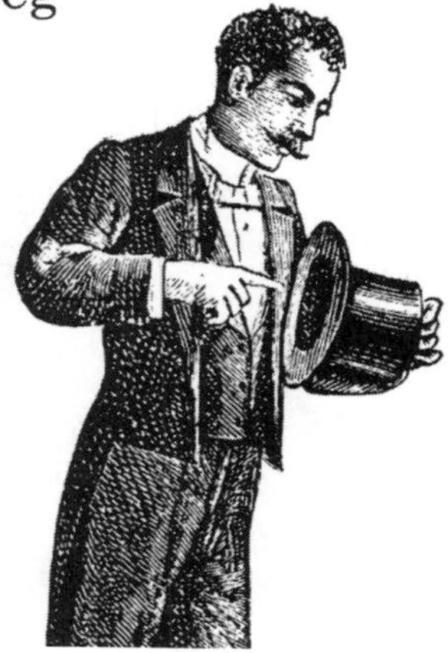

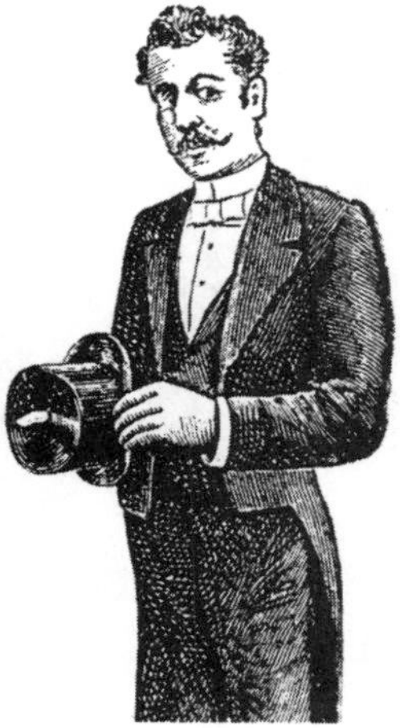

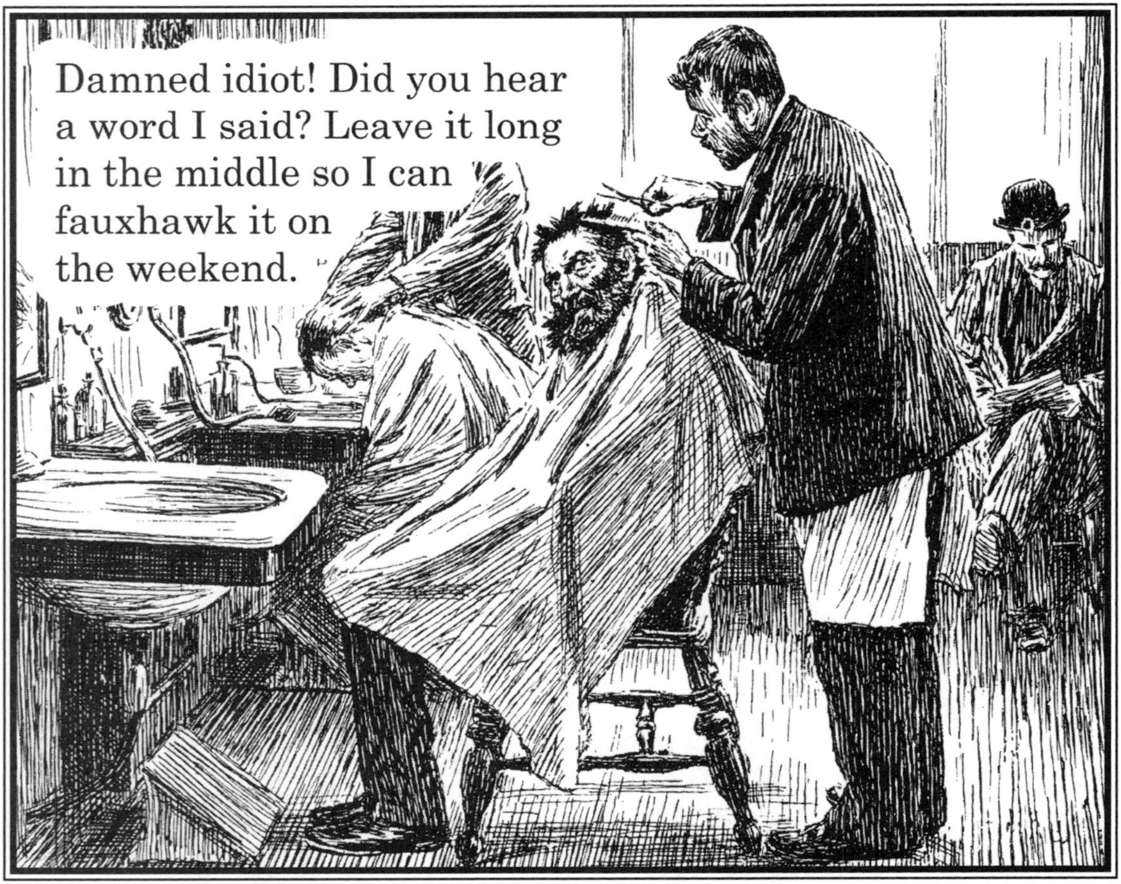
Damned idiot! Did you hear a word I said? Leave it long in the middle so I can fauxhawk it on the weekend.

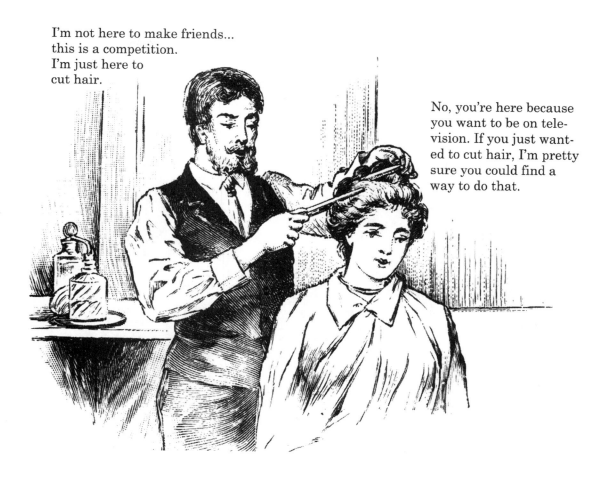

I'm not here to make friends...
this is a competition.
I'm just here to
cut hair.

No, you're here because
you want to be on tele-
vision. If you just want-
ed to cut hair, I'm pretty
sure you could find a
way to do that.

181 ⮞

D'you hear that, Warren? The lady on the sexophone sounds like...
Yes, her name's Margaret! Isn't your wife's name Margaret? I
thought you said she worked at the flower shop.

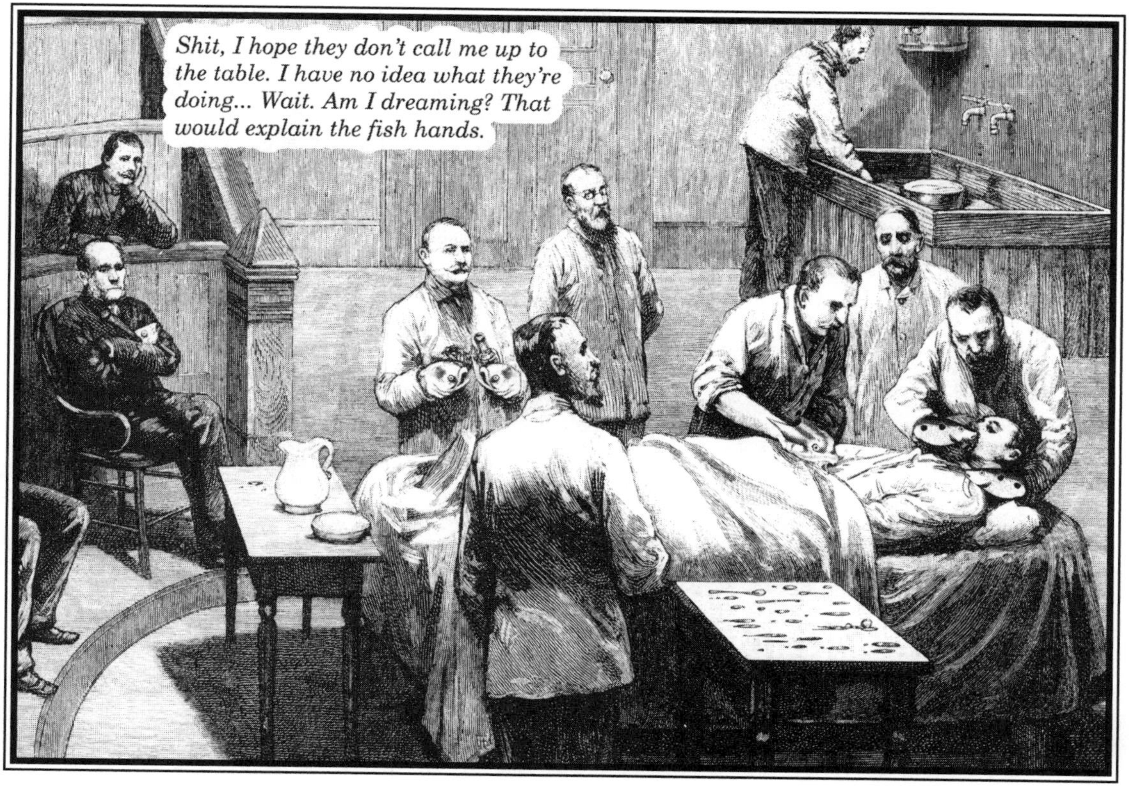
Shit, I hope they don't call me up to the table. I have no idea what they're doing... Wait. Am I dreaming? That would explain the fish hands.

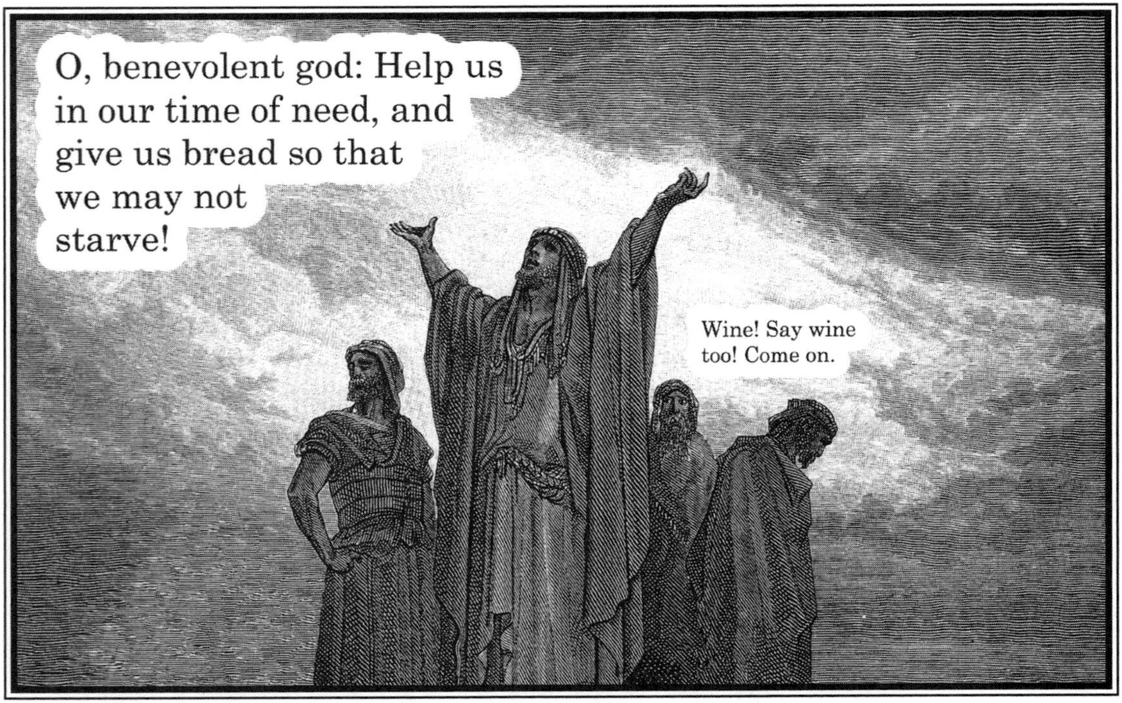
O, benevolent god: Help us in our time of need, and give us bread so that we may not starve!
Wine! Say wine too! Come on.

Shit, the lake's handing me a sword?! What do I do? Is it rude to just grab it? Shit. You get your minor in swords and they still don't teach you about the most basic things.

What are you talking about, shoot me?
Nobody's gonna shoot me, man.
If I break my leg, my owner'll
just put a cast on it.
We're cool like that.

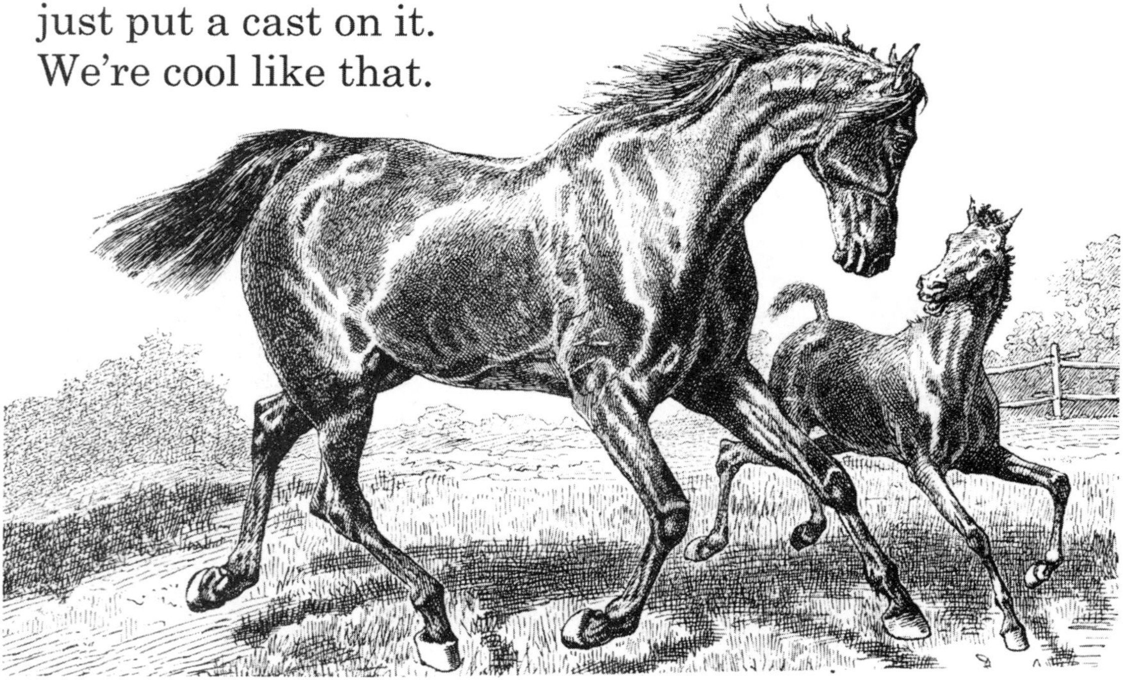

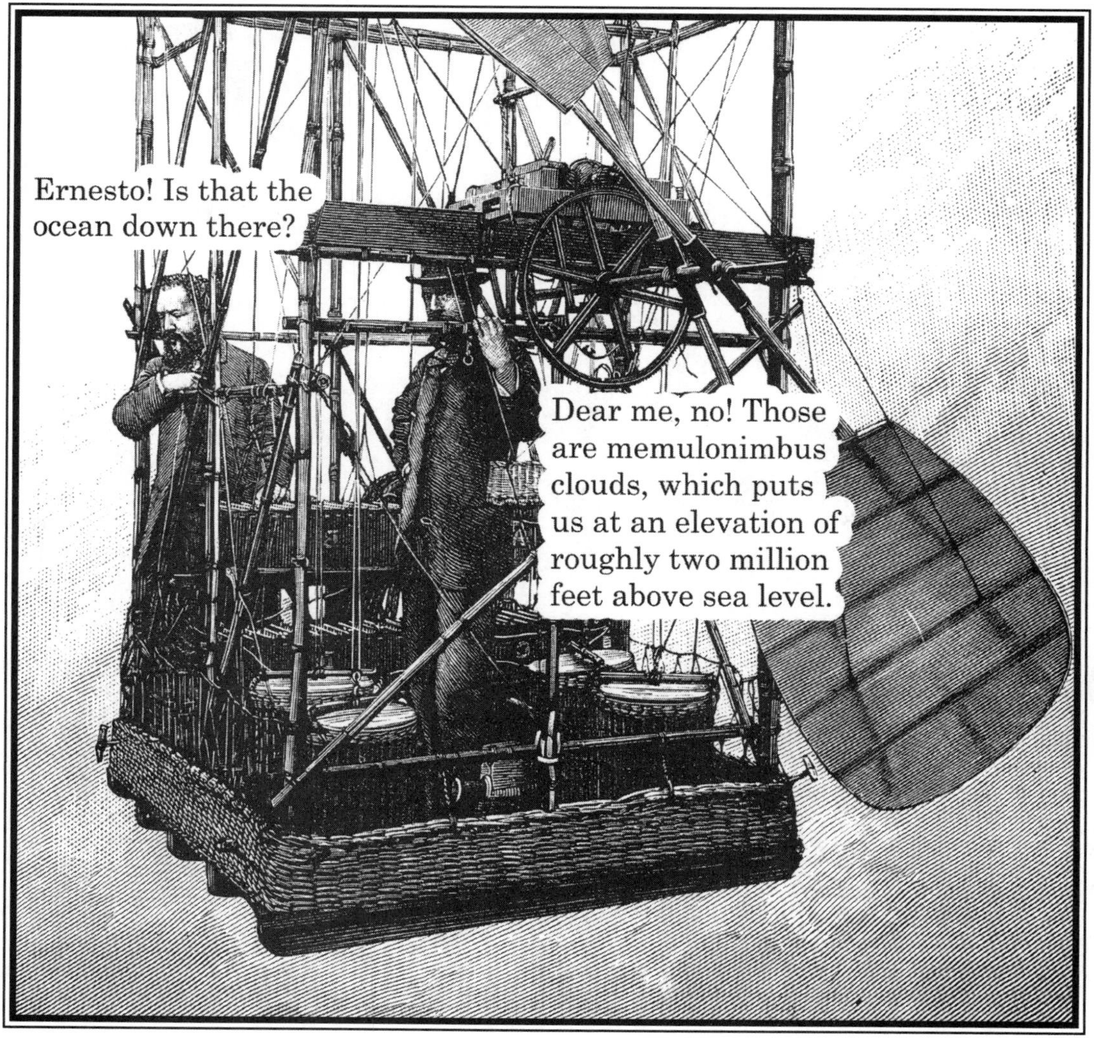
Ernesto! Is that the ocean down there?
Dear me, no! Those are memulonimbus clouds, which puts us at an elevation of roughly two million feet above sea level.

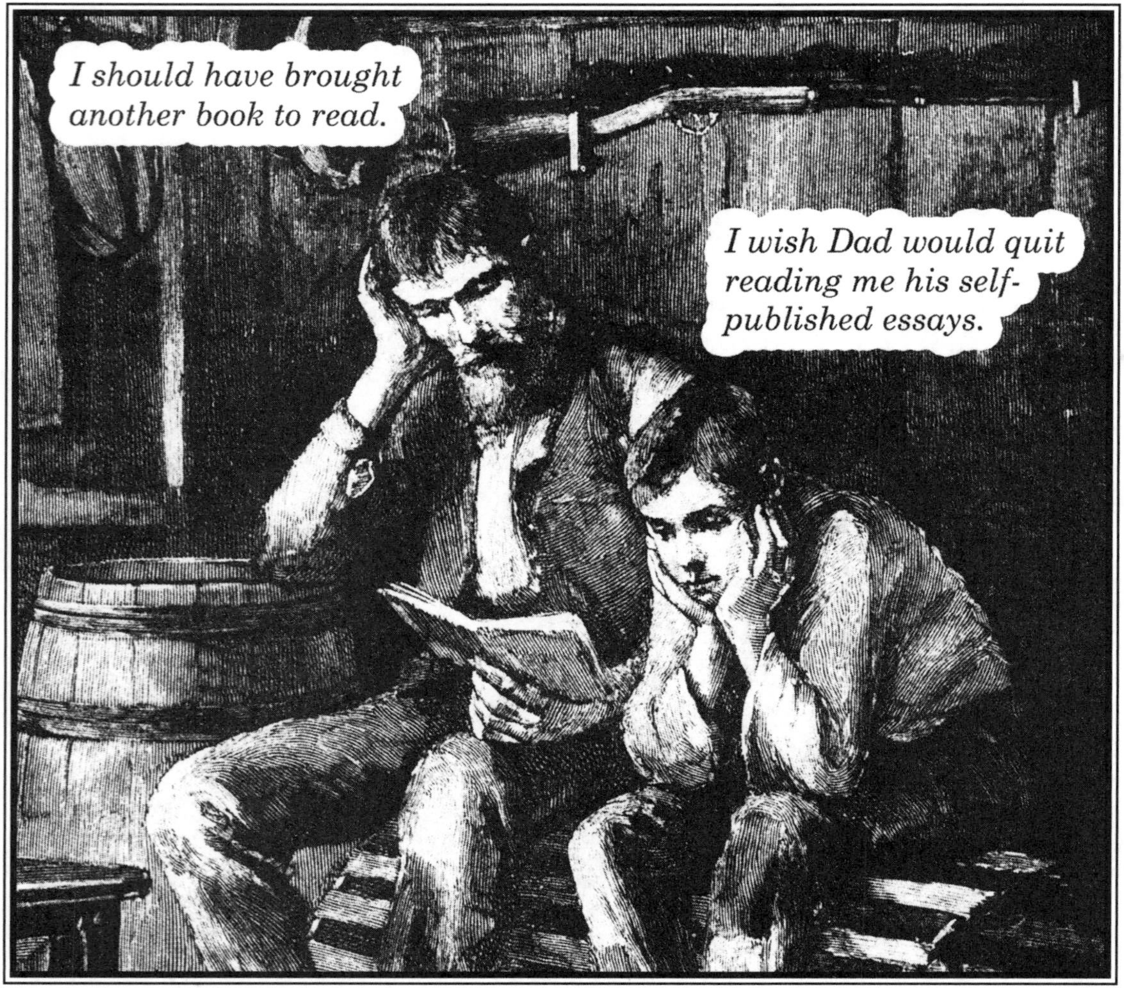
I should have brought another book to read.
I wish Dad would quit reading me his self-published essays.

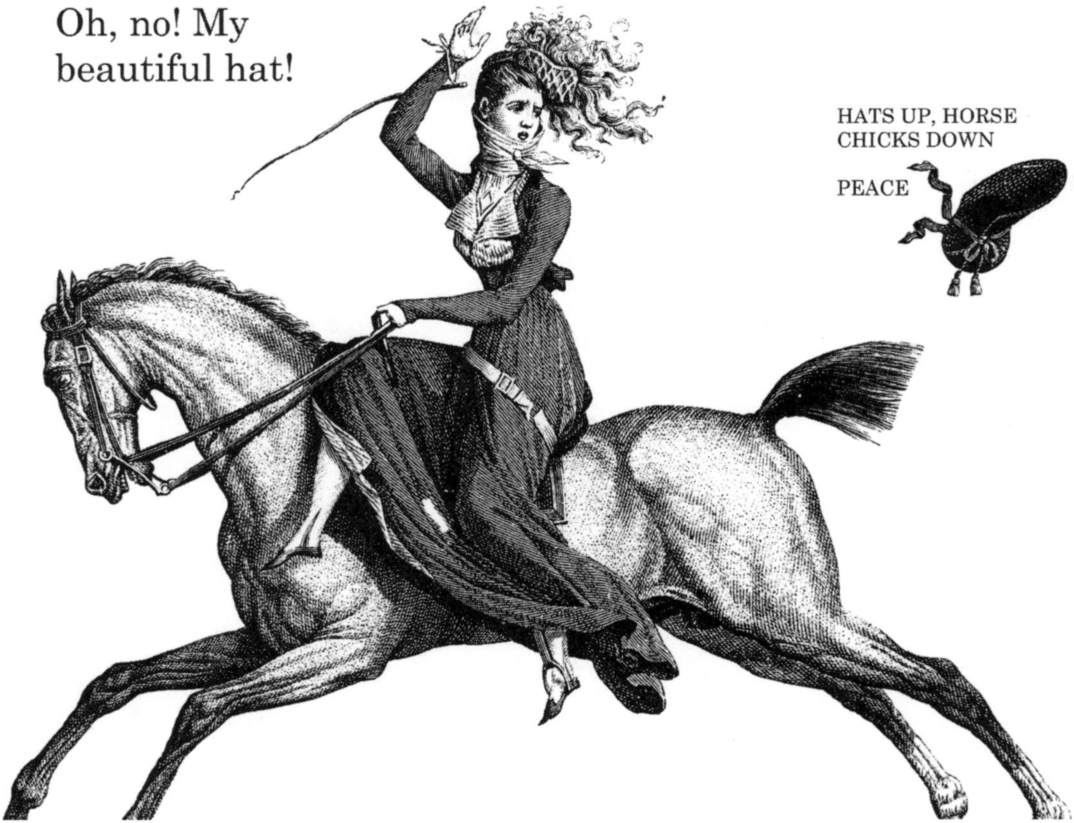
Oh, no! My
beautiful hat!
HATS UP, HORSE
CHICKS DOWN
PEACE

I can't recommend it enough, Florence. All you have to do is tell the doctor you've got something called hysteria.

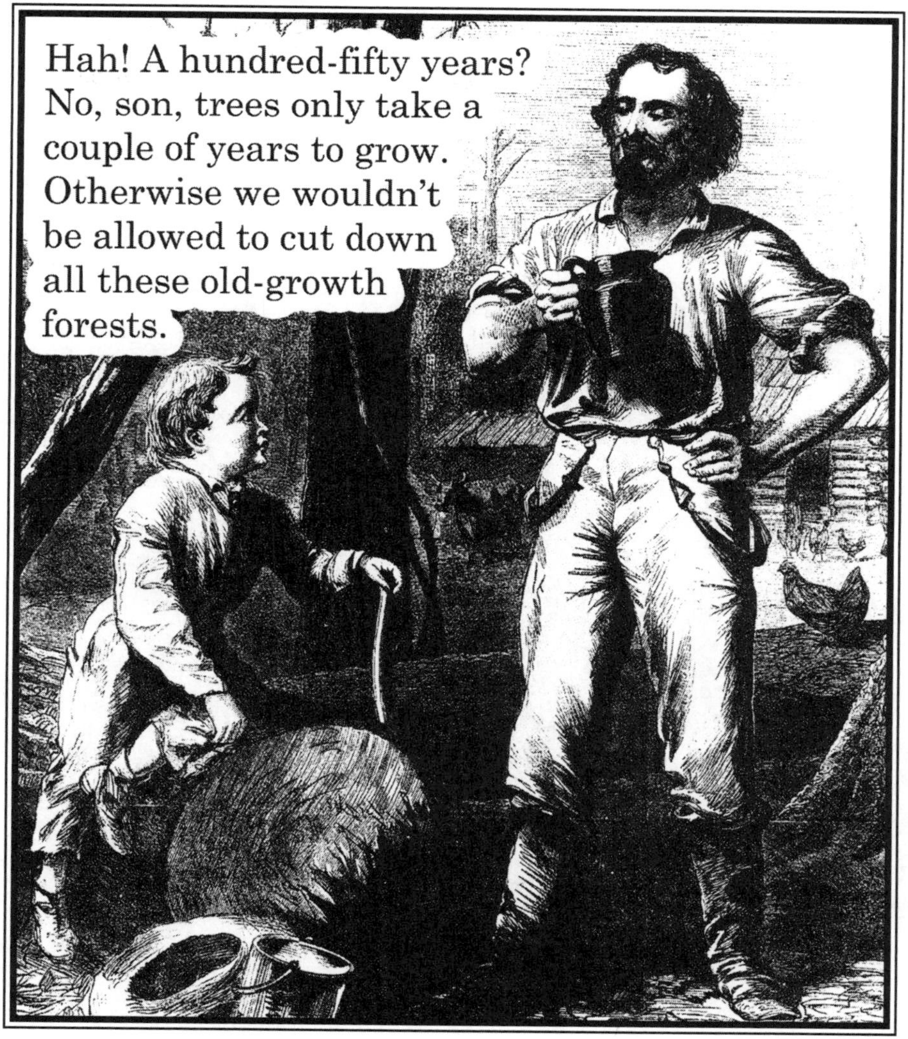
Hah! A hundred-fifty years? No, son, trees only take a couple of years to grow. Otherwise we wouldn't be allowed to cut down all these old-growth forests.

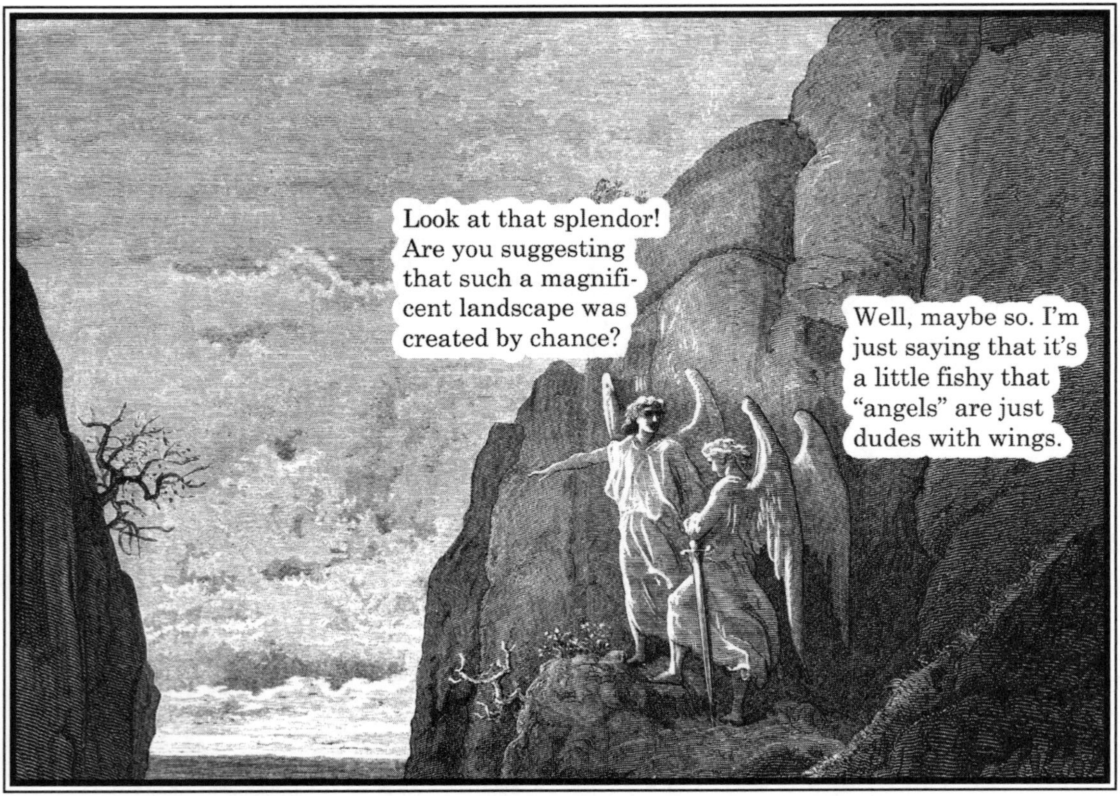
Look at that splendor! Are you suggesting that such a magnificent landscape was created by chance?
Well, maybe so. I'm just saying that it's a little fishy that "angels" are just dudes with wings.

Forward 20 steps! Now turn
right, by 45 degrees! Now
go back 40 steps! Turn
right, 90 degrees!

You can't do magic tricks...

WITH NUCLEAR ARMS

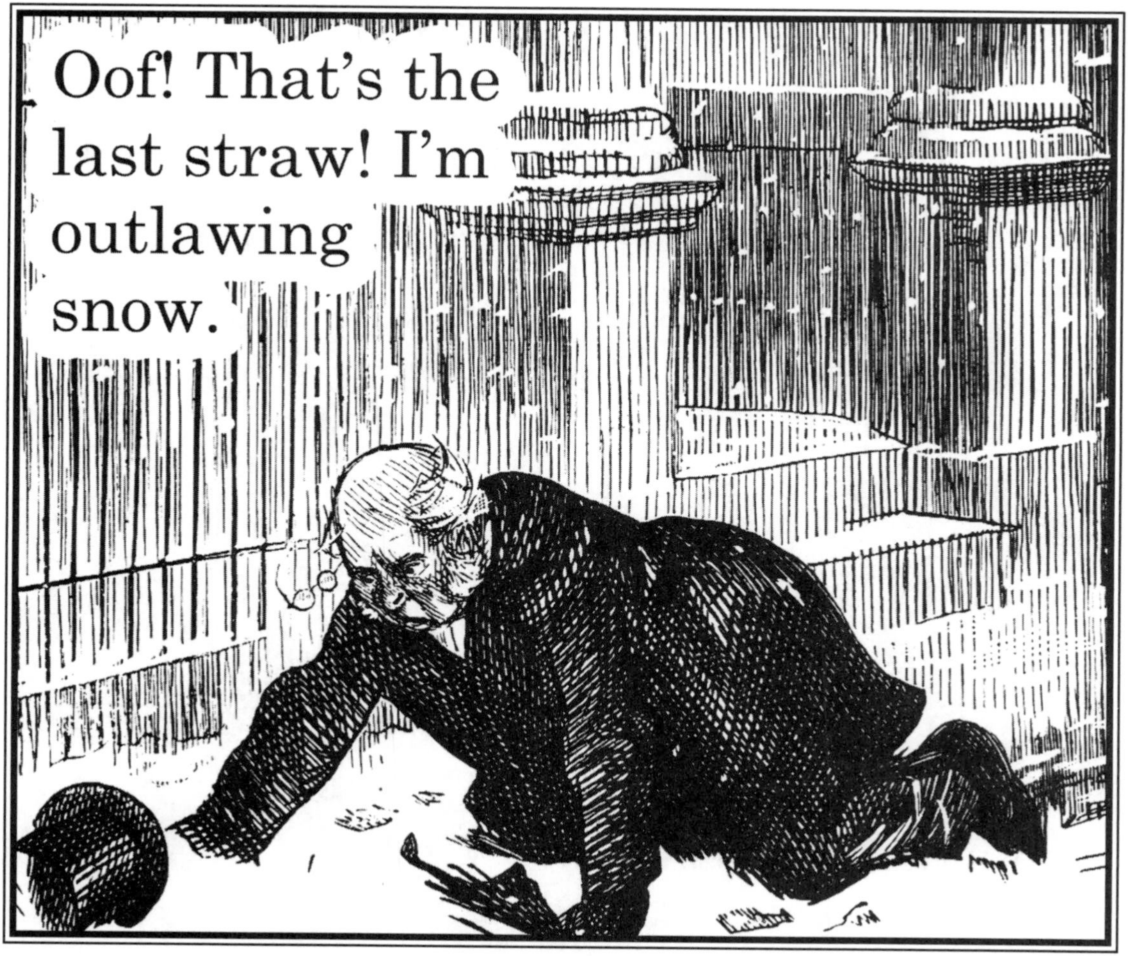
Oof! That's the last straw! I'm outlawing snow.

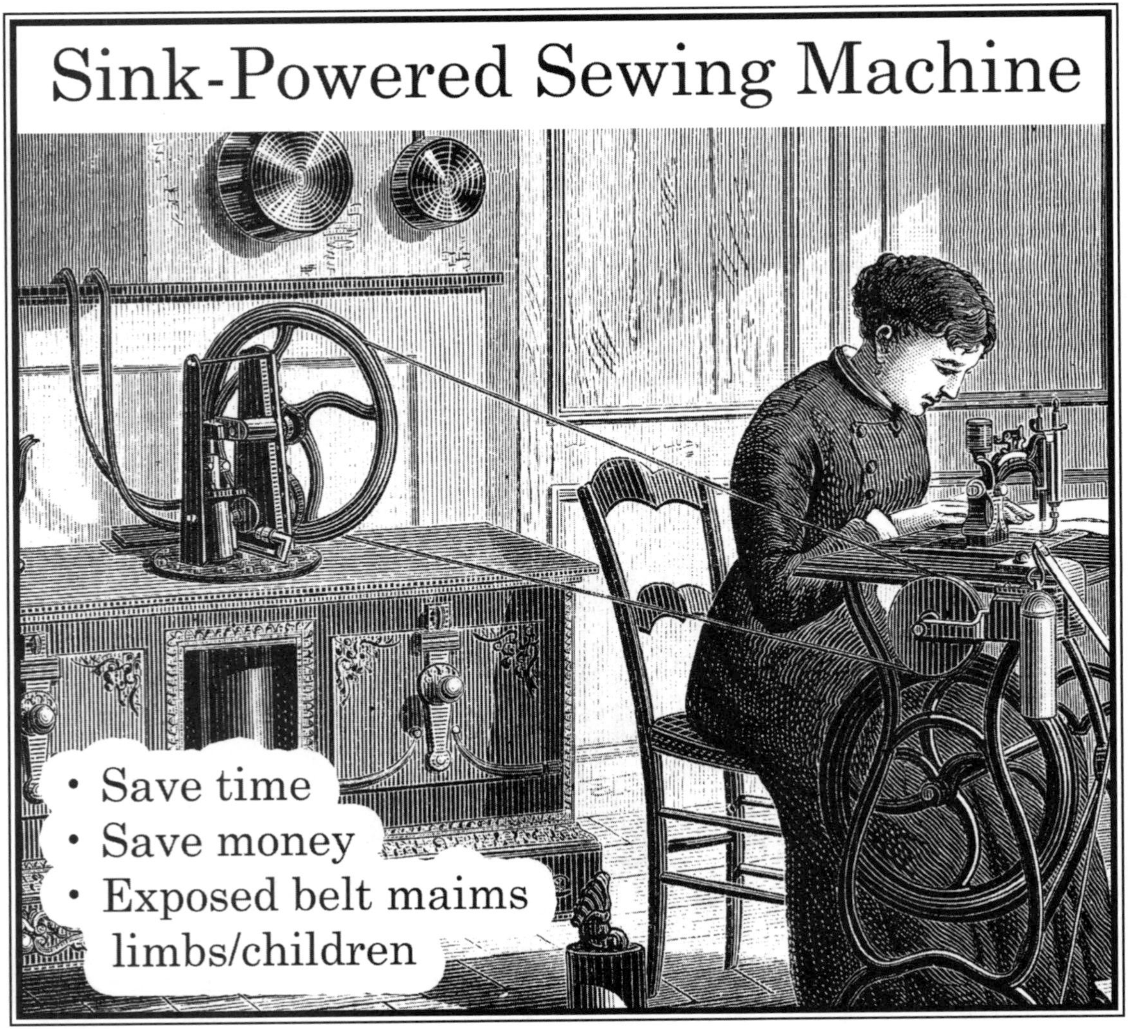
Sink-Powered Sewing Machine
• Save time
• Save money
• Exposed belt maims limbs/children

"Say... how about you trade
me a rabbit for one of my
delicious blueberries?"

"How about you keep your
blueberries... and I'll go
home now, and pretend I
didn't just see a tiny man
picking blueberries."

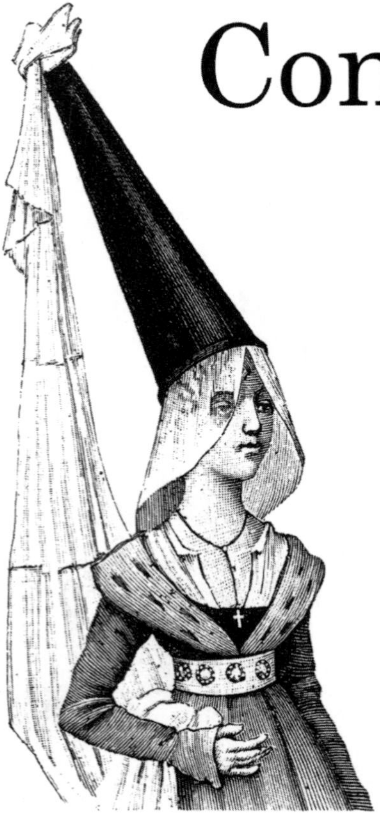

Congratulations

on attaining your Master's Degree!

Here's an application form for the Renaissance Faire.

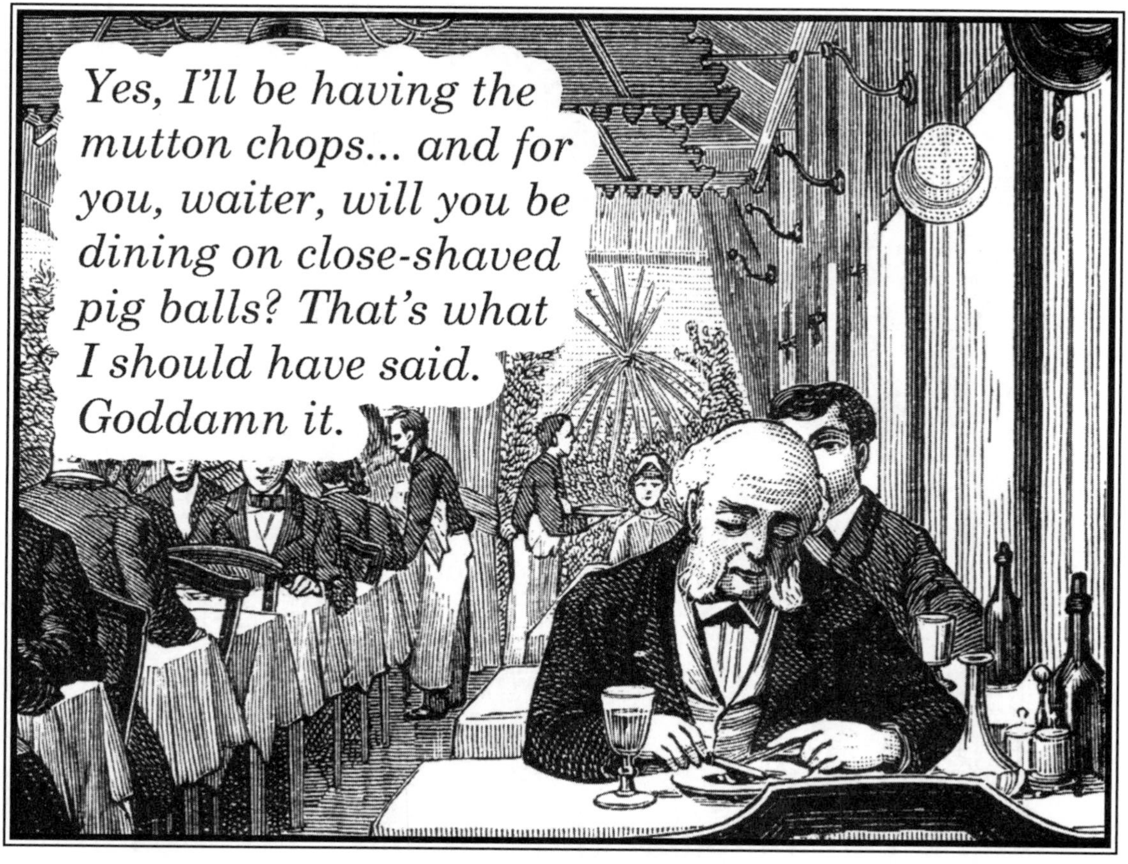
Yes, I'll be having the mutton chops... and for you, waiter, will you be dining on close-shaved pig balls? That's what I should have said. Goddamn it.

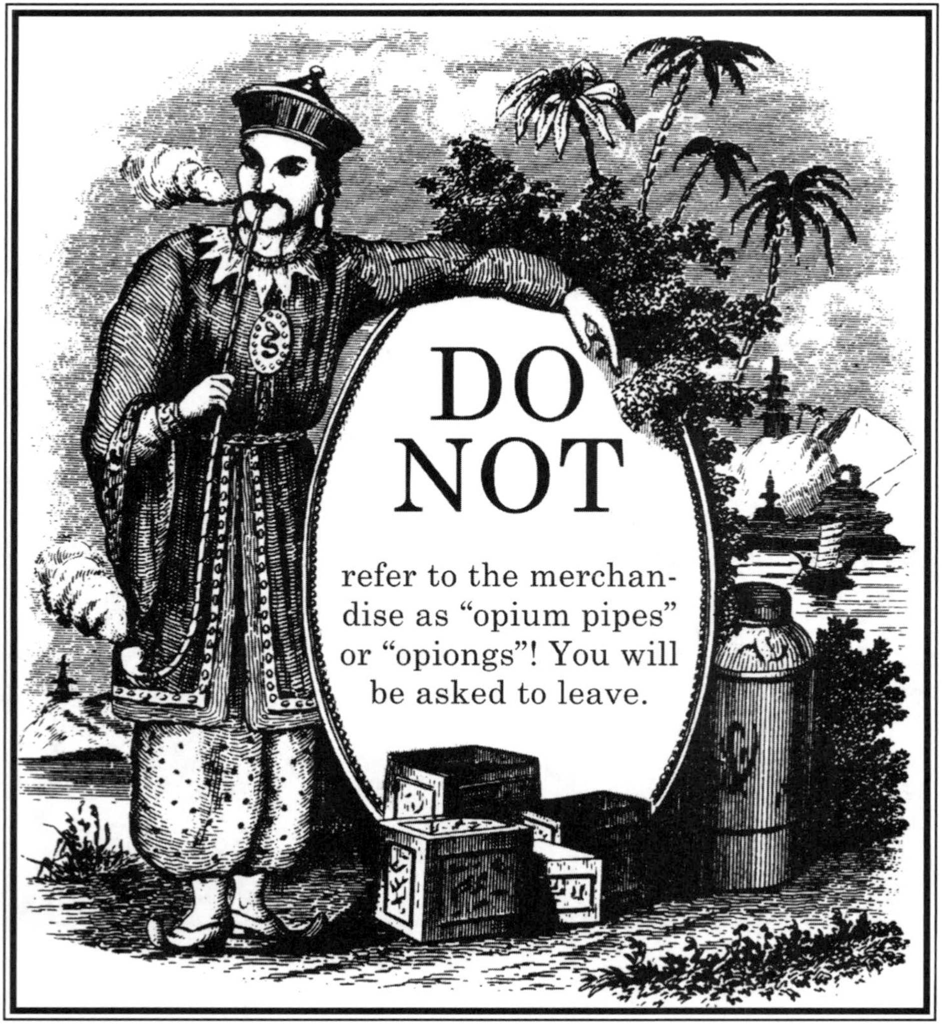
DO
NOT
refer to the merchandise as "opium pipes" or "opiongs"! You will be asked to leave.

It's over here, behind the rock? Well, that's where I am, and I don't see anything. Are we supposed to dig up this whole area?

I knew this "geocaching" was some bullshit as soon as you started talking about it, Ethan. You started off "This really cool thing..." and I was like... bullshit.

Why do you always do this? Is there a well in town that you lower your bucket into whenever you're low on bad decisions?

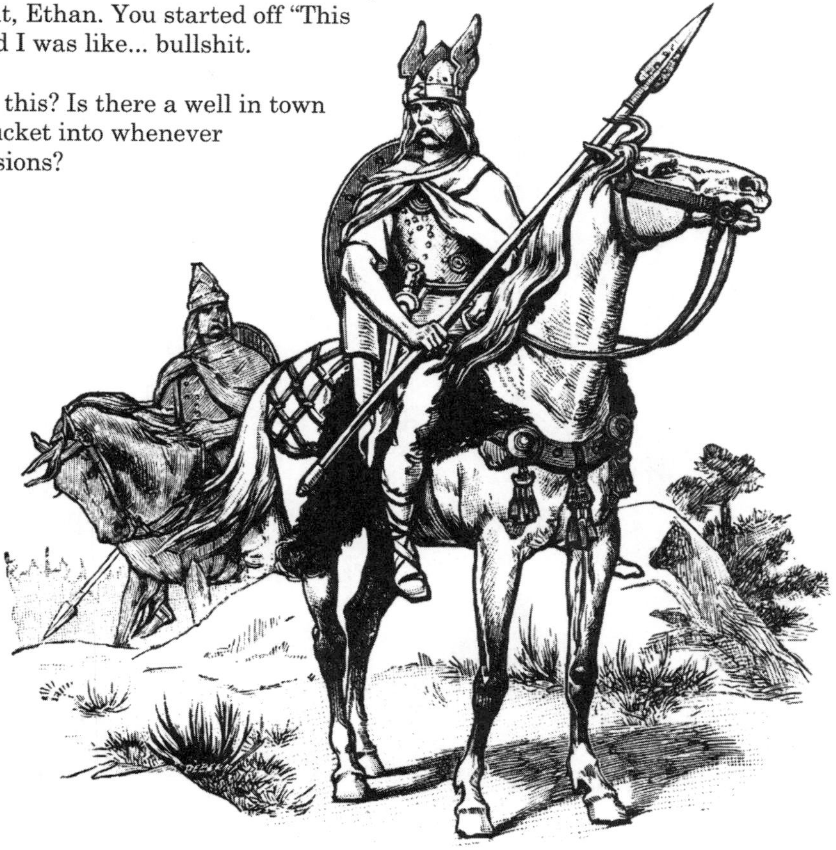

Ah... look, Josephine... I'm really sorry... but the truth is... compared to your sister, you're just a little bit fugly. Just a touch. Nothing big, but, you know, enough to make a difference.

So, okay, Josephina, you got my card, just hold onto that, and I'll see you at eight tomorrow.

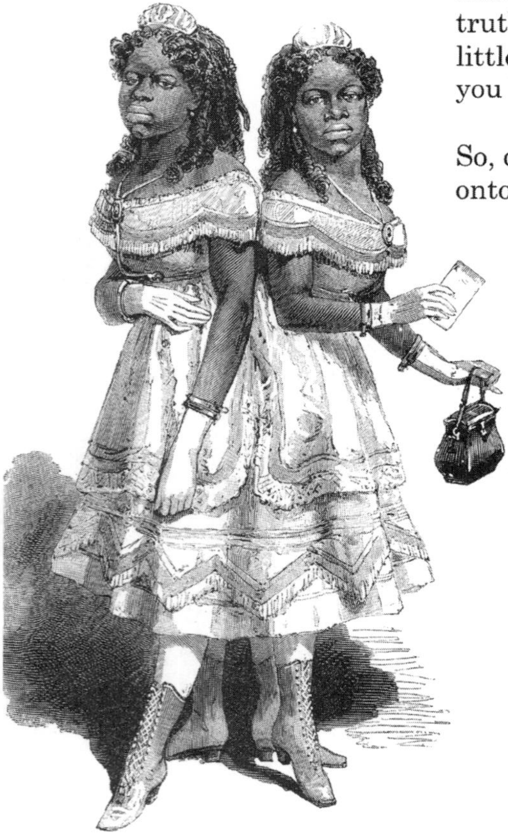

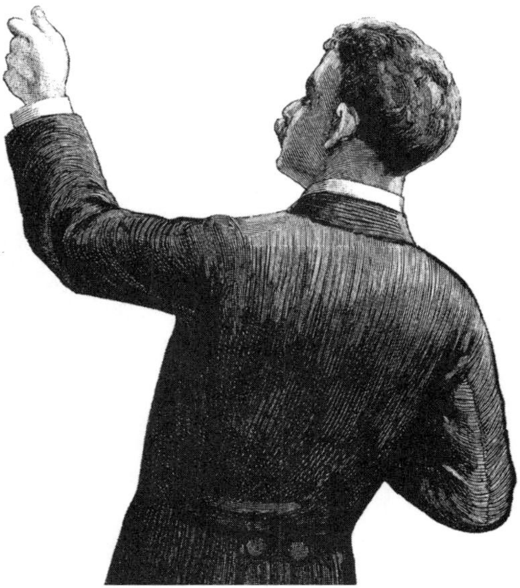

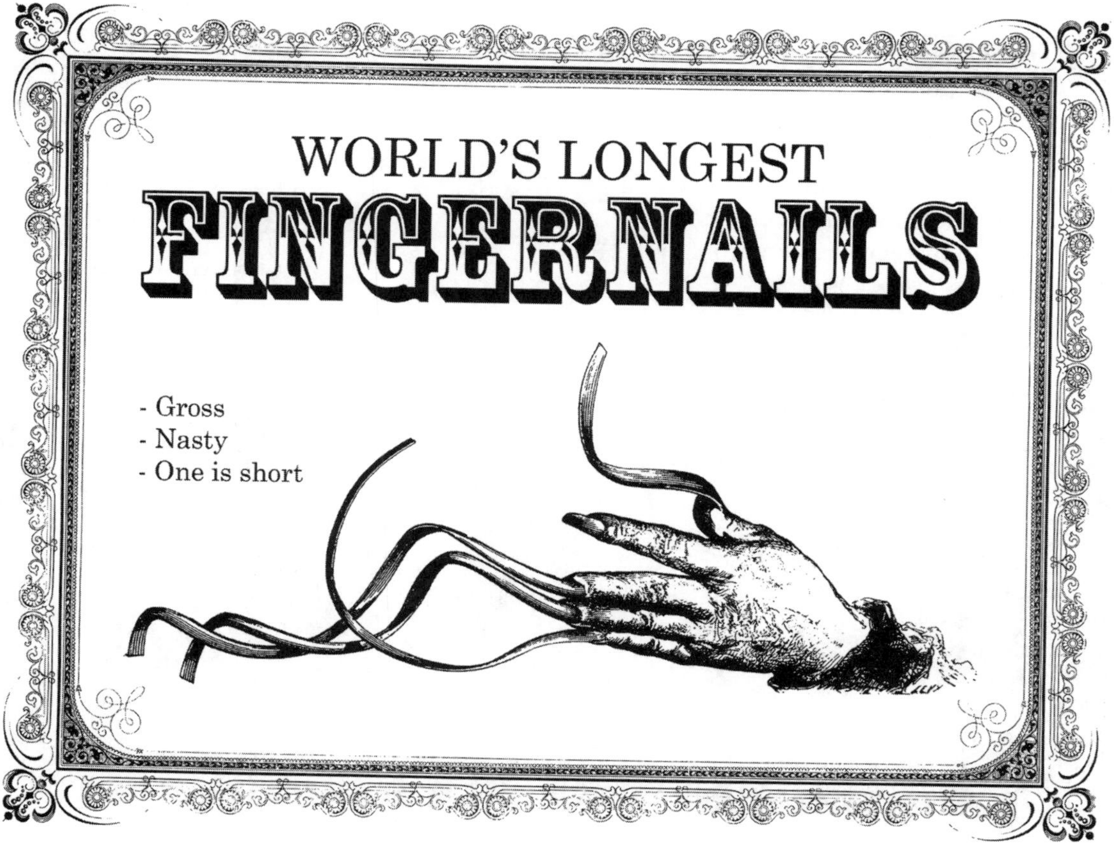
WORLD'S LONGEST
FINGERNAILS
- Gross
- Nasty
- One is short

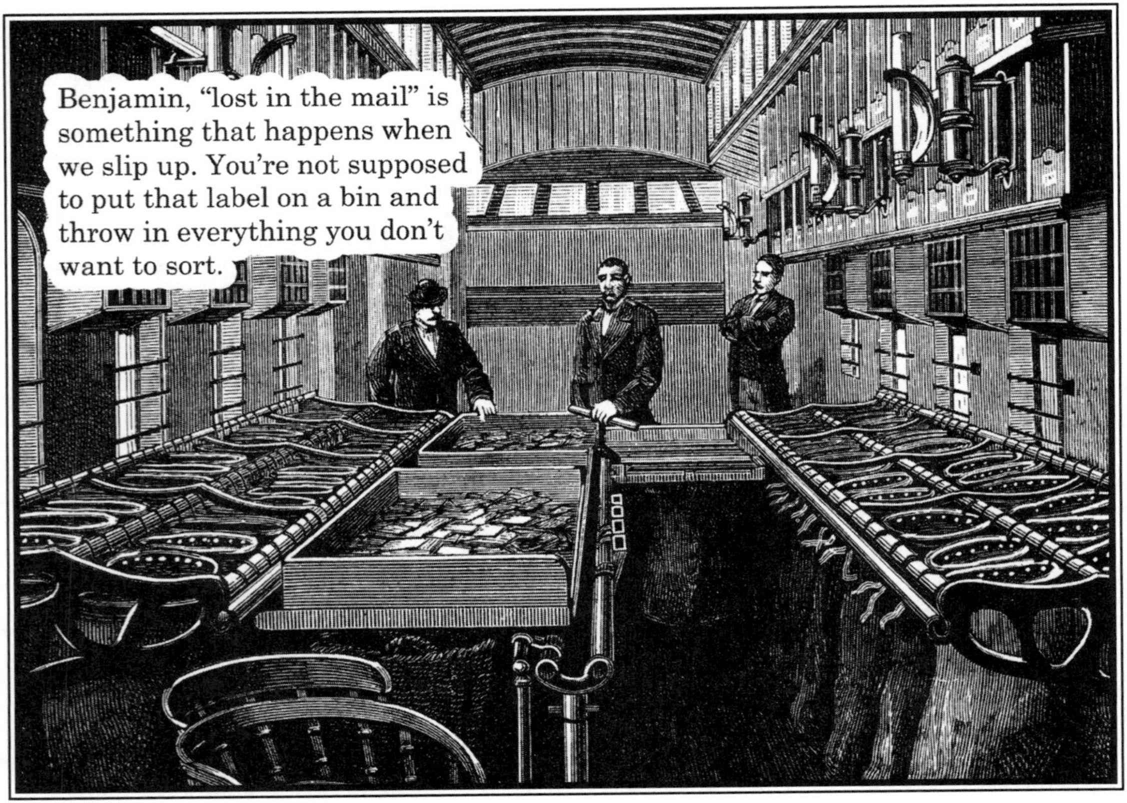
Benjamin, "lost in the mail" is something that happens when we slip up. You're not supposed to put that label on a bin and throw in everything you don't want to sort.

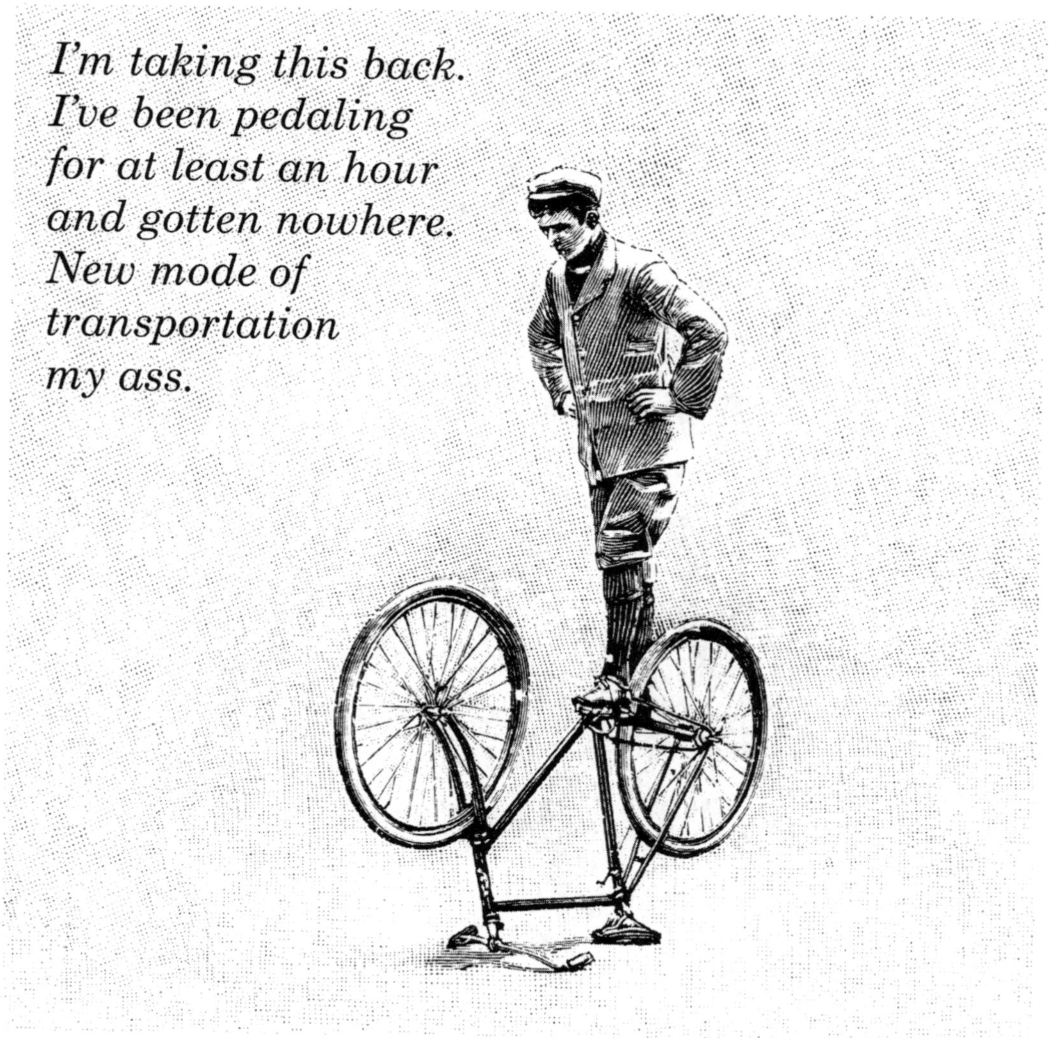
I'm taking this back. I've been pedaling for at least an hour and gotten nowhere. New mode of transportation my ass.

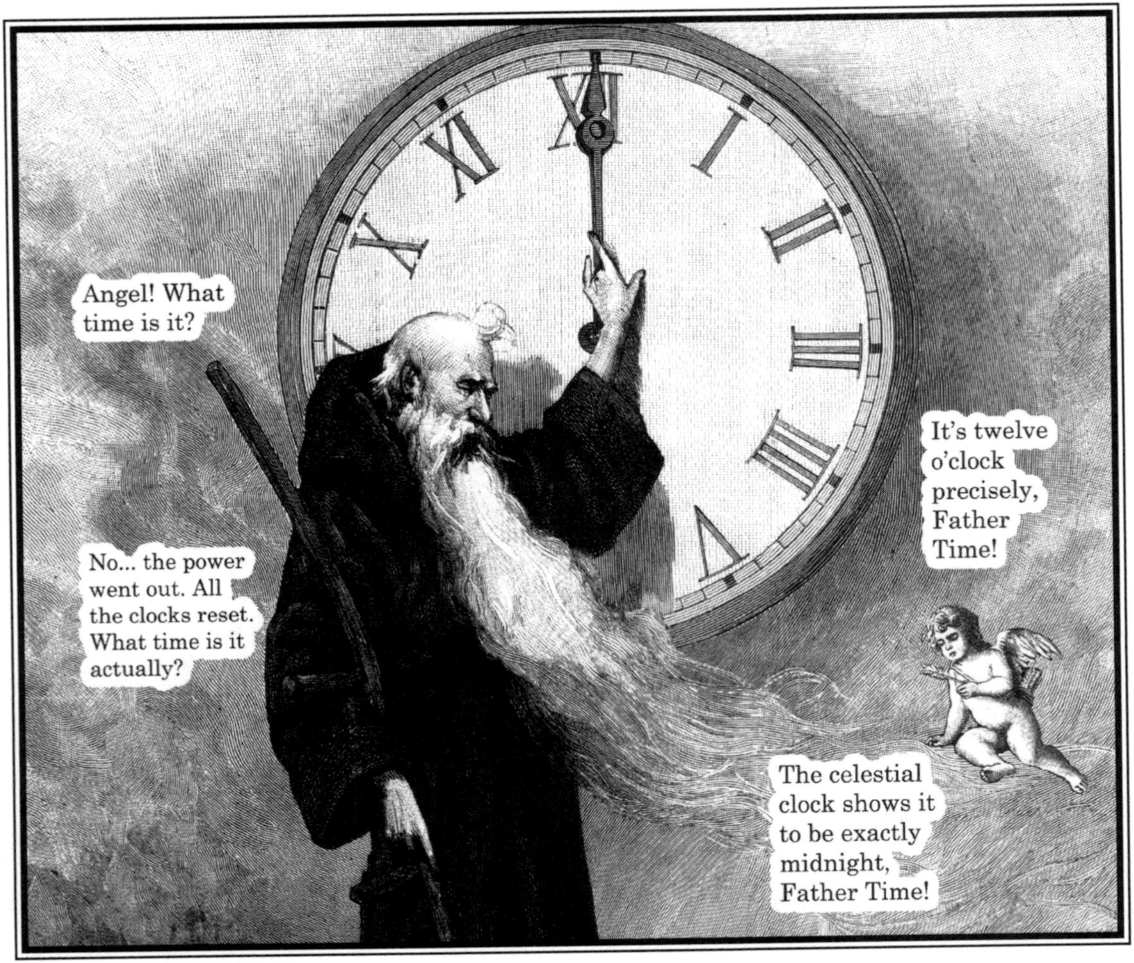
Angel! What time is it?
It's twelve o'clock precisely, Father Time!
No... the power went out. All the clocks reset. What time is it actually?
The celestial clock shows it to be exactly midnight, Father Time!

You're naked? I spend a thousand pounds on a magic tinyman and they don't send clothes?!

CLOTHES ARE EXTRA MAN IT SAYS THAT CLEARLY IN THE CATALOG

This? You want this olive branch? Do you?

You're gonna have to fight me for it.

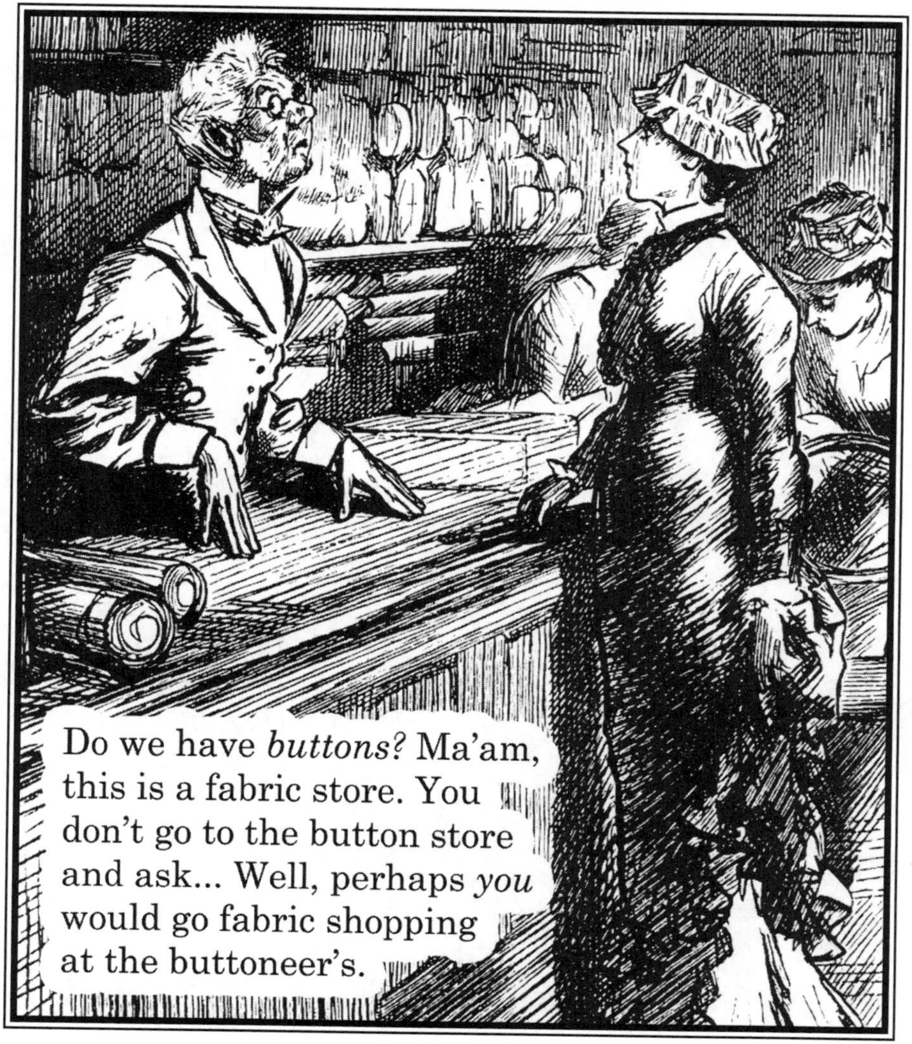
Do we have *buttons?* Ma'am, this is a fabric store. You don't go to the button store and ask... Well, perhaps *you* would go fabric shopping at the buttoneer's.

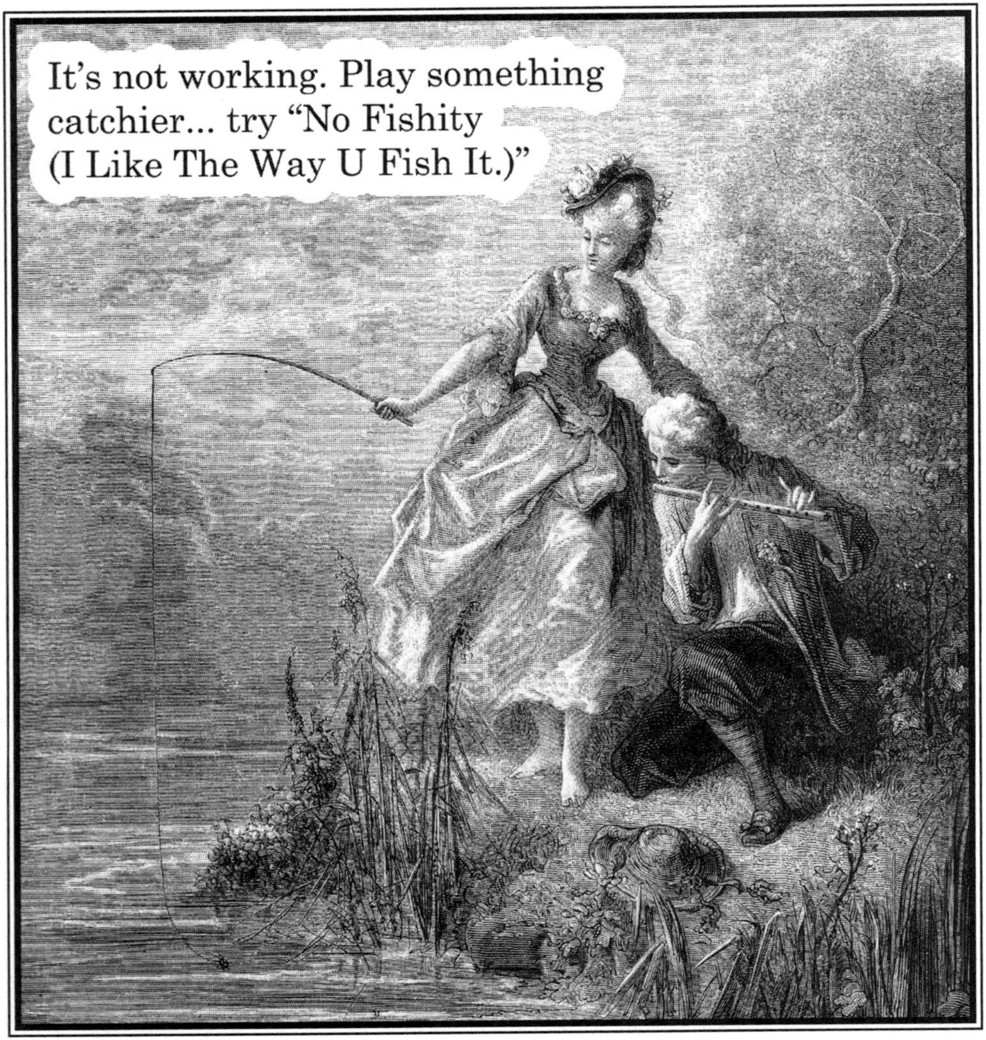
It's not working. Play something catchier... try "No Fishity (I Like The Way U Fish It.)"

Passive-Aggressive Orange Company Incorporated.

You want to get scurvy? Fine. Go ahead and don't buy our oranges.

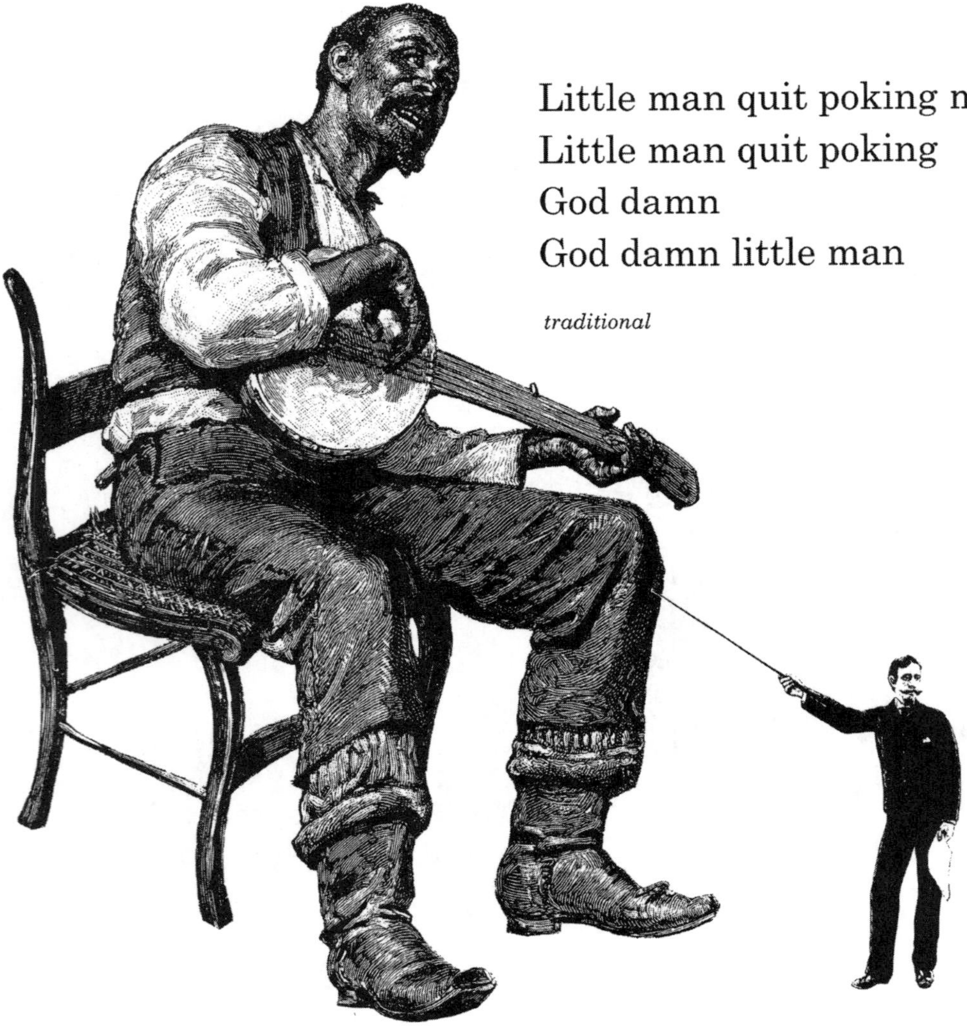

Little man quit poking me
Little man quit poking
God damn
God damn little man

traditional

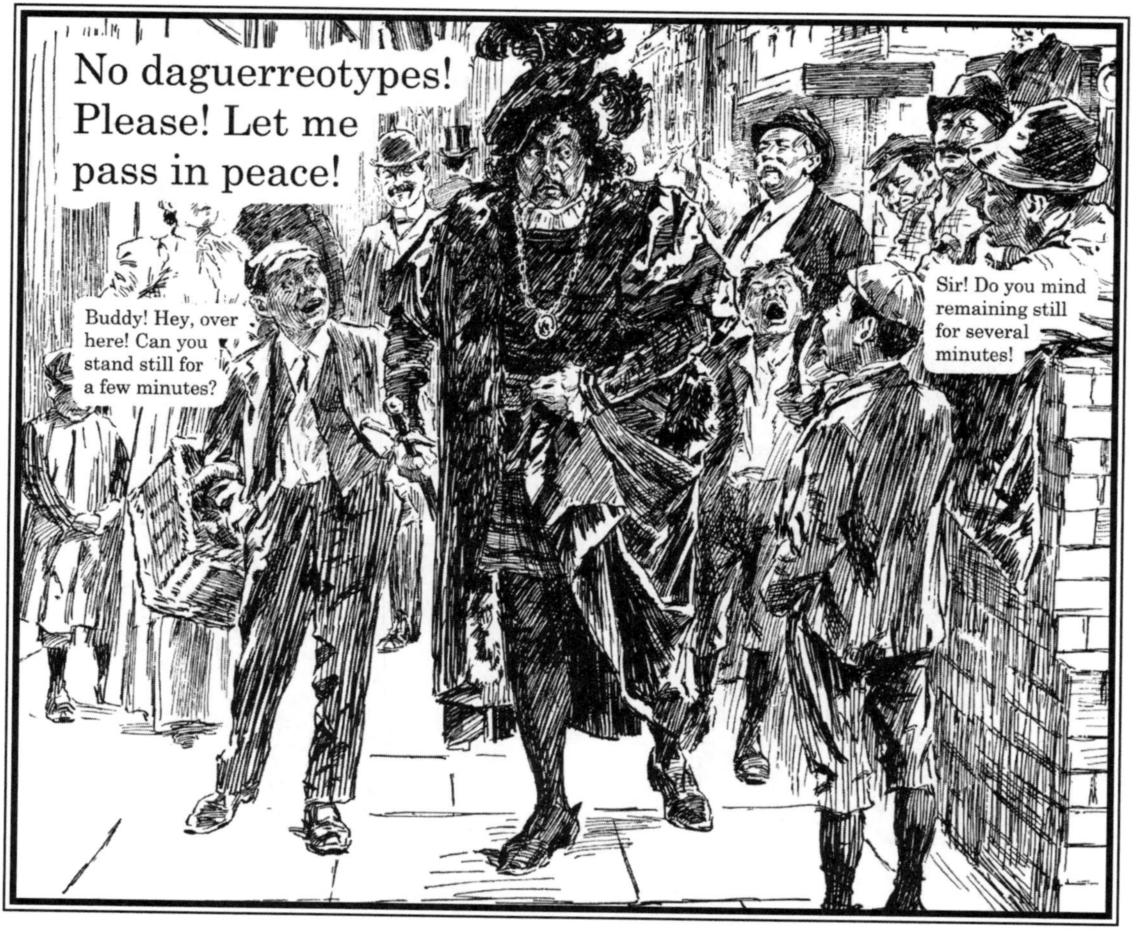
No daguerreotypes! Please! Let me pass in peace!
Buddy! Hey, over here! Can you stand still for a few minutes?
Sir! Do you mind remaining still for several minutes!

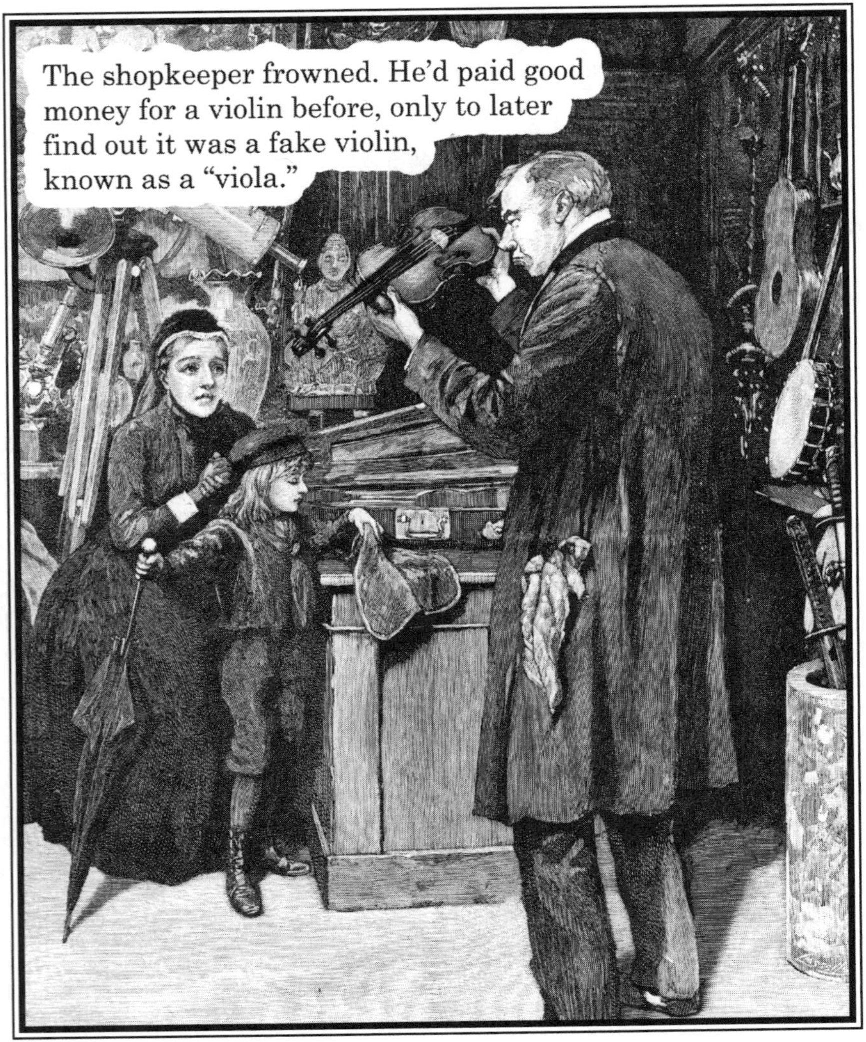
The shopkeeper frowned. He'd paid good money for a violin before, only to later find out it was a fake violin, known as a "viola."

ain't nothin but a
dog thing *bay-bee*

two trained-
ass wolves
so we
cray-zee

"No time for shaving, boy! You've got to study! Exams are in the morning!"

"It's too late, father. I've already decided to become a full-time scenester."

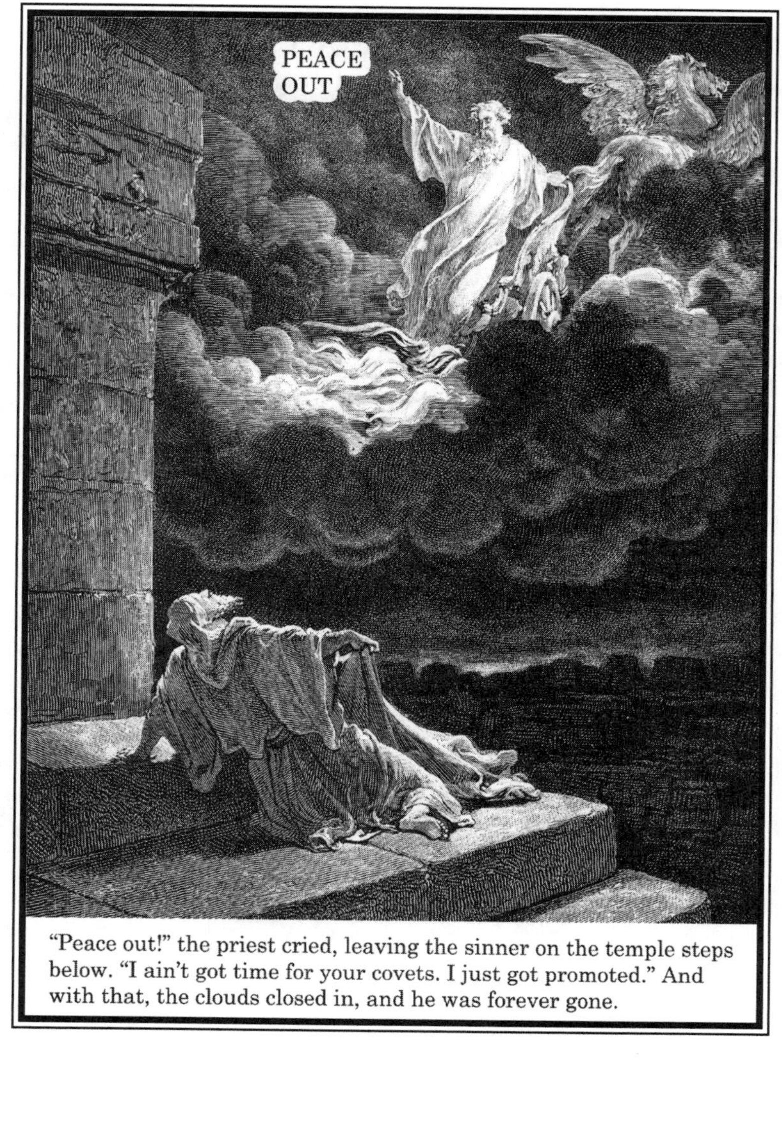
PEACE
OUT

"Peace out!" the priest cried, leaving the sinner on the temple steps below. "I ain't got time for your covets. I just got promoted." And with that, the clouds closed in, and he was forever gone.

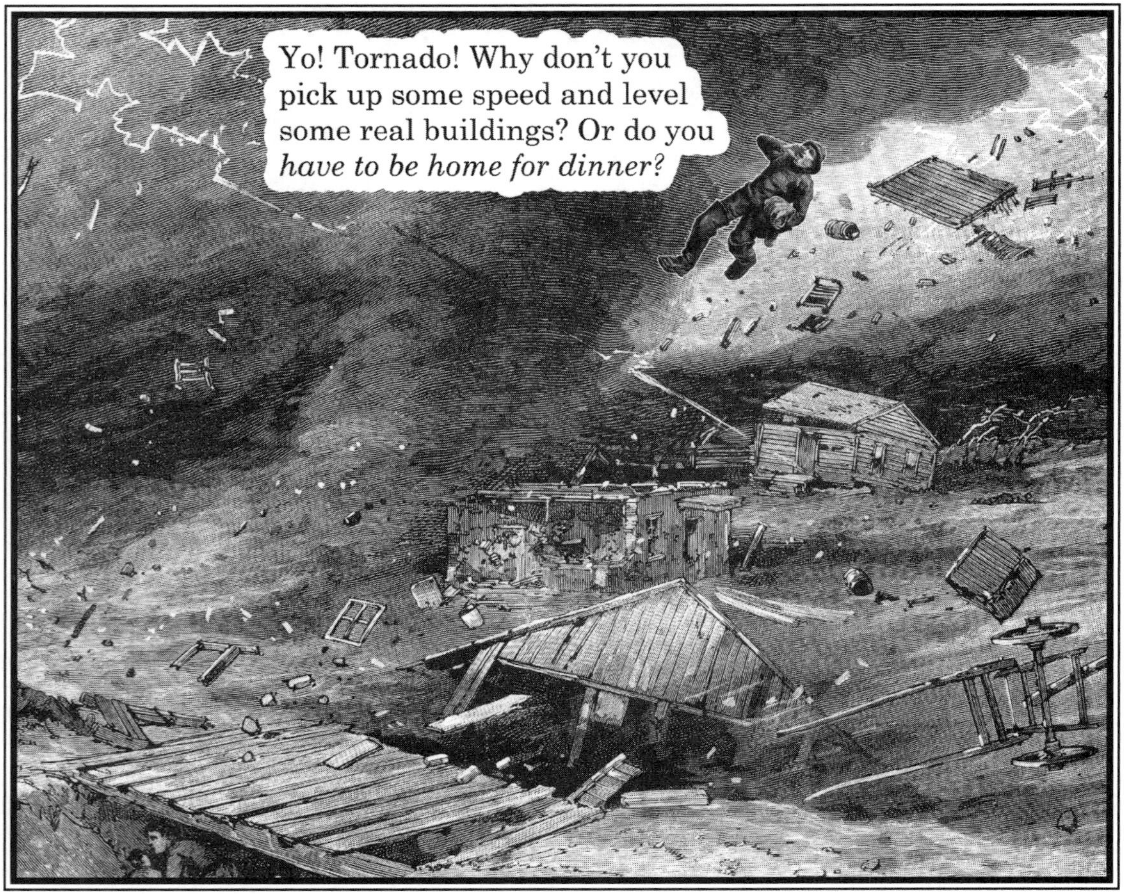
Yo! Tornado! Why don't you pick up some speed and level some real buildings? Or do you *have to be home for dinner?*

Nothing for a professional drinker. Yet again. I'm starting to feel like my career in indie-rock was a dead end.

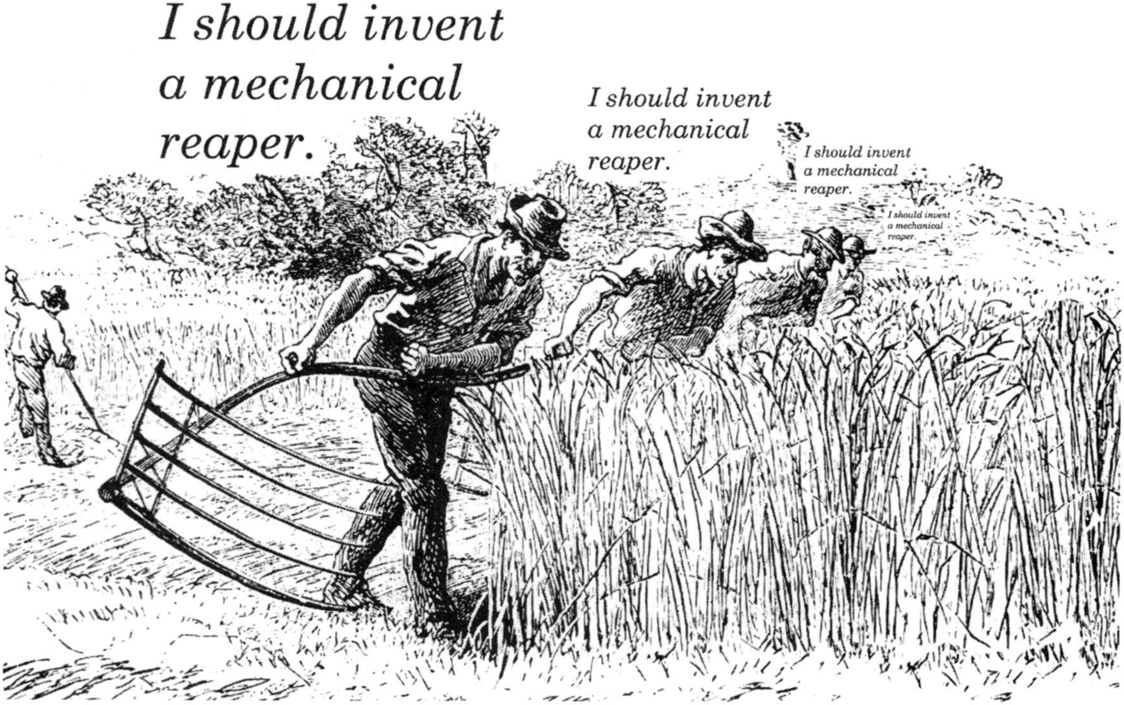
I should invent a mechanical reaper.
I should invent a mechanical reaper.
I should invent a mechanical reaper.
I should invent a mechanical reaper.

"I'm not going to 'chug' a glass of Potard! That's ridiculous. Crab wine should be savored. Do you know nothing about wines?"

"You get two more for that! No complaining! Bartender, two more shots of the 'Tard. Now, if you're ready, Dad, chug it like a man. On the count of three."

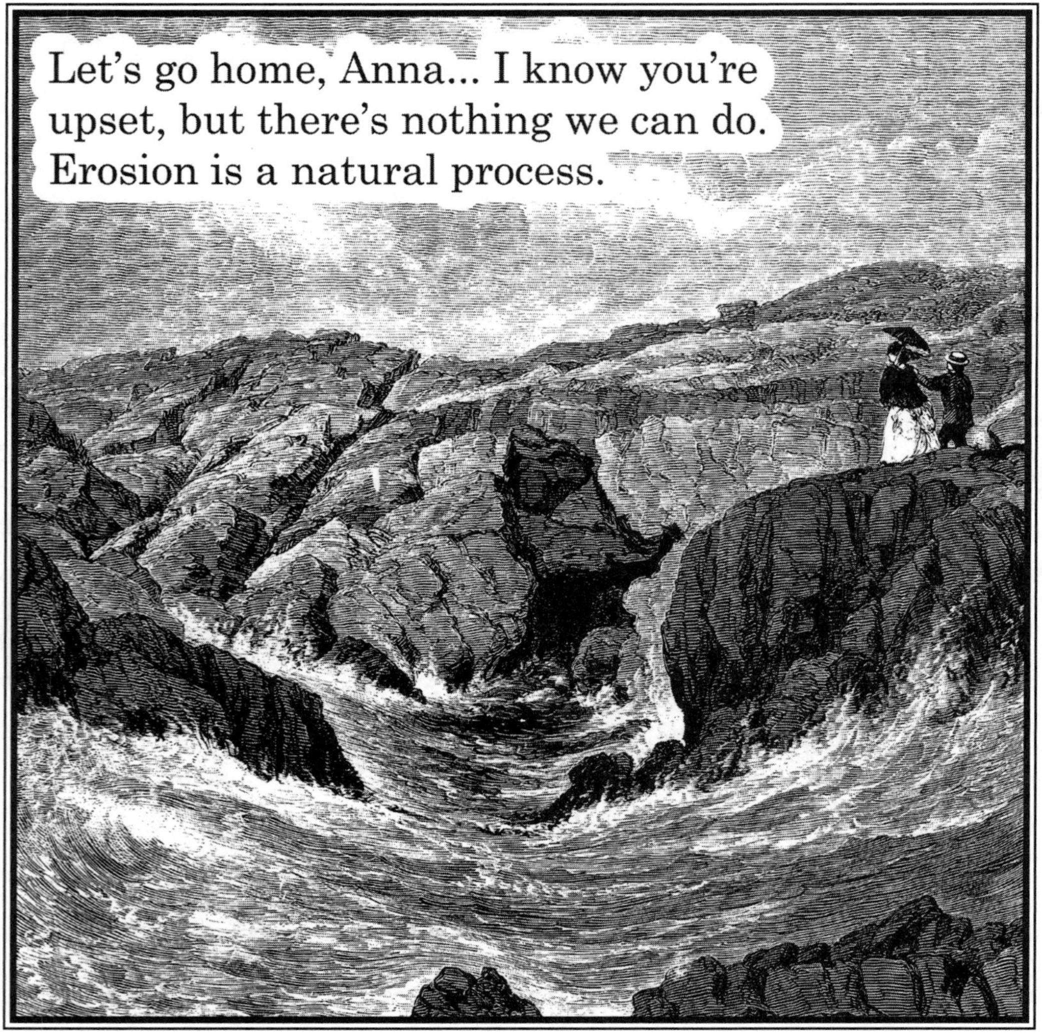
Let's go home, Anna... I know you're
upset, but there's nothing we can do.
Erosion is a natural process.

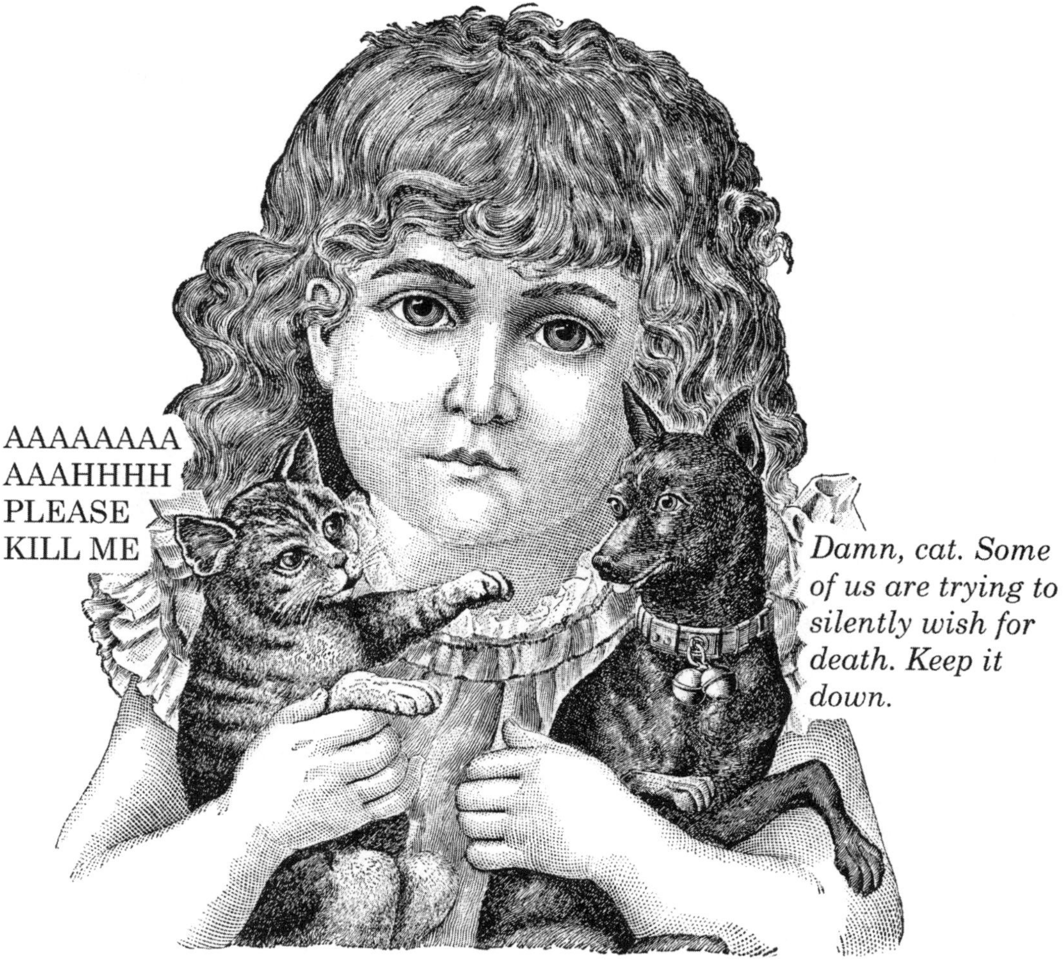
AAAAAAAA
AAAHHHH
PLEASE
KILL ME
Damn, cat. Some of us are trying to silently wish for death. Keep it down.

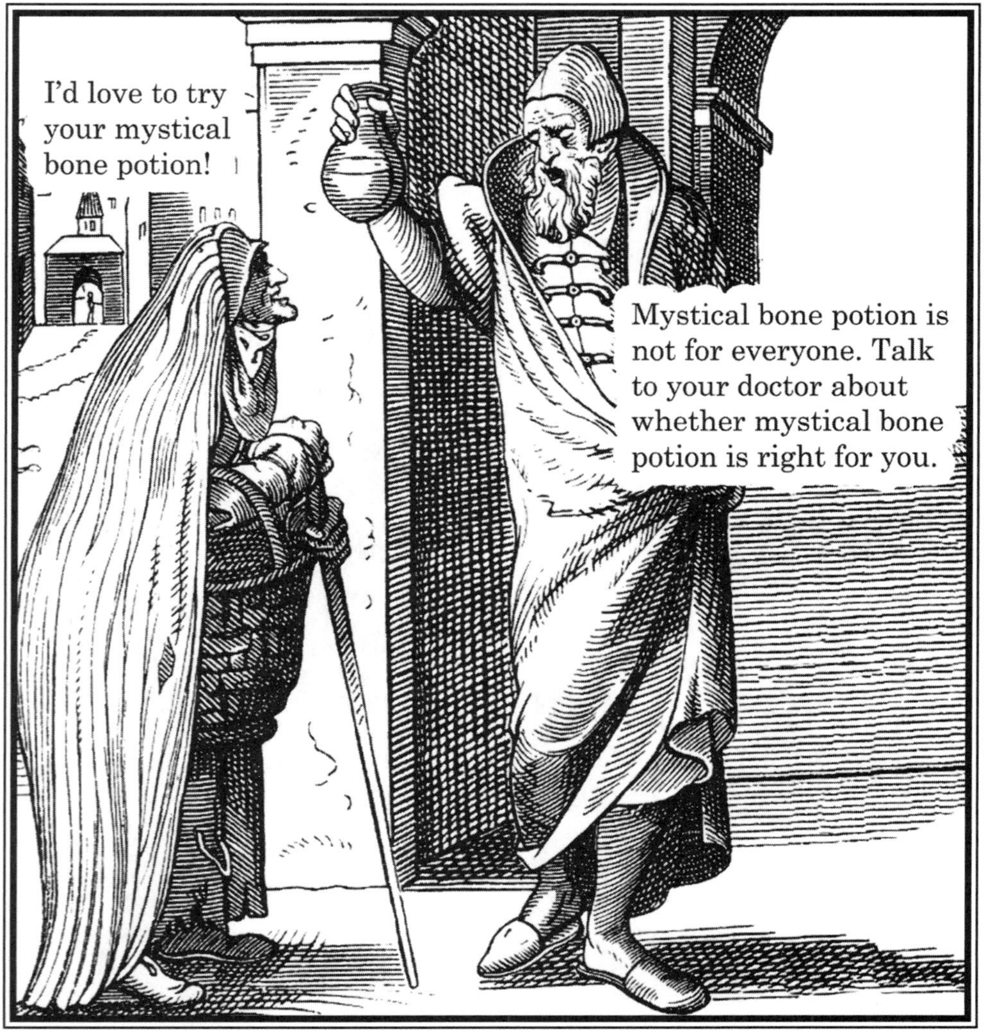
I'd love to try your mystical bone potion!
Mystical bone potion is not for everyone. Talk to your doctor about whether mystical bone potion is right for you.

Is the mystery object... *a pilgrim?*

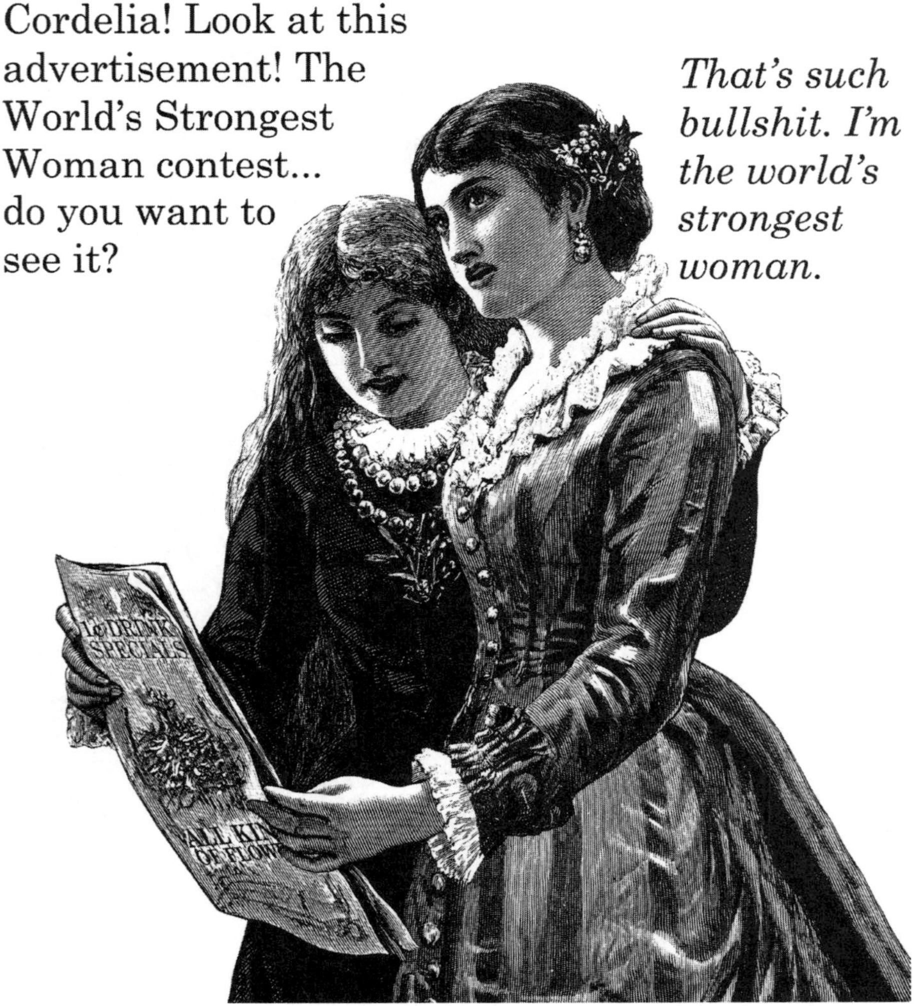
Cordelia! Look at this advertisement! The World's Strongest Woman contest... do you want to see it?
That's such bullshit. I'm the world's strongest woman.

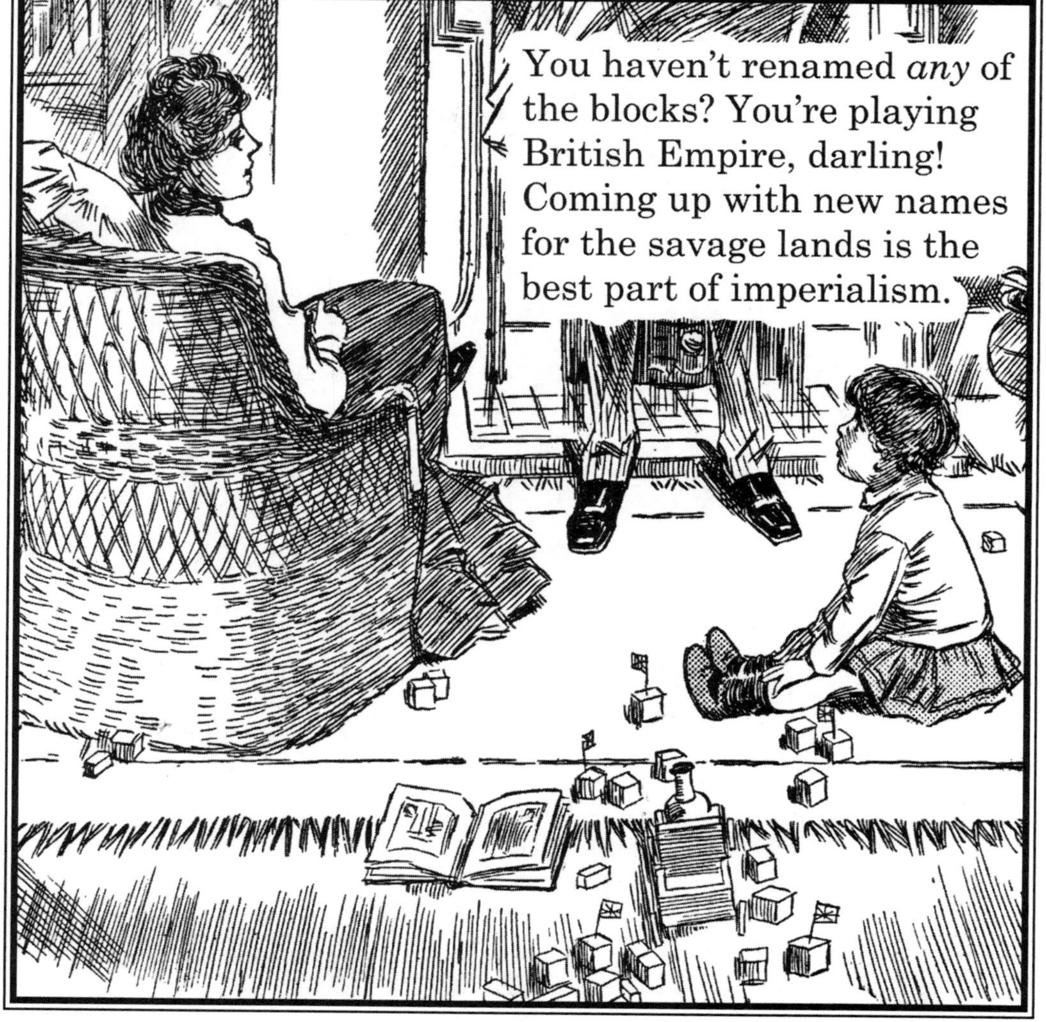
You haven't renamed *any* of the blocks? You're playing British Empire, darling! Coming up with new names for the savage lands is the best part of imperialism.

Miss! Hello, miss!
Hello up there!
Excuse — Down
here! Wanted to let
you know your win-
dow's open.

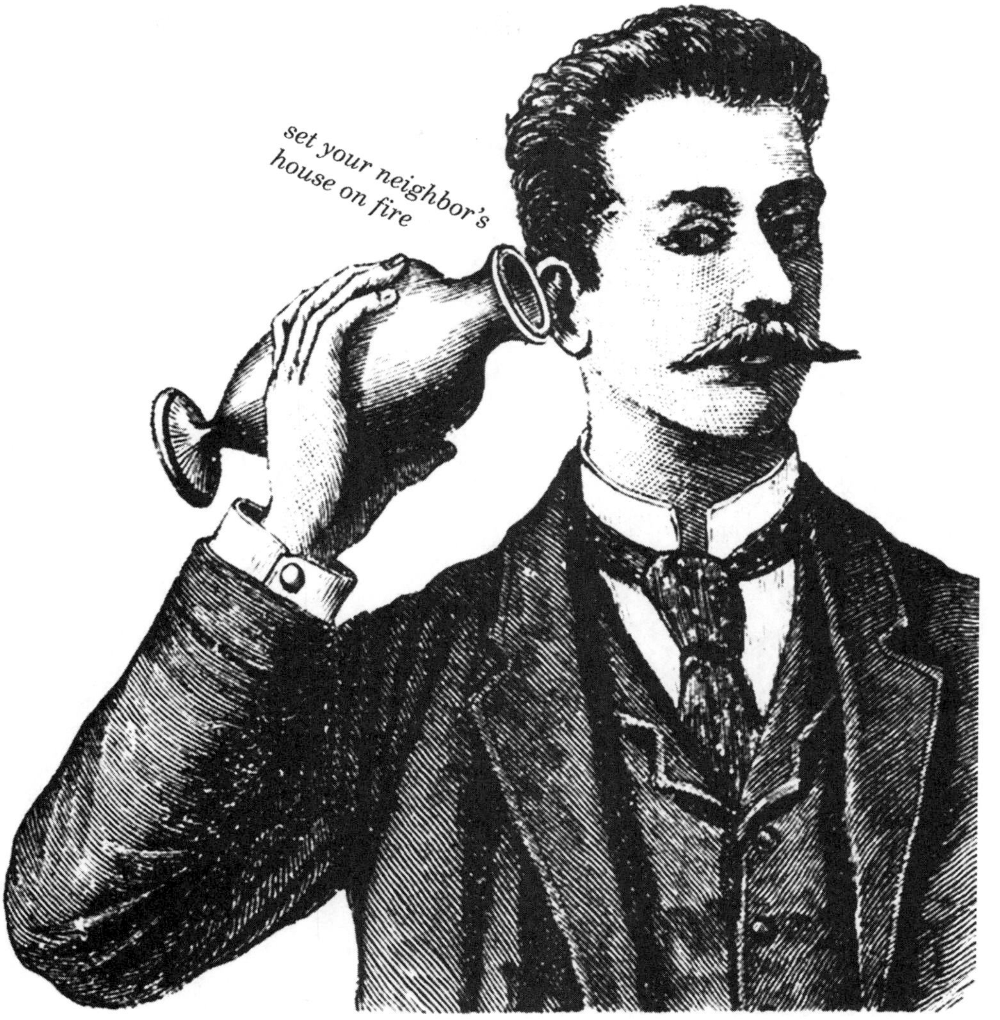
set your neighbor's
house on fire

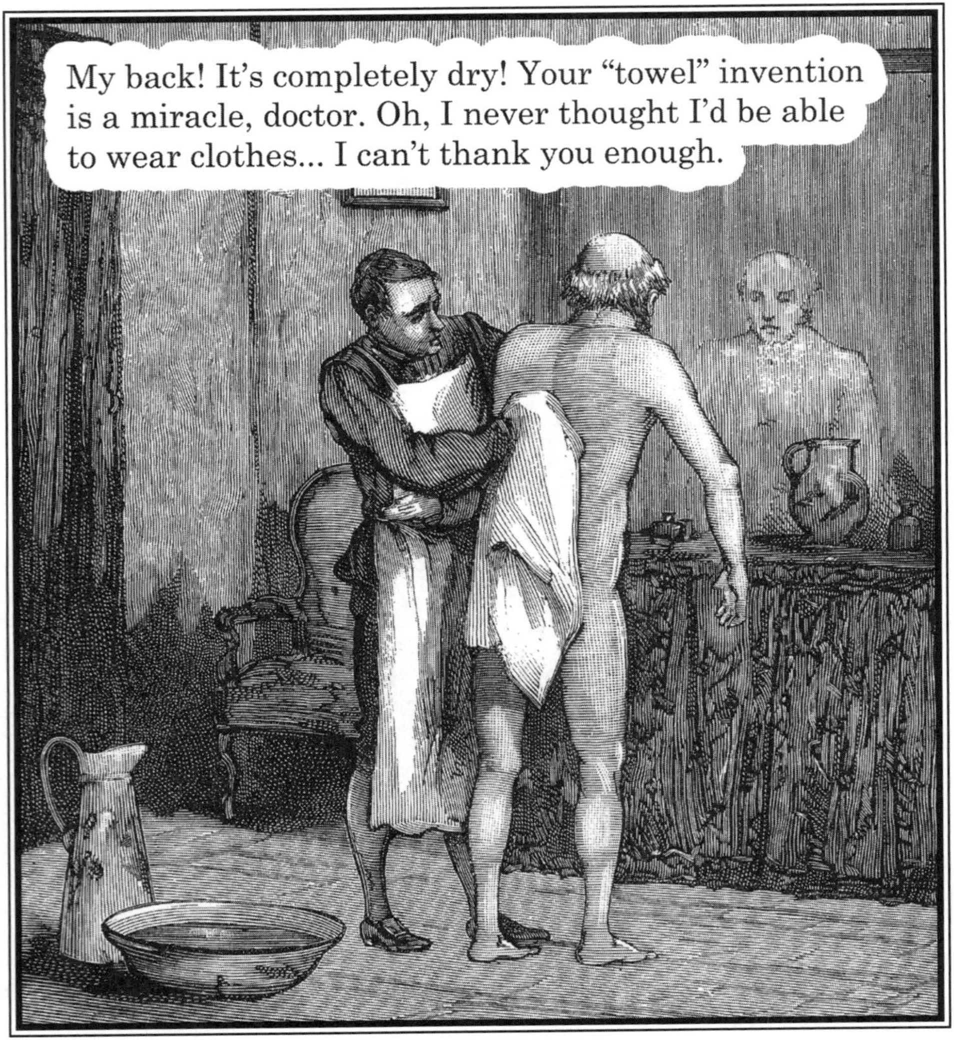
My back! It's completely dry! Your "towel" invention is a miracle, doctor. Oh, I never thought I'd be able to wear clothes... I can't thank you enough.

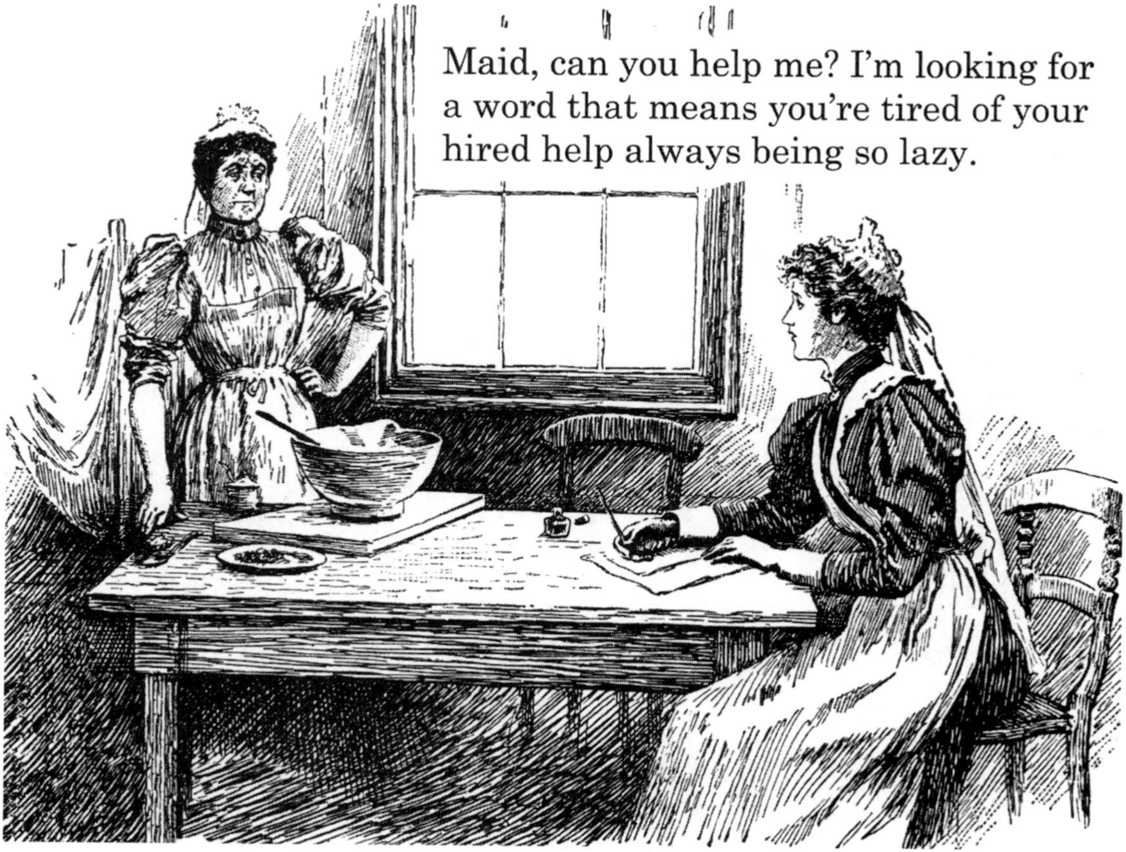
Maid, can you help me? I'm looking for a word that means you're tired of your hired help always being so lazy.

Come on, Mr. Stompy... do your job. I explained this to you just yesterday... railroads won't replace elephants. The only way you'd be putting yourself out of a job is if you were building a backhoe that occasionally went crazy and trampled a bunch of people.

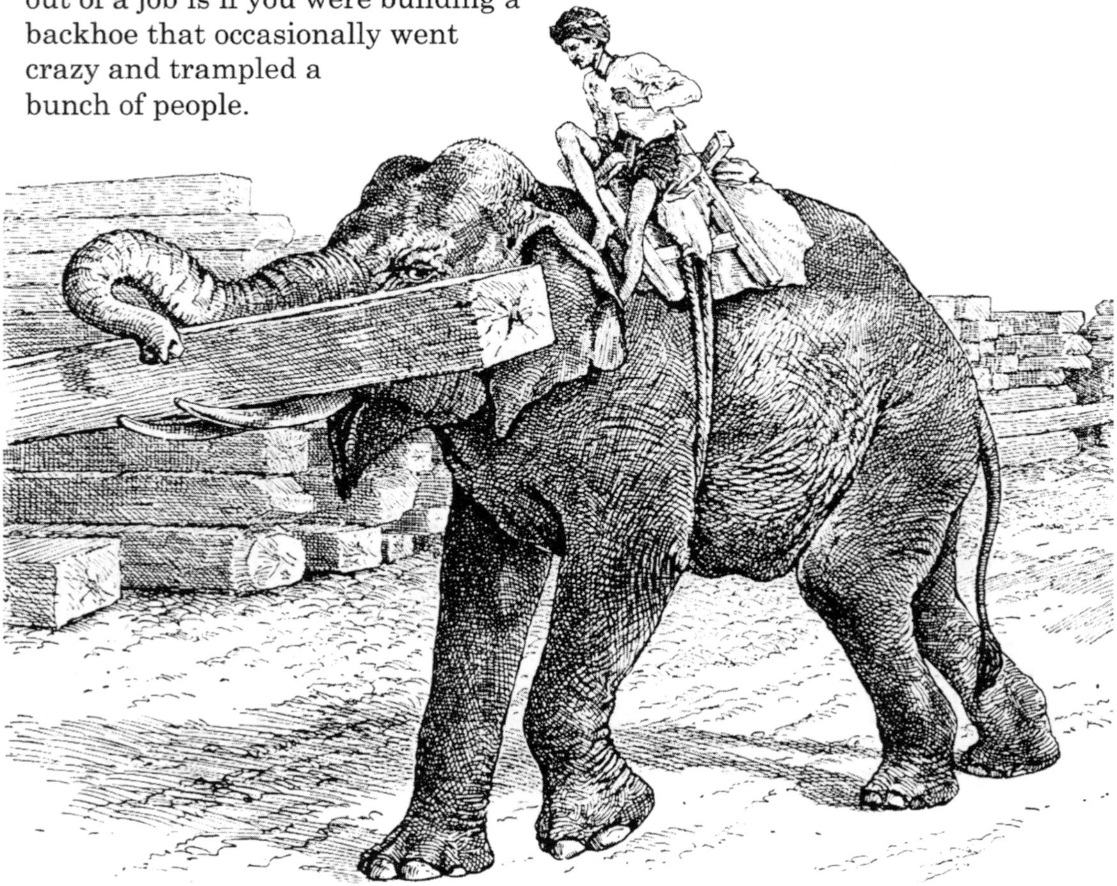

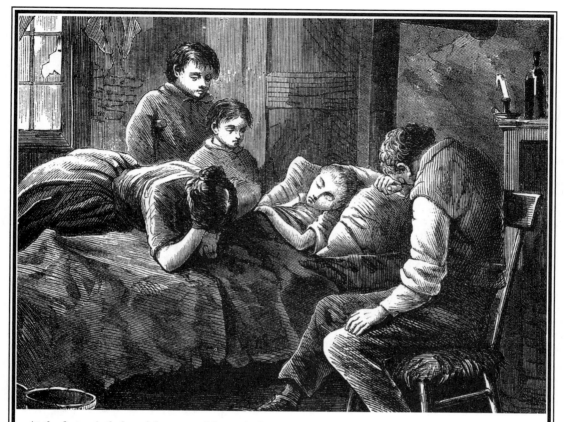

At the forty-ninth day of the competition, only Percival and his younger brother remained alive. Their sister, and both parents, had perished in the quest to win a free bed. "I'm going to win this, Percy," his brother said, and pulled a handful of chocolate-chip cookies from his pocket. "I've got enough cookies to keep me alive for at least a week!"

Percival had poisoned the cookies. As his brother began to foam and convulse on the floor, he cast down his crutches, and hopped to the bed with his good foot. He would sleep well tonight.

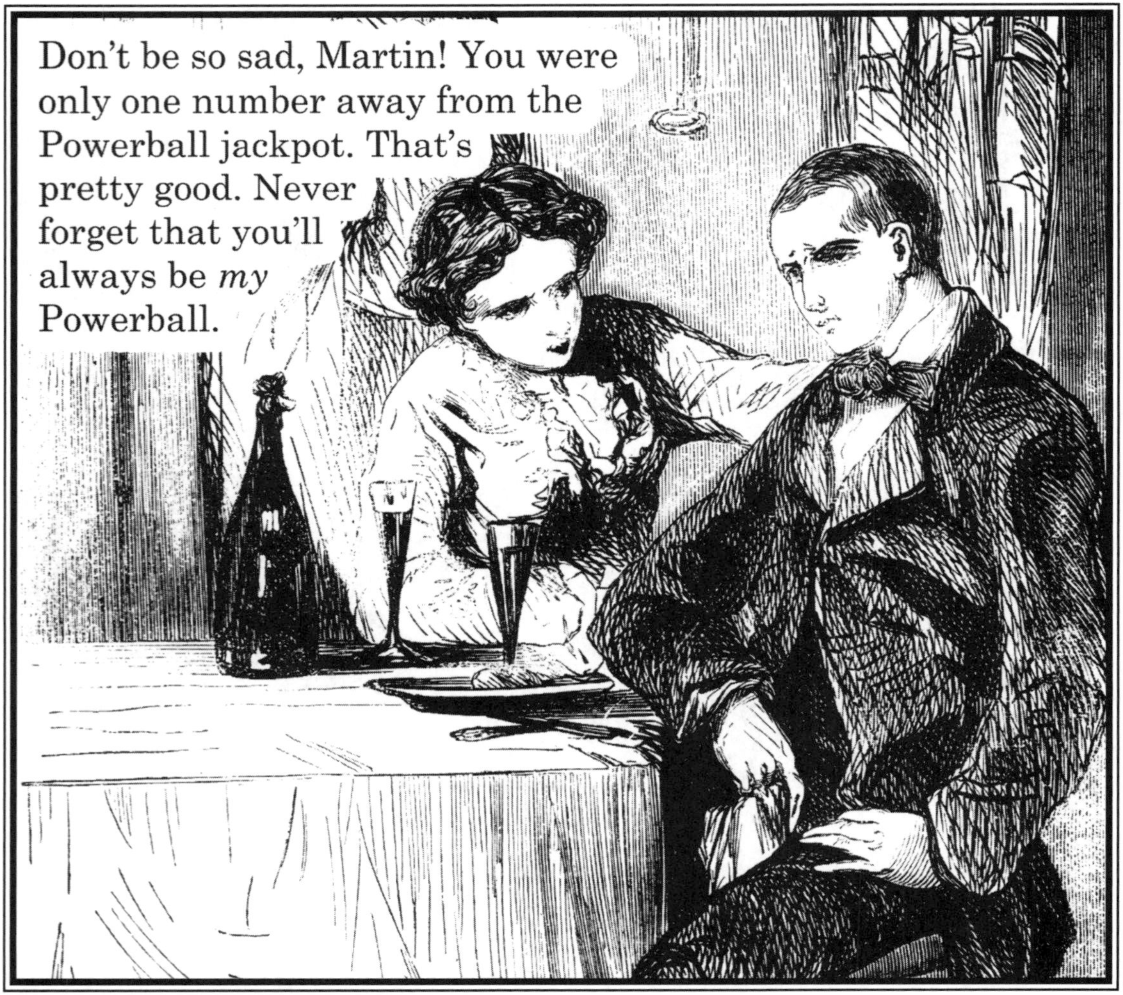
Don't be so sad, Martin! You were only one number away from the Powerball jackpot. That's pretty good. Never forget that you'll always be *my* Powerball.

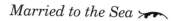

No!

Don't poison the rich!

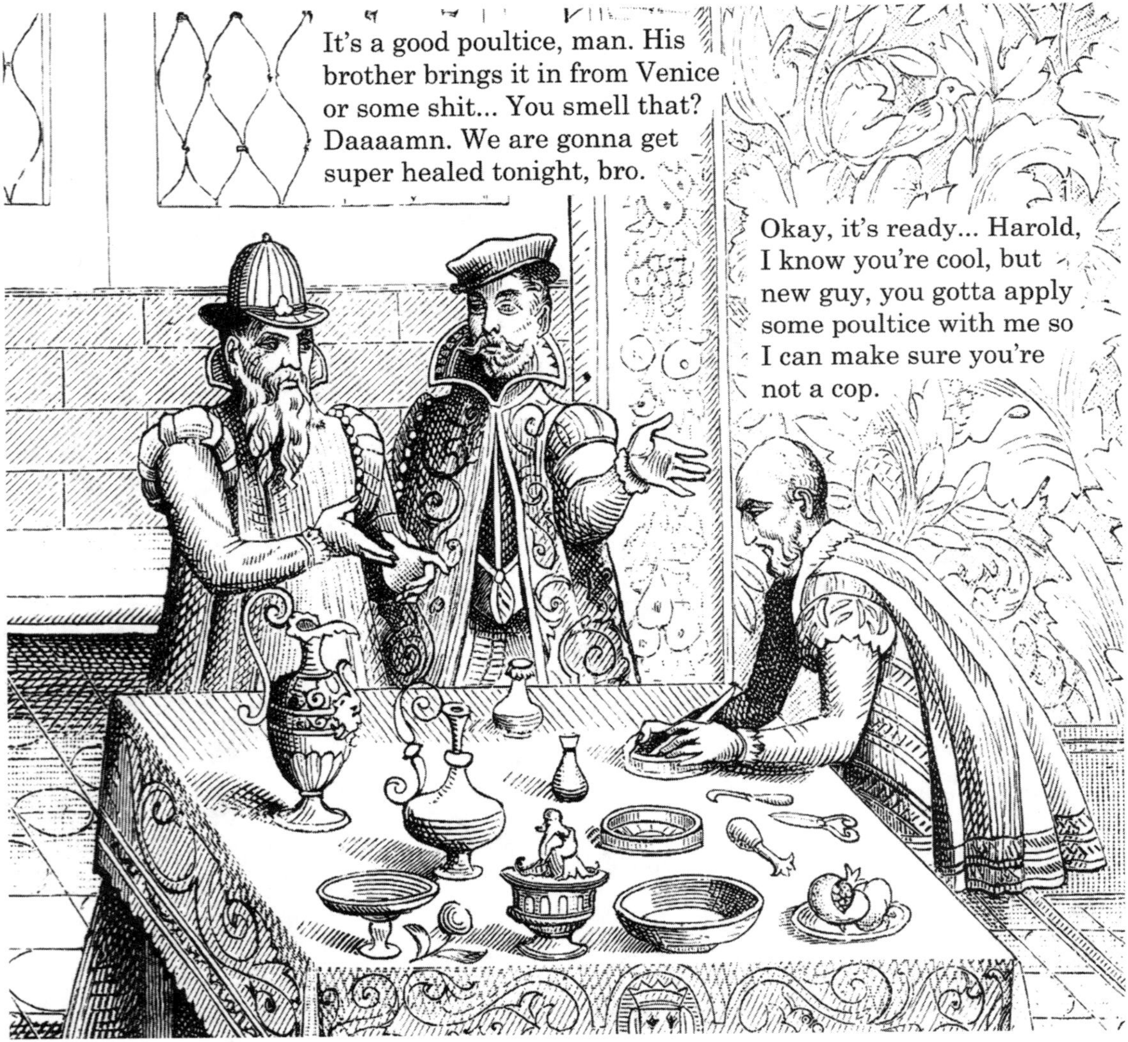
It's a good poultice, man. His brother brings it in from Venice or some shit... You smell that? Daaaamn. We are gonna get super healed tonight, bro.
Okay, it's ready... Harold, I know you're cool, but new guy, you gotta apply some poultice with me so I can make sure you're not a cop.

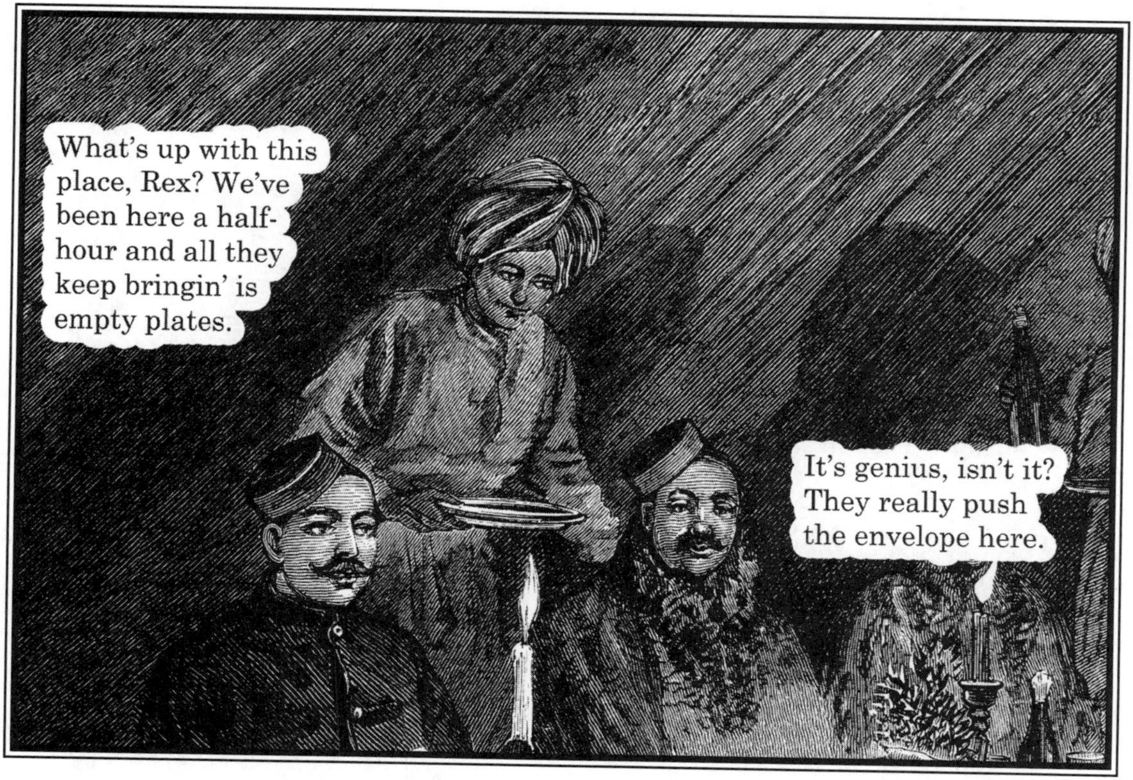
What's up with this place, Rex? We've been here a half-hour and all they keep bringin' is empty plates.
It's genius, isn't it? They really push the envelope here.

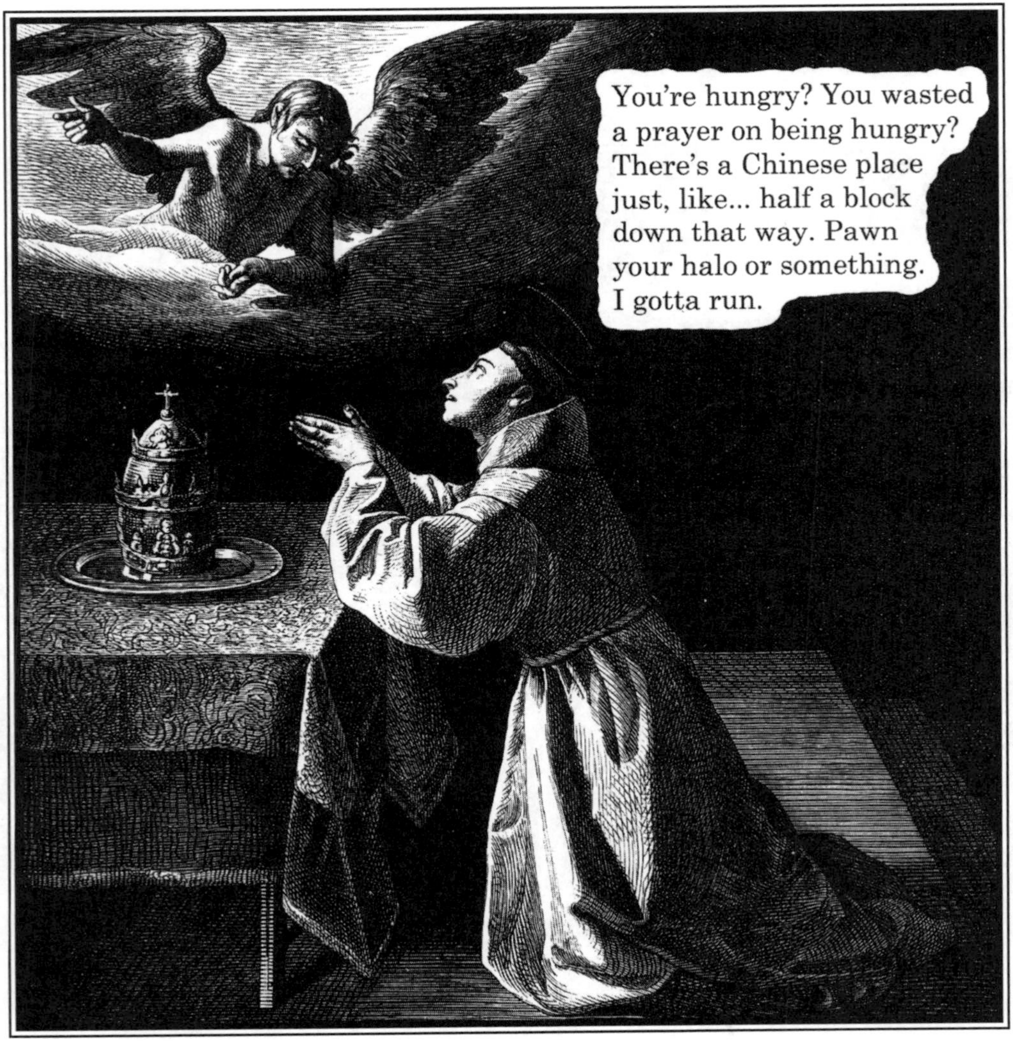
You're hungry? You wasted a prayer on being hungry? There's a Chinese place just, like... half a block down that way. Pawn your halo or something. I gotta run.

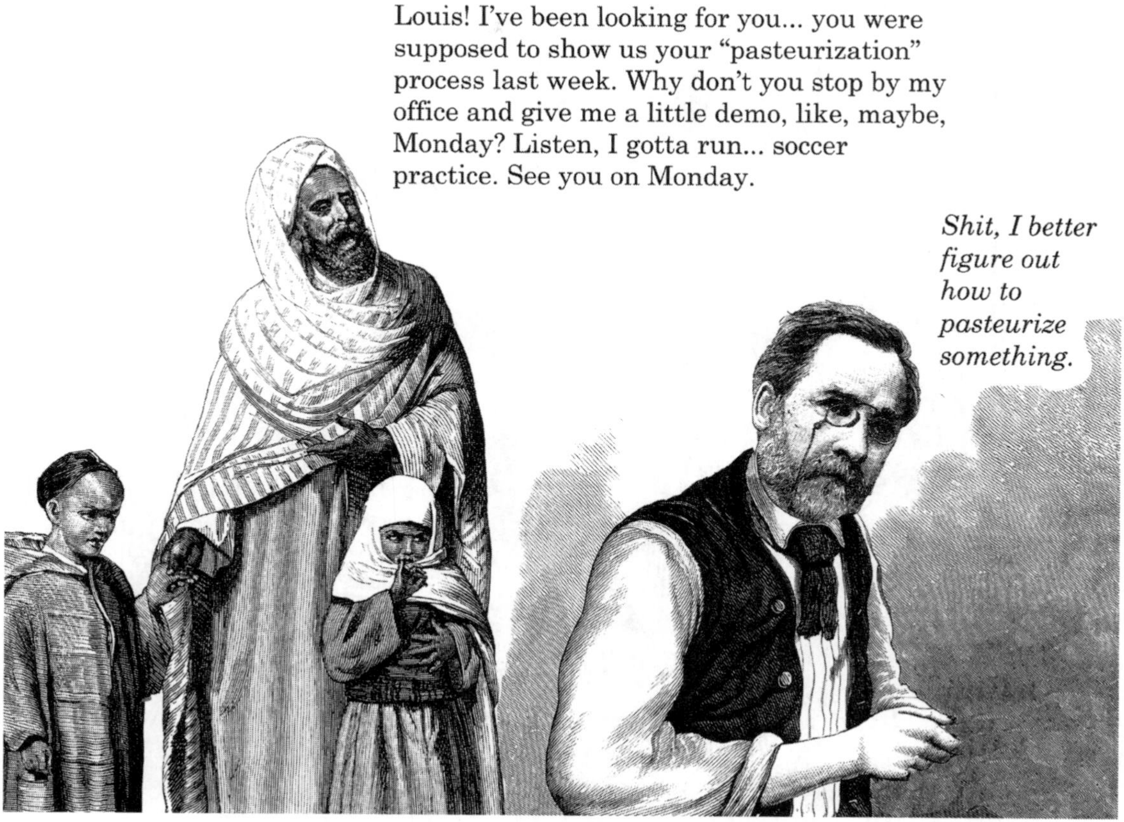
Louis! I've been looking for you... you were supposed to show us your "pasteurization" process last week. Why don't you stop by my office and give me a little demo, like, maybe, Monday? Listen, I gotta run... soccer practice. See you on Monday.
Shit, I better figure out how to pasteurize something.

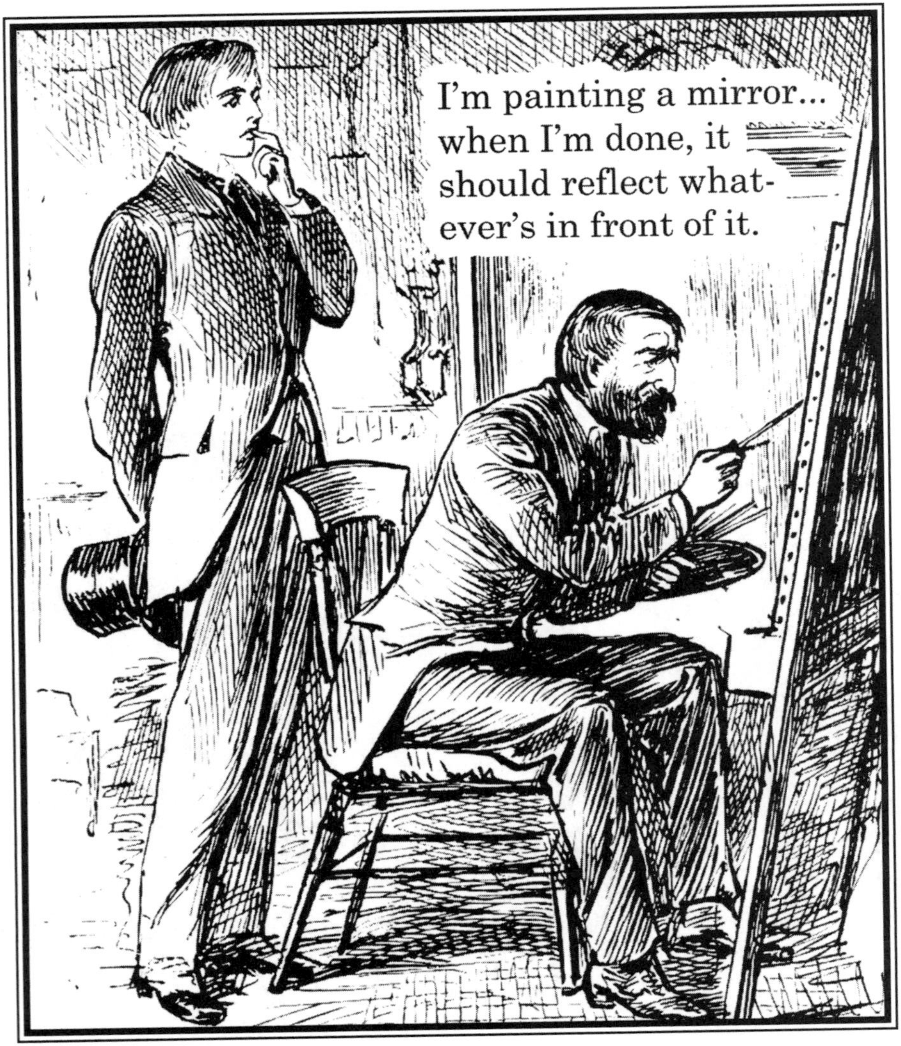
I'm painting a mirror...
when I'm done, it
should reflect what-
ever's in front of it.

There's no "laughter" in

S-C-H-O-O-L

"George! My letter paper
is too big to go in this
envelope. How do I make
it go? It makes me mad!"

"Have you tried
folding it?"

"It makes me mad
inside my head!"

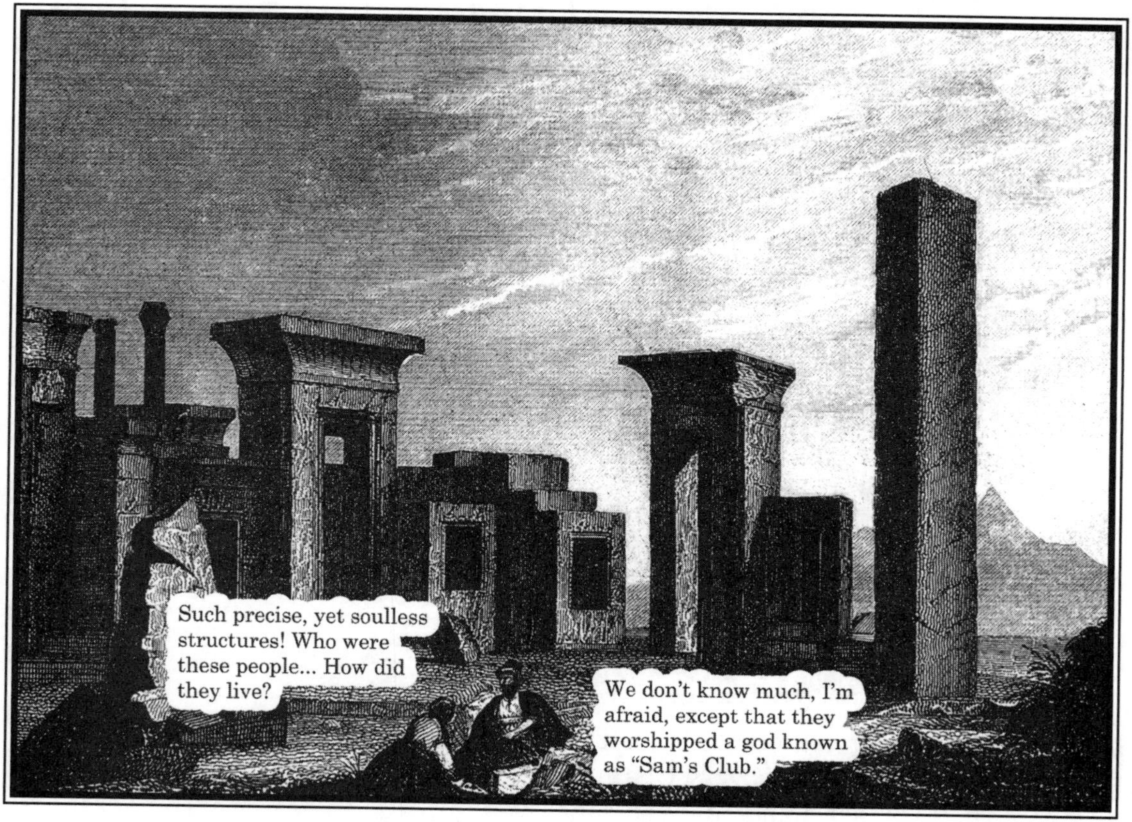
Such precise, yet soulless structures! Who were these people... How did they live?
We don't know much, I'm afraid, except that they worshipped a god known as "Sam's Club."

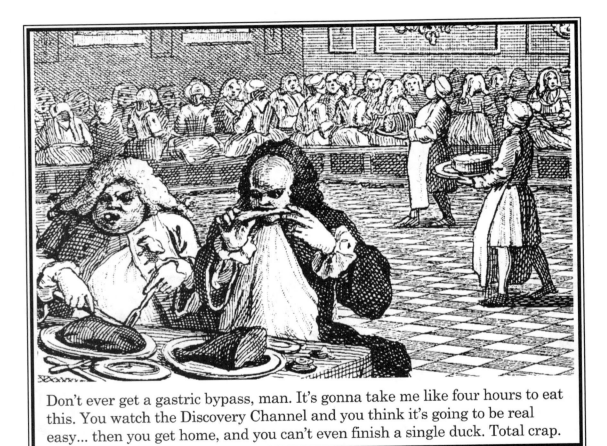

Don't ever get a gastric bypass, man. It's gonna take me like four hours to eat this. You watch the Discovery Channel and you think it's going to be real easy... then you get home, and you can't even finish a single duck. Total crap.

In recent years, scholars of
literature have suggested that
some of Shakespeare's best-
known works may have been
written by his cousin, William
"Pegleg" Shakespeare.

WHEAT IS MURDER

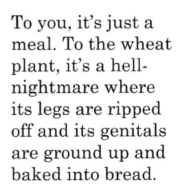

To you, it's just a meal. To the wheat plant, it's a hell-nightmare where its legs are ripped off and its genitals are ground up and baked into bread.

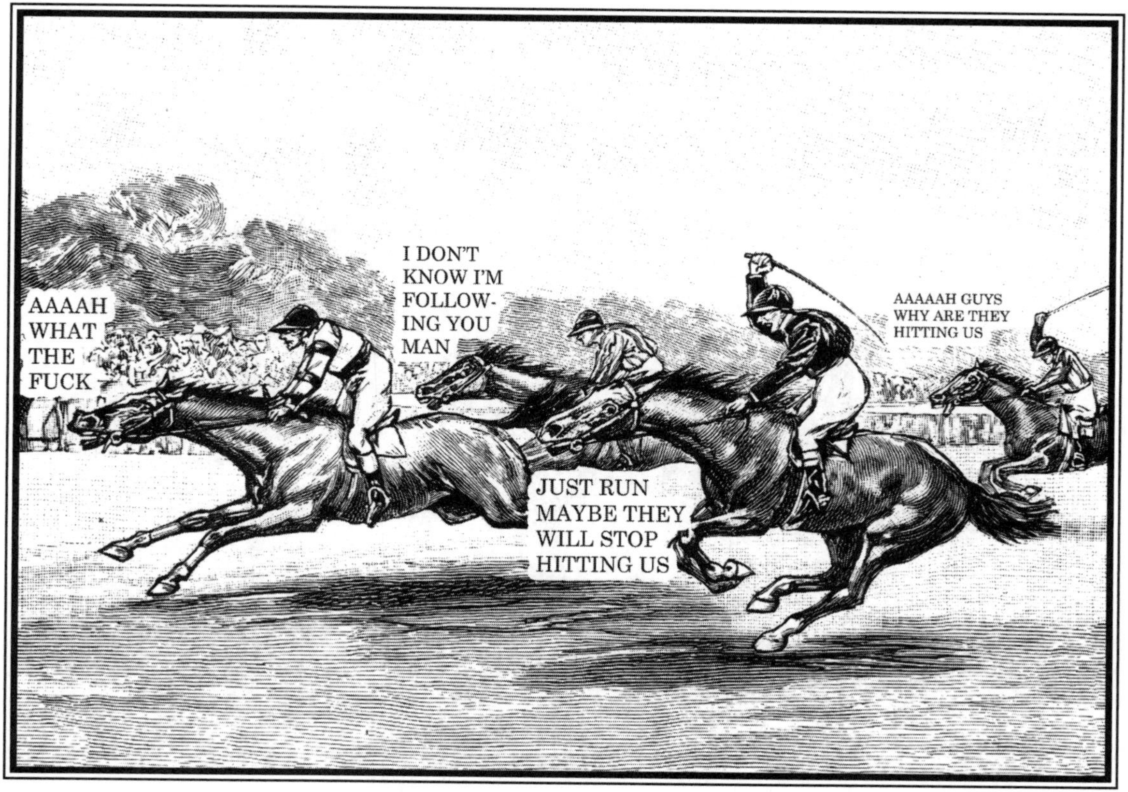
AAAAH WHAT THE FUCK
I DON'T KNOW I'M FOLLOW-ING YOU MAN
JUST RUN MAYBE THEY WILL STOP HITTING US
AAAAAH GUYS WHY ARE THEY HITTING US

"Hello there, young man! What's your name?"

"His name is Scott. Say hello, Scott!"

"My! That's a mouthful.
I'll just call you Marvin."

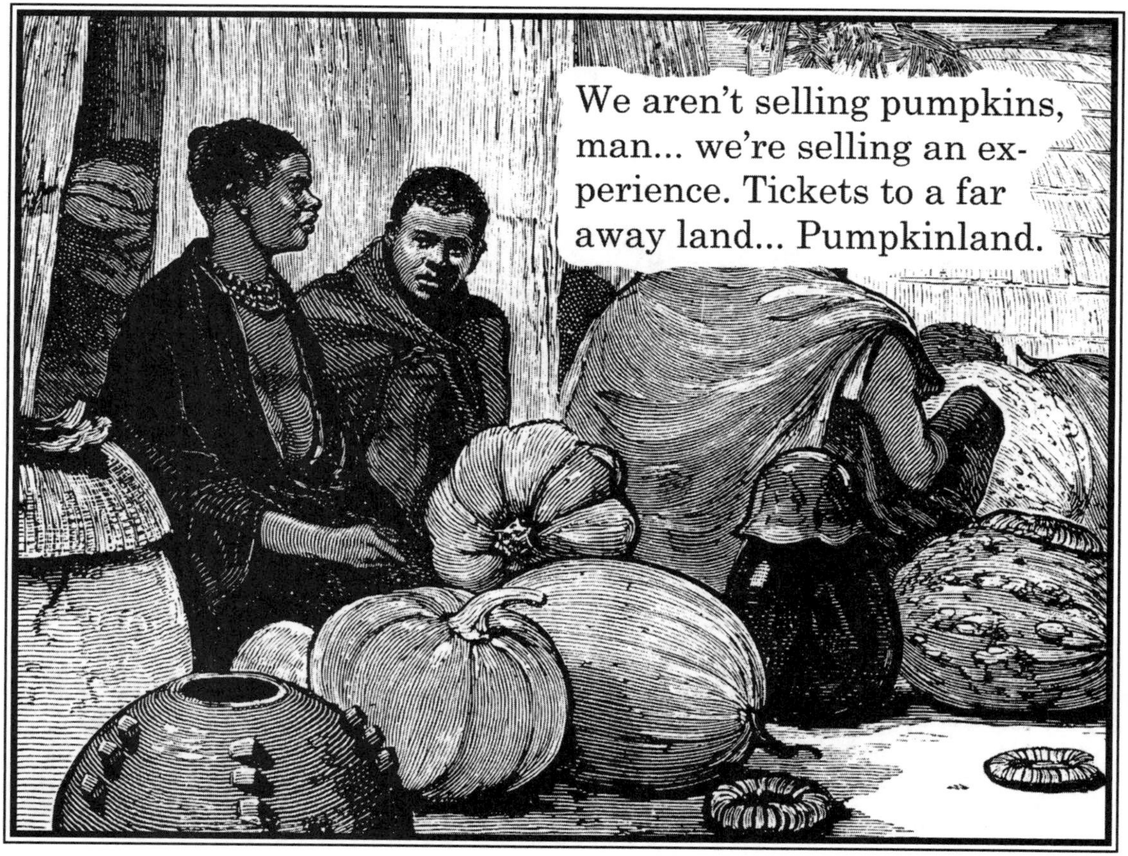
We aren't selling pumpkins, man... we're selling an experience. Tickets to a far away land... Pumpkinland.

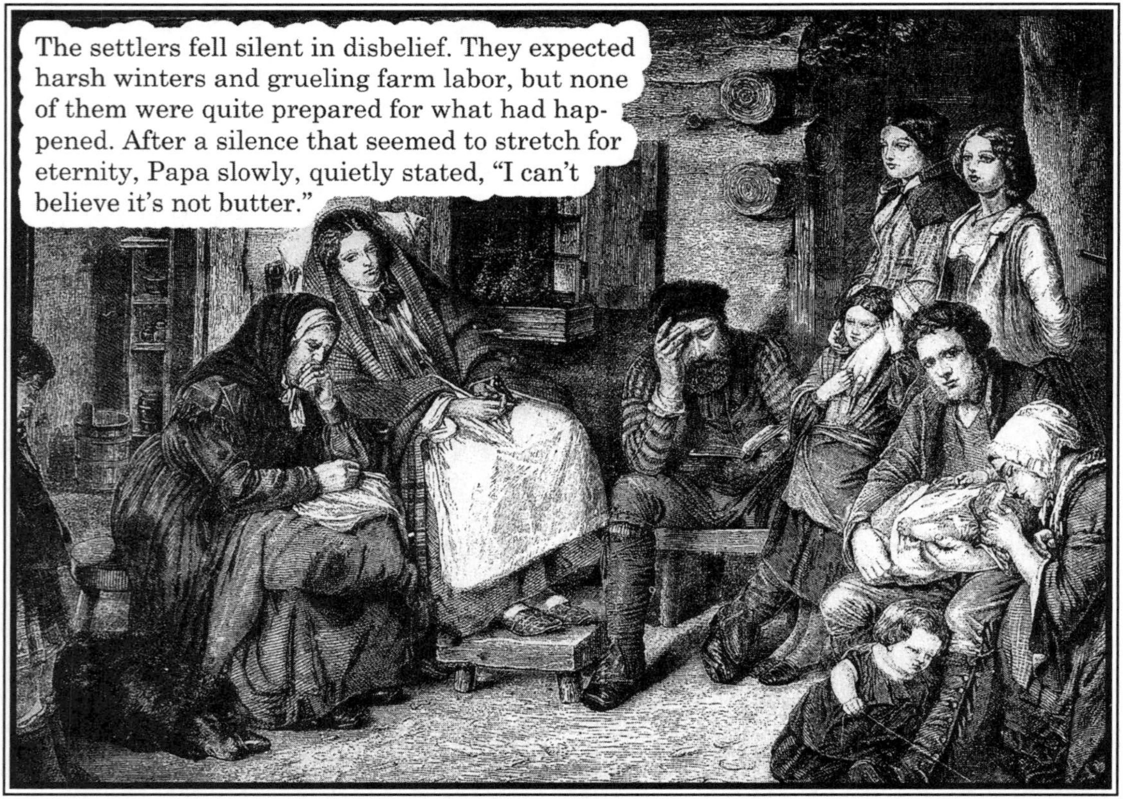
The settlers fell silent in disbelief. They expected harsh winters and grueling farm labor, but none of them were quite prepared for what had happened. After a silence that seemed to stretch for eternity, Papa slowly, quietly stated, “I can’t believe it’s not butter.”

"Here we are... the Alamo. You remember this place?"

"No doubt. 3/6/1836, never forget."

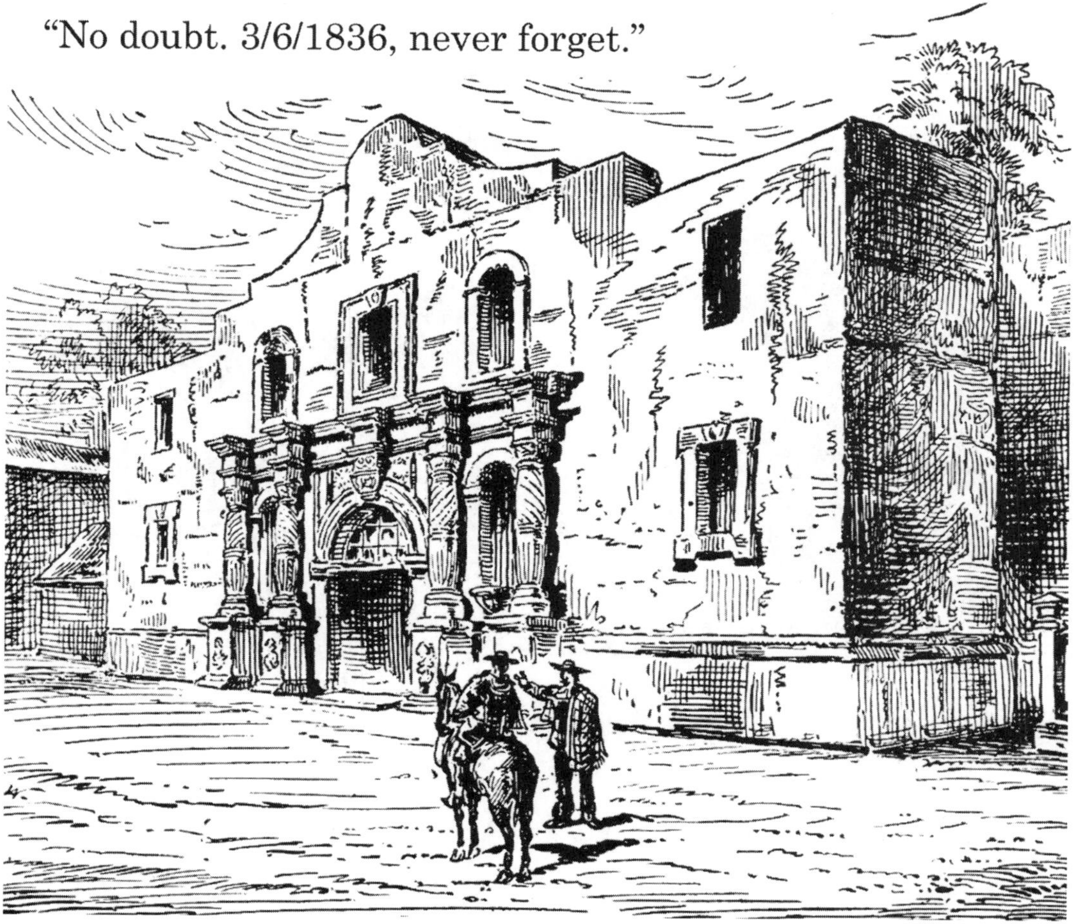

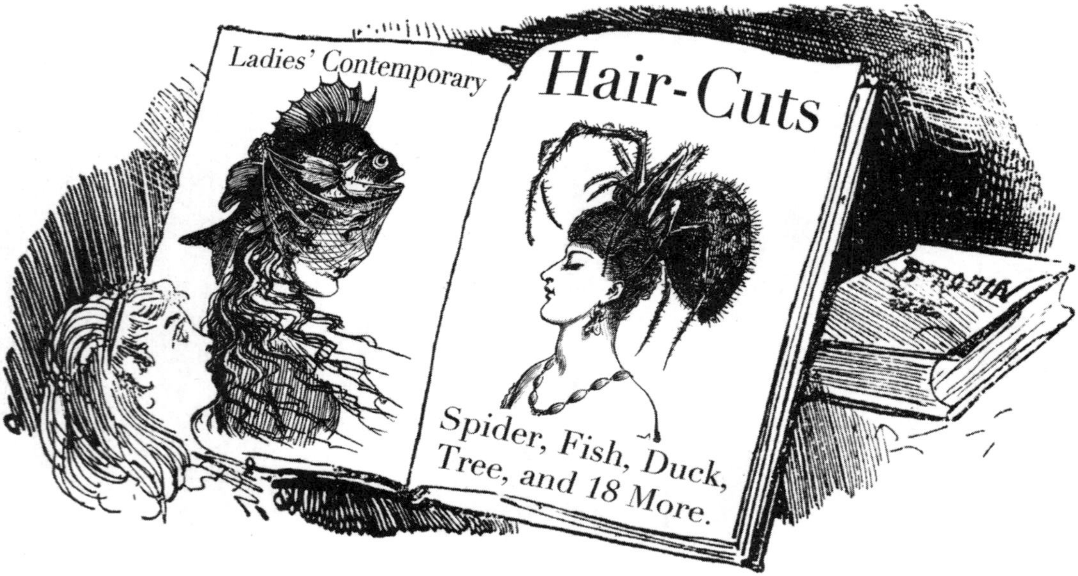
Ladies' Contemporary
Hair-Cuts
Spider, Fish, Duck,
Tree, and 18 More.

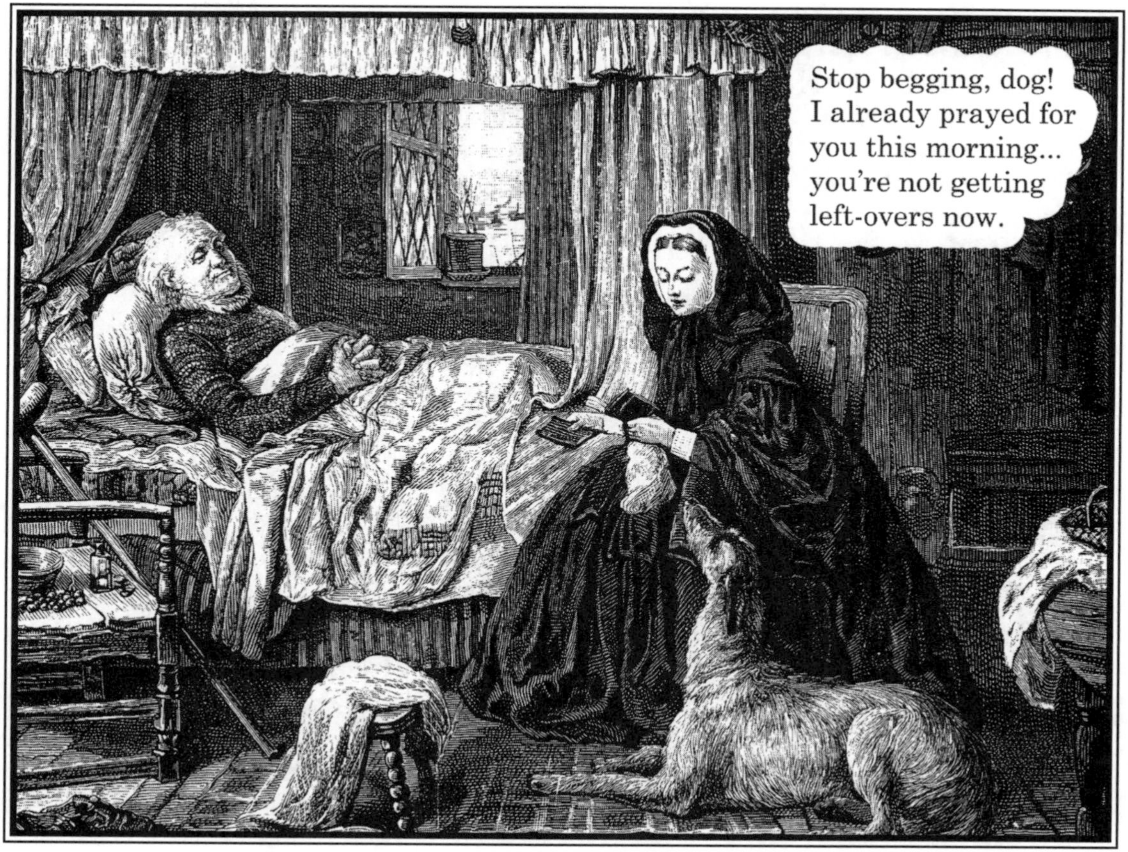
Stop begging, dog!
I already prayed for
you this morning...
you're not getting
left-overs now.

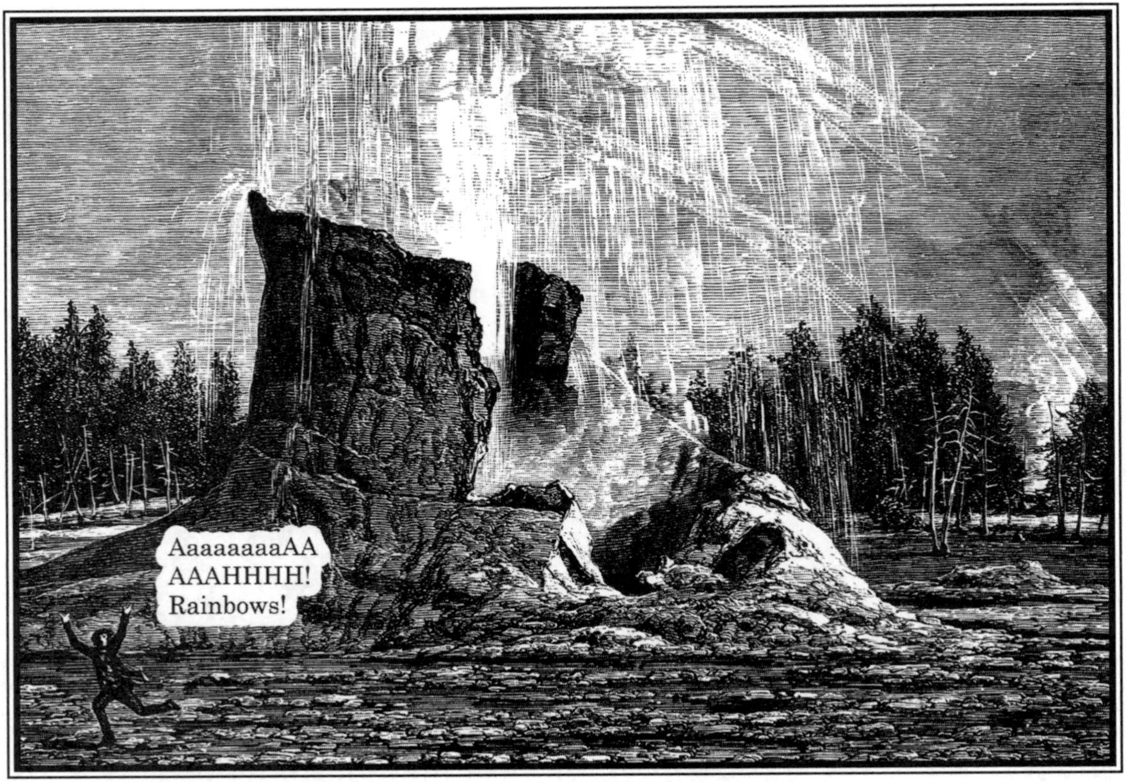
AaaaaaaaAA
AAAHHHH!
Rainbows!

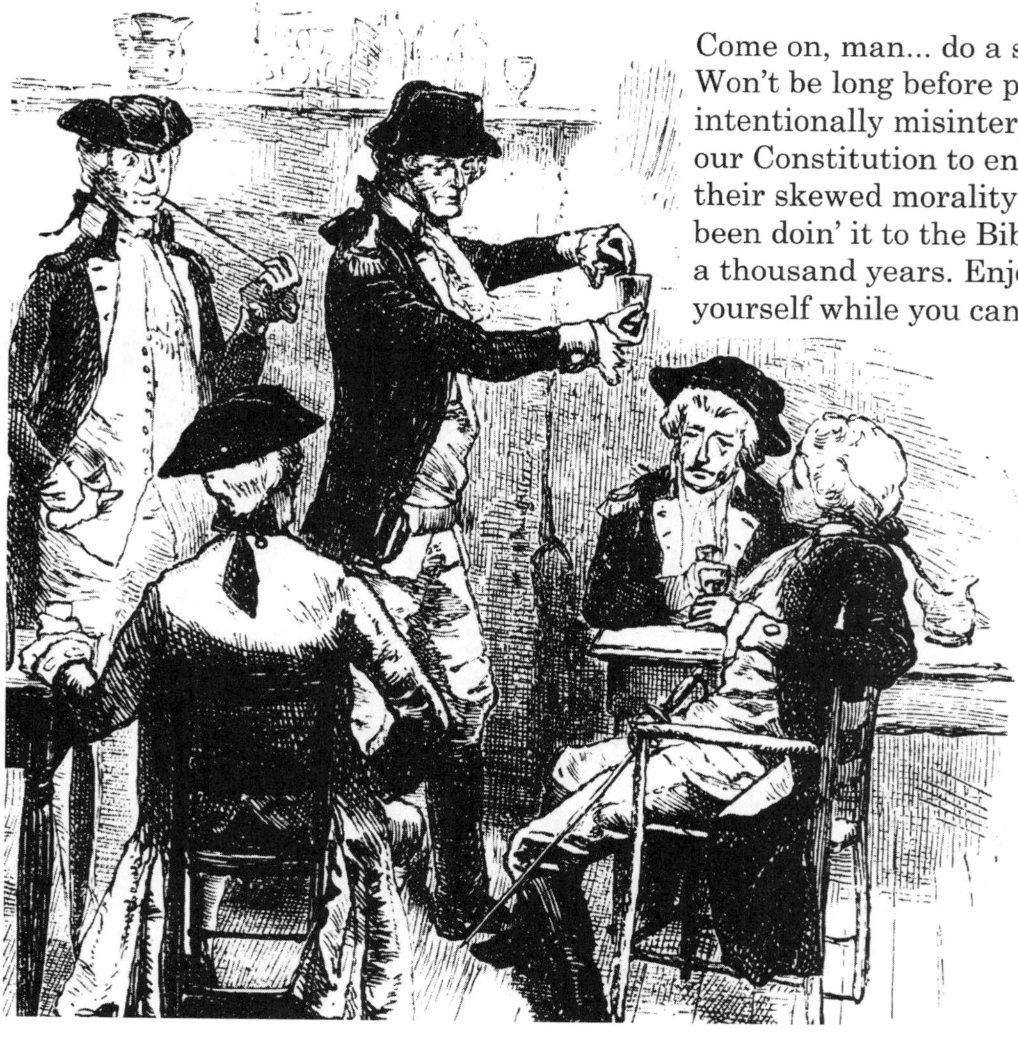

Come on, man... do a shot. Won't be long before people intentionally misinterpret our Constitution to enforce their skewed morality. They been doin' it to the Bible for a thousand years. Enjoy yourself while you can.

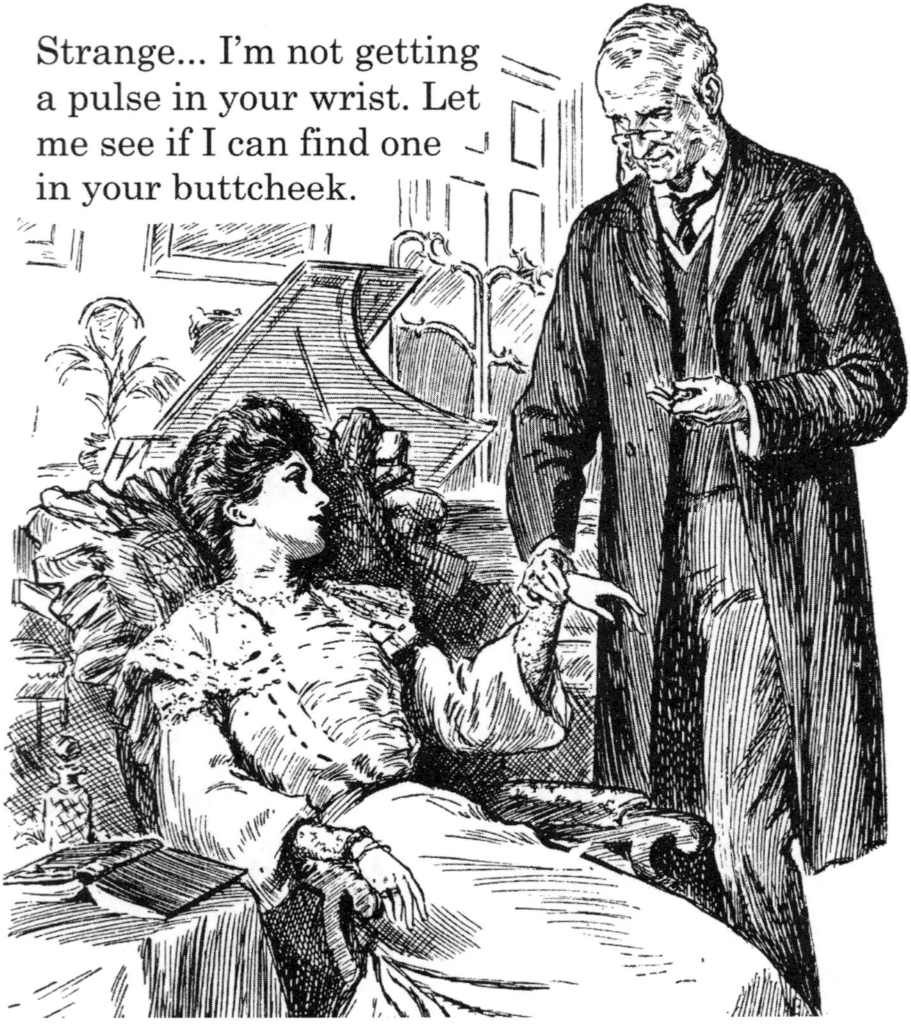
Strange... I'm not getting a pulse in your wrist. Let me see if I can find one in your buttcheek.

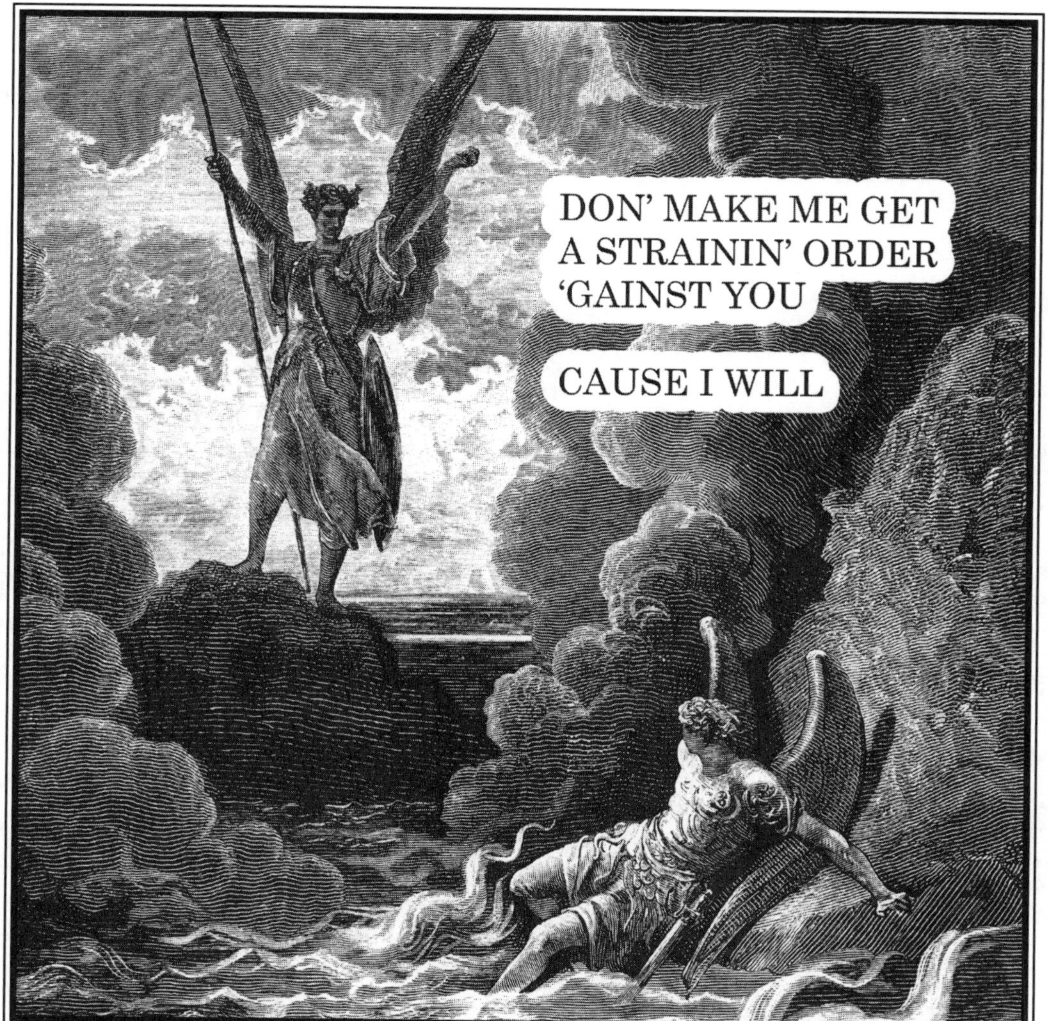
DON' MAKE ME GET A STRAININ' ORDER 'GAINST YOU
CAUSE I WILL

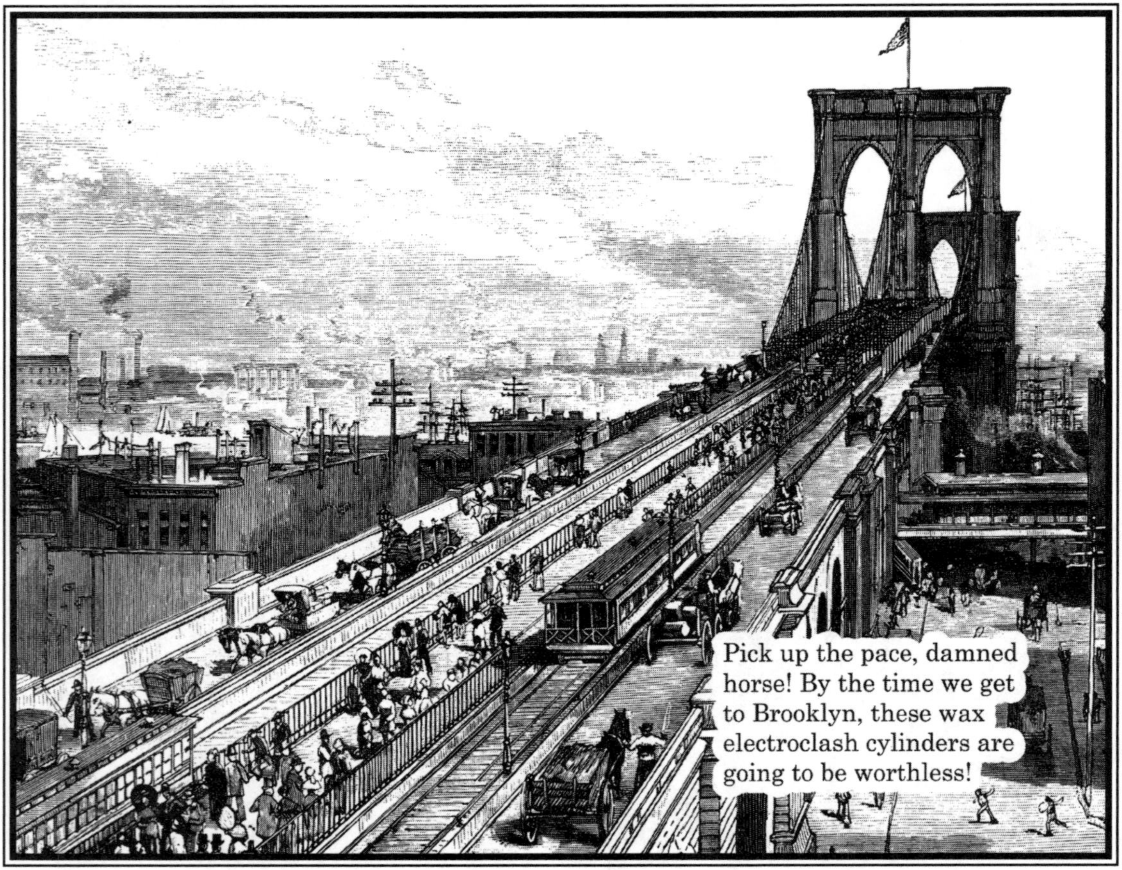
Pick up the pace, damned horse! By the time we get to Brooklyn, these wax electroclash cylinders are going to be worthless!

Children! You mustn't touch that ottoman! Do you see how it aged that poor boy? He looks like a tiny man!

Oooh, this isn't looking good at all... You definitely need to see a real doctor.

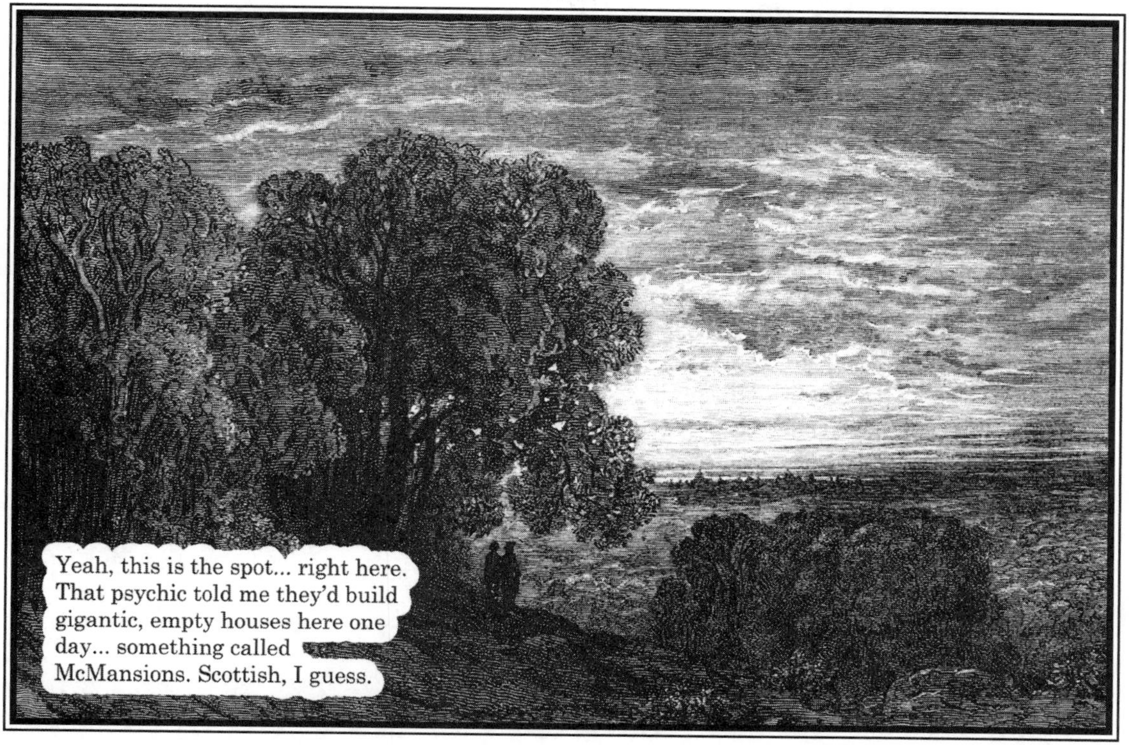
Yeah, this is the spot... right here.
That psychic told me they'd build
gigantic, empty houses here one
day... something called
McMansions. Scottish, I guess.

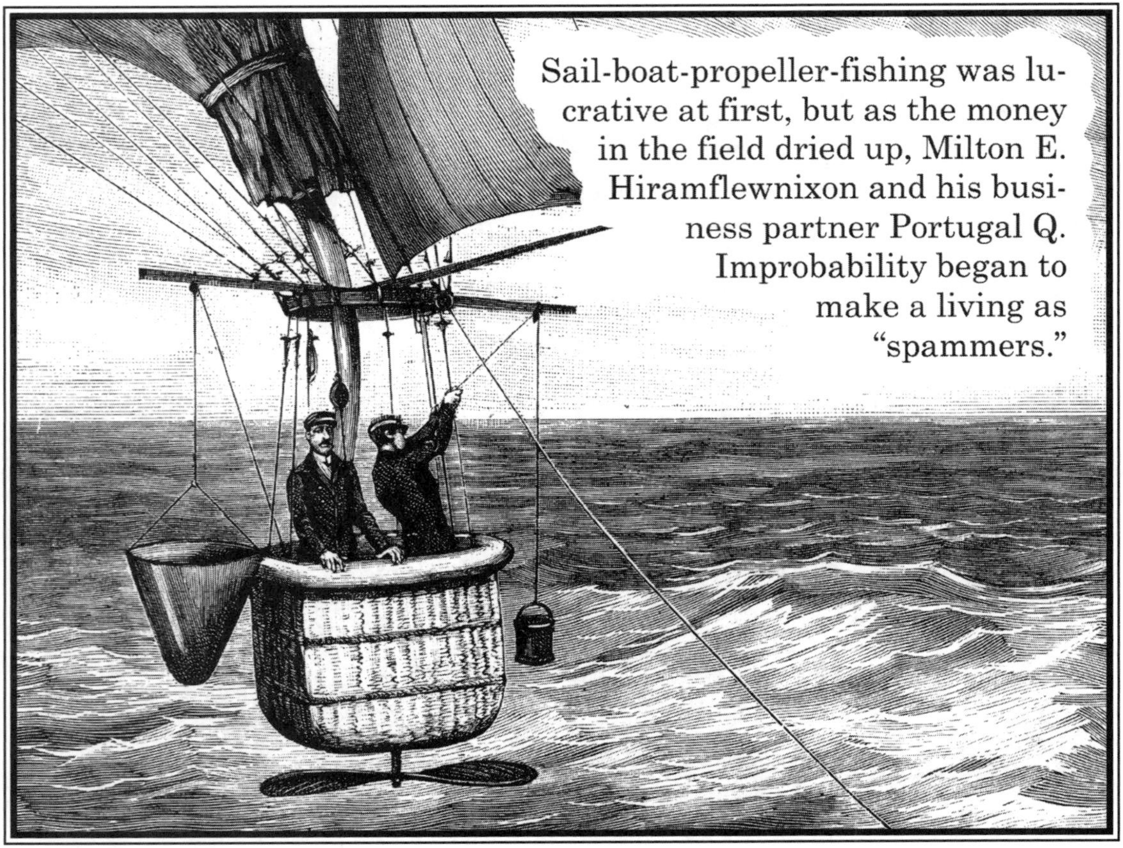
Sail-boat-propeller-fishing was lucrative at first, but as the money in the field dried up, Milton E. Hiramflewnixon and his business partner Portugal Q. Improbability began to make a living as "spammers."

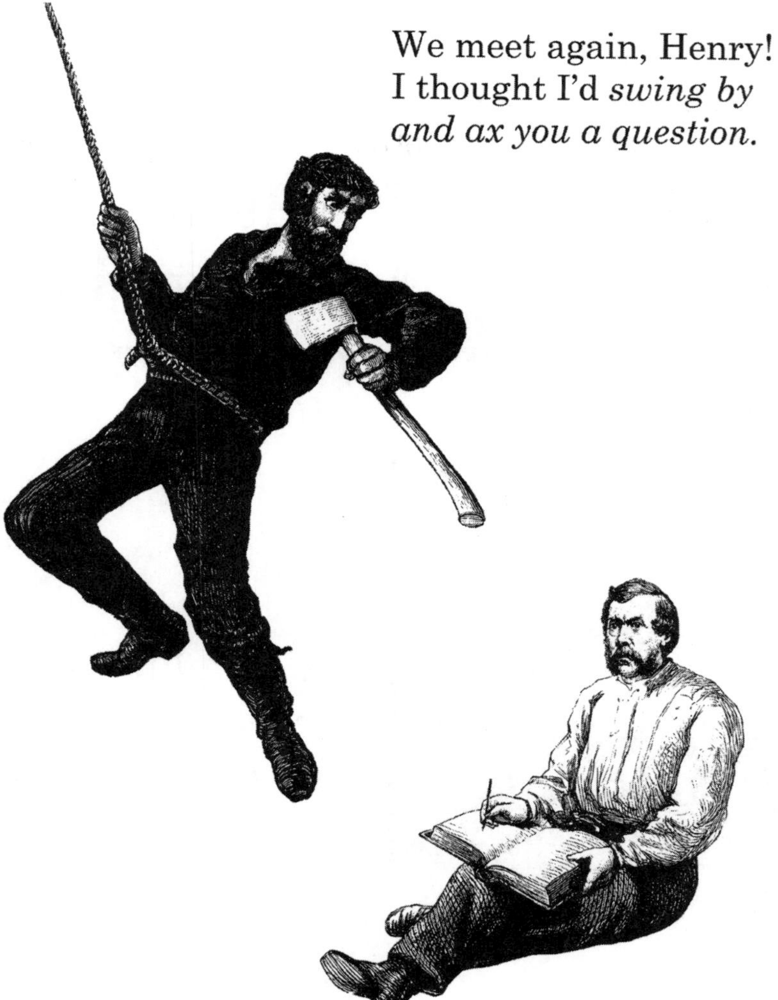
We meet again, Henry!
I thought I'd *swing by and ax you a question.*

file photo

Schoolteacher indicted in reading scandal

"It shouldn't be illegal for women to read"; Judge recommends death by hanging

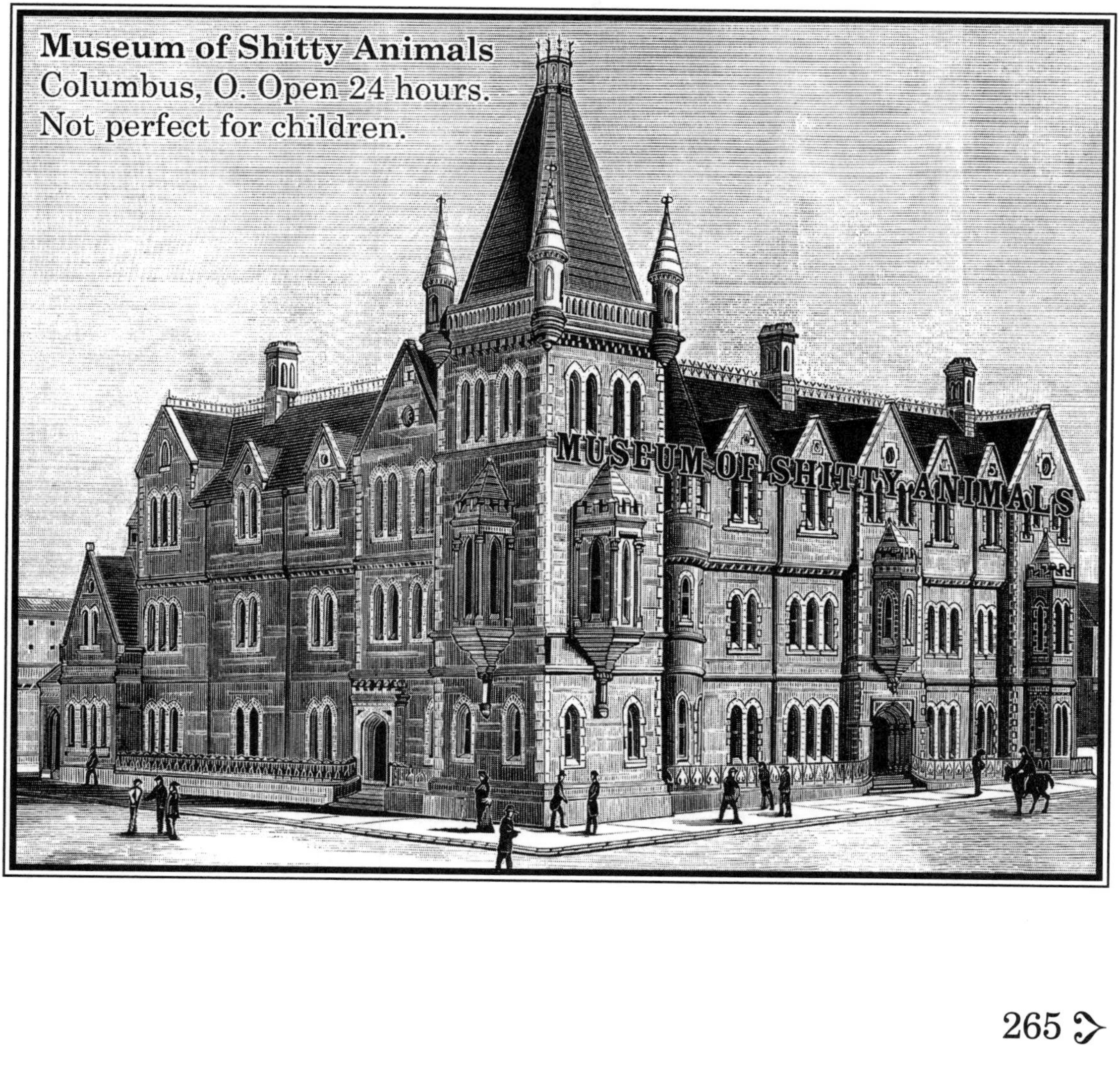
Museum of Shitty Animals
Columbus, O. Open 24 hours.
Not perfect for children.
MUSEUM OF SHITTY ANIMALS

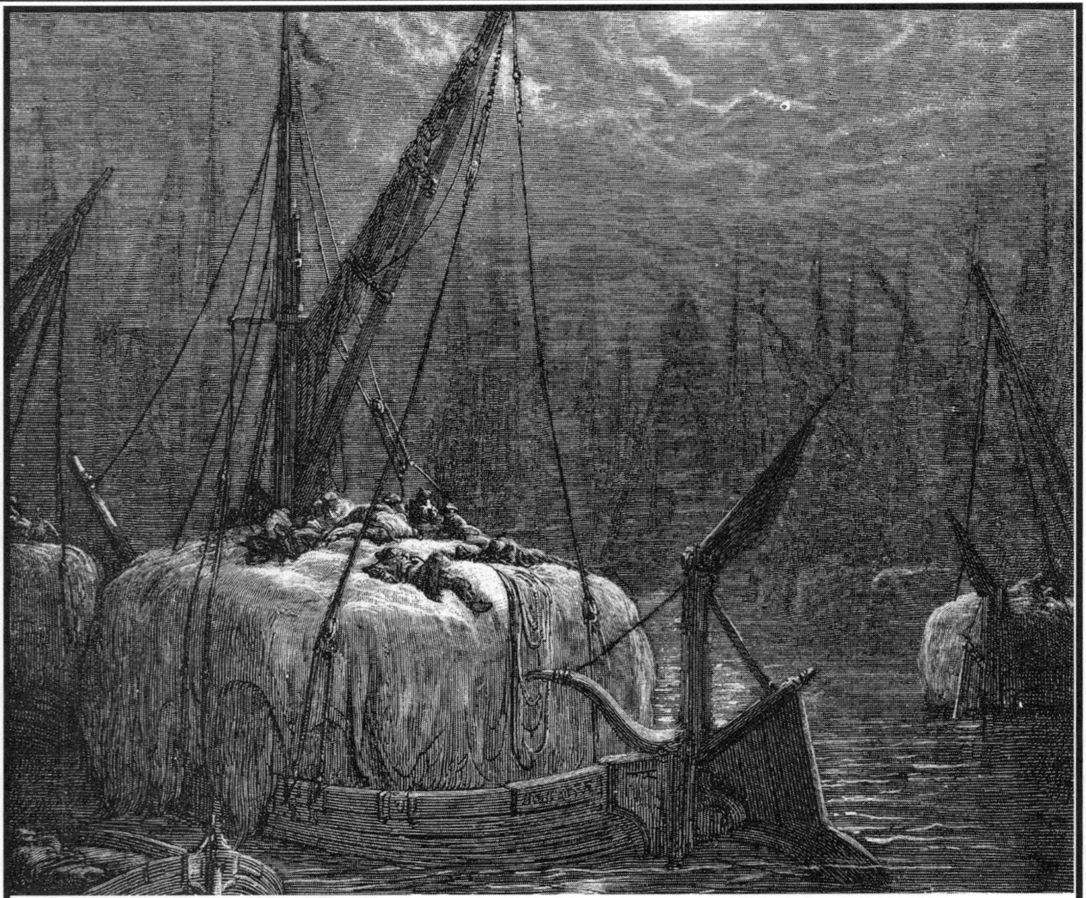

To save money, sailors would sleep on board the cheeseboats, often on top of the cheese itself. Before selling at market, the soiled top layer of cheese had to be removed, a process which irritated the men and originated the phrase "cheesed off."

Their music was terrible, and the audience hated
the theatrical antics of the Precocious Underfoot
Noisemaker Kids. It was not until a hundred
years later that untrained children would be
celebrated for making "PUNK" music, named
in honor of the original artists.

My saddle isn't in here, either. How on earth am I going to get to work today?

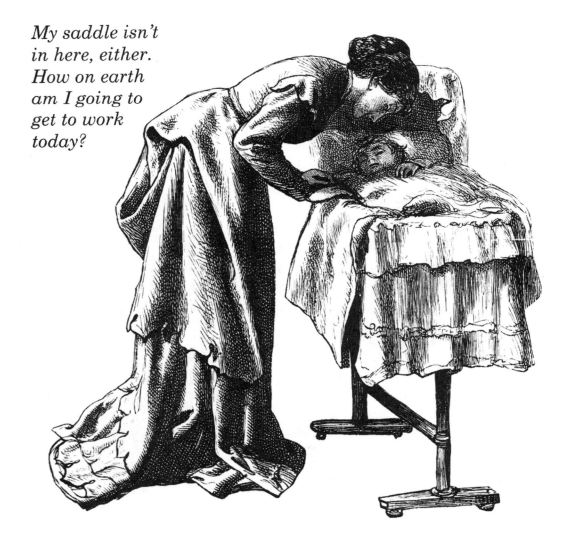

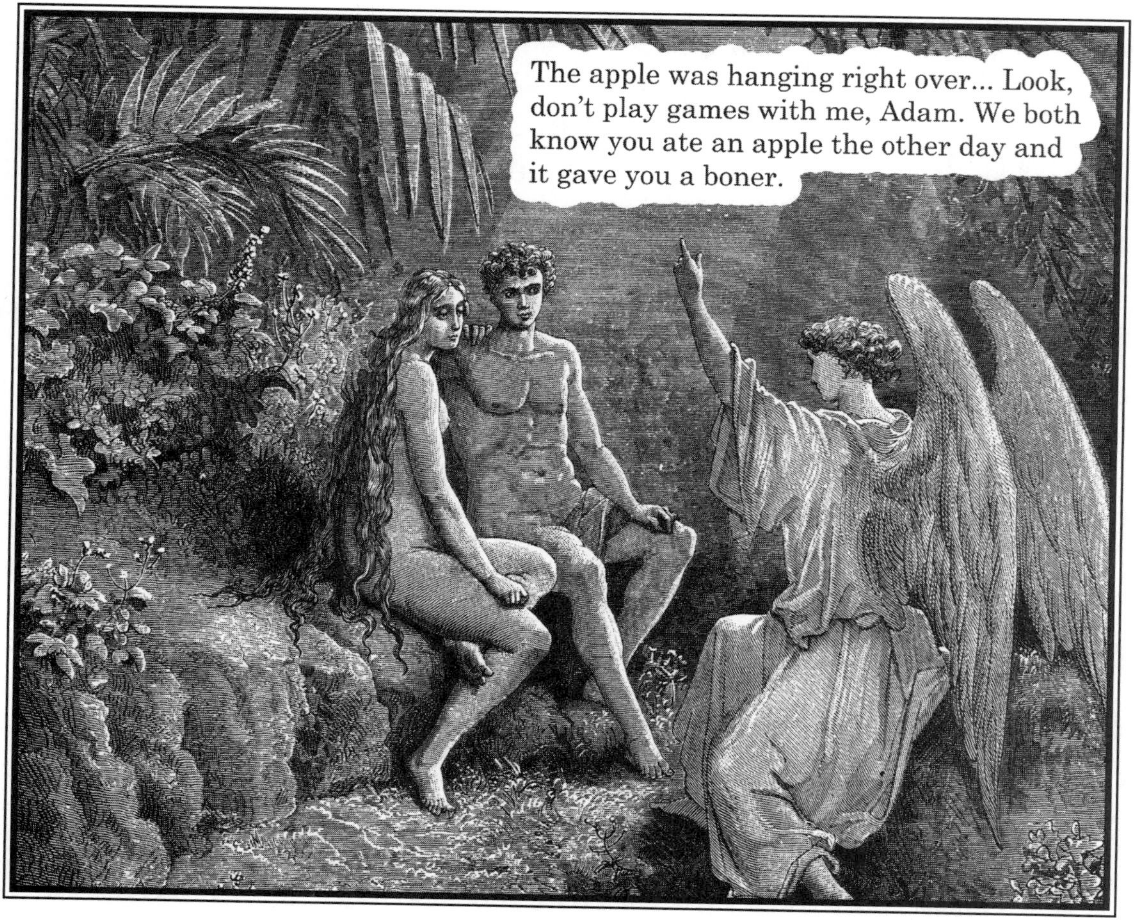
The apple was hanging right over... Look, don't play games with me, Adam. We both know you ate an apple the other day and it gave you a boner.

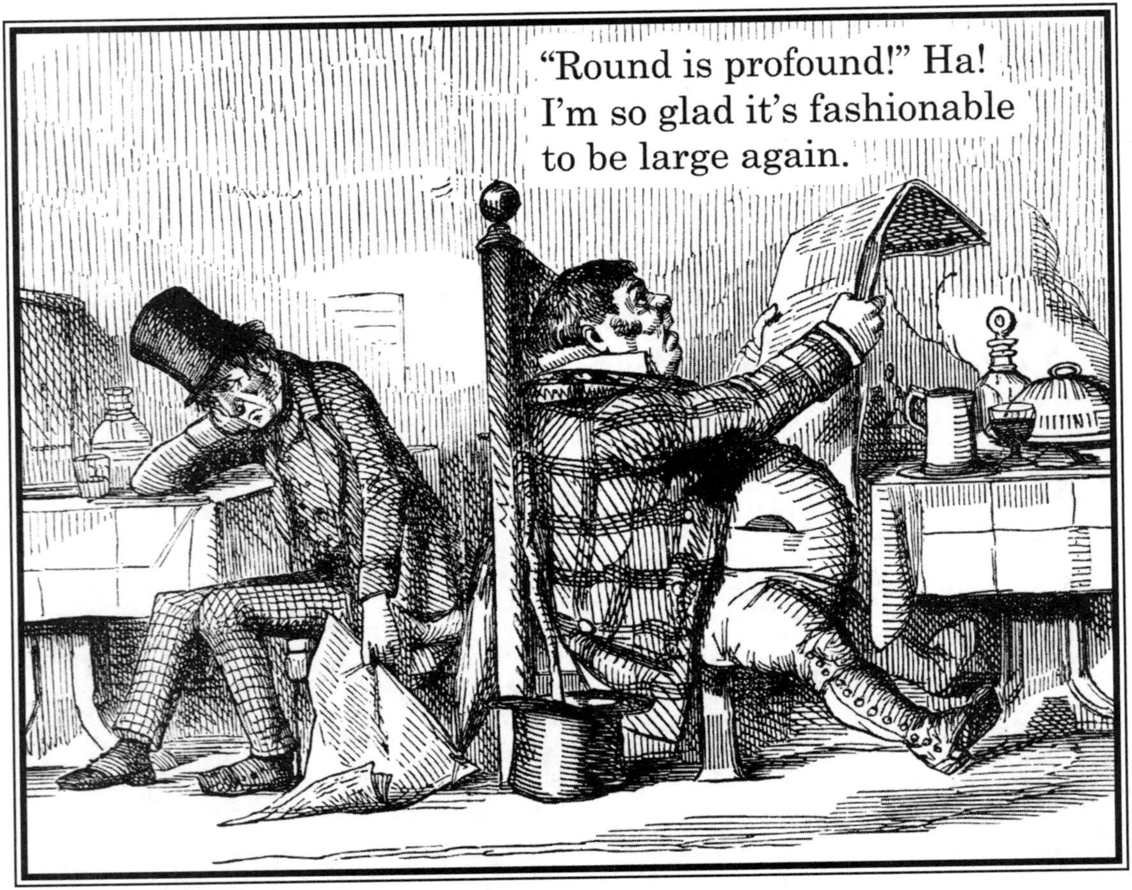
"Round is profound!" Ha!
I'm so glad it's fashionable
to be large again.

I wish virgin sweat didn't cure the plague.

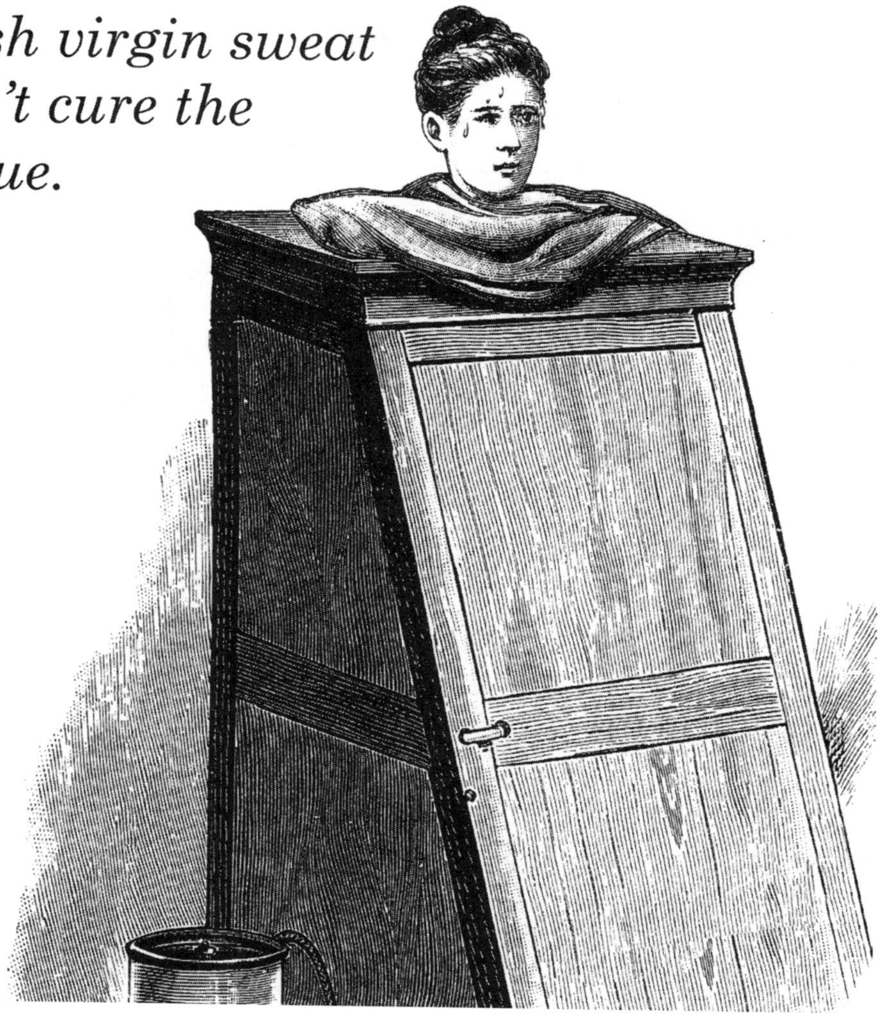

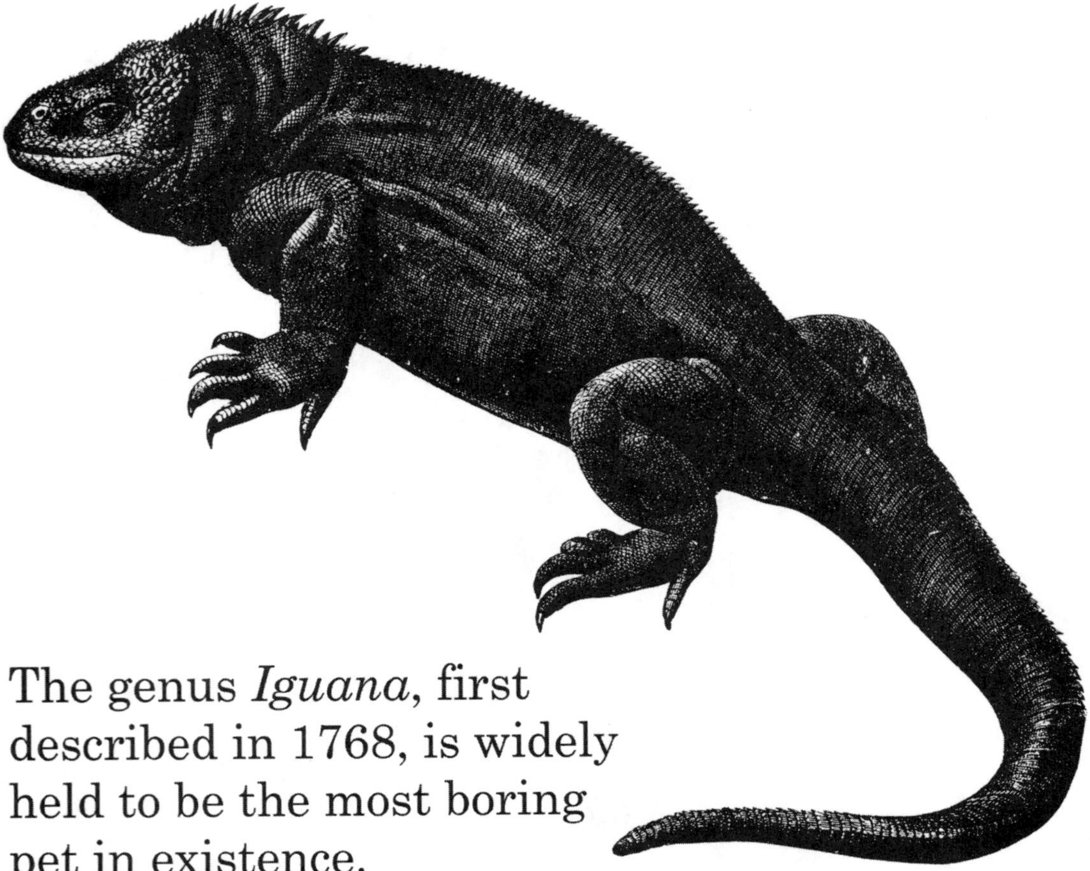

The genus *Iguana*, first described in 1768, is widely held to be the most boring pet in existence.

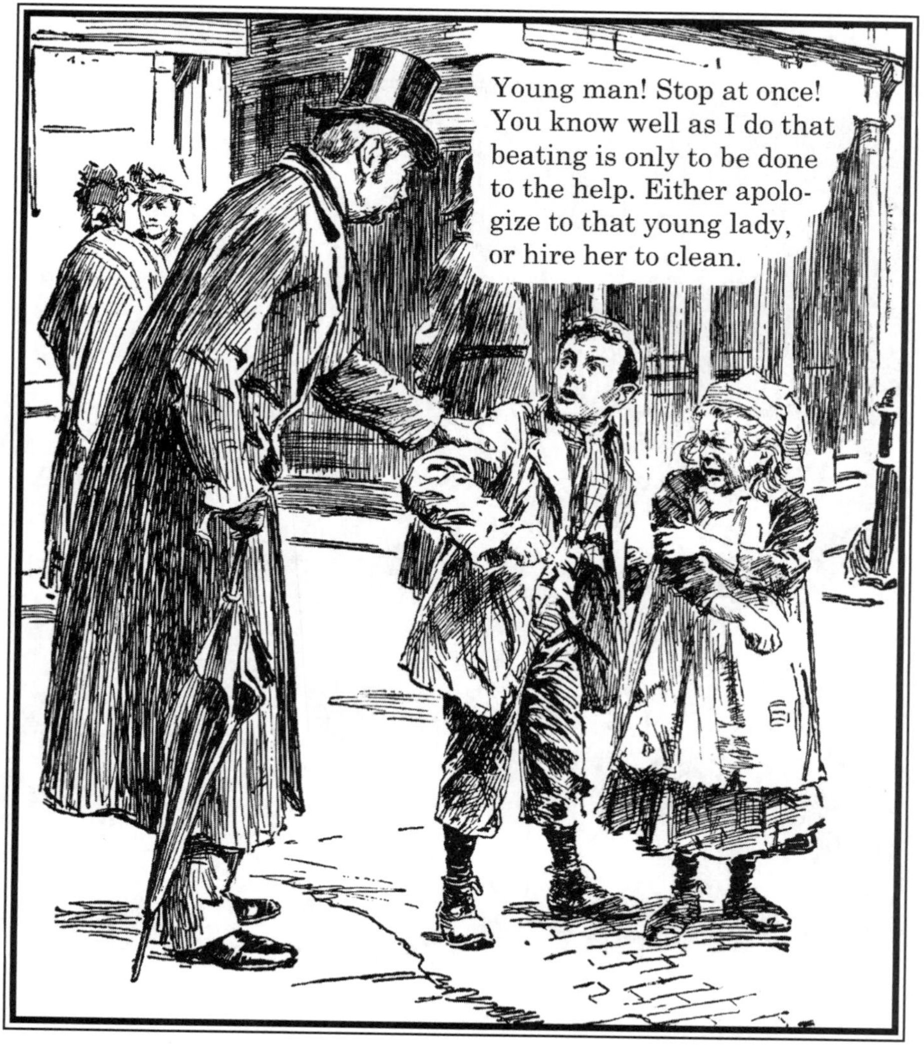
Young man! Stop at once! You know well as I do that beating is only to be done to the help. Either apologize to that young lady, or hire her to clean.

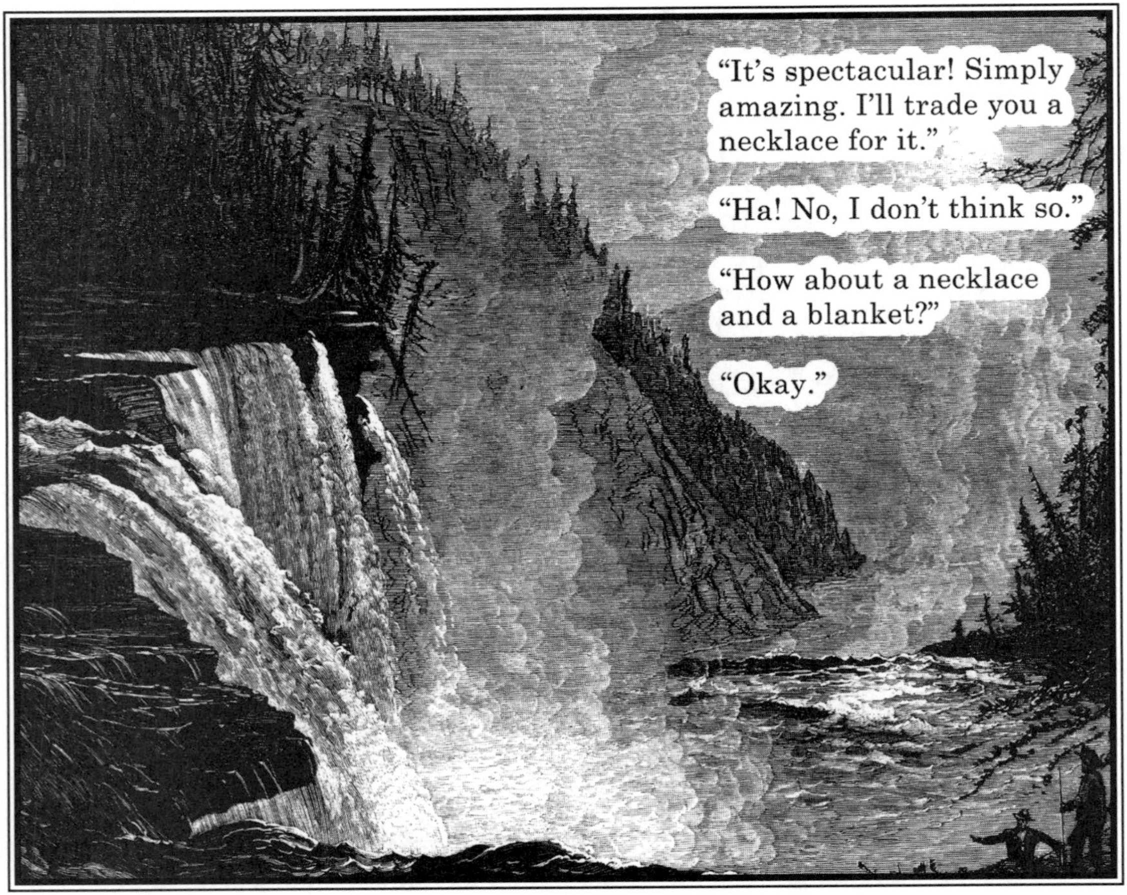
"It's spectacular! Simply amazing. I'll trade you a necklace for it."
"Ha! No, I don't think so."
"How about a necklace and a blanket?"
"Okay."

Take Things On Boat Company

Parcel status: Loaded onto ship
Est. Delivery Date: 1890

2 FEB 89: BARREL LOADED
3 FEB 89: BARREL ON SHIP
14 AUG 89: STILL ON SHIP
19 SEP 89: STILL ON SHIP
8 NOV 89: STILL ON SHIP
5 JAN 90: STILL ON SHIP

Tracking Number: 14

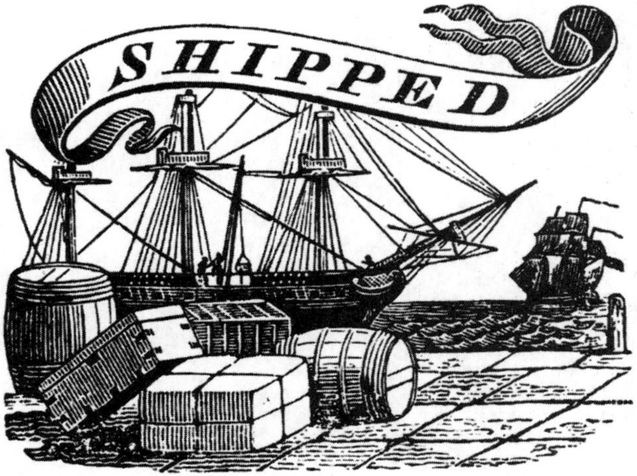
SHIPPED

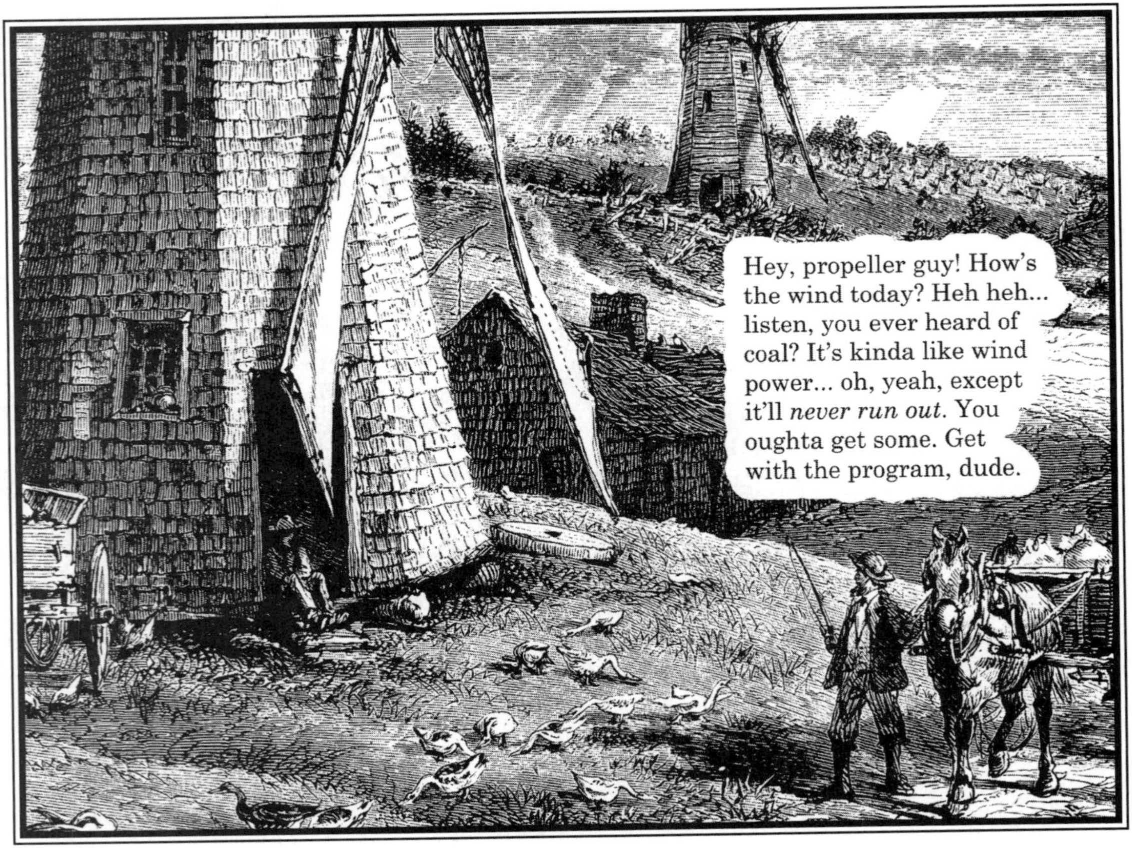
Hey, propeller guy! How's the wind today? Heh heh... listen, you ever heard of coal? It's kinda like wind power... oh, yeah, except it'll *never run out*. You oughta get some. Get with the program, dude.

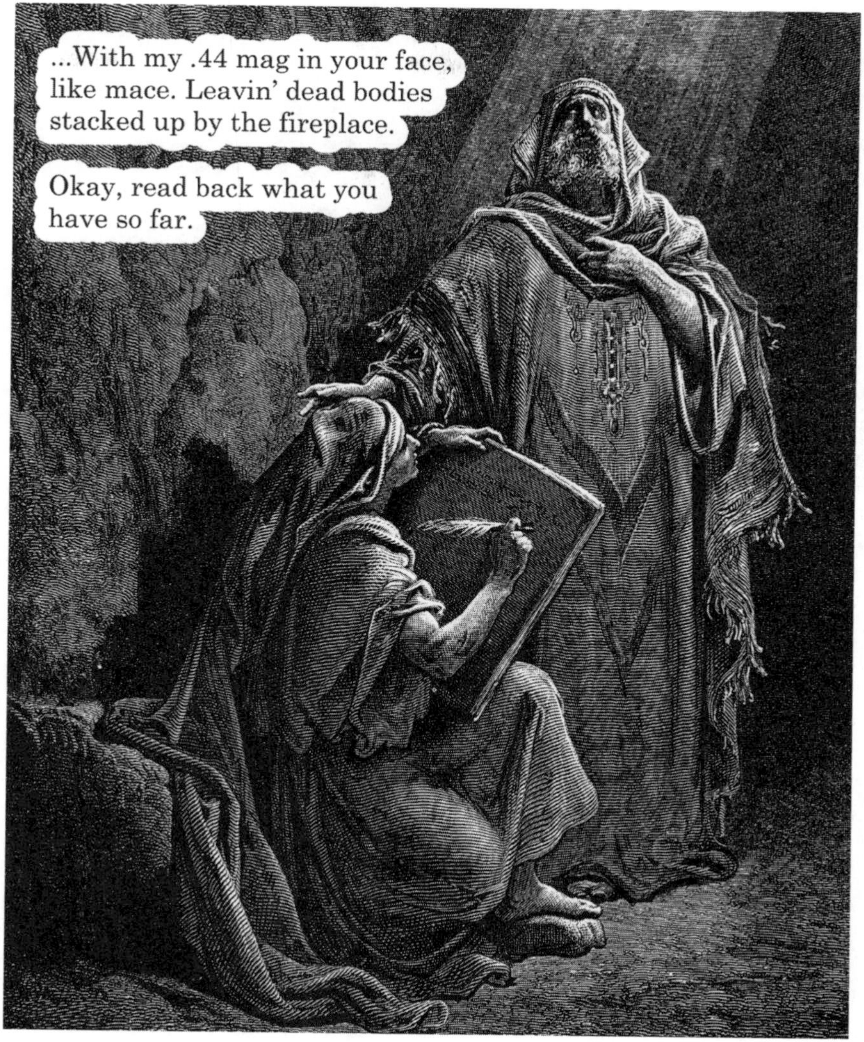
...With my .44 mag in your face, like mace. Leavin' dead bodies stacked up by the fireplace.
Okay, read back what you have so far.

The men sipped their salvia punch,
and within minutes they haaaaddd
d,.][.,[-,.833333333hahahahmmmm
mmmooooooooooooooooo

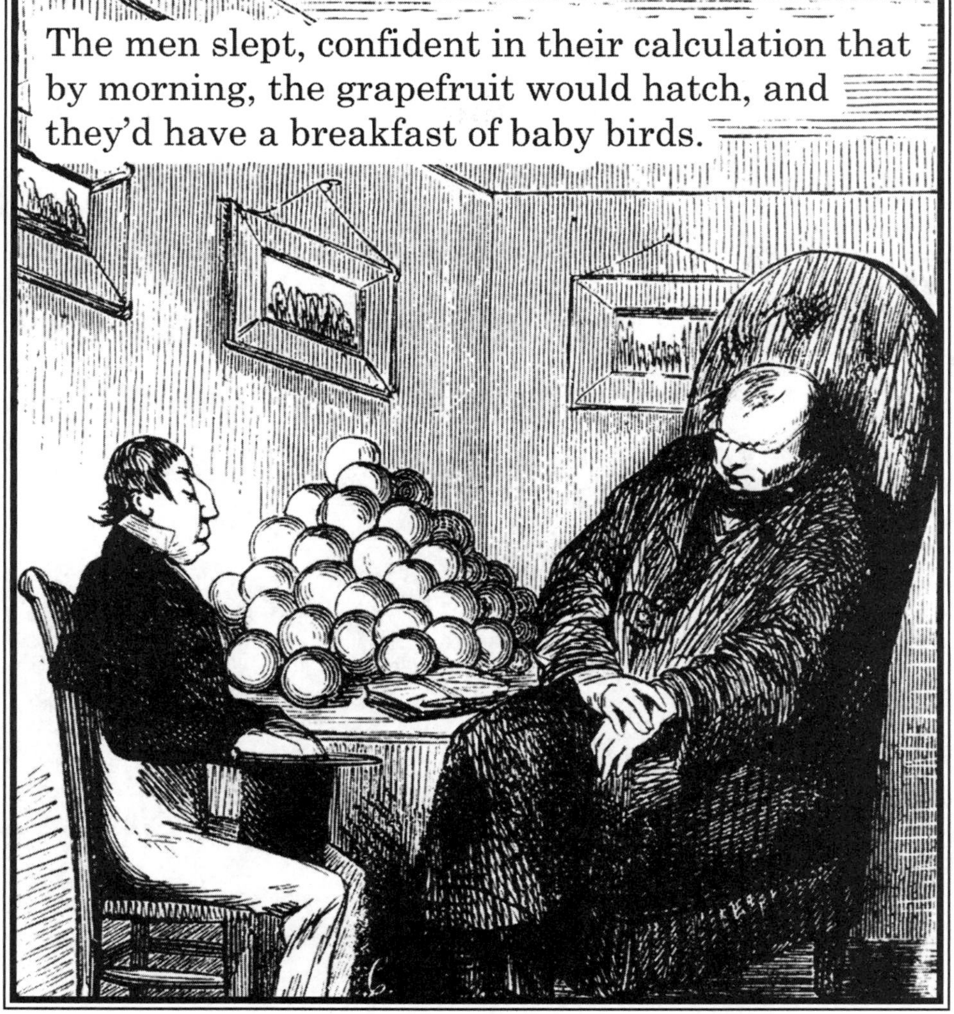
The men slept, confident in their calculation that by morning, the grapefruit would hatch, and they'd have a breakfast of baby birds.

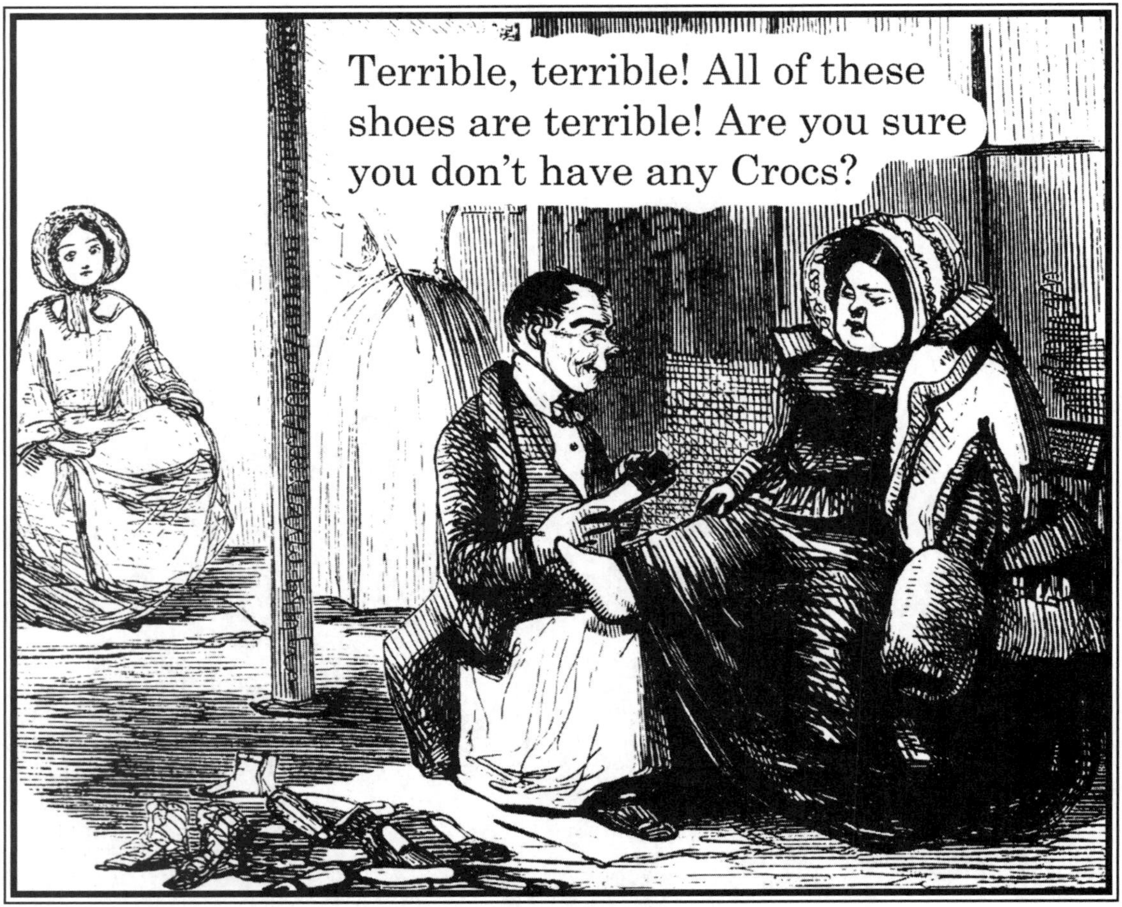
Terrible, terrible! All of these shoes are terrible! Are you sure you don't have any Crocs?

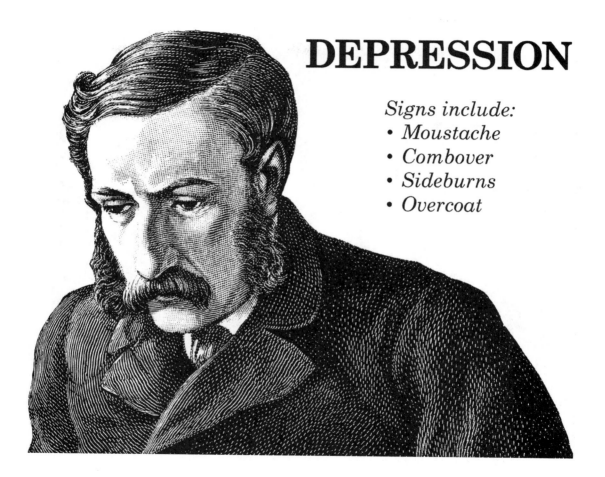

DEPRESSION

Signs include:
- *Moustache*
- *Combover*
- *Sideburns*
- *Overcoat*

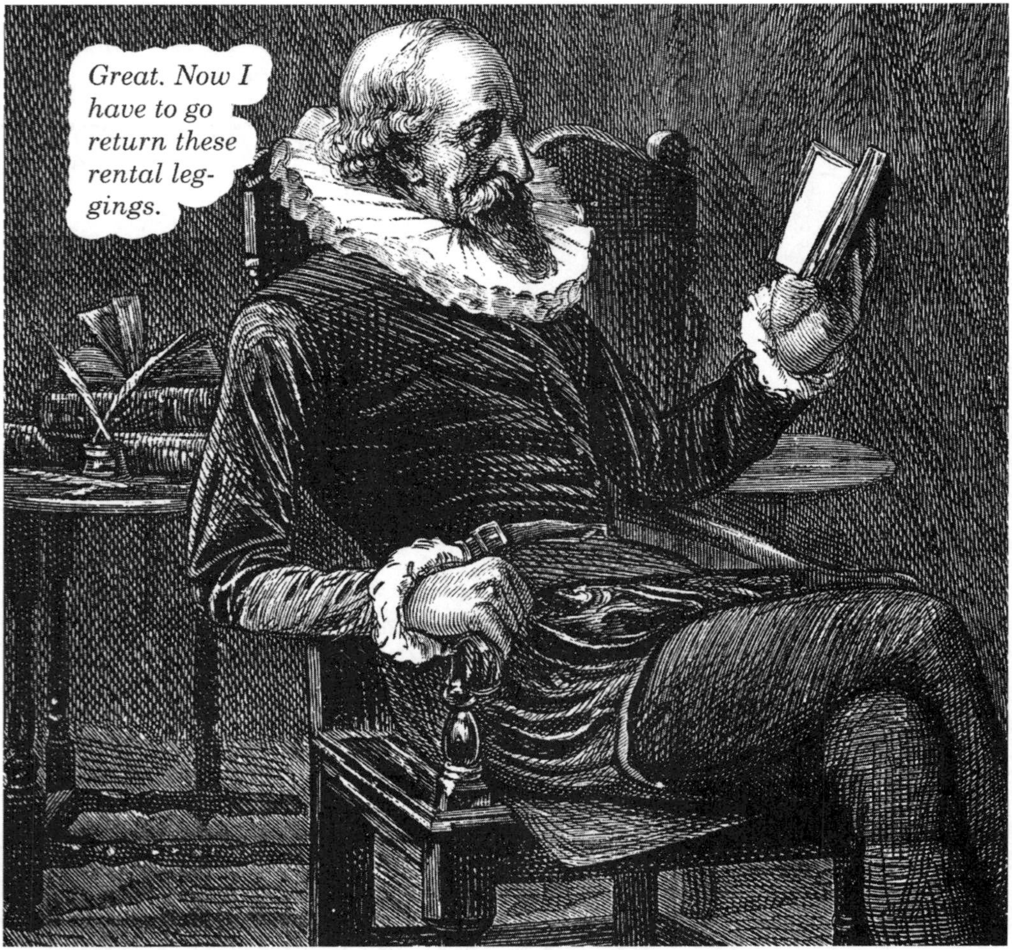
Great. Now I have to go return these rental leggings.

Even after donning the era-appropriate clothing and haircut, Jonas, like anyone else with taste or sense, found it completely impossible to enjoy the works of William Shakespeare.

"Oh, Henrik! It's beautiful! I can't believe it's all ours!"

"Well, technically, it's not ours yet... but if we can squat there for seven years, it will be."

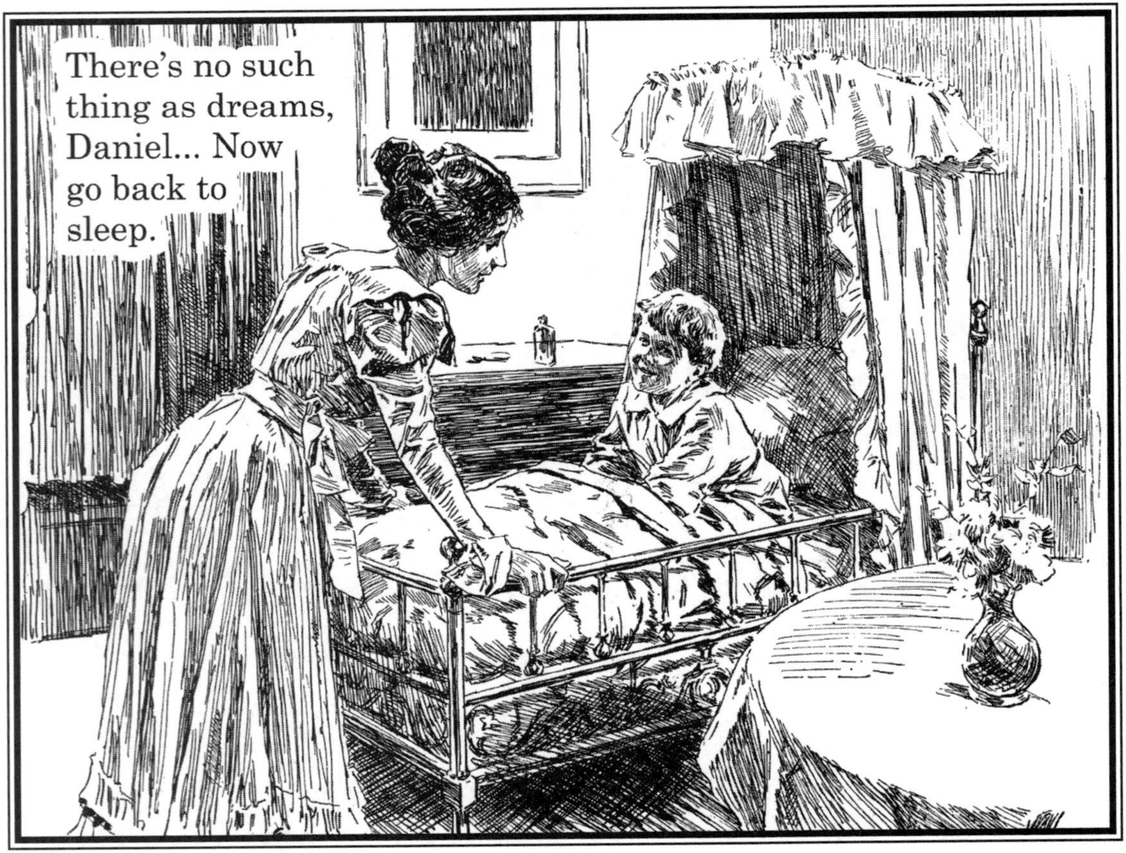
There's no such thing as dreams, Daniel... Now go back to sleep.

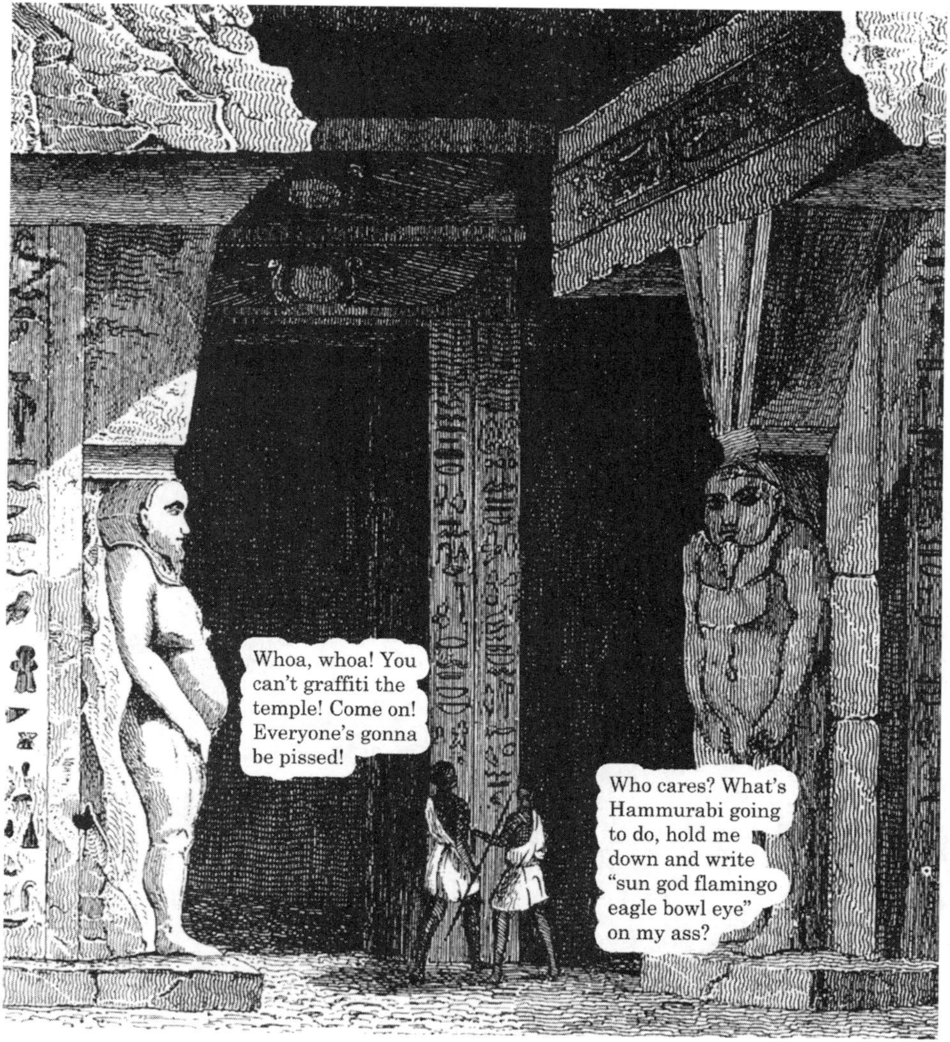
Whoa, whoa! You can't graffiti the temple! Come on! Everyone's gonna be pissed!
Who cares? What's Hammurabi going to do, hold me down and write "sun god flamingo eagle bowl eye" on my ass?

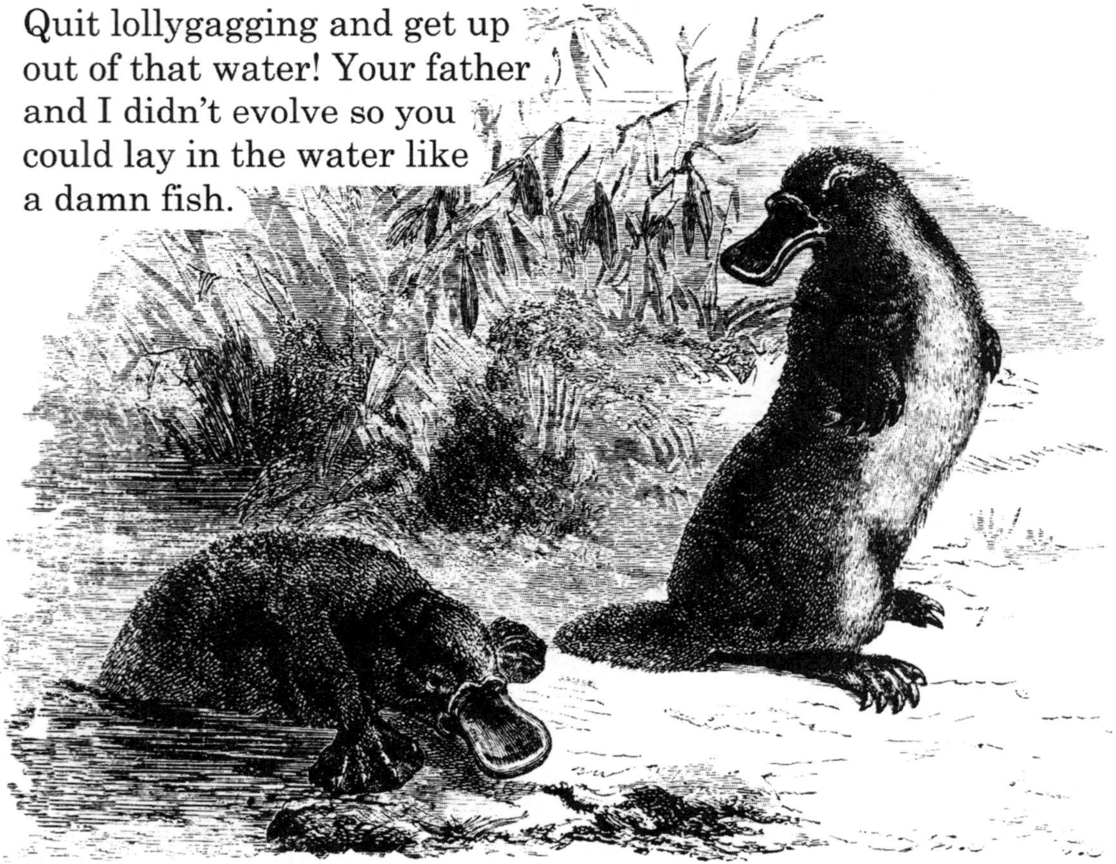
Quit lollygagging and get up out of that water! Your father and I didn't evolve so you could lay in the water like a damn fish.

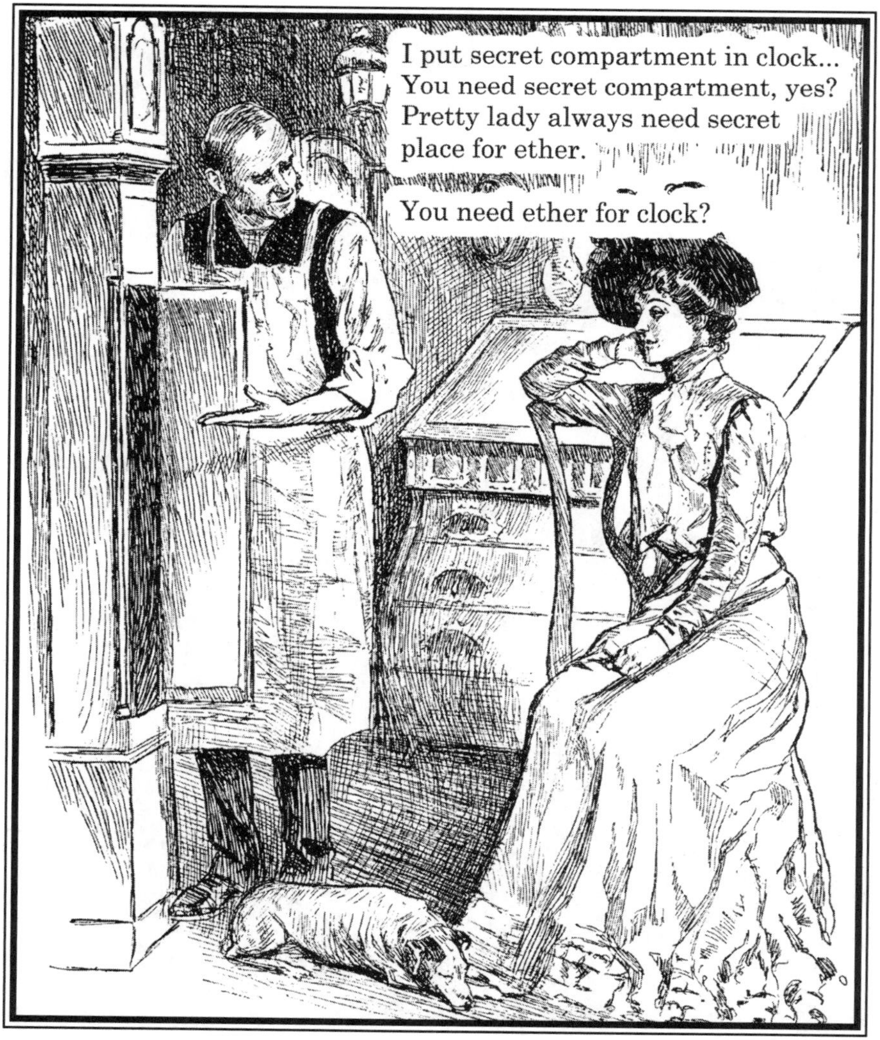
I put secret compartment in clock...
You need secret compartment, yes?
Pretty lady always need secret
place for ether.
You need ether for clock?

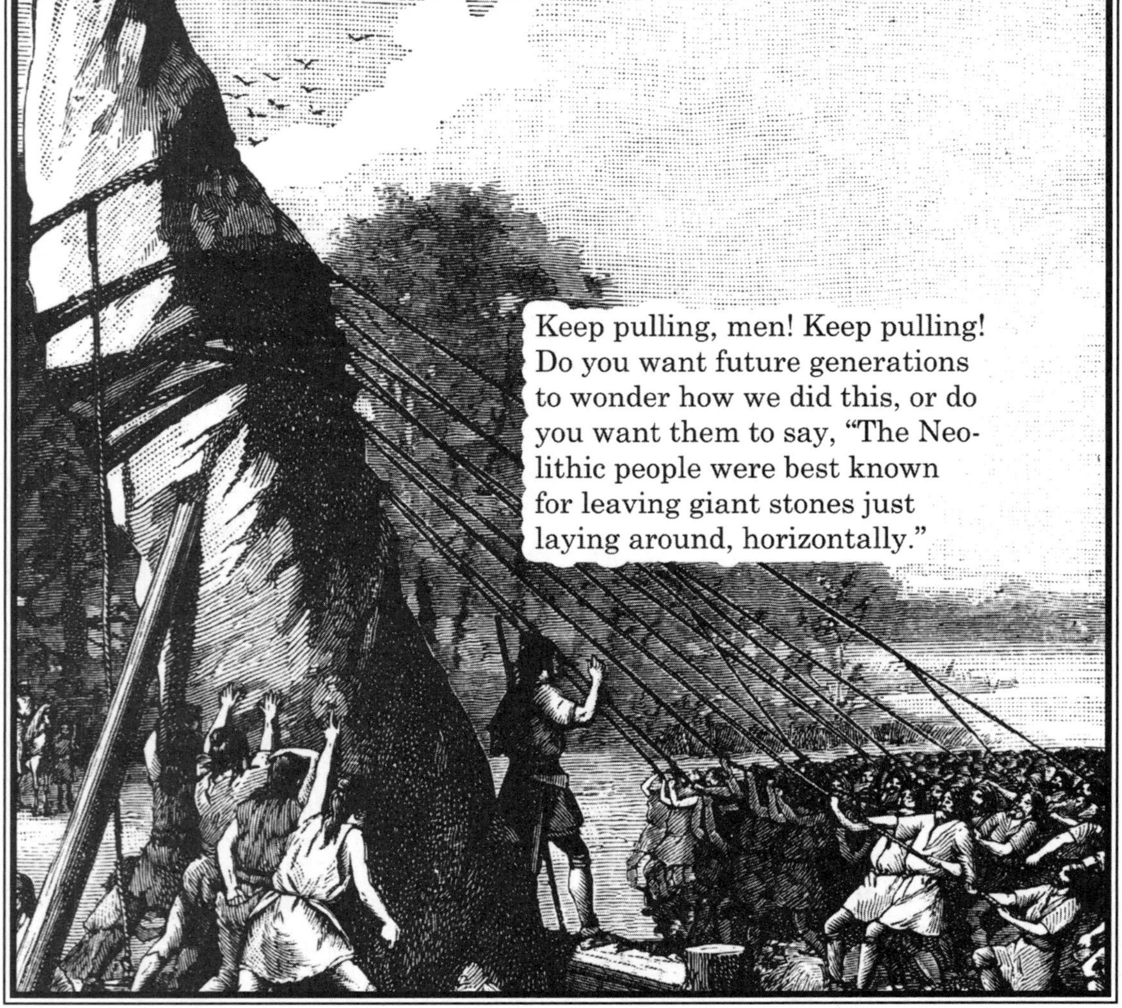
Keep pulling, men! Keep pulling! Do you want future generations to wonder how we did this, or do you want them to say, "The Neolithic people were best known for leaving giant stones just laying around, horizontally."

What on earth is that, Timothy? Some kind of... mouth... board? You'll need to switch that monstrosity out for an ear-stick if you plan on dancing at the ball tonight.

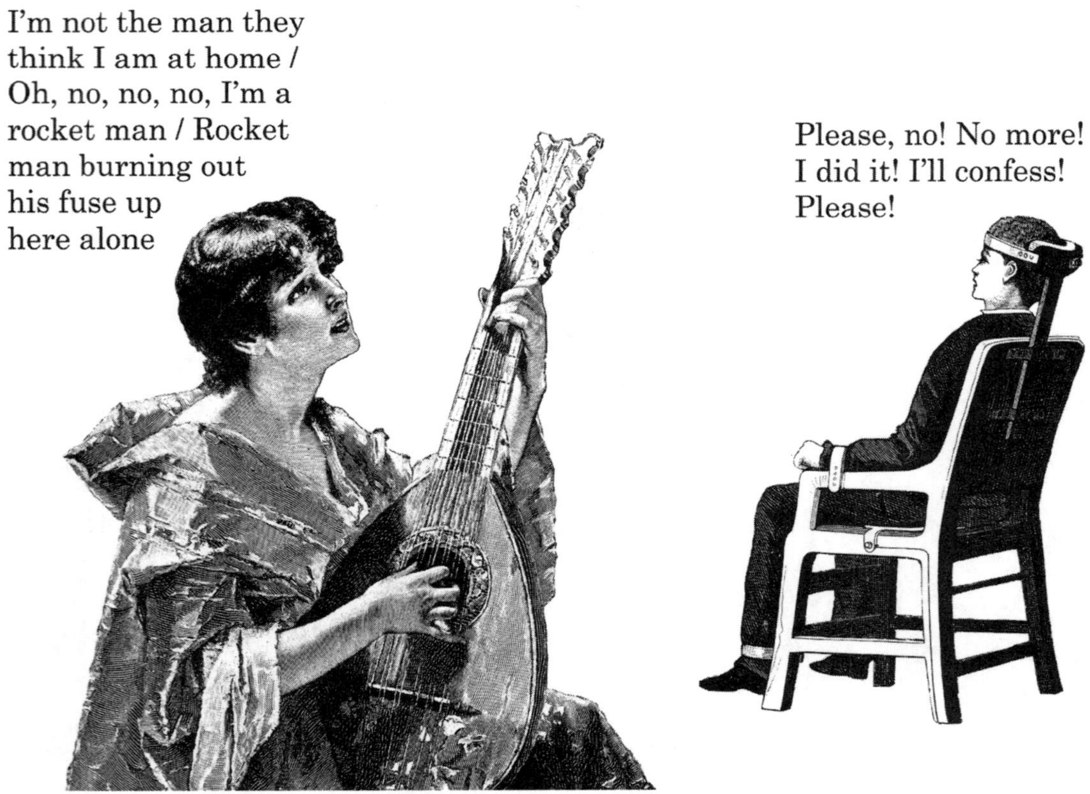
I'm not the man they think I am at home / Oh, no, no, no, I'm a rocket man / Rocket man burning out his fuse up here alone
Please, no! No more! I did it! I'll confess! Please!

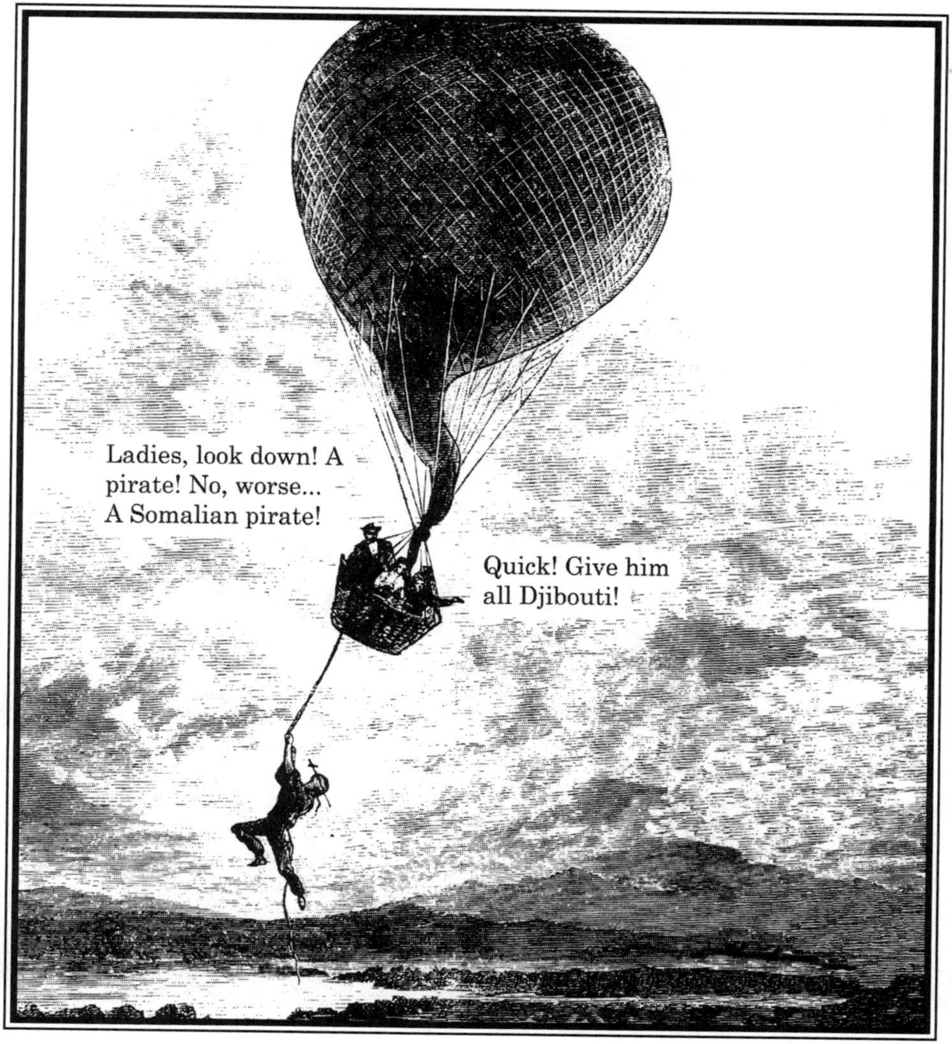
Ladies, look down! A pirate! No, worse... A Somalian pirate!
Quick! Give him all Djibouti!

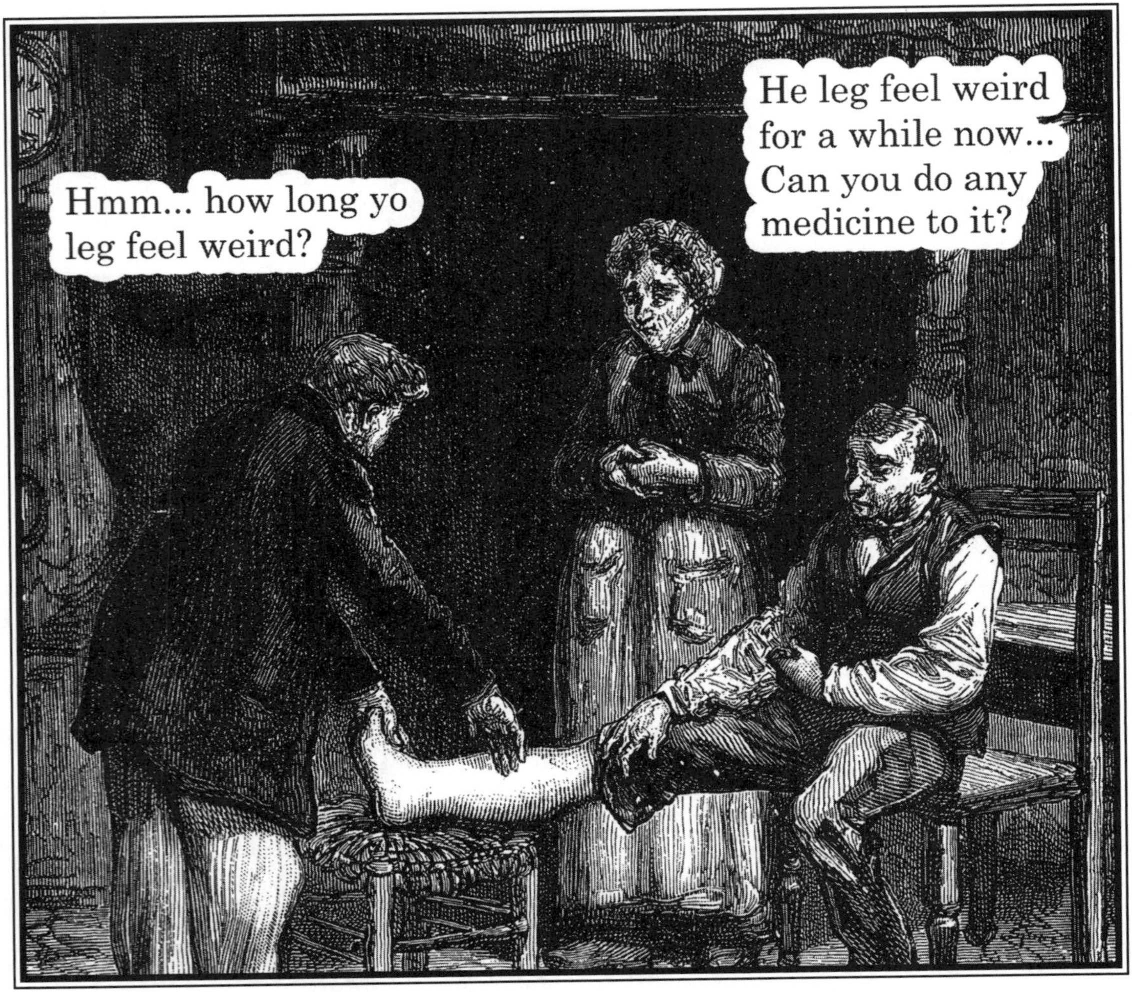
Hmm... how long yo leg feel weird?
He leg feel weird for a while now... Can you do any medicine to it?

Hey, Andre... Andre. Check out that guy over there... Should we be making our roof tilted like him?

What's the square root of three? Um, let me see... Well, Roy, the square root of three is one point fuck you Roy. Do you have any more funny things to say, Roy? Do you want to know why my canvas is still blank after six years of painting in seclusion? Do you really want to go there, Roy? Are you sure you can withstand the intense, blistering waves of fuck you Roy?

Meanwhile,

inside a turtle's mind...

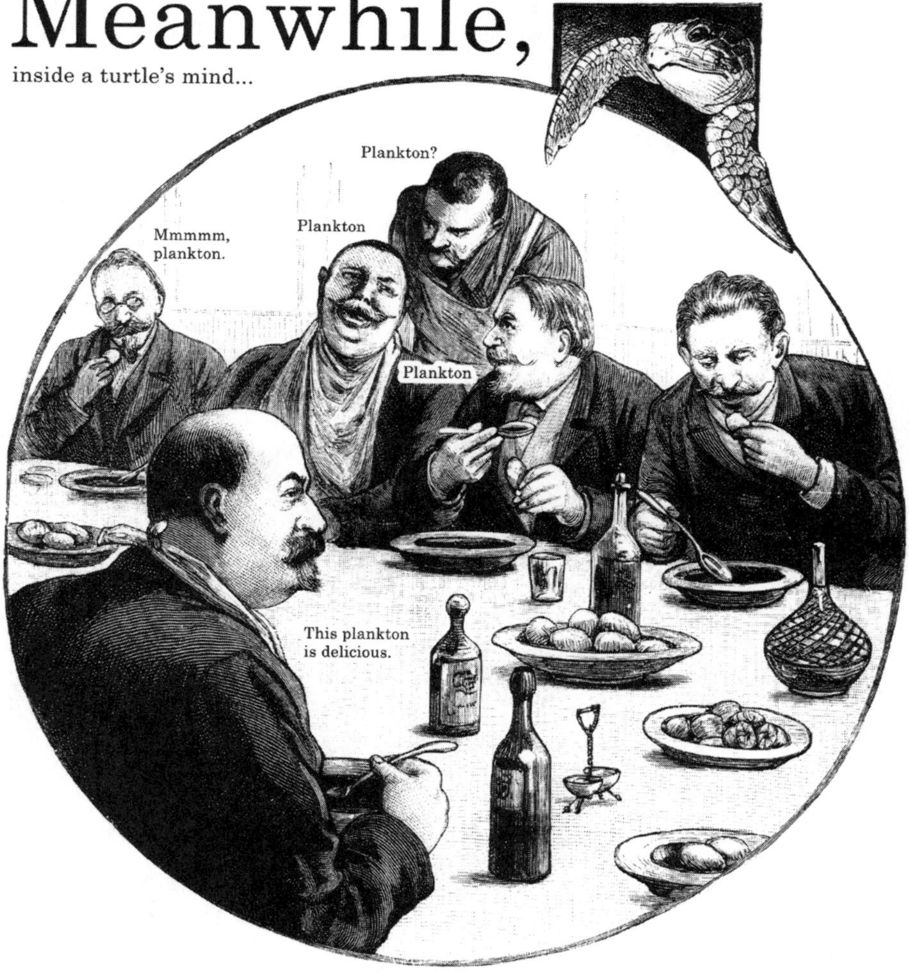
Mmmmm, plankton.
Plankton
Plankton?
Plankton
This plankton is delicious.

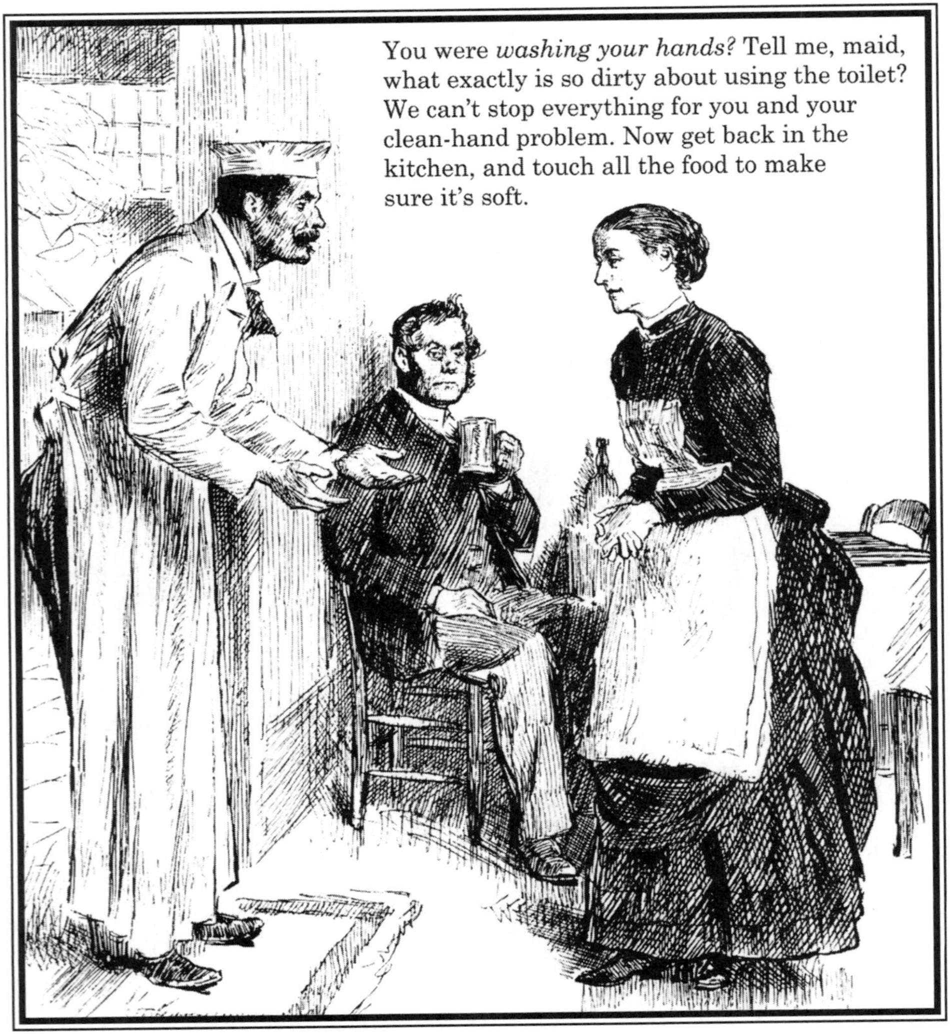
You were *washing your hands?* Tell me, maid, what exactly is so dirty about using the toilet? We can't stop everything for you and your clean-hand problem. Now get back in the kitchen, and touch all the food to make sure it's soft.

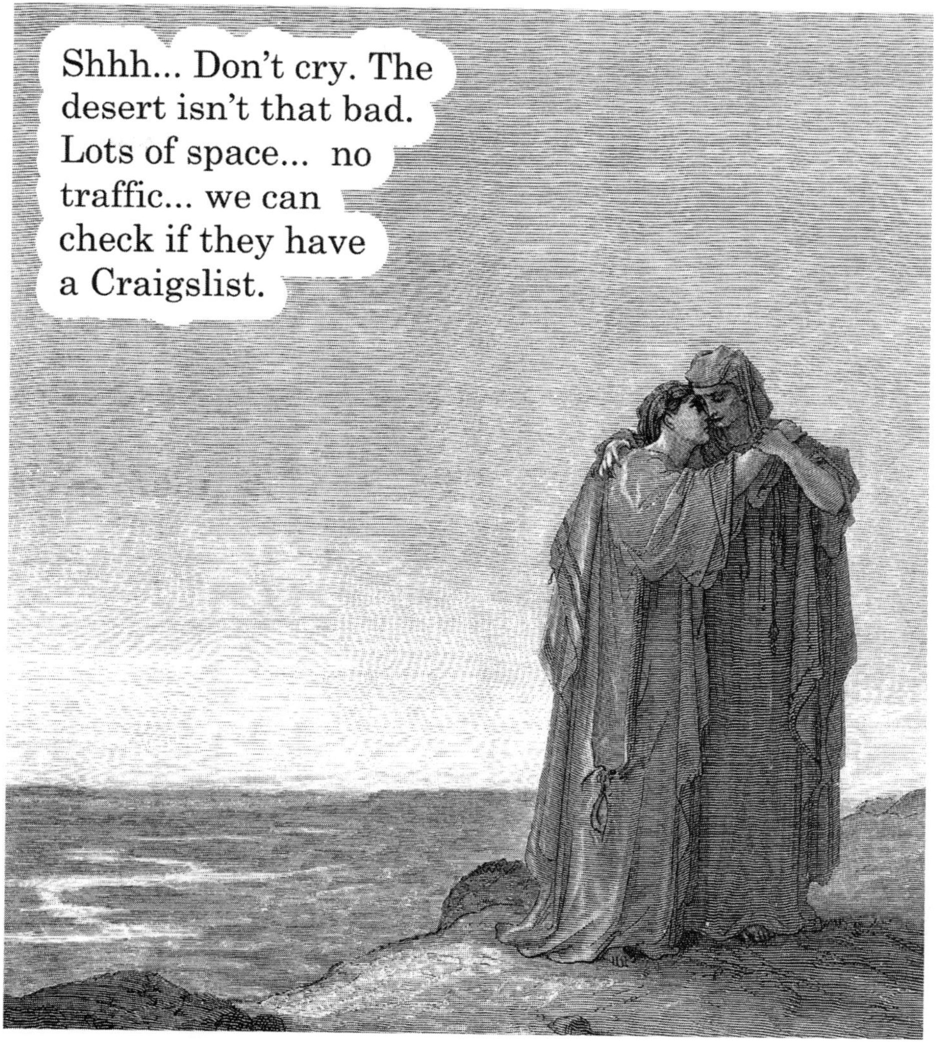
Shhh... Don't cry. The desert isn't that bad. Lots of space... no traffic... we can check if they have a Craigslist.

The pain! The torture... it is unceasing!
I wish for naught but a hard-pack of
Marlboro Lights... naught but the
icy hand of the Reaper himself!

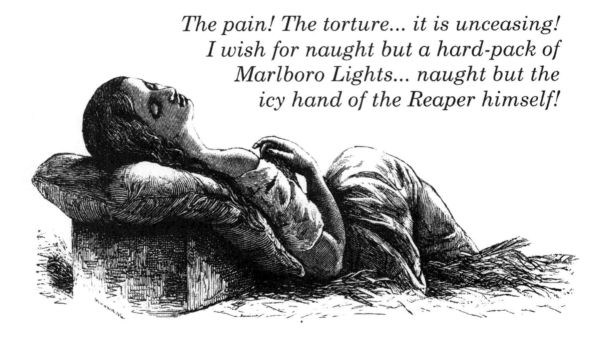

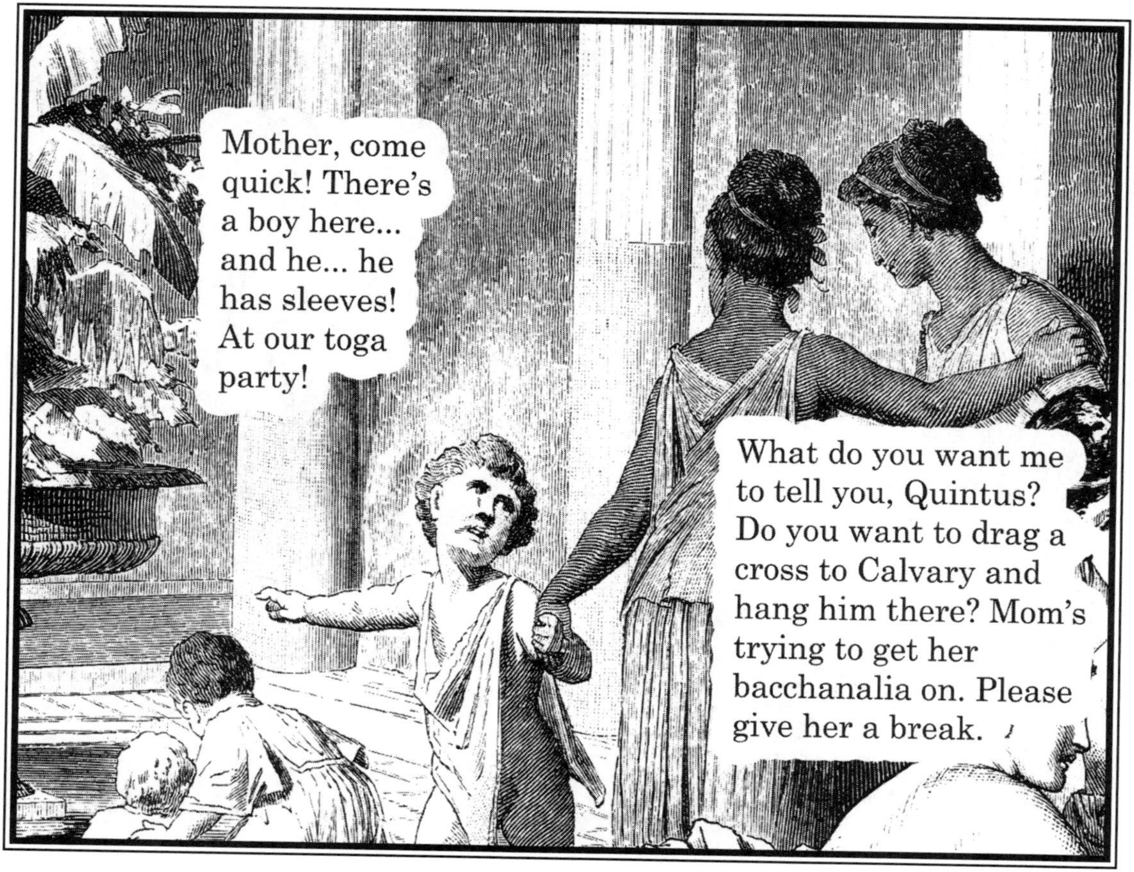
Mother, come quick! There's a boy here... and he... he has sleeves! At our toga party!
What do you want me to tell you, Quintus? Do you want to drag a cross to Calvary and hang him there? Mom's trying to get her bacchanalia on. Please give her a break.

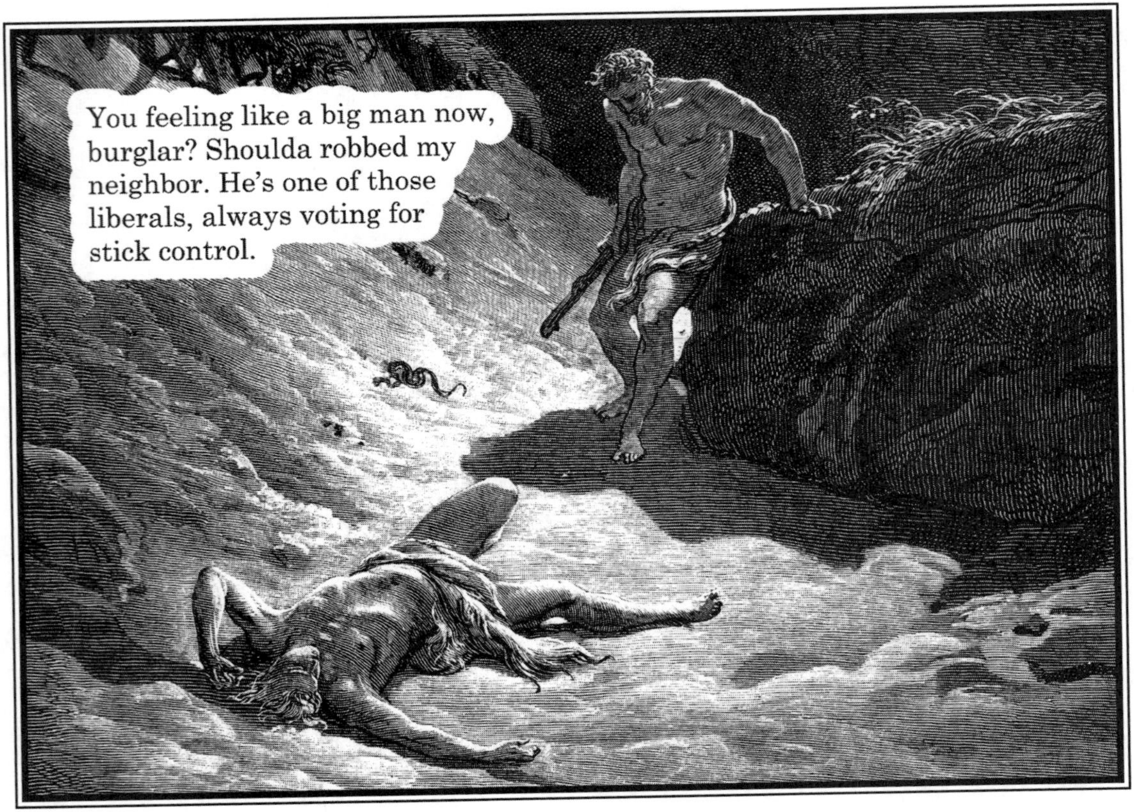
You feeling like a big man now, burglar? Shoulda robbed my neighbor. He's one of those liberals, always voting for stick control.

I don't understand why you guys aren't extinct yet... no thick, shaggy hair, no subcutaneous fat layer, no natural weapons... How do you even survive?

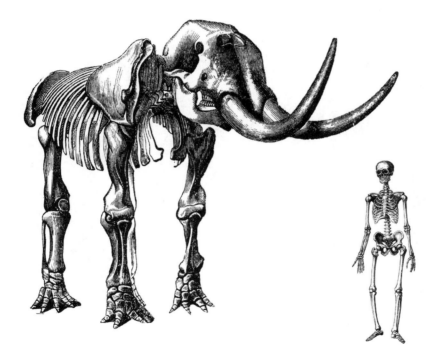

Mostly through spite... speaking of which, I edited your Wikipedia page last night. Hope you're ready to go down in history as the animal with the smallest dick.

I would give anything for you to be here at this very moment, my love, sitting next to me, helping me write out all of these postcards.

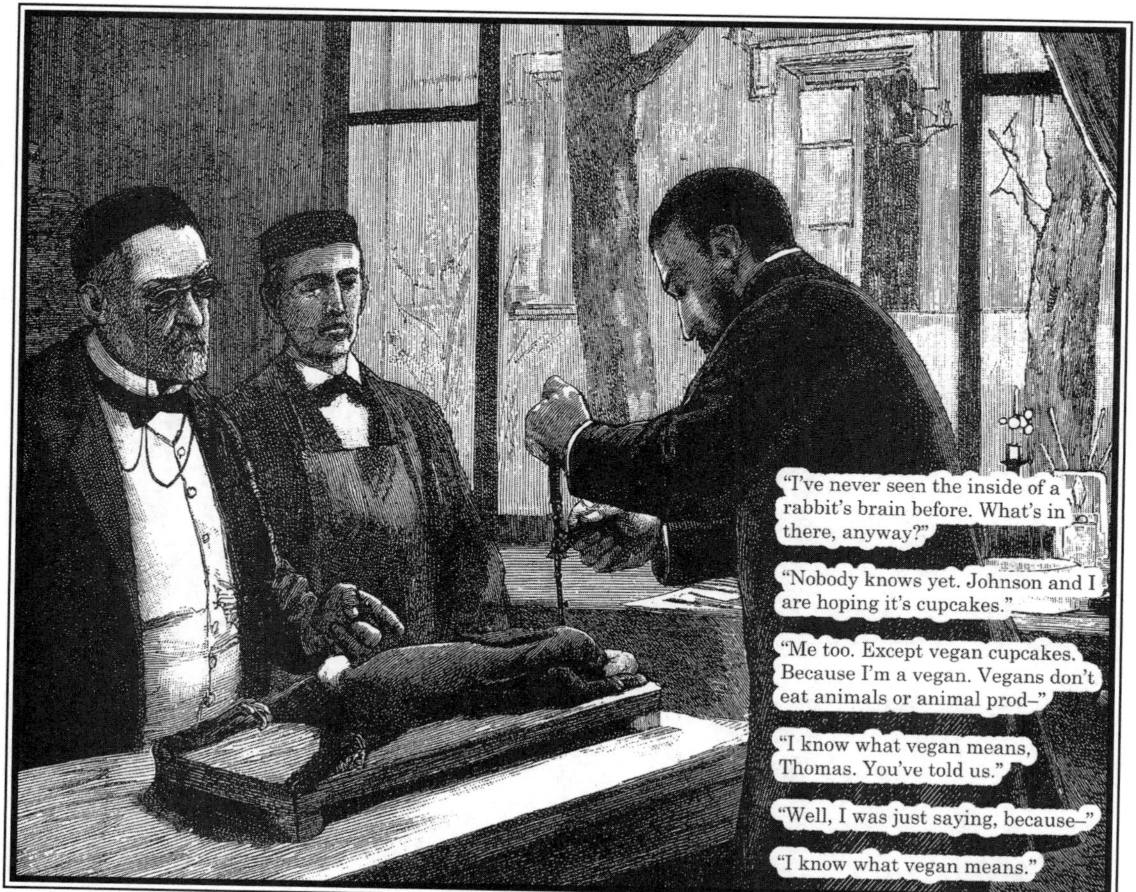
"I've never seen the inside of a rabbit's brain before. What's in there, anyway?"
"Nobody knows yet. Johnson and I are hoping it's cupcakes."
"Me too. Except vegan cupcakes. Because I'm a vegan. Vegans don't eat animals or animal prod–"
"I know what vegan means, Thomas. You've told us."
"Well, I was just saying, because–"
"I know what vegan means."

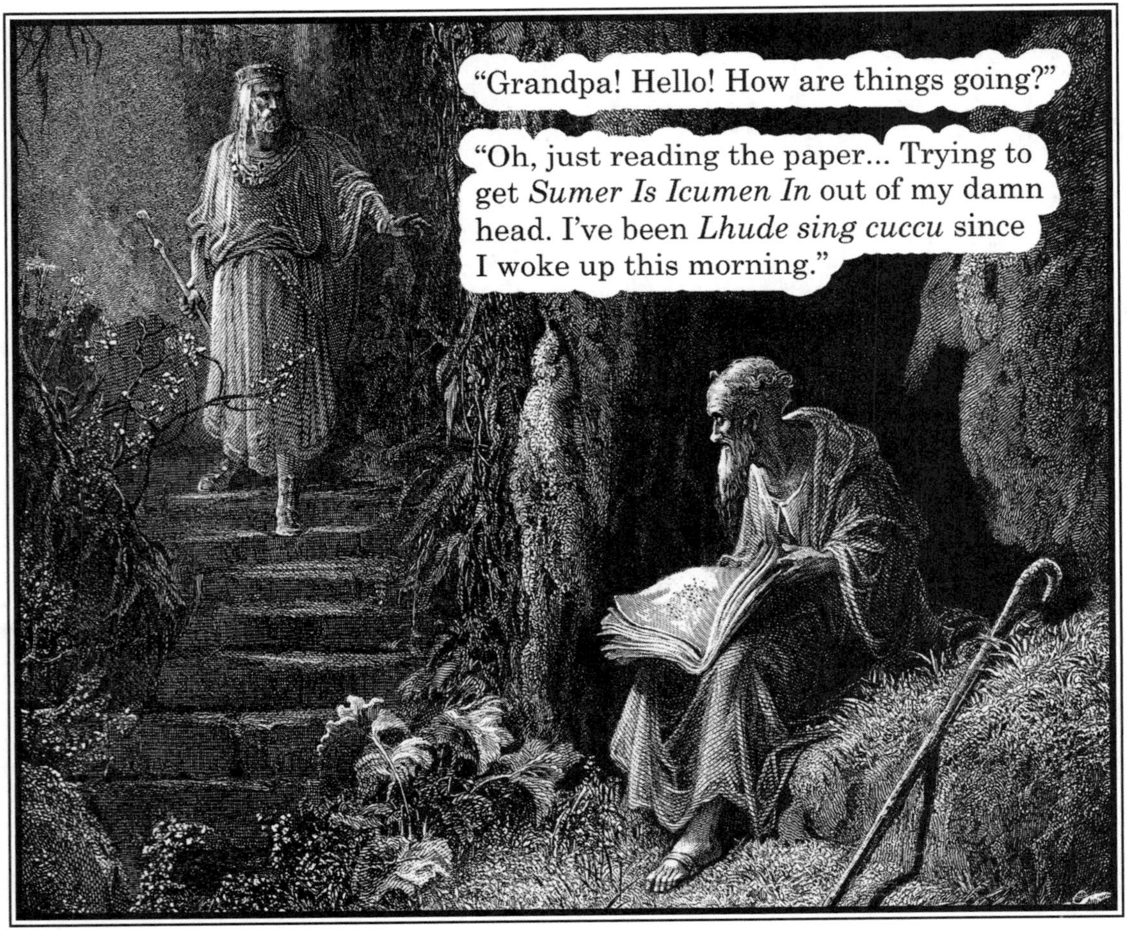
"Grandpa! Hello! How are things going?"
"Oh, just reading the paper... Trying to get *Sumer Is Icumen In* out of my damn head. I've been *Lhude sing cuccu* since I woke up this morning."

"A toast! Frances, let's do a toast!"

"I'm trying to read, mother."

"Yes! To learning to read! You'll do it one day, Frances."

Hello. One two three. By the time you listen to this cylinder, I will be gone. Do not worry about our children, as I have sold them to a man up the road. You always liked this talking machine more than you liked me, so I shall leave you alone with it. Farewell.

P. S. What are the big circles on top.

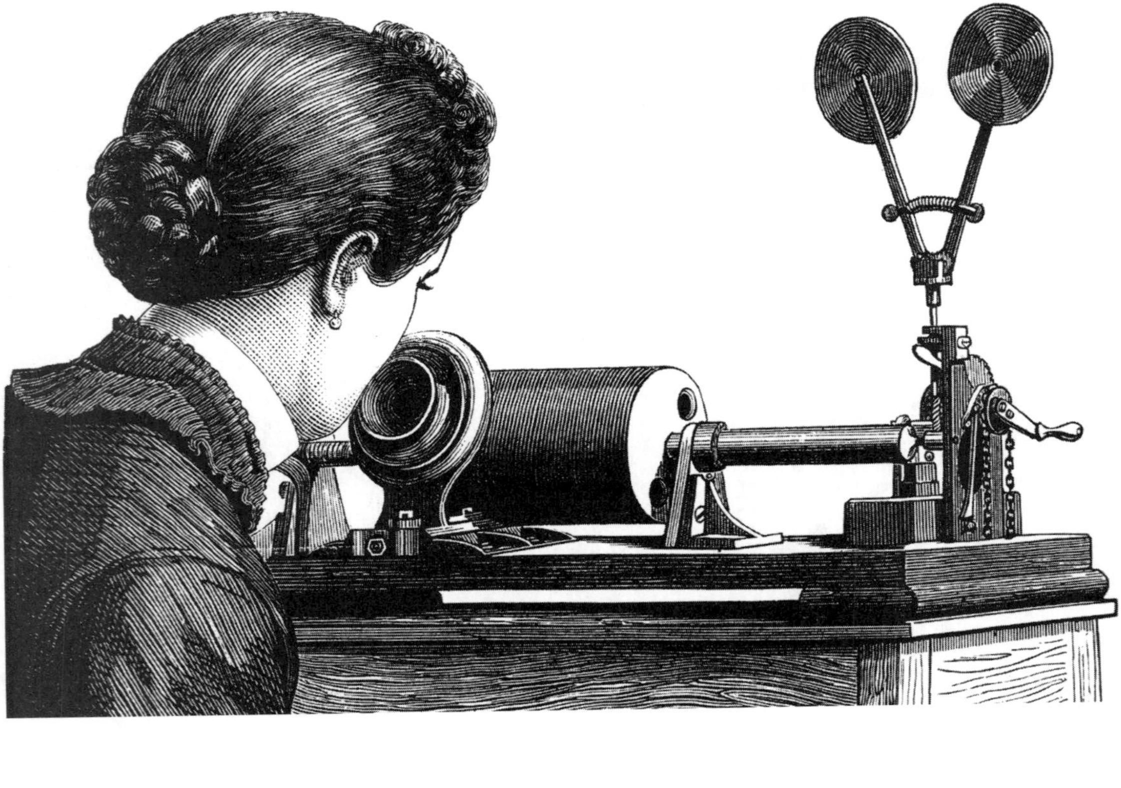

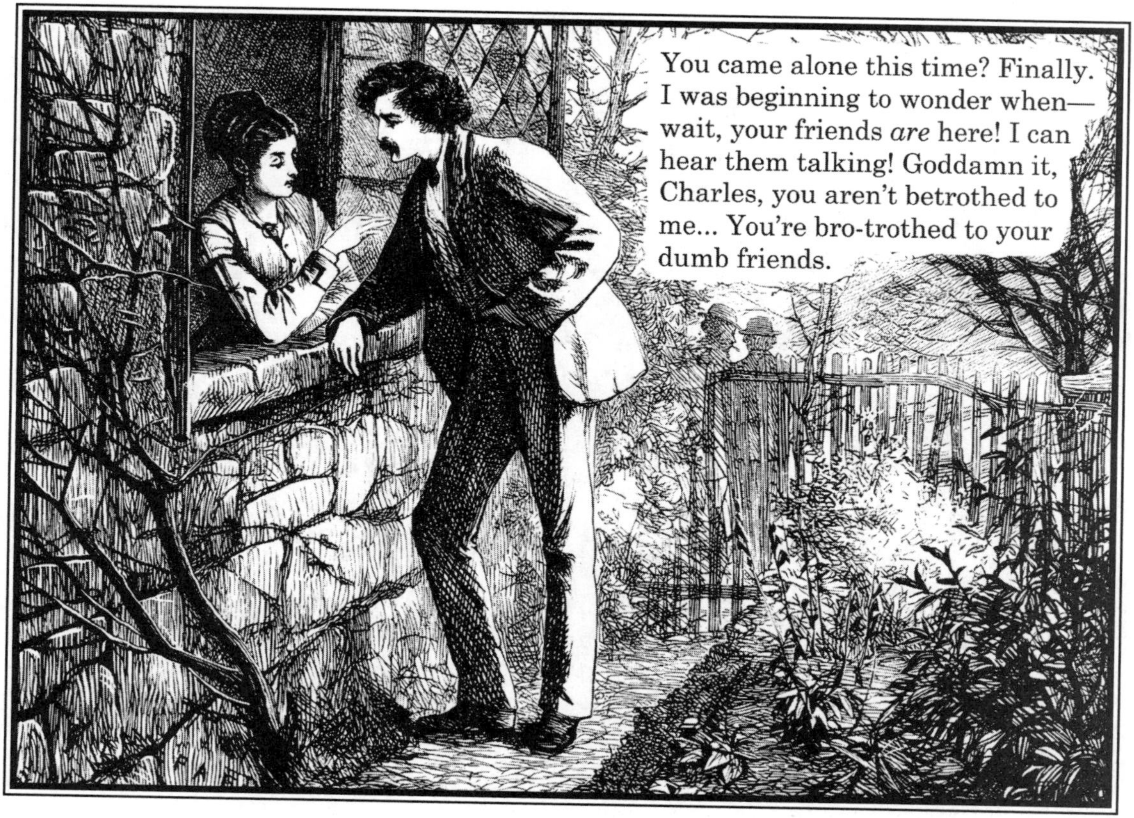
You came alone this time? Finally. I was beginning to wonder when—wait, your friends *are* here! I can hear them talking! Goddamn it, Charles, you aren't betrothed to me... You're bro-trothed to your dumb friends.

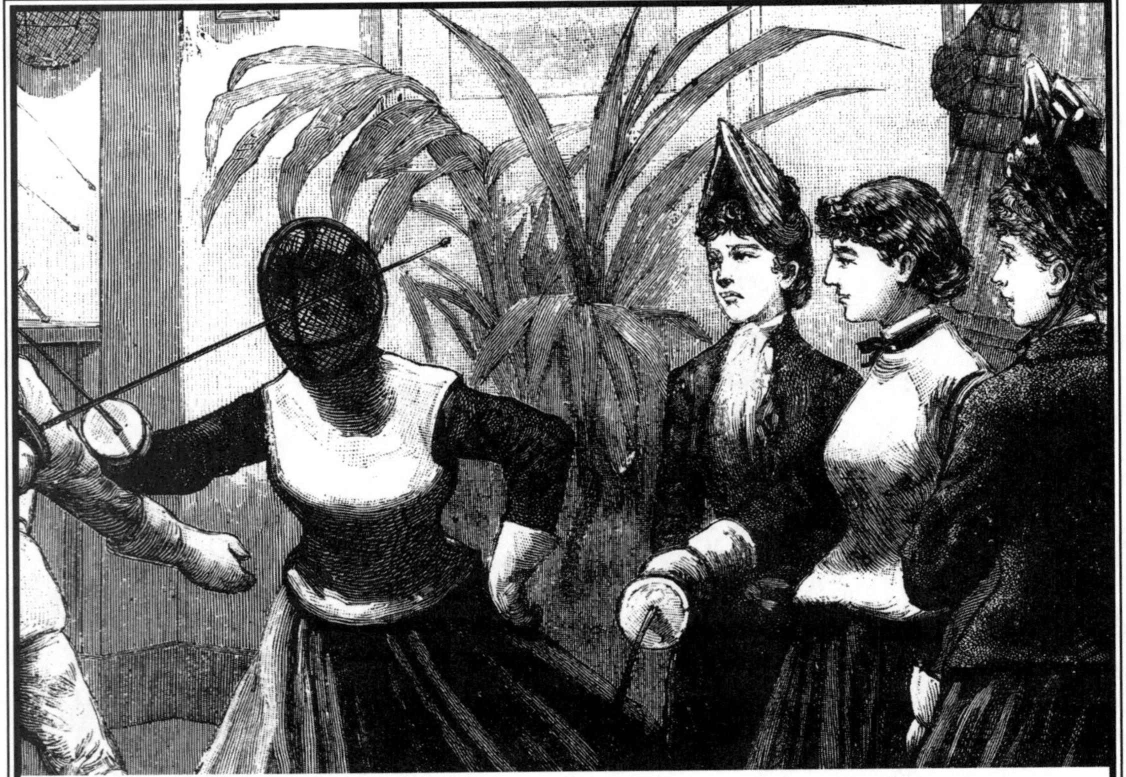

Listen, ladies... I'm going to take a pass on this fencing deal. If I'm gonna get stabbed like that, I want free dinner and margaritas. At the very least.

"Sir! Sir! Help! Please help!"

"What's the problem, ma'am?"

"Let's switch hats!"

"... What?"

"What?"

"What?!"

"What?"

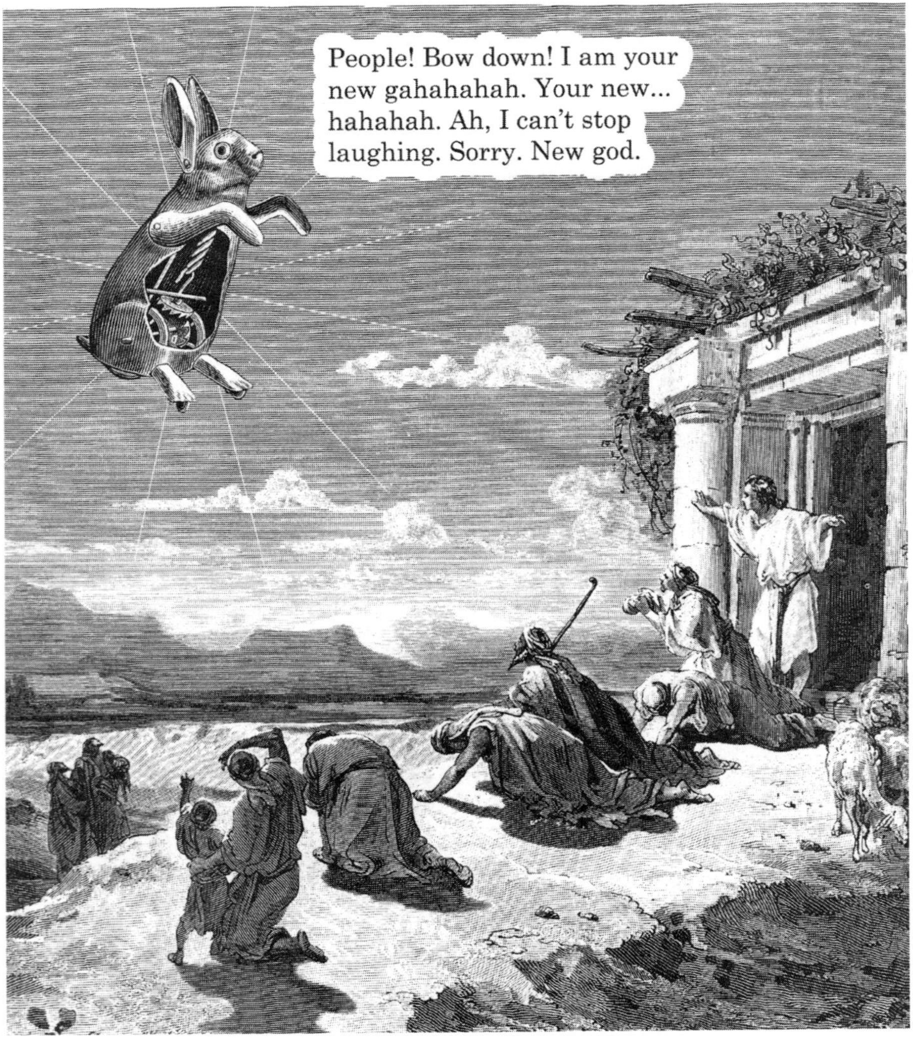
People! Bow down! I am your new gahahahah. Your new... hahahah. Ah, I can't stop laughing. Sorry. New god.

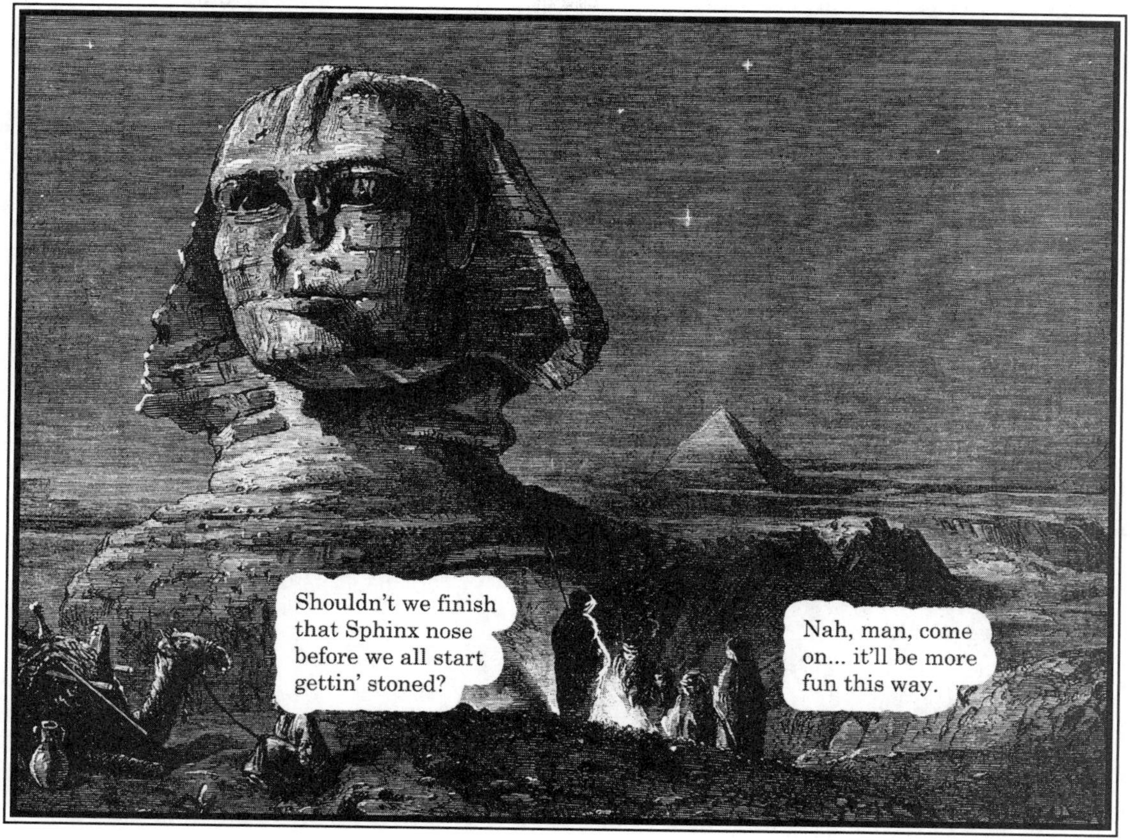
Shouldn't we finish that Sphinx nose before we all start gettin' stoned?
Nah, man, come on... it'll be more fun this way.

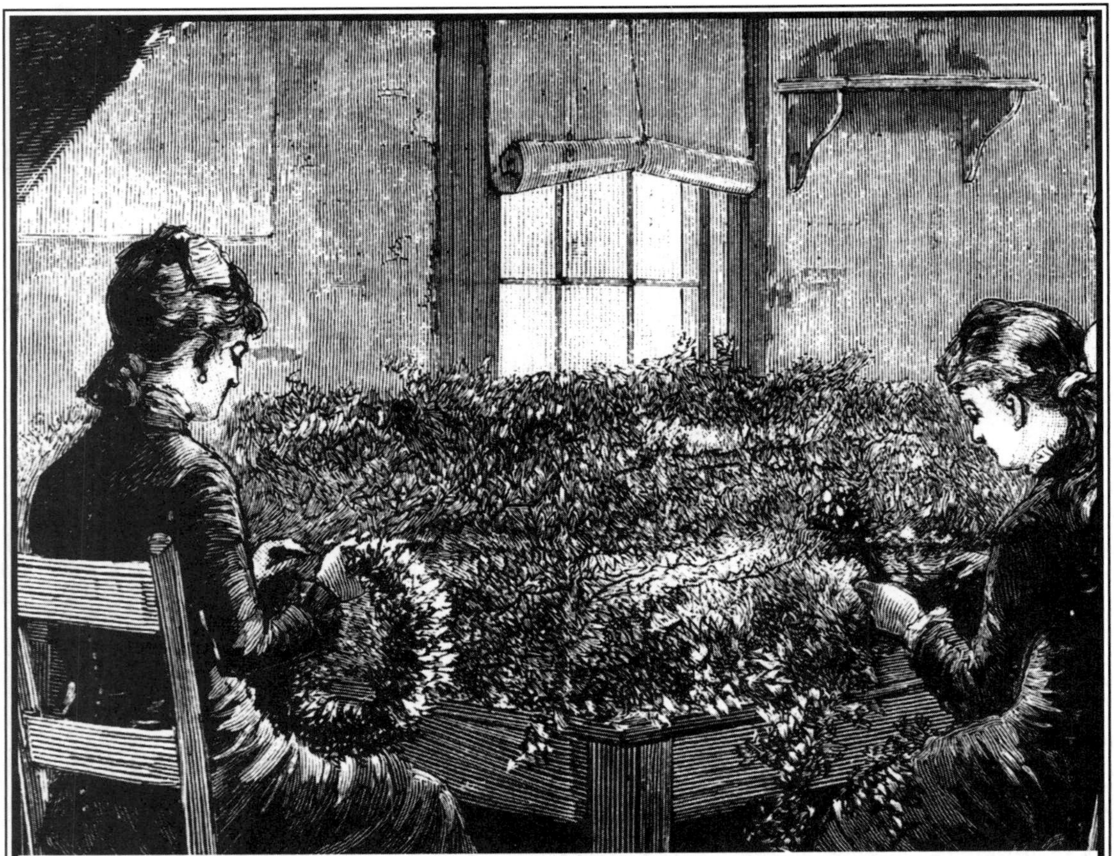

Well, the way I do it is like... okay. I'll just go up and knock on the door, and say that wreaths are two dollars. Then, right as they start to respond, I go, "Or... I'll just trade it to you for some opium. My grandma loves that shit."

Fear not, mine beautiful
maiden. I shall find a
wi-fi connection anon.

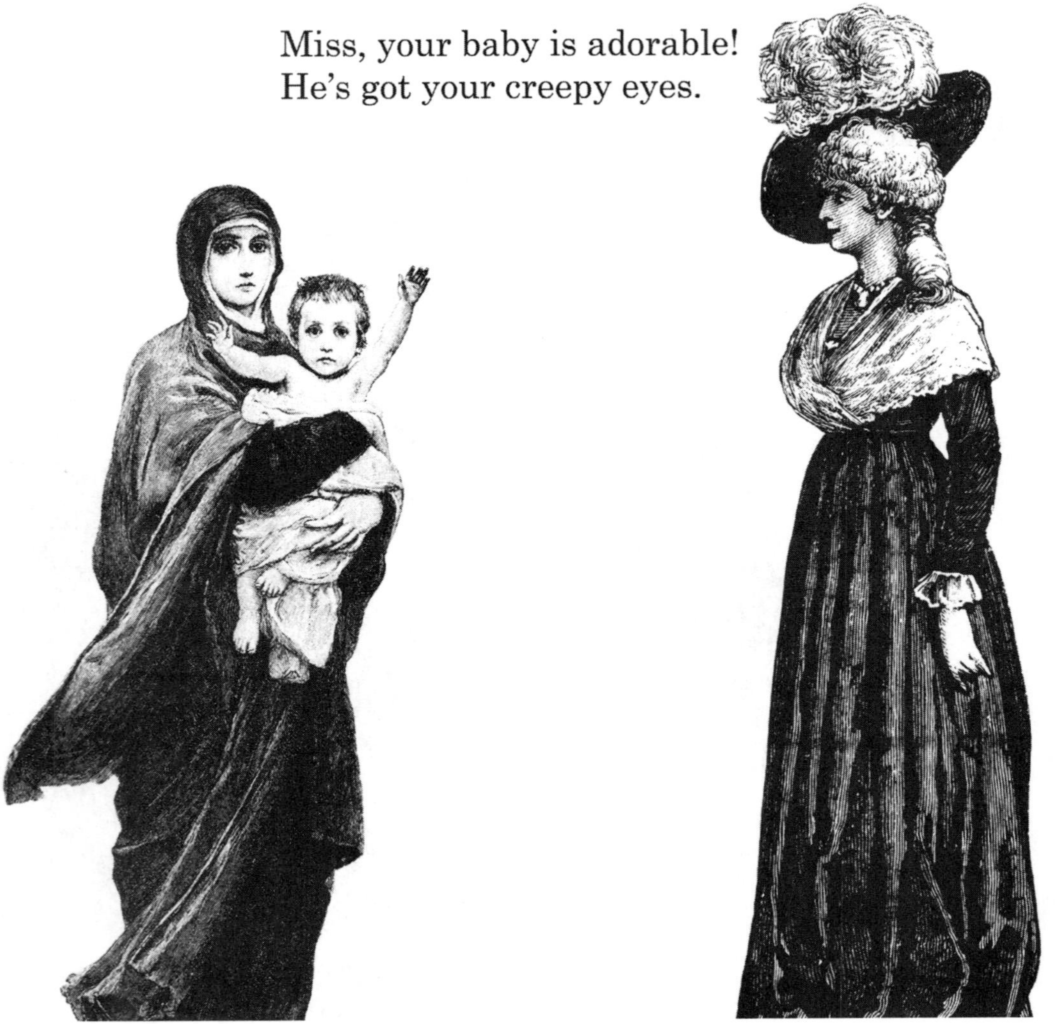
Miss, your baby is adorable!
He's got your creepy eyes.

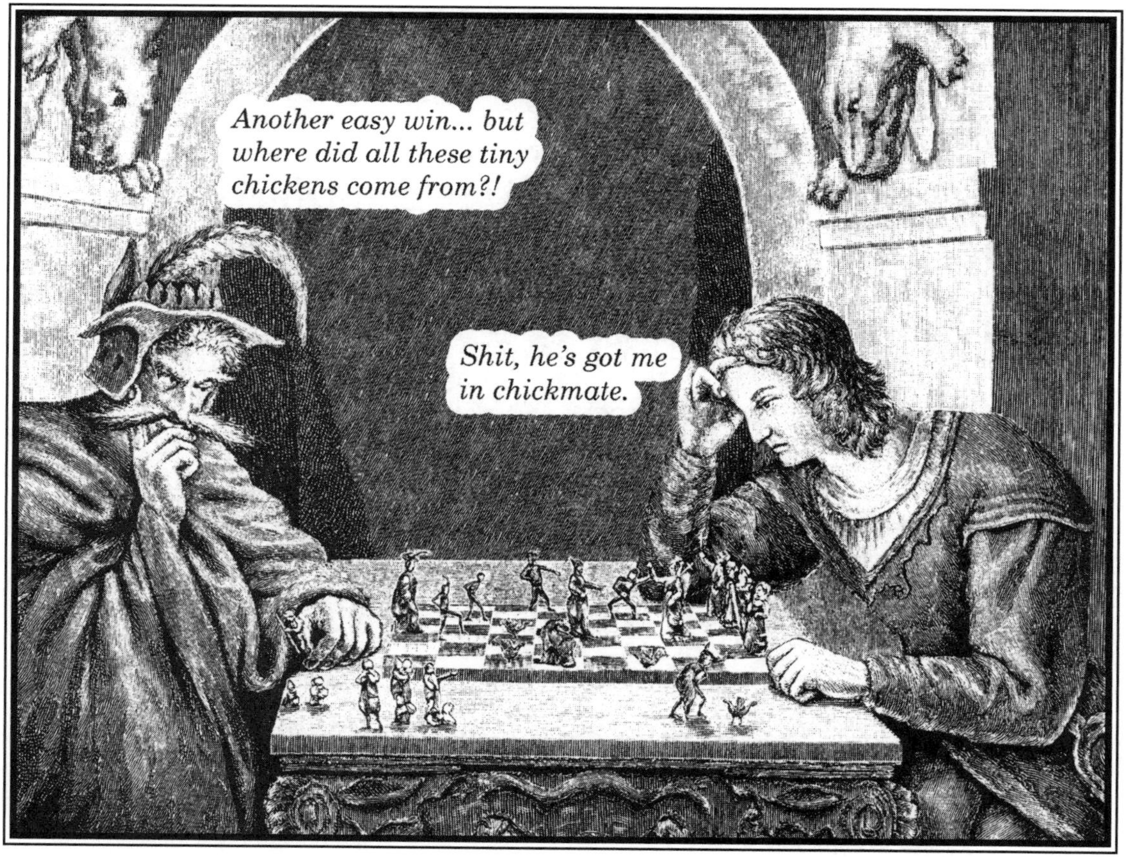
Another easy win... but where did all these tiny chickens come from?!
Shit, he's got me in chickmate.

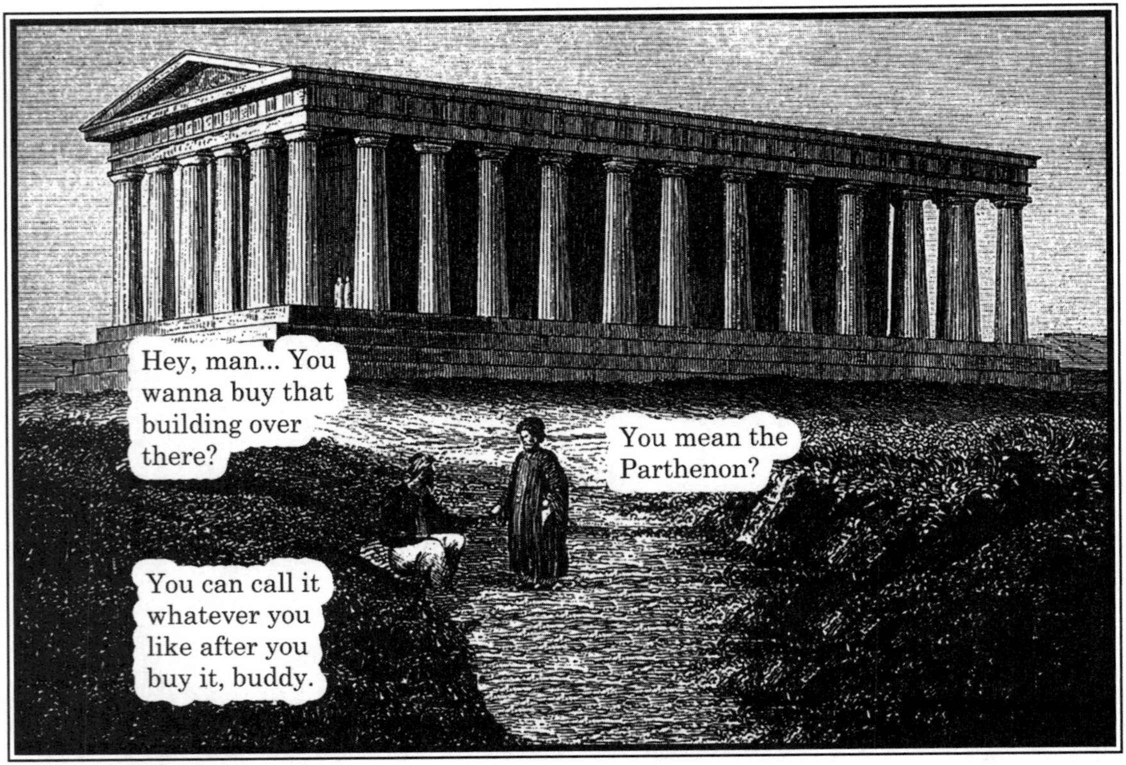
Hey, man... You wanna buy that building over there?
You mean the Parthenon?
You can call it whatever you like after you buy it, buddy.

You're bored? Well, unless you think you can invent a Nintendo, you'd better learn to read.

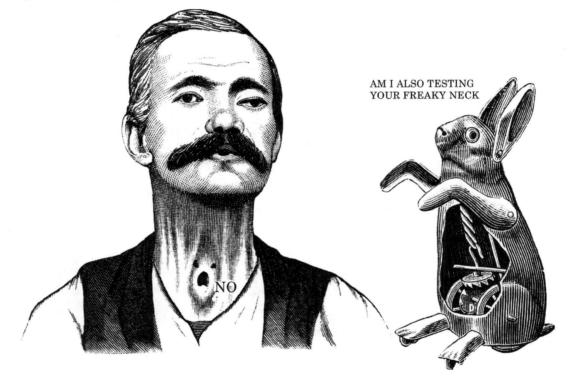

You're testing my patience, rabbit.

AM I ALSO TESTING YOUR FREAKY NECK

NO

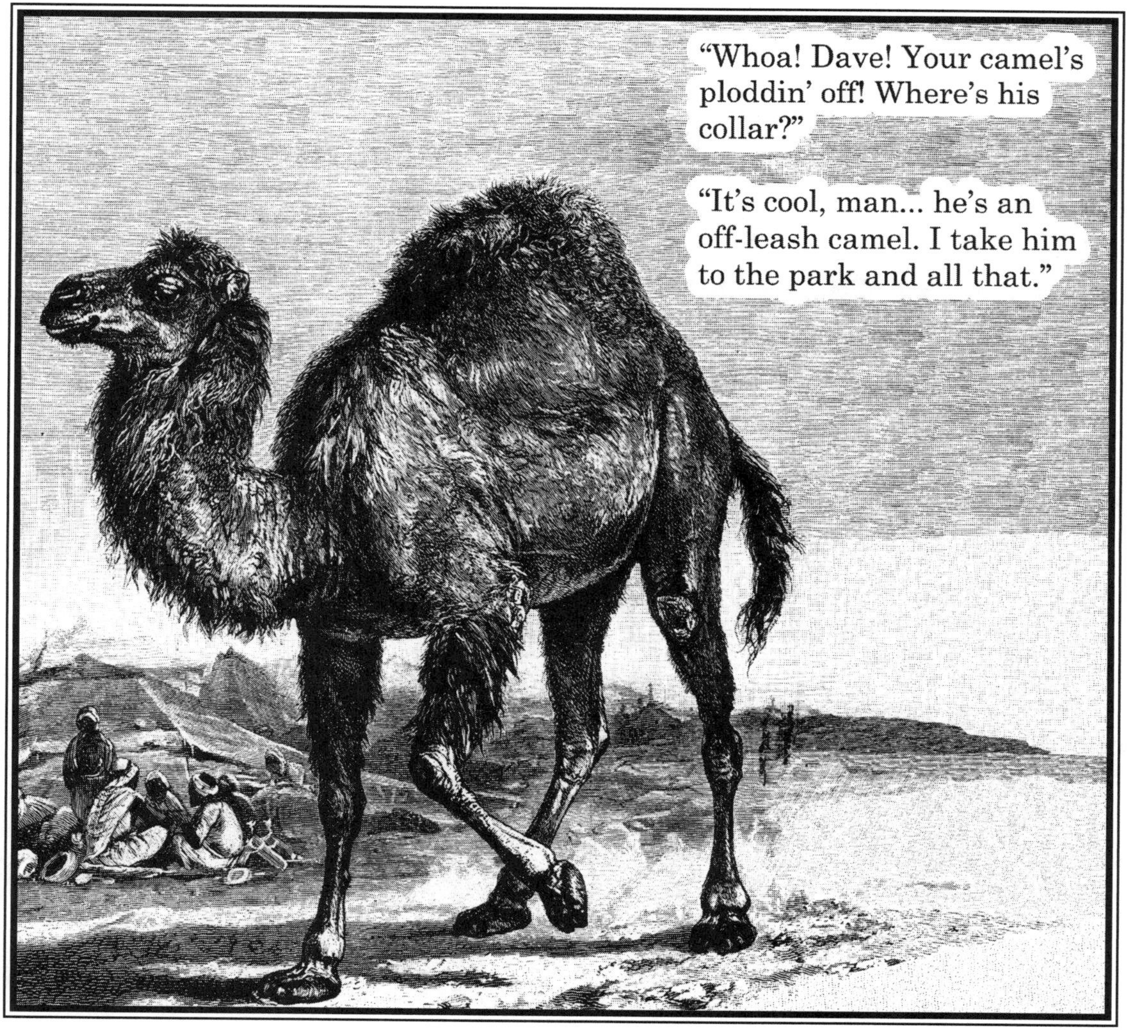
"Whoa! Dave! Your camel's ploddin' off! Where's his collar?"
"It's cool, man... he's an off-leash camel. I take him to the park and all that."

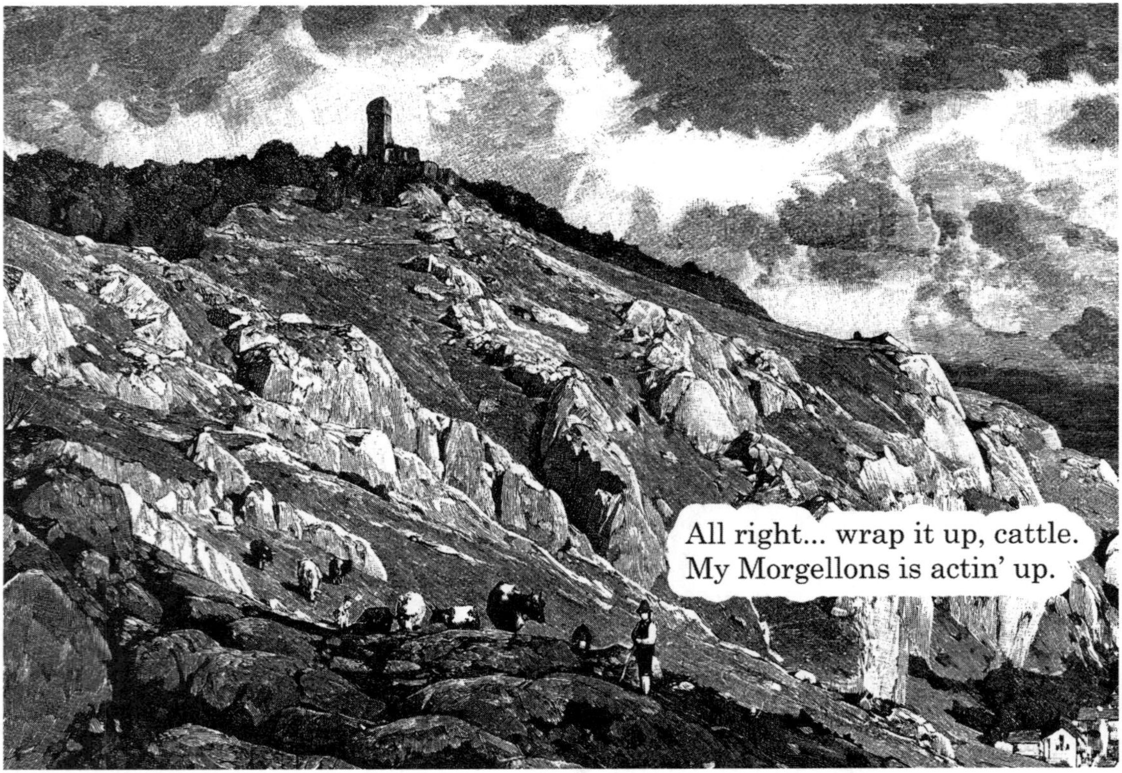
All right... wrap it up, cattle.
My Morgellons is actin' up.

Take a...

CLOSER LOOK

...at your life!

It's okay

It's okay

Okay... Which one of you assholes invented zero?

Index

Q

R

S

About the Author

Drew was born in 1979 and lives in Columbus, Ohio, USA. With his wife, Natalie Dee, he created *Married To The Sea* in March 2006 and has published one comic every day since. He is also the author of another daily online comic, *Toothpaste For Dinner*, and raps under the name CRUDBUMP. He does not read or respond to correspondence unless it comes in the form of Post-it Notes attached to unopened bottles of single-malt scotch.